Max Egremont was born in 194   History at Oxford University. As w the author of two biographical stud won the Yorkshire Post First Book .   _.jour: A Life of James Arthur Balfour. For this biography he was granted unrestricted access to Spears's extensive diaries and papers.

Max Egremont lives in West Sussex with his wife and four children.

UNDER TWO FLAGS

The Life of Major-General
Sir Edward Spears

Max Egremont

A PHOENIX GIANT PAPERBACK

First published in Great Britain by Weidenfeld & Nicolson in 1997
This paperback edition published in 1998 by Phoenix, a division of Orion Books Ltd,
Orion House, 5 Upper St Martin's Lane, London WC2H 9EA

A CIP catalogue record for this book is available from
the British Library.

ISBN: 0 75380 147 7

Printed and bound in Great Britain by
Butler & Tanner Ltd, Frome and London

For Richard Usborne

CONTENTS

ILLUSTRATIONS

PREFACE

Few people knew the most significant twentieth-century leaders of Britain and France as well as Edward Louis Spears. A friend and ally of Winston Churchill, he could claim, at different times, friendship with, and close knowledge of, Marshal Pétain and General de Gaulle. As a young liaison officer in 1916, he took Churchill on a tour of the French section of the western front, inspiring in the politician an admiration for his ability and courage; Spears was, Churchill wrote in October of that year, 'a Paladin worthy to rank with the truest knights of the great days of romance'. In Paris in 1917 he saw the first outbreaks of mutiny in the French armies, observed the tactics used by Pétain to quell these and worked with Georges Clemenceau during the German offensive of 1918 when the allies came near to defeat.

It was Spears's position as a link between the British and the French that led to his unique closeness to the commanders and policitians of both countries. From this came his appointment in June 1940 as Winston Churchill's personal representative to the French Prime Minister, Paul Reynaud. He was a horrified observer of the fall of France, then a champion of de Gaulle whom the General judged to have been essential to his cause. Later this alliance shattered when, as British minister to the Levant states of Lebanon and Syria, Spears found himself embroiled in a quarrel with de Gaulle that led almost to war.

Spears wrote brilliantly about some of his exploits, in books admired by critics as diverse as George Orwell, Cyril Connolly, A. J. P. Taylor, Winston Churchill, Harold Laski and Edith Wharton. Exceptionally articulate on paper as well as in conversation, he kept a diary during most of the key moments of his career and expressed his thoughts, prejudices and ideas constantly in letters or memoranda. Yet to many of his contemporaries Edward Louis Spears was a man of mystery. He spoke immaculate French, of a kind that could seem almost excessively ornate, but said that he had not a drop of French blood; he was, he declared, Anglo-Irish in origin, and certainly not Alsatian Jewish as other rumours hinted. He wanted to be remembered for his achievements: not for the vagaries of his ancestry.

The origin of these achievements came in 1914 when, as a young liaison officer with the French, he became the first British officer at the western front and found himself thrust into close contact with the commanders of the two allies. His career continued through the First War at the front until 1917 and then in Paris. Between the two wars, as a member of parliament and writer, Spears tried to act as an interpreter of French anxieties to the British and watched in despair as the two nations failed to stop the rise of Nazi Germany. As friend, adviser and confidant of Winston Churchill and Charles de Gaulle, he lived through the troubled Franco-British relationship of the Second World War.

De Gaulle thought that Spears understood France as well as any foreigner can, having for the country of his childhood 'a sort of uneasy, dominating love'. He was enchanted by *Peter Ibbetson*, George du Maurier's story of a boy who grows up in the Passy district of Paris, speaking a curious blend of French and English called Inglefrank. In the book, the boy's childhood is beautiful, both in reality and in remembrance, in contrast to a later, much rougher life in England. The young Spears's paradise of his cousins' château in Burgundy where he learnt the ideals of French medieval chivalry left an abiding sense of an ideal which neither he nor the France of his later experience would ever reach. It made him also, as with the hero of *Peter Ibbetson*, an outsider in both countries: not quite English and certainly not French.

Spears hoped that his feeling for France was without the sentimentality that often characterises British francophilia. He would tell scornfully how a British admiral, Lord Keith, after accepting the surrender of Marshal Masséna during the Napoleonic Wars, had exclaimed in a sudden fit of emotion that if the French and the British worked together they could dominate the world; to which the Frenchman answered with a withering froideur: 'La France suffit.' Yet he had a deep, emotional attachment to the country of his childhood and early youth. Memories of the suffering and bravery of the French troops during the First World War stayed with him always, like that of the story of the soldier, struck down by a bullet, saying as he died to his commanding officer: 'It's a good thing it wasn't you, mon capitaine.' He saw in this response a uniquely French combination of expressive elegance, sentiment, simplicity and courage even at the moment of death. In the Second World War the grating of these recollections against the reality of a defeated and collaborating nation set up a tension that led to feelings of betrayal and anger.

Spears was a man of ambition and ideals, and these often clashed. In the Levant, from 1941 until 1944, he saw himself as someone who might succeed where T. E. Lawrence had failed in bringing freedom to the Arab nations. With these high aims went a ruthlessness in his determination to achieve them. He was, he felt, ultimately alone, unable to depend upon the loyalty, affection or protection of others. His marriage to a woman of independence and fortune who became one of the leading popular novelists of her time proved to be difficult, sometimes stormy. For years, Winston Churchill was his patron, only, in 1944, to let him down, at least in Spears's estimation. This seemed to confirm what Spears had always felt: that he could rely only on his own capabilities and that these should be used with the greatest possible vigour and determination. After 1945 he went into business, embarking, in Africa and elsewhere, on a second career that proved to be as strenuous, and almost as controversial, as his years as a soldier, diplomat and politician. In 1973, a year before his death, he was involved in a public battle with the tycoon 'Tiny' Rowland.

Spears's life stretches from the late Victorian age, when Britain was the greatest power in the world, to a time of national self-doubt and comparative economic decline. It reflects many aspects of this extraordinary transformation, not least through his links to France and the complex psychology of official and personal Anglo-French relations. But above all it is the story of a man who sought power and success and tried also, not always successfully, to keep to those tenets of honour that he had learnt as a boy. Articulate, determined, occasionally brutal and often the cause of suffering in those close to him, he had also the imagination to write beautifully, and sometimes with great tenderness, of his struggles and experiences. This is perhaps what makes Edward Louis Spears unusual: the combination of a life of action with the temperament, mercurial brilliance and vulnerability of an artist.

Many people have helped me with this book. I am particularly grateful to Duff Hart-Davis, Major-General Sir Edward Spears's step-grandson, for having suggested the subject to me and to Colonel Anthony Aylmer, Spears's heir and literary executor, for help and encouragement in every conceivable way. To Richard Usborne, I owe an immense debt. Having worked for some years on a biography of Spears, he not only made the result of his researches available to me but offered help and advice at every stage. Without our many conversations, I doubt if my book could have been finished, not least because often, by a subtle remark or even a single word, he illuminated a previously dark corner. Sir John Stokes, another enthusiast for the life and work of Spears, showed me invaluable contemporary letters from his time on the Dakar expedition and in the Levant and spoke evocatively of these days.

Others who have given freely of their time and knowledge are Correlli

Barnett, the Princesse de Beauvau-Craon, Béatrix Beck, Antony Beevor, the late Sir Alfred Beit, Claude Blair, Brian Bond, Henry Boyd-Carpenter, George Bull, Etienne Burin des Roziers, Colin Campbell, Viscountess Camrose, Hugh Cecil, the late Lord Colyton, Baronne Martine de Courcel, Cedric Cremière, Isabel Cobbe, Artemis Cooper, Nigel Davidson, General Jean Delmas, Baron Jehan Drouas, the late Nicholas Elliott, David French, Lieutenant-Commander Tom Foden, M. R. D. Foot, Sir Martin Gilbert, Howard Gotlieb, Lord Hailsham of St Marylebone, Simon Head, Andrew Hislop, Richard Holmes, Lady Iliffe, Douglas Johnson, John Kelly, Laurence Kelly, Alan Kucia, the late Marie-Antoinette Ladd, Richard Lamb, the Marquis of Lansdowne, Joan Pirie Leclerc, James Lees-Milne, Wing-Commander Ian Madelin, Douglas Matthews, Virginia May, Lieutenant-Colonel Robin Merton, Patricia Methven, Alexander and Charlotte Mosley, Elizabeth Nelson, Anne Oakley, Kate O'Brien, David Ogilvy, Lieutenant-Commander Tony Orchard, Burnet Pavitt, Ann Payne, William Philpott, Robert Pirie, David Pryce-Jones, Jean Rafinesque, the Countess of Ranfurly, Anthony Rhodes, Simon Robbins, Andrew Roberts, John Rogister, Belinda Ruck-Keene, Thérèse de Saint Phalle, the late Lord Sherfield, Kathy Stevenson, Sarah Stockwell, Bernadette Szapiro, John Terraine, Sir Günther Treitel, John Tusa, Lieutenant-Colonel Peter Upton, Philip Ziegler, the Hon. Lady de Zulueta.

I am very grateful to the staffs of the British Library; the British Library newspaper collection at Colindale; the Churchill Archives Centre at Churchill College, Cambridge; the French Foreign Ministry archives at the Quai d'Orsay; the French military archives at Vincennes; the House of Lords Record Office; the Imperial War Museum; the Institute of Directors; the Liddell Hart Centre at King's College, London; the Liverpool City Library; the London Library; the Middle East Centre at St Antony's College, Oxford; the Ministry of Defence; the Mugar Memorial Library at Boston University; the Public Record Office at Kew.

My agent Gill Coleridge has been characteristically encouraging and helpful throughout and Ion Trewin and Benjamin Buchan of Weidenfeld and Nicolson showed enthusiasm, wisdom and admirable objectivity. To my wife and children I owe more than I can say, not least for their tolerance of a biographer who became obsessed by his subject.

1

A Divided Boyhood

The family background of Edward Louis Spears was often said to be mysterious.

He had a different name until he was thirty-two, starting life as Edward Louis Spiers and changing in 1918 to Spears. Later he gave his reason as a long exasperation at the mispronunciation of Spiers and claimed that Spears had been the spelling used by his forebears. But his great-grandfather, his earliest traceable paternal ancestor, was known at various times as Spires or Spyers, never as Spears, at least not in the surviving records. Irritation at mistaken pronunciation may not have been the only reason for the change. In 1918 there was possibly also a wish for an identity appropriate to his position as a brigadier-general, the head of the British Military Mission to the French War Office and husband of an American heiress. Spiers had a German ring to it, perhaps a hint of Jewishness. He did not like to be thought of as a foreigner.

France was his first home, the country where his parents and grandparents lived, the scene of most of his childhood. He was born in Passy, a smart district of north-west Paris near the Bois de Boulogne, at 7 chaussée de la Muette on 7 August 1886, the son of Charles McCarthy Spiers and Melicent Marguerite Lucy Hack, his father being described on the birth certificate as 'commission agent'.[1]

His father had been born in 1858, the son of Alexander Spiers and Victoire Dawes Newman. As a young man, Alexander had studied in England, Paris and Germany, where he gained a doctorate of philosophy at Leipzig. In 1853 he married at the parish church of Camberwell a Miss Newman, the daughter of John Newman, an architect residing at Rye Lane in Peckham.[2]

Alexander Spiers settled in Paris and taught English at the Ecole de Commerce, the Ecole des Ponts et Chaussées, the Ecole des Mines and the Lycée Bonaparte. His greatest monument is an English–French and French–English dictionary, published in 1846. Years later Alexander

Spiers's grandson admitted somewhat grudgingly that he still consulted the work.

It was to his mother's ancestry that Spears looked with pride and romantic feeling, for the Hacks were linked to the Anglo-Irish Aylmers and their castle, baronetcy and estates at Donadea in County Kildare. Spears remembered that although his maternal grandmother had liked Alexander Spiers's wife Victoire, a descendant of a lord mayor of London, his mother had looked down on her in-laws because they were tainted by trade.[3]

Alexander Spiers had been born in Gosport in 1807, the son of Isaac Spiers, and died in his house in Passy, Paris, in 1869, having suffered a severe attack of dysentery. He had five sons, one of whom was Charles, the 'commission agent' and Edward Louis Spears's father; another, Victor, followed his father's profession and became a professor of French at London University; a third lived openly with a mistress in London and was shunned by the rest of his family, whose members seem to have alternated between rakishness and a propensity for harsh judgement.[4]

Alexander Spiers's dictionary, his appointments as an examiner at the Sorbonne and an *inspecteur général de l'université* and the award of the cross of the Legion of Honour by Napoleon III made him a considerable figure in France. He spoke seven languages, edited editions of Sheridan's *School for Scandal*, Bacon's *Essays*, anthologies of English prose and poetry and a manual of commercial English. He also had a belligerence that was to be one of his grandson's characteristics and in 1857 unsuccessfully sued his own publishers for pirating his work.[5]

Edward Louis Spears denied that he was Jewish, but there is in the papers of the Alien Office of the Home Department for 1803 a reference to Isaac Spiers, Alexander's father and his own great-grandfather, that would have shocked him. On 25 June of that year, at the height of the spy fever of the Napoleonic Wars, the Reverend Richard Bingham of Gosport wrote to the Home Department in London to complain of 'an alien who resides & has done for some time in this Town'. This 'Isaac Spires' had apparently married a woman with the indisputably Jewish name of Hannah Moses who kept a shop. 'Spires' said he was Jewish; 'but he acknowledges that he is by Birth a Frenchman & he appears to me to be a very suspicious Character.' Bingham declared: 'I have every reason to believe that he was a Soldier in the French Army.' 'Spires' had been also 'much concerned in procuring lace & other contraband articles' in Gosport and was 'a very bad Member of Society'.[6]

The Alien Office had a declaration by 'Spyers' that he was 'a native of Frankfort'. Even apes were hung as possible spies at this time and

Isaac sounded at least as likely an offender. Bingham wrote again on 1 August to report that Spyers 'says he was born in Germany & lived there till he was four years old, but that from that Time till just before he obtained permission to dwell here, he lived in France'. The connection with the French army was hard to prove but 'a Man of this place, who owned & commanded in the Peace a Packet from hence to Havre ... was told by many Persons in France, that Spyers had been in the French Army'; the man also told Bingham that Spyers 'was continually going backwards & forwards to France, & his having been a Soldier appeared to be a matter of no doubt ... he adds also, that Spyers has a Mother & Brother now residing in Paris.' This was enough to damn Spyers. On 10 August Bingham reported that he had been arrested.[7]

The investigation foundered; perhaps evidence was too circumstantial or hysteria died down with the passing of the French threat. By 7 March 1807 Isaac had established himself as a loyal citizen and was granted denization. But the imbroglio has later resonances in the life of Isaac's great-grandson. Spears was accused of dubious financial dealing and of having links with France strong enough to cast doubt on his patriotism. He often spoke opaquely of his own espionage work, leaving an impression of romantic mystery.

Alexander's son, and Edward Louis Spears's father, Charles McCarthy Spiers (usually called 'Charlie'), was more easy-going than his lexicographer father and nearly wrecked his engagement to Melicent Marguerite Hack when he was seen escorting a certain Miss Bulloch in Liverpool.[8] The Hacks, the family of Charlie Spiers's wife, were originally Quakers from the south coast of England; Spears's Hack great-grandfather had moved to a house in Dieppe where his mother's father, Edward Louis Hack, was brought up with his sisters. Here their father would announce periodically that he was ruined, but Edward Louis Hack escaped the gloom to work as a railway engineer in continental Europe. He and his wife Lucy Aylmer were married in a protestant church near Rome and Hack received a papal decoration for his work on the Italian railways. A daughter, Melicent Marguerite, their only child and Spears's mother, was born in Cannes and the family went soon afterwards to Sicily, where Edward Hack built the railway. Here brigands ruled the interior, water was more expensive than wine and the baby's nurse threatened Mrs Hack with a knife. During meals Mr Hack kept a pistol on the table from fear of attack. Even the priests carried guns.[9]

Spears wondered if his mother's childhood in this terrifying country might have permanently affected her. At first the instability lay hidden.

She was a gifted artist and while her father was working near Paris won a prize for piano-playing at the Conservatoire. Spears recalled her enchanting renderings of French lullabies and her beauty. But his mother later failed him, and his grandmother Lucy Hack became the dominant figure in his childhood, particularly after the death of her husband in 1889.[10]

Born an Aylmer, Lucy Hack had seven sisters and one brother and the family grew up as strict protestants in Ireland. She kept her religion to herself, like her brother Michael, who became rather a rake; Spears's Aylmer great-aunts were less reticent. On their visits to Menton, where the Hacks had a villa, they would try to convert the local peasantry by leaving low-church tracts, translated into the local patois, in lunch baskets in the Provençal hills, hoping the food might act as bait.[11]

Charles McCarthy Spiers and Melicent Marguerite Hack were married at the British embassy church in Paris on 18 May 1885. On 8 August in the following year Charles McCarthy Spiers wrote to tell his father-in-law about the birth of 'our dear little Edward Louis', who had been named after him. Edward Hack instructed his son-in-law from Evian, where he was working at the time, that the event must be registered at the British embassy so that the child would be a British subject.[12]

The birth had been difficult, and this was a bad omen. Kathleen, a sister for Louis, as he came to be called, was born exactly two years later in August 1888 and, long after he had grown up, Spears found a letter from his mother in which she accused his father of trying to have her put away in an asylum because she had been treated in a Swiss sanatorium for a post-natal breakdown. He did not believe this, for she was prone to fantasies, but a separation took place while her children were still young. As if to make up for this, his adoring grandmother, Lucy Hack, certainly spoilt Spears. In February 1889 his father wrote to her after his return from a visit to the Hack villa at Menton to say that the child 'did not come up to my expectations. I dislike him very much to whimper for a thing until he gets it.'[13]

The boy was often on the move, usually with his grandmother, from Menton to Aix-les-Bains – both haunts of the expatriate British – to Switzerland, to the Aylmer castle of Donadea in Ireland, to Brittany and to Voutenay, a medieval château in Burgundy on the River Cure, near the Morvan hills, owned by the Rafinesques, a Protestant family of the French provincial nobility into which his Hack grandfather's sister had married. An attack of diphtheria in Switzerland at the age of two nearly killed Louis and this was followed by a bout of typhoid. Designated a delicate child, he spent winters at his grandmother's Menton villa in the Mediterranean warmth with a series of tutors and did not mix with children of his own age. The sense of isolation lasted all his life.

At Voutenay there was companionship, with his cousins Marcel and Gaston Rafinesque. Marcel was older, so Gaston, or 'Ton Ton' – 'the loveliest child imaginable, kind, humorous & intelligent' – was his friend. Spears, 'much less of a mixer and much shyer', never forgot how he suffered when the angelic French boy seemed to spurn him.[14] Always he craved outward signs of affection or love, quickly imagining the worst if these were not forthcoming.

The Rafinesques' father, a slow pessimistic man also called Gaston who practised as a doctor, was kind to Spears although clearly more loving with his own sons. It was from Gaston Rafinesque that Spears learnt a code based on stories of French chivalry and honour; the contradiction between this and his powerful ambition led later to an almost unbearable strain. Gaston's bible, he told the young Louis, was Alfred de Vigny's *Grandeurs et servitudes militaires* and his dutiful treatment of his hysterical wife, Cis, who died in an asylum, reflected his high ideals.

There were idyllic days at Voutenay, especially in the summer when the children ran wild in the woods and bathed in the river. In Spears's memory, it became a place of enchantment: tranquil and secure. Near by were reminders of history: the abbey of Vézelay, where St Bernard had preached the third crusade, and the landscape through which the Black Prince's armies had marched on their French wars of conquest. Tutors, governesses and the village schoolmaster came to the château. 'England is Carthage,' the schoolmaster would say, prophesying the decline of the great Victorian empire.[15] French was the language of his childhood, so much so that Spears developed an inability to pronounce the English *r*. He believed this to be a handicap later in the House of Commons for when he saw *r*s floating towards him he became hypnotised by the need to avoid them and this often put him off his speech.

While travelling by sea to Ireland, on the way to Donadea, he was lifted up and passed around a group of sailors, their strong grips giving a wonderful sense of reassurance; his grandmother provided this but no one else, certainly not his father.[16] Charles McCarthy Spiers bought some land in Brittany and built a house there near the Atlantic. At this place, called St Marguerite, he imposed his boisterous energy on his frail son by throwing the child into the sea to teach him to swim. It was a shock when this apparently heroic figure wept while telling his two children that their mother was leaving him.

Her apparent breakdown was only part of the trouble. Charlie Spiers had been blatantly unfaithful to his wife and scarcely concealed his pursuit of the various maids and governesses in the household. The Rafinesques and Hacks turned against him, Spears's grandmother in particular detesting her son-in-law. But the children continued for a while to go to St Marguerite, where a nursemaid called Gaidic told them of the area's legends and creatures of myth. She also revealed an hereditary distrust of the British in her stories of du Guesclin and the Hundred Years War, of the abortive landing of the Redcoats at Quiberon Bay during the revolution and their failure to aid the Breton royalists. For Gaidic and many of the French whom the young Spears met the English were always the enemy.[17]

Melicent's feelings turned to hatred. She sued her husband in the Paris courts, kept the children out of his hands and did her best to ruin his business prospects. When Spears joined the Kildare Militia in 1903, the estrangement between father and son was complete, for Charlie Spiers had not wanted him to go into the army. In 1905 the marriage was officially dissolved and Spiers died soon afterwards, leaving a sense of frustrated energy and some melancholy letters to his children and their implacable mother. Spears felt keenly the lack of a father and in later life turned often in filial hope to older men such as Sir John French, Philippe Pétain, Georges Clemenceau and Winston Churchill.

In Ireland he learnt to ride, and in the castle at Donadea there were hints of ghosts which, with Gaidic's tales, fostered a fascination with the supernatural. Superstitious by nature, he carried as a talisman throughout his life a leopard gadling which the Black Prince had reputedly taken from his own gauntlet and given to an Aylmer ancestor at the battle of Poitiers. Often he was watched over by his grandmother, a snowy-haired, dignified, cheerful, very silent woman who spoke little French in spite of her years of exile; to her at least the little boy had to speak English. It was she who supervised his physical hardening by weaning him away from winters in the south of France, first to Paris, then to Switzerland and ultimately for two years to a spartan boarding school run by monks in Germany. Spears became a strong swimmer and an athlete, easily capable of running up to ten miles. The childhood frailty had gone, leaving only a life-long tendency to infections of the throat.[18]

His education was sketchy. But he learnt much poetry by heart – particularly French poetry – and became well read later through his own curiosity. From early on he eschewed any obvious manifestation of an inner life and seemed to crave activity, decision and the role of leader. It was as if he had tried to bury his sensibility, the part of him that engendered fantasy, intuition and dread. In his books these would be revealed; in his life they were concealed from all but his closest associates and friends.

His mother took drugs for insomnia which aggravated her vindictive nature. She openly preferred her daughter Kathleen, whom she later tyrannised, to her son Louis; his sense of the charm of her presence began to be replaced by distrust and anxiety. Her marriage in 1905 to a rich Frenchman called Raymond Duval de Maratray seemed to offer a chance of happiness. For a while de Maratray made a cult of her, then turned elsewhere to seek solace in Sufism and philandering.

Spears was a fighter. As a child he owned a Savoy terrier and when at Voutenay his older cousin Marcel Rafinesque taunted him about the dog and struck out at his face with a riding crop, Spears bit his assailant in the thigh, refusing to let go until some grown-ups plunged the biter and the bitten into a bath of water; only when half suffocated did he relent and then he had to be brought round by artificial respiration.

There was something odd about this bellicose side. Boys often like stories of battles but Spears's memories of the Breton nursemaid Gaidic's stories have an unpleasant edge: knights prising open the armour at a wounded opponent's neck 'as a cook opens a sardine tin' to plunge a dagger into his throat, squires telling their dying masters who called for water to drink their own blood, revolutionaries at Nantes tying up terrified aristocrats and hurling them into the Loire.[19] Later, people saw flashes of cruelty in Spears, also of sadism, a tendency to dwell on the vicious and the macabre.

In 1903 he joined the Kildare Militia, the 3rd Battalion of the Royal Dublin Fusiliers, when only sixteen and a half, and in 1904 was gazetted a second lieutenant. Stationed at the regiment's depot at Naas, he had to overcome an upbringing presided over mostly by old ladies. On the first day in the mess he ordered a soda and water and was brought a glass of milk on the instructions of a scornful captain.

The Aylmer connection helped a little. The family knew the Colonel but it was clear from the start of Spears's army life that a foreign education and accent set him apart. In the mess he was given the nickname of Monsieur Beaucaire after a popular play about an urbane Frenchman which had opened in London in 1902; many of his friends called him this always, sometimes shortened to B.

It took up to three years of cramming before Spears passed the examinations for a commission in the regular army and in 1906 he was gazetted to the 8th, the Royal Irish Hussars. His grandmother followed him, taking flats in Colchester when his regiment was stationed there, or in London. A young officer's life was expensive and she gave what she could from the depleted Hack inheritance, much of which had now passed to his mother, to help him keep up with the extravagant habits of his peers. In his determination to get on, Spears chose the route of hard work.

Cavalry training had been only partly reshaped by the sinuous tactics of the Boers. Few officers thought beyond the traditions of courage, light-heartedness, the *élan* of the full-blooded charge and pride in display: the much vaunted ideal of the 'cavalry spirit'. This might, they believed, be traduced by too much emphasis on musketry and dismounted action. Spears's intelligence rebelled against this. His fellow subalterns must have been astounded when in 1906, the year he was commissioned, he published a translation of the French officer General François de Négrier's book, *Lessons of the Russo-Japanese War*, which tried, and failed, to take the French cavalry into the twentieth century.

It was a remarkable start, particularly as, at the outset of his career, Spears had little guidance. In England the Aylmer influence was limited to General Sir Fenton Aylmer, holder of the Victoria Cross, who kept a distant watch over his young cousin. However, his grandmother had some friends called Dr and Mrs Sebastian Evans and took Spears to stay with them at their house near Canterbury. Mrs Evans was rich, the daughter of a successful City merchant called Goldney; her money enabled the doctor to lead a life of ease and to dabble in literature, politics and art. Dr Evans was the first person with serious intellectual tastes whom Spears knew well. He had a large library, particularly strong on medieval French, had known Burne-Jones and the Pre-Raphaelites, once stood for parliament against Joseph Chamberlain in Birmingham and wrote books on the legend of the Holy Grail. Evans talked enthusiastically, treating the boy 'as a son' in his expositions on France in the age of chivalry, on his former editorship of a Conservative journal, the *People*, and on terrifying Birmingham election meetings when the riotous Irish would intimidate and assault the speakers.[20]

Mrs Evans was less appealing. A sharp-tongued, spoilt woman, she rather repelled the young Spears, but her adored son, Francis Bennett-Goldney, who had taken her family name because of an inheritance, played a much more prominent role in his early life. An ambitious and clever bachelor, Goldney showered his mother with diamonds and lace and pawed her as if she were a tame cat; his taste for over-ripe pears and passion for interior decoration made Spears shudder at first. He had come under suspicion in connection with the theft of the Irish crown jewels from Dublin Castle in 1907, but this did not stop him from being mayor of Canterbury from 1906 until 1911 and member of parliament for the city from 1910 until his death in 1918. Goldney's two sides are shown in the way he helped Spears as if the young officer were his son and later tried to swindle both him and old Mrs Hack. After his death it was discovered that he had stolen books and manuscripts. When he learnt of this dishonesty Spears felt ashamed that he had been Goldney's protégé. It was another contradiction between the ideals he hoped were behind his high ambition and a murkier reality.

Spears bought a small bulldog bitch called Mrs Gamp, an unsuitable pet for a cavalry officer because she tried constantly to nip the heels of the horses. By 1908 he had a car and terrified a colleague by taking him on drives round Aldershot at breakneck speed. Spears told the man a story of how on manoeuvres he had charged 'bald-headed' with his sword drawn at a subaltern of the 20th Hussars on the other side, making his opponent flee in terror, and was cheered by the watching troops.[21]

The incident is significant for its perpetrator's aggression and his later boastful account of it. Modesty was not his way, as he felt that unless he told the world of his achievements these might not be noticed. His solitary youth had not prepared Spears well for human contact. He could be tactless and his quick intelligence ruthlessly pierced weak argument. The ideals of the mess were those of courtesy and effortless amateurism, neither of which he adopted. An outsider from the start, he stayed one all his life.

It all almost came to nothing. On the afternoon of 17 June 1908, while Spears was playing polo at Colchester, the ball knocked him unconscious. Taken to hospital, he quickly became delirious and Francis Bennett-Goldney rushed to his bedside.

Goldney demanded that Sir Victor Horsley, the most eminent neuro-surgeon of the day, should be summoned to Colchester.[22] Horsley diagnosed concussion and a haemorrhage of the brain, noting a partial paralysis of the left side of the body and the face. He operated, then moved the patient to a nursing home in London for a long con-valescence. The army put Spears on half-pay, and in November, at Horsley's suggestion, he left to spend the winter in the south of France with his grandmother, where they stayed in a villa at St Raphaël owned by his mother and her French husband. The accident seemed likely to end his military career, so he started to prepare for the examination for the diplomatic service, a process made more difficult when his mother suddenly let the villa and they had to move into an expensive hotel.[23]

The London nursing home at 9 Mandeville Place was run by two women, one of whom – Miss Jessie Gordon – led Spears into a love affair that lasted for several years. Jessie, who won Goldney's approval, had no money, was very lively, older than the young subaltern and did not have rich tastes, which suited the impecunious Spears. Only gradually did another side emerge: that of an extreme ruthlessness when crossed.

In the south of France Spears had a flirtation with an English girl who was staying near St Raphaël. On his return to London Jessie routed her with a fierce display of possessiveness. By May 1913 she was relaxed enough about their friendship to write soothingly to old Mrs Hack, who wished her adored grandson to marry a girl of spotless background and reputation: 'I hear you are worried fearing that I should marry Louis. Please put such an absurd idea out of your head once and for all. I have no intention of doing such a foolish thing, had I wished to do so I could have done it long ago and I should be only too pleased to see him happily married to some suitable girl' – a statement that was clearly untrue.[24]

The convalescence dragged on. Goldney turned from kindness to dishonesty and persuaded Mrs Hack to advance him money for Louis's medical expenses, at the same time not paying rent for the use of her London flat; the bills were less than the amount Spears's grandmother gave the Mayor but she received none of it back and he extracted a loan from Jessie Gordon as well. As for the patient, his cure was gradual. Always prone to nightmares, Spears suffered violent nocturnal fits. By the end of 1909, still on half-pay, he sought employment as a king's messenger or a military attaché, perhaps in Japan; then Goldney, reverting to kindness again, introduced him to Colonel G. M. W. Macdonogh, who was chief of MO5, the War Office's intelligence department.[25]

Macdonogh saw a use for Spears's languages and set him to work translating foreign documents and articles from journals. Spears still had time to travel at his own expense to Belgium to see the terrain of a possible future European war and to attend French manoeuvres with his cousin General Sir Fenton Aylmer. To him, the French army seemed unprepared for modern warfare. He noted a dislike of digging trenches and an insistence on bayonet attacks over open ground with drums and bugles and troops clad in red caps and trousers. This would put them at the mercy of rapid rifle fire and reinforced Spears's belief in musketry training.

Macdonogh took to Spears. Winston Churchill described this austere, shy man as 'an officer of brilliant attainments',[26] Lloyd George tried to make him permanent under secretary at the Foreign Office in January

1918 and Curzon proposed in 1922 that he should be appointed Chief of the Imperial General Staff.[27] Macdonogh's ability, however, was of a flinty, unobtrusive kind; his taciturnity and extreme secretiveness made him an often bleak master. His support was very useful to Spears, whereas the interventions of Henry Wilson, another senior officer whom he met at this time, were far more equivocal.

Wilson, then a brigadier-general, became the director of military operations in August 1910. Having grown up in a protestant family in County Longford, he was a passionate Irish Unionist. His opposition to the Liberal government policy of Home Rule for Ireland divided him from Macdonogh, who was not only an Irish Roman Catholic and (worse still in Wilson's eyes) a convert from Methodism but believed that the army should obey its political masters.

Wilson and Spears came to loathe each other, Spears comparing his erstwhile master to Quint, 'the semi-spooky, entirely evil valet' in *The Turn of the Screw*.[28] In fact there were certain similarities between them. Like Spears, Wilson had entered the army through the Irish Militia and was regarded more for his political and diplomatic ability than for military or tactical skills. Another parallel was Wilson's belief in an alliance between Britain and France, an idea that owed much to his friendship with the French General Foch.

Tall, grotesque in appearance ('the ugliest man in the army'), with a deep scar above his right eye from a wound obtained in action against Burmese bandits, Wilson had a booming geniality of manner and the deviousness of a born intriguer.[29] He was a brilliant staff officer who showed ferocious zeal in getting his way, combining this with skilful communication: 'a real ability to make military matters clear in the simple language of civilians'.[30] Unashamedly political, he despised the Liberal Prime Minister Asquith, but his influence was immense because the attitude of the army towards the French depended very much on individuals.

In January 1906 the War Minister Haldane had obtained the consent of the then Prime Minister Campbell-Bannerman for preliminary joint staff talks; since then the French Military Attaché in London, Colonel Victor Huguet, had tried to entice the British into closer co-operation. Some senior officers had previously refused even to meet Huguet socially, such was their fear of an unnecessary and catastrophic involvement in continental Europe. Wilson changed this. His francophilia pervaded every department over which he had control, including the intelligence work of Colonel Macdonogh.

Spears returned to active service, having been passed fit in June 1910.

But the 8th Hussars had been sent to India, where the heat and sun might harm his still fragile condition. Luckily the authorities agreed to his request for a transfer to the 11th Hussars.

Here the officers were smarter and grander than those of the 8th. During his early days, Spears was admonished by the Senior Subaltern for having a handkerchief up his sleeve: 'No gentleman ever has anything up his sleeve,' drawled the older man.[31] As in the 8th Hussars, the atmosphere was one of intense philistinism, for intellectual interests and literary inclinations were thought to denote either affectation or effeminacy. Osbert Sitwell, then a younger subaltern suffering at Aldershot, observed Spears at this time, noting 'lingering cobwebs of unpopularity' because he was 'an unusually intelligent man, liked conversation and, worse yet, talked French as easily as he spoke English'. Sitwell saw a vanity and exoticism alien to Aldershot in 'his shrewd, keen, rather thin face as he pared his nails, much in the way I have seen Italian officers do'.[32] Spears seemed remote and always busy, having become the regiment's assistant adjutant. It was not until much later that he told Sitwell of his memories of Aldershot, 'half of pleasure, half of pain': the pleasure from 'the love of horses and the deep feeling of solidarity engendered by the regiment itself', especially potent for one who came from his disjointed background; the pain, or tension, from his 'two separate lives', the one of 'books, study, friendship with people who thought in other terms than those of horses and dogs', the other among the limited occupants of 'those fog-shrouded barracks'.[33] Another harsh feature was the occasional drunken brutality. Once he went to bed on a mess guest night before the last guest had left and a group of young officers hauled him out and forced him to fight them; as the party included two heavyweight army champions he emerged from the encounter in an extremely painful state.

Spears tried to make his troop of thirty to forty men 'a perfect Lilliputian army'.[34] While the regiment was at Shorncliffe in Kent he did a musketry course at Hythe and passed with distinction, to be made regimental officer in charge of musketry training. He made sure there was not a bad shot among his pupils and in 1914, at the Aldershot Command meeting, the 11th Hussars won the Hemming Cup for the best cavalry regiment in the competition.[35]

Success of this kind brought disfavour: 'it led me to forget that it was very bad form in the Army of those days to seem to take anything seriously, particularly one's profession'. Perhaps the worst rebuff came when he technically wiped out the 1st Cavalry Brigade on manoeuvres at Aldershot with the aid of six machine guns firing blanks. 'You are all dead, sir,' Spears reported delightedly to General 'Black Jack'

Kavanagh, the Brigade Commander, who roared, 'Never have I seen a lack of cavalry spirit more blatantly displayed!' Furious at this hypothetical annihilation of what he believed to be the finest mounted force in Europe, Kavanagh made the youth dismount and walk home. On the long trudge back, his top boots agonisingly uncomfortable, Spears thought of resigning but stayed on because he felt sure of the imminence of war and the opportunities it would offer.[36]

In October 1911 Spears was summoned from Shorncliffe to the War Office. Macdonogh and Henry Wilson wished to involve him in a project known to very few people: the compilation of an Anglo-French codebook that could be used by the two sides in the event of war.

The intense secrecy meant that Spears could not reveal the nature of the work and he was suspected of taking the easy option of a staff post. In fact the job proved to be very hard, particularly as the French would not allow the British to see any of their codebooks. Taken away from his regiment until April 1912, he was sent back by Henry Wilson only after the Colonel had accused him of being engaged in 'licking stamps' and putting an unfair burden on the other subalterns by his absence.[37] Spears became close to some of his secret allies and showed Aldershot to a French officer who was horrified by its discomfort. The War Office had also given a glimpse of the future. Working in the same room as Spears was another of Macdonogh's assistants, Captain Anthony Henley, and through him and his wife Sylvia he saw 'really intelligent, intellectual people'. It was in the Henleys' drawing room that Spears first met Winston Churchill.[38]

The codebook seemed to have passed out of his life. But in 1913 he was summoned to a remote part of the south coast where a small van containing wireless equipment was perched on the edge of white cliffs. Even the wireless operators were not told what they were doing, which was to try to communicate with a similar French station across the Channel; they guessed only when they observed the unusual form in which morse was being transmitted from the other side. During the war Spears saw the code lying on a desk bound in soft blue morocco and called 'Le Code W' by the French, perhaps after Henry Wilson. Probably its greatest significance is as an example of secret Anglo-French co-operation before 1914.

In 1913 Spears suffered further sickness, this time sinus trouble, which needed an operation. At the end of that year, still unfit for general service, he was given permission to spend part of the winter of 1913 to 1914 in Berlin.

In one of those links of the pre-war world that now seem strange, the German Crown Prince, the Kaiser's eldest son, was colonel-in-chief of the British 11th Hussars. He encouraged exchanges of officers with his own country's cavalry and, because of this, Spears had already had some experience of the German army on a short cavalry course at Hanover and ballooning expeditions with an artillery regiment at Mainz and Wiesbaden.

Now in the opulent and bombastic Wilhelmine Berlin of 1913, he spoke to officers at the German Staff College who, once he had penetrated their stiffness, talked easily and professionally about soldiering. They assumed that there must be a war with France; if the British army came in, they declared, its effect would be 'negligible', for England's continental allies would be crushed before she could develop her full strength. This was not said in a threatening way: simply as an obvious fact.[39]

The Crown Prince was attending a course at the German Staff College. Spears found him 'generous and chivalrous' under a flippant manner; others were not so impressed by this dissolute and shallow man who would later flirt with the Nazis. The half-Russian Crown Princess he liked also, noting her twisting of the tail of a gold pig that concealed a shrill bell to summon the servants. Once the staff officers drew for Spears an outline of their proposed advance through Belgium, an approximation of the Schlieffen plan, which he passed to the British Military Attaché, who 'was horrified and would not listen' and to his French equivalent, who 'was enormously interested' but failed to convince his superiors of its worth. Spears was shocked by the brutal treatment of the German soldiers, particularly the raw recruits, by their officers; he also thought that such cruelty checked initiative by inducing a stifling terror of making mistakes.[40]

In 1914 he followed his 1906 translation of the de Négrier book with a translation of another French military text, *Cavalry Tactical Schemes* by Colonel Monsenergue. Again the emphasis was on the importance of musketry training, and Brigadier-General H. de la P. Gough, a senior cavalry officer, wrote an introduction praising the work. In prefaces to this and the de Négrier book Spears thanked Francis Bennett-Goldney for his help.

Then in May 1914 Colonel Macdonogh ordered him to return to the War Office. Here he was told to go to Paris, to the Ministry of War, to work alongside the French and to make contact with British intelligence agents in Belgium. His only form of accreditation was a letter of introduction from Henry Wilson and he was outside the control of the British embassy. The secrecy was vital, for officially Britain was not bound by a military alliance to France.[41]

He left a brilliant London season dimmed only by the Irish crisis. In

Berlin the officers he had seen were laughingly confident about the coming smash. Crossing the Channel in plain clothes, his uniform packed as a precaution, he found a tense and nervous Paris.

In a sense he was coming home, to the country of his childhood. His mother, however, was not there to greet him. Moving restlessly between Touraine, the south of France and Paris, anxious about her second husband's financial improvidence, she had turned viciously and irrationally against her son and her daughter, her former favourite Kathleen. Two years younger than Louis, Kathleen escaped to live in poverty. She worked in a library and then married Christian Beck, a Belgian whom Spears described, wrongly, as 'detestable' and (even worse) 'a bogus literary man'.[42]

In fact Beck was a poet much admired by André Gide, who used him as a model for the shy Lucien in *The Counterfeiters*; the Hacks and the Aylmers may have disapproved of him because he had a previous child, whom he fully acknowledged, out of wedlock. When Kathleen and Beck met, he was already ill with tuberculosis. Sensing perhaps that he had not long to live, he tried to persuade his wife's relations to give her at least a part of the Hack inheritance. The family, at the behest of Kathleen's mother, ignored him and Kathleen was again pushed into the wilderness. In 1916 Beck died in Switzerland, his grim decline watched over by his wife. Two years earlier they had had a daughter, Béatrix, to whom Kathleen devoted the rest of her tragic life.

In July 1914 Spears turned to the Rafinesques, staying with them in the family flat at Passy near the Bois de Boulogne. Gaston again assumed the paternal role and on warm evenings in the city spoke of his memories of the Franco-Prussian War and the siege of 1871 when he had been a student in Paris. France wanted peace now: not to fight for the return of Alsace-Lorraine, although she would respond if attacked. Unlike in Germany, there was no bombast. Spears sensed the French hope in their alliance with a supposedly unconquerable Russia. News came of the German and Austrian preparations for mobilisation. On 28 July Austria declared war on Serbia.

In the Ministry of War Spears worked alongside two French officers of the General Staff in a small stuffy room. Their suspicions of him, and of Britain's equivocal position, took the form of an icy courtesy and an insistence on reading his letters back to the War Office in London. In the Passy apartment, stocks of food were laid in, for Gaston remembered the diet of rats in 1871. Spears tried to avoid the question of when Britain was going to come out in support of France. On 29 July the collective anxiety burst into a tumultuous reception of the French President, Raymond Poincaré, and the Prime Minister, René

Viviani, on their return from Russia after a reaffirmation of the alliance. On the 30th the French cabinet withdrew its troops six miles from the German frontiers to advertise its peaceful intentions and did not respond to a German cavalry incursion. On no account must the British be given the excuse to say that they would not help an aggressor nation. The constrained fear had the quality of unnatural silence. Then on the evening of 1 August Spears saw the Order for the General Mobilisation, its ink still wet and shining in the sun, on the wall of the Palais Bourbon: 'it was to be war after all'.[43]

As a soldier of a power not yet involved in the coming conflict, he found his position at the centre of the French military machine awkward. The French demanded that he should at least be accredited to the Military Attaché at the British embassy, Colonel Yarde-Buller, a man whom Spears had avoided. At the embassy, Yarde-Buller admitted that he knew about the young Lieutenant but would have nothing to do with him; 'this would teach the War Office not to short circuit the Military Attaché'.[44] Fearing that if he was thrown out the position of the agents in Belgium might be jeopardised, Spears sent a private cable to Macdonogh, who insisted that Yarde-Buller should help. Spears wanted to be recalled by the War Office and to return to his regiment.

At last, on 4 August, after the German invasion of neutral Belgium, came the British ultimatum to Germany and the declaration of war. French criticism turned to doubts about the strength of the new ally's volunteer army; there were, however, already reassuring rumours of barges full of British troops at Rouen on the Seine.

Spears unpacked his khaki uniform. Two huge conscript armies, the French and the German, faced each other in western Europe and the infinitely smaller British Expeditionary Force embarked for the continent, following the plans formulated by Henry Wilson. The longed-for war had started. For Spears it would bring, sometimes almost simultaneously, visions of hell and of previously unimaginable glory.

In a large house on the borders of Scotland and England, there was a rather different approach to the European crisis. A young American heiress sat among her circle, a literary group most definitely not 'bogus' at all. Ford Madox Ford was talking; he and his wife were guests of the American in the house she had taken near Berwick with her husband, a worthy man called Douglas Turner who had been a missionary in India.

The American woman's lover, Percy Wyndham Lewis, the painter and writer, observed the scene as Mary Borden, or Mary Borden-Turner (as a believer in women's rights she had joined her husband's name on to her own), listened to Ford hold forth on the prospect of war. Small, very attentive, with large serious eyes, she had, according to Lewis, 'the attractive freshness of the New World, and of a classless community', which made her seem different from the more jaded denizens of Mayfair.[45]

Then she spoke. 'There won't be any war, Ford. Not here. England won't go into a war.' Ford said exactly the opposite, that England would fight, to which Mrs Turner's riposte was that a Liberal government 'cannot declare war'.[46] So definite was her tone that Lewis admired her political sagacity, which had previously revealed itself in a suffragette assault on the Treasury in 1913 when Lloyd George was chancellor of the Exchequer; she had broken a window, spent five days at Bow Street police station – where her family sent in heavy lunch-baskets and light novels – and been fined twenty-five shillings, which, to her fury, her husband had paid without consulting her.

Within a few days the Liberal government declared war. Wyndham Lewis brought out the second number of *Blast*, joined the army and broke off his relationship with Mrs Borden-Turner.

Mary Borden had found him exciting, having grown tired of the prosaic Turner. She wanted to be a great writer and had published two novels under the pseudonym of Bridget Maclagan: *The Mistress of Kingdoms* in 1912 and *Collision* in 1913. The artists who came to her house at 33 Park Lane, where she commissioned Lewis to decorate the drawing room, were polite about these, Ford declaring that 'the delightfully dainty little blonde lady' was 'a novelist of really great gifts and authenticity'.[47] Later, in the way writers have with rich patrons, Lewis would caricature Mary Borden in the figure of Mrs Wellesley-Crooks, the pretentious literary hostess from Chicago, in *The Roaring Queen*.

Advanced for its time in its expression of feminine frustration and passion, Mary Borden's first novel, the obviously autobiographical *The Mistress of Kingdoms* (the title is taken from the book of the prophet Isaiah), has as its heroine the American heiress Barbara Witherow, who seeks experience and sensation. At college she meets the painter Anthony Ladd, surely based at least partly on Lewis, and they talk 'ardently and constantly of sex and marriage, and the national conscience'. Ladd pierces Barbara's 'incredibly sensitive attitude to her own body', but she is confused by his art ('I have simply painted a square little man made up of triangles') and goes to India and meets the missionary Colin Traive (surely Turner), who 'lives like a Fakir' and is 'all heart'. Her devout mother encourages a passionless marriage ('she felt not even physical repulsion') and their child dies in infancy in France. Seeking spiritual depth, she goes back to India, Colin having already returned there, and they achieve happiness through his humility and abnegation of the self. The novel is strong, rather clumsy, obviously honest until the end when the (for the time) brave attempts to transmit a woman's predicament run into mawkishness, with Colin even calling Barbara his 'dear bonnie bairn'.[48]

Collision, her second novel, is set in India, where Imogen Daunt, 'the famous socialist', has been asked out for the winter by her friend Mrs Susan Digby, the wife of an administrator of the Raj, to observe British rule. Colonel Digby, Susan's husband, is fascinated by Imogen and not stupid, unlike other members of his local Gymkhana club who have faces 'stamped with that subtle negation of curiosity or of understanding or even bare intelligence, which is the Englishman's pledge of fine feeling'. But it is Imogen's sexual strength that draws the Colonel, not her political views.[49]

Mary Borden spiced up *Collision* with assassination attempts and Russian and Islamic plots against the British empire. Imogen ultimately seems rather pathetic, and her idealism no match for other people's dishonesty or the strength of the Raj. As with *The Mistress of Kingdoms* the novel's chief interest now is in its depiction of the frustrations and limitations forced upon women by feminine emotion, their position in society and the way men see them, even when they have every intellectual and material advantage. Mary Borden's life-long impatience with this, and her search for a belief or fulfilment in work and action, made her a difficult and demanding partner.

Born in 1886, the daughter of William Borden of Chicago, a millionaire with interests in mining and dairy products, Mary Borden grew up in a large house in that city, on the corner of Lake Shore Drive and Bellevue Place. Later she looked back with longing to the high ceilings, the view out towards Lake Michigan and the memory of her exotically dressed parents coming up to her room to say goodnight before a party. Summers in Camden, Maine, completed this idyllic childhood built on a burgeoning American prosperity. Then suddenly a new note entered with her mother's conversion to fundamentalist Christianity.

The pleasure-loving William Borden tried to understand his wife's beliefs. 'He loved the world,' his daughter Mary wrote, 'to him it was a treasure house; while to her it carried the threat of eternal damnation and she feared and hated it.'[50] The characters of their children seem to have been split between those of the parents; one son devoted himself to missionary work, another became a reckless playboy, and Mary (or May as she came to be called) showed parts of both sides.

She had immense obstinacy, great determination and a craving for experience and adventure.

May was educated well, first by German and French governesses at home and later at Vassar. An early sense of the shortness of life, and a wish to pack as much as possible into it, made her weep on her thirteenth birthday. At the age of sixteen she wanted to be missionary to China, but at college to be a great writer seemed suddenly better. In 1906, on her twentieth birthday, May wrote from Vassar to tell Mrs Borden that she wished to devote several years to 'writing hard – in serious preparation. Then I would know whether it was in me to do a really great work that way.' The alternative was a life dedicated to charity. In any case she had 'no regrets or desires to go back to sweet sixteen. I suppose it's that I have you and so many people to love me – and the conviction that I have something vital to do here – to make my life tell for eternity. It's a wonderful thought to me that – to have our little innocent lives last forever in Christ.'[51]

Mr Borden had died when May was eighteen. Tensions arose in the home because of Mrs Borden's increasingly dogmatic opinions; May loved her but found these hard to accept. After Vassar, in an attempt to nurture her daughter's faith, Mrs Borden arranged for May to go on a world tour with a Mr and Mrs Bausher, who shared her religious views, and the journey was planned to include the many Christian missionary settlements to which the Bordens had given money. May was now extremely rich, her father having settled enough capital on her to produce an annual income after tax of £10,000. Intent of helping others, particularly in the field of women's education, she used some of this to endow a scholarship at Vassar in William Borden's memory which paid for one student a year to travel in Europe.

In Lahore she and her chaperones met an Englishman called George Douglas Turner, the son of a Scottish clergyman. Turner's early life had been spent partly in British Guiana and Jamaica – where his father had worked as a missionary – and Scotland; he had finished his education in France. Now he was living in deliberate poverty in 'a native bazaar' in order to carry the Christian message to Indian children, and he served as secretary to the local branch of the Young Men's Christian Association.[52]

The Baushers and May were captivated by his piety and quiet zeal and within a week she became engaged to him, leaving soon afterwards for Bombay and Egypt to continue her tour. Turner joined them in Switzerland, as did Mrs Borden, and, partly in response to the enthusiasm of the Baushers and her mother, May married Douglas Turner in Lausanne on 28 August 1908 when she was twenty-two.

Their early years together involved much travelling, partly because of Turner's missionary work, partly also because of May's reluctance to put down roots and deny her wish for adventure. Joyce, their first daughter, the eldest of three, was born in August 1909 in Camden, Maine; the second, Comfort, a year later at Gulmarg in Kashmir; the third, Mary Borden, in November 1915 in London. May was brave and adaptable. In India, soon after their marriage, she learnt Hindustani, lectured Indians in their own language and kept open house for potential converts. At one time fifty missionaries were sleeping in tents in her garden.

The contrast with her London life, which began in 1911 when she and Turner took a furnished house in Park Lane, was striking, for here she indulged her other side: that of a worldly and original hostess who brought Bernard Shaw and Wyndham Lewis to her dinner table, 'an intelligent and quick, witty' woman whose parties 'were always remarkable'.[53] Turner, a gentle, rather dim man, did not shine in this world of high bohemia, although he seemed content to abandon the ascetic life. He added the cause of social reform to his religious activity and worked with Rowntree and Tawney. He became honorary secretary of the Persian Society, touring Persia on his own, and in 1913 went on an extended trip to the Balkans, again without his wife. Turner was financially dependent on May; she took a house for his parents in Paddington and had him made British representative of an American company partly owned by the Bordens. Gradually she lost interest in him, a process accelerated by her excited admiration for artistic and literary achievement.

In London she backed plays, including one of her own, and became known as a writer. Wyndham Lewis found the small, large-eyed May attractive and she was enthralled by his energy and genius, offering to build a gallery for his pictures. When Turner was away, May slept with Lewis in his run-down flat and wrote afterwards in obsessive anxiety:

> It doesn't matter, does it, whether I understand your technique or not as long as I adore you, not too stupidly? If I'm an artist at all it is in living ... You are a genius and you might be cruel to me some day were it not for this. Anyhow – I don't care ... I lay awake last night and heard you snoring peacefully in the place that was once a brothel but I didn't want to cut your throat.[54]

But Lewis felt May was not 'primitive' enough. He accused her of vanity, of having an absurd fascination for bohemia while living a life of luxury in Mayfair. They quarrelled, he showing his irritation in harsh words. 'I love you,' May wrote, admitting that she had been 'tactless, inconsiderate and stupid', not to mention 'vain and spoiled, but I am also fine enough to know that you are a great artist', although 'you are also a faulty human being and you have hurt me, many times.'[55]

Then the war kicked away her old world. Turner joined up as a private in the London Scottish Territorial Regiment and went to France in October 1914 to be an interpreter with the Indian troops. May, still unsettled, thought of how she might use her great fortune. She put her name down with the London committee of the French Red Cross and was interviewed by its president, the Vicomtesse de la Panouse, the wife of the French Military Attaché. Admitting that she had no nursing experience, she volunteered to go to Dunkirk to work in a hospital where there was an epidemic of typhoid.

May offered her services free and paid for two English nurses to come with her. She left her three young daughters in London and arrived at the casino at Malo-les-Bains near Dunkirk, a makeshift typhoid hospital where patients lay in conditions of terrible squalor. There was very little equipment; the contrast with the gilded mirrors and vast gas chandeliers of the Belle Époque seemed absurd. The stench sickened her, an accompaniment to pain and death. Such scenes became the backdrop to her life for the next four years, crowding out memories of Lewis and those pre-war explorations in London's bohemia, for she believed that she had at last found something to make her life 'tell for eternity'.

2

Liaison 1914

Spears would say that he was the first British officer at the front in 1914.

He left Paris in a car for Vitry-le-François, the French Grand Quartier Général or headquarters, on 5 August, still under the orders of Colonel Macdonogh, and the driver stopped on the way to buy a Union Jack, which he fastened to the bonnet, to the surprise of some spectators who did not believe that Britain was now their ally. At Vitry, a small town on the Marne, he found wild optimism. German shells were said to be bursting harmlessly high, a sign of defective munitions; apparently German prisoners complained of 'starvation', enemy cavalry was 'absolutely inefficient'[1] and French officers spoke poetically of 'dying in white gloves'.[2] The dark blue coats and red trousers of the army had the pathetic elegance of 1870, the year of the last catastrophic German war.

What had happened was that the French, in a gallant but outmoded belief in 'offensive à outrance', had struck eastward across the German frontiers into the lost territories of Alsace and Lorraine.[3] But the Germans had stuck to the Schlieffen plan, first promulgated in 1905 and modified since, which denuded their eastern front, where they faced the Russians, for a massive strike of fifty-four divisions through Belgium and northern France. These would pass to the west of Paris and then east to encircle the French and smash them against their own frontier defences. The French concentration on the east at the expense of the north was precisely what the Germans wanted. The trap had been set for a quick victory in the west.

Spears saw Joffre, the French Commander-in-Chief, walking with an ADC outside his headquarters. The heavy General paused placidly to greet the young Englishman. Behind him stood his *chef de cabinet*, the impressively cool young Major Gamelin, who would be commander-in-chief in 1940.

In 1914 the French and British armies knew little of each other and contacts were often bedevilled by mutual incomprehension. Even Henry

Wilson, the arch-advocate of Franco-British co-operation, had been said to declare that he saw 'no reason for an officer knowing any language except his own',[4] and when Sir John French, the commander of the British Expeditionary Force, spoke from a prepared French text at manoeuvres in France in 1910 his listeners thought he was speaking in English. On the French side few of the commanders spoke good English, with the exception of Nivelle and Foch. It was in this linguistic fog that Spears flourished.

At Vitry he had a symbolic meeting on 9 August in the mess with the suave Colonel Victor Huguet, head of the French Mission to the British army. Then came the message from London. Spears was to move to Rethel, the headquarters of the French Fifth Army under the command of General Lanrezac. Colonel Muller, Joffre's ADC, joked that the British would have to hurry up if they were going to see any of the fun, since General Lanrezac was not going to delay for slow-coaches.

As the Germans approached, there was another duty for Spears: that of making use of his pre-war intelligence work. Under Macdonogh's orders he tried to keep in touch with agents in Belgium by visiting them in a car with a French chauffeur and a soldier as an escort. Once they ran into a troop of German cavalry which chased the car back to the French lines.

On 14 August Spears arrived in Rethel, a pleasant town on the slopes of the Ardennes. He was to act as a link between the French Fifth Army of over a quarter of a million men and the British Expeditionary Force of only 111,000 on its left. The neighbouring allied commanders, Sir John French and General Lanrezac, were very different. Before the war, Lanrezac, a flabby faced man whose dark complexion showed his mulatto blood, had taught at the Ecole de Guerre, where his nickname was 'Le Voyou' (the hooligan) on account of his fierce manner. A theoretician, he spoke as if delivering a lecture, with his eyeglasses hitched absurdly over his right ear. Sir John French, on the other hand, was a brave, emotional cavalryman who had won his reputation in the Boer War. A small, bulky, red-faced figure with a snowy moustache, in appearance a caricature of the brainless army officer, French relied on intuition, a belief in the old cavalry spirit and the gift of inspiring loyalty in his troops. Sir John had charm; he loved women and could show a soft, almost caressing, side but he was neither imaginative nor astute.

Much of the character of the alliance had already been decided. In a confusion that went back to the first joint talks in 1906, the French believed that they with their huge armies had command over the tiny

British contingent, whereas Sir John French saw his position as that of an independent commander; he felt also the need, pressed upon him by Lord Kitchener, the Minister of War, not to waste the lives of the British Expeditionary Force before the arrival of reinforcements.

On 17 August Sir John French came to Rethel to make his first call on General Lanrezac. The two commanders met alone, without interpreters. Spears and some French officers stood in the square outside imagining a conversation restricted to such phrases as 'what has become of the penknife of the gardener's uncle?'[5] But it was worse than that. Lanrezac's son challenged Spears's account of the meeting in *Liaison 1914*, claiming that his father's most scathing comments had been delivered to a group of his staff officers that evening. Even if it is an exaggeration, the story conveys the arrogance on the French side.

The two generals emerged from Lanrezac's inner sanctum, their linguistic reserves exhausted. In the room where his staff were waiting, Sir John French saw a map. Observed by a British officer, who later told Spears, he pointed at it. 'Mon Général,' he began, 'est-ce que ...' and then he broke down, asking one of his staff, 'How do you say "to cross the river" in French?' before, in true cavalry spirit, charging again. 'Est-ce que les Allemands vont traverser la Meuse à ... à ...?' The next word, Huy, might have trapped a more accomplished French speaker; for Sir John it came out in an oddly triumphant shout of 'Hoy!' The mystified Lanrezac asked, 'What does he say?' When told that Sir John wished to know if the Germans were going to cross the River Meuse at Huy he said: 'Tell the Marshal that in my opinion the Germans have merely gone to the Meuse to fish.' The meeting lasted little more than twenty minutes.[6]

Oddly enough, and this is why Spears may have exaggerated Lanrezac's rudeness, Sir John French seems to have left with respect for the Frenchman, writing that night in his diary of 'a very capable soldier' who 'struck me very much by his nerve and decision of character'. He also wrote: 'we fully discussed the situation and arrived at a mutual understanding'.[7] What could not be denied, however, was Lanrezac's contempt for the reluctant British, and this surely must have communicated itself even to the obtuse Sir John, who was later very uncomplimentary about him in *1914*, his account of the campaign.

On the night of 17 August, Spears met a captured German aviator at the headquarters of the French Fifth Army who was astonished to see a British uniform, not knowing that Britain had entered the war. In the French mess there were jokes about British officers taking three-year leases on houses in Rouen, absurd behaviour because the war could not last beyond Christmas. Was this an excuse to reconquer France? The question was only partly a joke. One French officer said: 'If the English get into Calais they will never leave it at the end of the war. They were too upset when they lost it before.'[8]

On 18 August Lanrezac moved north to be closer to his advancing troops. Spears and his bandy-legged French servant Boisvert followed in a car of his own, a small Sunbeam with faulty headlights, and observed the French units. With their disorganised appearance, heavy packs, apparent inability to march in step and *capottes*, which combined both a tunic and a greatcoat, often unbuttoned, they looked 'much more like a mob than like disciplined men'. Mostly workers from the land, they seemed bigger than their British counterparts, who came generally from the industrial cities.[9]

He and the Basque Captain Fagalde were told to find the British and searched Picardy without success. Some French staff officers laughed, wondering if their ally's presence was just a myth. The forces of the enemy were more in evidence. On the evening of 20 August, from a hill overlooking the industrial area of Charleroi, with the River Sambre below, Spears and a French officer saw the sky to the north aflame as the Germans surged southwards.

Lanrezac would not get out to see his troops, choosing instead to sit in his room, wander around his offices or pace up and down outside. On the 21st the Fifth Army moved its headquarters north to the small Belgian town of Chimay. Here Spears found a population barely aware of the war, unlike in France, where people remembered the Prussian invasion of 1870. He had his first sight of troops of the British Expeditionary Force: a detachment of the Irish Guards and a column of artillery, very smartly turned out.

Lanrezac and his staff were obsessed with secrecy and told the Englishman very little. He had to watch, listen and delve for information, relying on friendly staff officers, overheard conversations or his own observations. His journeys by road to find out what was happening or to report back to British headquarters involved cars that constantly broke down and frequent challenges by aggressive French territorials at roadblocks and sentry posts. Communication by telephone was unreliable; the system often collapsed and even picked up the German lines by mistake. Added to these was the astonishing speed of the enemy.

In response to French reverses in Alsace and Lorraine, Joffre ordered Lanrezac to attack in the north. Spears did not know that the battle of Charleroi had started until Chimay started to fill up with refugees.

Quickly he went north, to find evidence of French retreat, of German mastery of the heights south of the Sambre river. At a crossroads Spears saw two British cars, one of which contained the Commander-in-Chief Sir John French. The party, which included Henry Wilson, was on its way to see Lanrezac at Chimay. They signalled to Spears to stop and went with the nervous subaltern into a nearby cottage. Some French soldiers resting on the verges looked suspiciously at these strange, khaki-clad beings.

The cottage was also some kind of café or estaminet. Its proprietor, an open-mouthed woman, was made to clear dirty cups and plates off a table so that maps could be spread out; as the British peered at these she began to wash up loudly in a tub, ceasing only when asked to do so by one of Sir John's staff. Spears's news was vital. Lanrezac's forces, he said, had suffered in an encounter with the Germans and would not be able to stave off the huge, far-flung enemy manoeuvre to the west, which intelligence reports suggested must now fall on the isolated, vastly outnumbered British. The only French support the British could depend upon was General Sordet's cavalry, which would move up from the south to reinforce their left flank. Lanrezac, Spears said, had left Chimay for his battle position at Mettet.

Sir John stared at the map. Mettet, he decided, was too far for him to go; perhaps also he dreaded another incomprehensible conversation. Spears was distraught. The need for the two neighbouring commanders to speak to each other had never seemed so great. How otherwise could they hope to co-ordinate their armies, now mutually dependent? For the British in particular, with their tiny force, support was vital. Communications should not be left only to himself, an overwhelmed young officer. He begged Sir John to go and later blamed himself for having been too diffident. Instead the Field Marshal told Spears to come back with them to the British headquarters at Le Cateau, where they were met by Colonel Macdonogh with an intelligence report of an imminent German descent on the British left wing. 'Now we knew,' Spears wrote later.[10]

He left in his car for Mettet where, in front of the church, Lanrezac stood with his staff in apparent silence. He refused to see Spears but one staff officer said that the French infantry could not stand against German troops who had had three years of training instead of the French two; the only course was to shelter behind the artillery. By driving to the front and speaking to staff and fighting officers, he learnt that the French had fallen back, leaving the British isolated about nine miles ahead of the French line. There would be an annihilation if the German might crashed into Sir John's tiny army.

Spears knew he must report to Le Cateau and set out at 7 p.m. On his arrival, faint with exhaustion, he was revived by Colonel Macdonogh and half a bottle of champagne. He then went to the château, where the Commander-in-Chief was having a late dinner. When Sir John French and Sir Archibald Murray, his Chief of Staff, appeared, Spears, anxious not to be too pessimistic, said simply that Lanrezac would not attack and the British were isolated on his right, about half a day's march north of him. Macdonogh added intelligence of a German corps marching down on the extreme left of the British line.

Spears and Macdonogh were asked to leave. They went into the dining room, where other members of French's staff were looking at plans laid out on the table, and Spears thought of Nolan at Balaclava, who had brought the order for the charge of the Light Brigade. His task was to stop an advance but if he failed the consequences would be even worse. After twenty minutes Murray returned. 'You are to come in now and see the Chief,' he said to the staff officers. 'He is going to tell you that there will be no advance. But remember there are to be no questions. Don't ask why. There is no time and it would useless. You are to take your orders, that's all. Come on in now.'[11]

Spears and Macdonogh left, feeling relieved. At Chimay, on his return in the early hours of 23 August, there was not much rest. At 6 a.m. the French General left for a new advance position at Phi-lippeville. With him went Spears, who had embarked upon the most momentous day of his young life.

How terrible Philippeville seemed in the cold mist of that early morning. The jammed carts and tired columns of refugees, the old women with bleeding feet, the weeping children and stunned elderly couples helping each other, stifled Spears's sense of the romance of war; now it seemed 'only a dreary massacre, a stupefying alternation of boredom, fatigue and fear'.[12] Lanrezac watched this in the Place all morning, a heavy figure in a black tunic, red breeches and black gaiters, his legs apart and hands behind his back. Worn-out troops tried to sleep on the pavements. From time to time gendarmes arrested a soldier whom they suspected of desertion and brought him up to the General.

Some vestiges of normal, even comfortable, life remained. Spears had a good meal in a local hotel but the interlude was short. At 3.10 p.m. he received a message from Colonel Macdonogh over the telephone for Lanrezac, apparently dictated by Sir John French, which said that the British would support the Fifth Army in its forthcoming attack.

Now this seems an astonishing communication, not least because of its apparent ignorance of what was happening elsewhere. First, since early that day Sir John's own forces had been engaged in the battle of Mons, a fact of which he seems to have been unaware. Second, Lanrezac's stance was anything but offensive in character. Third, the message implied a wild underestimation of the size of the German forces with which the British were faced. At 6 p.m. Macdonogh brought a more realistic assessment of the position and a message arrived from Joffre to say that three German corps were threatening the BEF. Sir John would have to change his plans, but he still hoped to avoid retreat. To his north the BEF, vastly outnumbered, was trying to hold its own by superior rifle fire.

At 4.55 Spears received another message from the British. GHQ had heard that at least one other French corps was in full retreat. He rushed to the post office, found only one clerk and after frenzied efforts got through to Le Cateau to say that he had been assured the French troops had only fallen back slightly; the observers in the British aeroplanes must have mistaken the long lines of refugees for fleeing soldiers. On leaving the post office he found an almost empty square, heard that Lanrezac had moved back to Chimay, and quickly followed. Previously Sir John had offered to draw the pressure off Lanrezac by attacking; now the need seemed to be for the French to attack to relieve the British. At about 9 p.m. the staff were called into the General's room at Chimay and Spears felt 'a current of excitement' pierce 'the atmosphere of sickening inactivity and apprehension' at last.[13] The conference broke up. He asked for information, to be told that Lanrezac was about to issue orders for the Fifth Army to retire.

The decision had been made without any reference to the British and would expose them to certain destruction. Lanrezac seemed indifferent to their fate. They were in advance of the French and were proposing to stand their ground. Sir John must be warned. Spears drove to Le Cateau, arriving there at about 11 p.m. From Lanrezac's decision Sir John deduced that, further to his right, the French Third and Fourth Armies were also retiring, and so he must retreat as well. By his action, and closeness to the French, Spears had saved the British Expeditionary Force. An acting captain, in reality a subaltern, had saved an army.

Henceforth Sir John French would never trust Lanrezac; and this distrust grew into a general suspicion of the French. A determination to preserve his forces had changed almost to fear.

Sir John saw Spears again at Le Cateau, shortly after one o'clock in the morning of 24 August. Lanrezac, he said, should be informed that the BEF would retire on its lines of communication, 'in which case General

Lanrezac must look after his own left flank, as the British would no longer be responsible for covering it'.[14] At Chimay, just after dawn, Spears was shown into Lanrezac's bedroom to deliver his message. Standing to attention, he saw the big man sitting on his bed, gazing in silence at the carpet. The allies were now retreating independently of each other from what seemed to be an inexorable German advance.

Spears was still worried. Could the British disengage in time to catch up with the French Fifth Army or would they become an isolated target for German encirclement? He confided in the French officers Duruy and Girard, who said he must speak to Lanrezac to urge a short counter-attack by a part of the Fifth Army to deflect the Germans. They would accompany him in silent support. Spears felt overwhelmed by the responsibility, but, on seeing Lanrezac sitting at a table in what had once been a classroom in the Belgian training barracks, he was overcome by a strange fluency: 'I have never got over my astonishment at my sudden and quite unusual eloquence.' 'Mon Général,' he concluded, 'if by your action the British Army is annihilated, England will never pardon France, and France will not be able to afford to pardon you.' Lanrezac exploded in anger and banged his fist on the table. Spears and his two French friends left quickly, not catching the words. Once outside, Duruy said: 'You did well.'[15]

The French General issued orders, of which Spears took a copy immediately to Le Cateau, but these merely postponed the withdrawal of one corps of the Fifth Army and held out the hope of an attack by this the next day. Sir Archibald Murray told Spears that the British retreat must go on. That evening Spears went to the new headquarters of the Fifth Army at Aubenton, an hour and a half's journey from Le Cateau, to give this message to a disgruntled Lanrezac.

It was a time of immense physical exhaustion. The British marched back in step, the French in a more irregular way, their regiments passing by 'to a sound like the rain of pebbles on a drum'.[16] The Germans, also weary, surged onwards in the August heat but with one huge difference: they were advancing towards Paris and an expected victory.

On the 26th, Spears heard more bad news, sent this time from the French liaison officer Colonel Huguet, of a British corps under Douglas Haig in a state of 'irremediable defeat', streaming back towards the Fifth Army while the Germans poured through the gap.[17] Wearily, Lanrezac ordered help to be given. In fact Haig had repulsed the enemy and carried out his retreat in good order and it was at Le Cateau, further to the left, that the danger lay. Here Sir Horace Smith-Dorrien stood (Sir John French later claimed against his orders) against the enemy: a British force of 55,000 against 150,000 Germans.

Spears went in search of Lanrezac, threading his way through the refugees on the clogged roads. He found the General at Le Nouvion in a bad mood, complaining that if only the British and his own head-quarters would not interfere with him he could beat the Germans. Spears did hear, however, that Huguet's message had been alarmist and that there was to be another attempt at allied co-operation. With Joffre, Lanrezac went to see the British at their new headquarters at St Quentin.

At the conference, the atmosphere was cool, Sir John insisting on the continuation of his retreat. Lanrezac left early, having annoyed the British by his pedantry, but Joffre stayed and became genial over lunch, admitting that his plans had failed and he was not pleased with Lanrezac. Outside, Spears was told that the liaison work could be left to Huguet and occasional visits to the Fifth Army by Colonel Bowles, a French scholar on the British staff. As this did not take the form of an order he ignored it. He learnt also that on hearing of Haig's rumoured disaster General Sir Archibald Murray had collapsed.

That evening he arrived in the drenching rain at the new Fifth Army headquarters at Marle, to hear news which turned the town into 'one of the most dreadful places I have ever been in': that of the apparent complete defeat of the British army.[18] The message had again come from Huguet. In fact Smith-Dorrien's stand at Le Cateau had delayed the German forces, and an orderly British withdrawal had been possible.

On 27 August Huguet's reports were still depressing, this time to the effect that the British might have to withdraw all the way to Le Havre to give them time to reorganise. Over the next two days, to Spears's disappointment and shame, the French planned to attack while the British remained fixed on retreat, and Murray collapsed again. Lanrezac said 'terrible, unpardonable things concerning Sir John French and the British Army', and Spears had to admit he had 'every excuse for exasperation'.[19]

Arriving in Laon, the new Fifth Army headquarters, on the evening of the 28th he felt overcome by misery. The city with its high-towered twelfth-century cathedral stands on a ridge in a naturally fortified position which had defied besiegers for centuries. Emboldened perhaps by a new impression of security, Spears sent a telegram to the British to encourage participation in the proposed attack. But the day before, Henry Wilson, who was gaining influence over Sir John, had dismissed Joffre's plan as 'mad'.[20] Then on the 29th Spears saw a French victory at last when Lanrezac fought the battle of Guise and General Franchet d'Esperey's division marched forward, flags flying and bands playing, to throw the Germans back over the River Oise. Later Spears told of the 'stern, silent' Brigadier Philippe Pétain, whom he saw for the first time during the battle, watching this daring display. Pétain had been a lecturer at the French Staff College and the dashing Franchet d'Esperey called out mockingly to him: 'What do you think of this manoeuvre, Monsieur le Professeur à l'Ecole de Guerre?' It was the man of action addressing the schoolmaster.[21]

Lanrezac sent Captain Fagalde to the British GHQ, now in the palace of Compiègne, to give Sir John news of the victory at Guise and ask for British support on the left. Once again the answer was that the British would continue to retreat; Joffre had also made the request and had also been rebuffed. On 30 August Duruy took Spears as support to Compiègne to ask similarly for a pause in the retreat. Sir John listened to them without giving an answer; by now he had developed so strong a distrust of Lanrezac that he did not believe the result of Guise until he sent an emissary to speak to the commanders who had taken part. The retreat went on.

Spears had another glimpse of the enemy forces, this time from a French aeroplane. He went up from Laon, above St Quentin, piloted by an officer shaking with malaria, and saw the German columns 'for endless miles' like 'black laces spread along the long white roads'. They released steel arrows, a new invention, on to the invader. On another trip, Spears fired a French cavalry carbine at a German plane, which fired back: 'the usual thing in war, each tries to kill the other for fear of being killed himself'.[22]

The rain at Marle passed; the retreat took place mostly in scorching heat and Spears's memories were of dust and hard blue skies, of narrow roads blocked by refugees, of bands of unarmed soldiers looting and terrorising civilians. Once, searching for Lanrezac, he found himself in a village where no one could tell him the way to the Mairie because all the inhabitants had gone south, to be replaced by those of another village further north also in flight from the Germans.

Leaving Laon, Lanrezac established his headquarters in a dispiriting château at Craonne where Napoleon had stayed a hundred years before while trying to stem another invasion. When he came to the château during dinner, Spears saw the General and his party on a terrace looking out to the River Aisne and the distant lights of Reims. In the soft summer air the voice of Lanrezac could be heard, low, almost musical, reciting some Latin verses: 'Oh how happy is he who remains at home, caressing the breast of his mistress, instead of waging war.'[23]
A German aeroplane had dropped leaflets on Paris announcing the

arrival of the enemy in three days' time. As for the British, Sir John French's plan to retire behind the Seine was overturned when Lord Kitchener, the Minister of War, came to the French capital and ordered him to stay in line with his ally.

On 2 September the Fifth Army made its headquarters at Châtillon-sur-Marne, on the north bank of the river. As Spears and some French officers stood outside the staff offices, they heard Lanrezac's furious voice. 'Nous sommes foutus, nous sommes foutus!' it raged, reflecting the despair of a commander 'to whom a quarter of a million men looked to lead them to safety and ultimately to victory'.[24] The same day the French government moved from Paris to Bordeaux. On the 3rd the British army crossed the Marne. The German right swung eastwards in front of Paris, away from the British, and Joffre prepared to attack at last.

The Fifth Army headquarters now moved to Orbais, then to Sézanne, where in the late afternoon General Joffre suddenly appeared. The two generals walked together in front of the school which served as headquarters, Lanrezac seeming to talk in an expostulatory way, Spears and others noting his depressed air, the collapse of his shoulders. Joffre was fatherly, almost soothing. They walked out of the school playground. Lanrezac did not reappear, for he had been dismissed and was on his way to Paris. At once there were rumours that he would be court-martialled; in fact the only obvious sign of disgrace was that he received no further command in the field for the rest of the war. The British were happy to see him go.

On 4 September Spears saw Franchet d'Esperey, the new Fifth Army commander: a short, square man with hair *en brosse* and head shaped like a 'howitzer shell', entirely different to the morose Lanrezac.[25] Authority emanated from him, as well as intolerance and fierce energy. He was, Spears felt, a leader, the right man at last.

Franchet d'Esperey, christened 'Desperate Frankie' by the British, wished to meet Sir John that afternoon at Bray-sur-Seine with a plan which was the basis for Joffre's order to stand against the Germans on the Marne. But Sir John did not come to Bray, having baulked at the crowded roads and possibly also at another unequal encounter with a French general, sending instead Henry Wilson and Colonel Macdonogh, who arrived late, having stopped on the way to help a French woman whose car had run out of petrol.

Spears listened as Franchet d'Esperey spoke forcefully but cour-teously, with none of the abrupt impatience of Lanrezac. Wilson appeared to be lost in detail and it was left to Macdonogh to say how enemy movements seemed to the British. Franchet d'Esperey wanted a concerted attack eastwards and northwards with the British advancing to fill the gap between the French Fifth and Sixth Armies. Henry Wilson said he would take the proposals back to Sir John French.

Once again there was Franco-British confusion. Sir Archibald Murray had agreed with Gallieni, the Military Governor of Paris, that the British would start from a position further back, fifteen miles from where Franchet d'Esperey and Joffre wanted them to be. Sir John seemed unable to make up his mind. Huguet reported that the Field Marshal would do what Joffre wished, but the French Commander-in-Chief needed to be sure. He would meet Sir John at the British headquarters, ostensibly to thank him for his support.

Franchet d'Esperey ordered Spears to observe the meeting. The liaison officer endured the usual traffic jams on the way, arriving in time to see Joffre getting out of his car. In the château of Vaux-le-Pénil, the British contingent was waiting: Sir John, Generals Murray and Wilson and the 'keen-faced and intelligent' liaison officer at the French head-quarters, Major Sidney Clive.[26]

Joffre spoke, in 'a low, toneless, albino voice'. He said first that he wished to thank Sir John for having taken a decision 'on which the fate of Europe might well depend'. He then described his plan and the role of the British in it, his eloquence growing until Spears for one believed absolutely in victory. The retreat was over; 'those who could not advance were to die as they stood. No man was to give way even as much as a foot.' In his peroration, the words became more intense, and the sentiments too. 'Monsieur le Maréchal, c'est la France qui vous supplie,' Joffre declared, his voice thick with emotion, then waited, rather breathless, for the British response. Everyone looked at little Sir John, on whose cheeks they could see tears. First he tried French, always a mistake, then turned in despair to his officers. 'Damn it, I can't explain. Tell them that all that men can do our fellows will do.' Murray completed the anticlimax. It was, he said, impossible for the British to advance at 6 a.m. as Joffre had asked; they could not be ready until 9 a.m. This was translated to the French Commander, who shrugged his shoulders. 'It cannot be helped,' Joffre said. 'Let them start as soon as they can. I have the Marshal's word, that is enough for me.'[27]

Spears found that the liaison between the BEF and the French General Maunoury's Sixth Army was working well, a sign, he believed, of how much the problems between Lanrezac and Sir John had owed to personal incompatibility. Then he and Girard set out for Romilly-sur-Seine, Franchet d'Esperey's new headquarters. Outside the town they were stopped by a British officer. He said that Spears must immediately go to see Franchet d'Esperey, who was in a terrible rage, having heard from another British officer, Colonel Jack Seely, a former Liberal war minister, that the British were continuing to retreat. If this was so, the French Commander had declared, he would stop the advance of his own army.

In spite of Spears's assurances that there was no doubt of Sir John's intention to advance, Franchet d'Esperey raged on, saying 'some very bitter, some unacceptable things concerning the British commander-in-chief in particular and the British in general'.[28] Horrified, Spears telephoned the BEF's headquarters and found out that the advance was still in place. This was accepted and the Fifth Army's orders were not changed. He could not, however, let the slur on the British stand and bravely approached Franchet d'Esperey's chief of staff for an apology. This was duly given. Spears suggested that an end to the misunderstanding would come only if Sir John visited Franchet d'Esperey. He did so a few days later.

On 6 September the battle of the Marne began. Observing the change in tactics and morale of the French, Spears thought that no other people but 'the most intelligent and adaptable race in the world' could have changed so quickly 'or learnt so much'.[29] The loss of officers had been serious, but conscription and the high standard of education in the ranks ensured enough men to take their place. He moved between the British and the French, often with Girard, as the allies advanced through the devastated towns and villages with their shocked or ecstatic inhabitants, the dead cattle and the wreckage of war. The German corpses, he noted, turned black a few hours after death; some said this was the result of the explosive power of the French 75 gun, others that it came from drinking too much red wine. By 10 September the Fifth Army was at Vielmaison, and here on the 12th Spears heard General Gallieni's staff officers mock the slow British progress.

One occasion should have been impressive: that of General Franchet d'Esperey's entry into Reims. The Germans hung on and not until 1 p.m. on 13 September was the grand liberation thought to be possible; even then the enemy was still in the hill forts surrounding the city. Franchet d'Esperey and his party left their cars in the suburbs and got on to horses, Spears riding directly behind the General to represent the British. At first the streets were empty, for the cowed people had not dared to emerge; those who did seemed bewildered. The planned triumph fell flat, leaving a 'pathetic and rather depressing' impression, not improved by a few shouts of 'Vive le Général Pau!' for the crowd believed its liberator to be the popular one-armed French officer of that name. The Fifth Army's chief of staff's horse reared up and, fearing that officer might fall off, Franchet d'Esperey shouted at the people, 'Taisez-vous!'[30] Spears found a German notice which declared that if there was any disturbance in the city seventy named hostages would be shot. He took a copy of this later to GHQ and later heard that it had been read out in parliament by Asquith.

In Reims the Fifth Army came under astonishingly accurate German bombardment centred on the headquarters and on the cathedral, which the Germans wrongly claimed the French were using as a signalling station, and it turned out that spies were speaking by telephone to the German batteries, the French having neglected to cut the wires. The town hall, known to be full of German prisoners, remained untouched. The French moved the German wounded to the cathedral, but the bombardment went on, brave priests doing what they could to save the infirm enemy. It was Spears's first experience of being helpless in a shelled town. He tried to smoke his pipe which tasted vile, apparently a symptom of nerves.

The Fifth Army headquarters moved out, to 'the horrible little village' of Romigny, and a spy hunt began. That night he watched refugees pour out of Reims as the city burned, 'wrapped in flames', the fire rising above the huge cathedral, which stood dark against an orange sky.[31] It was 14 September and the allied advance had died out at the River Aisne. The war of movement became the impasse of the long line of the western front.

3

'Think I Will Shoot Myself'

In 1914 the duties of a liaison officer were poorly defined and Spears acted often on his own initiative. During the exhausting days of the great retreat, he learnt the importance of moving fast, of seeing immediately the point or possible result of orders, information or rumour. This need to report rapidly, either in person or on paper, came easily to his agile mind; less suited to his character were diplomacy or tact, although he had seen the essential need for good personal relations between allied commanders.

His work came to involve much dangerous travelling to and from the front line and the different headquarters (he was wounded four times) and contact with British and French of all types and ranks. To be effective, the liaison officer had to know about many subjects: transport, supplies and artillery or the movement of infantry and firepower. The physical and mental strains were very great; most of the driving took place at night, for this was thought to be safer, with few chances of sleep. In the course of the war Spears had fifty-six motor cars, British and French, issued to him.

He was between two uncomprehending armies, each often ignorant of the other's movements; as late as 1916 Spears found French troops who did not know that the British were fighting within a mile of them. In 1915 his British uniform was mistaken for a German one by a French detachment only a mile from the British lines. When he pointed to the ribbon of his Legion of Honour, the French corporal said: 'We thought you might have been given that for surrendering.'[1]

Food was a source of tension and he observed a curious scene once at Verdun. The French fed some of the British and the British fed some of the French; quickly the entente became stifled by dry lumps of meat or exotic sauces. An understanding of national sensibilities was vital. On the French side, there were suspicions that went back through Fashoda, Michelet, Napoleon, Louis XIV, Joan of Arc and the Hundred Years War, for 1914 was the first time in the long history of wars in France that a French soldier could answer 'Friend' to the challenge of a British sentry. As the British contribution grew, parts of northern France became a huge British camp. In 1918 a French officer told Spears that he could not wait for the British and the Americans to get out of Paris so that it could be a French city again.

In August 1914 Spears saw French soldiers in their red trousers and heavy coats, sweltering in the heat, victims of out-of-date tactics and equipment. But the first defeats changed the French army and brought out an astonishing ability to adapt. The French, he observed, could tolerate worse conditions than the British and were more inventive, although a French idea, like the quick-firing rifle or the steel helmet, was often improved upon by the British, who eventually introduced the most significant new weapon of the war: the tank.

Often those old caricatures of one nation loomed high in the thoughts of the other: the lofty, slow, patronising, devious British and the unreliable, quick, selfish, shifty, too-clever-by-half French. In January 1917 a British staff officer told Spears that the policy of the French was to win the war for themselves and to keep the British playing second fiddle. Spears thought that as the war progressed there seemed to be a reversal of what he saw as the usual national characteristics. In 1917, the year of the Calais conference and the disastrous Nivelle offensive, the French seemed to be ruled by their heart and the British by their head.

To Spears, his position had one great drawback. Although often in danger, he was bracketed with the despised staff officers and their easy life and he tried constantly to get a command at the front. The compensations were his proximity to the great, the sense of the importance of his work and his new friendships with the French officers on the staffs of the generals to whom he was attached.

Spears's relationships first with Colonel Macdonogh and Henry Wilson, then with Sir John French, had their origins in the nature of his job. There was something paternal in the response of Sir John to this young messenger from Lanrezac who had saved his army from almost certain annihilation. With the young French officers, however, Spears formed stronger bonds of shared risk and tragedy. A man of France himself by upbringing and early cultural influence, he saw the first hopes of victory by Christmas turn into a rout. When writing of his French colleagues he evokes the world of Dumas, of gallantry and romance, of chevaliers guided by those principles of chivalry he had learnt at Voutenay. The Marquis de Rose, a daring aviator later killed in action; Captain Wemaëre, once a cavalry instructor at Saumur, who held the bridge at Château-Thierry during the retreat; the Jewish interpreter Captain Helbronner; the Basque Captain Fagalde; and the 'sensitive, affectionate' partly Irish Colonel des Vallières, also killed; the Mun brothers from Normandy: these took the place of his old comrades from the prosaic peacetime soldiering of the 11th Hussars.[2] The outsider seemed to have been accepted at last.

After the Marne, Spears stayed for a while with General Franchet d'Esperey before moving at the end of September to act as British liaison officer with the French Tenth Army under General de Maud'huy in the area of Ablain, near Arras and the notorious killing ground of Notre Dame de Lorette. Overwrought after his experiences during the retreat and still only an acting captain, he felt lonely and neglected. He asked if he might go back to his regiment but was refused. 'I have noticed for the last ten days that you were a bit off colour & am not surprised,' Macdonogh wrote on 21 October from British headquarters. 'No one can work day & night as you have been doing without getting worn out. You are quite mistaken in supposing that your work is not appreciated. I can assure you that I appreciate it most highly & so do others.'[3] Spears craved praise and recognition as an antidote to the doubt hidden beneath his strength of will.

Maud'huy came from an old Lorraine family that had produced over forty generals and marshals. He had vowed never to go into a theatre or place of amusement until Metz, his birthplace, had been liberated from the German conquest of 1870. Like Gaston Rafinesque, Maud'huy had a code of honour based on the French heroes Bayard and du Guesclin, those knights *sans peur et sans reproche*; unlike Rafinesque, he was a strong Roman Catholic. A fighting general rather than a tactician, he courted danger and was quick to defend himself; before the war he had fought a duel with a journalist who had impugned his honour. Sir John French liked Maud'huy and congratulated Spears on getting on with the General so well. Huguet, however, said he was to be sent to General Foch, which annoyed him because 'it is a long way from the fighting', although the more responsible job might have led to promotion.[4] But Maud'huy would not let him go.

Near the end of 1914 Spears saw Maud'huy at his best. The French commander stopped a firing squad to ask what the condemned man had done, to be told that he had abandoned his post. Maud'huy went up to the prisoner and explained the need for discipline and the setting of an example. Failure in war put the lives of others at risk and therefore demanded the highest sacrifice. The execution was necessary so that others should not fail; 'yours also is a way of dying for France,' the General said. The victim's face showed a glimmer of redemption, 'a real hope'. The party marched off and, minutes later, the sound of a volley announced that it was all over. Turning away, General de Maud'huy wiped his brow. Over dinner in the mess at the Tenth Army's headquarters at St Pol, Maud'huy would tell 'l'ami' Spears that he could not conceive of defeat so long as a single Frenchman remained alive.[5]

Spears wrote almost daily to his grandmother and often to Jessie Gordon, whose unresponsiveness made him 'v hurt and fed up'.[6] He started to keep a journal, rushed jottings in small notebooks that evoke the dangers and moods of those extraordinary years: a sign of the urge to capture feelings and events, to turn these into words, which is the beginning of the development of a writer. Maud'huy recommended that he should be made a Chevalier of the Legion of Honour and on 3 November President Poincaré decorated him with this, beside a French Chasseur who had had an arm blown off and had to be carried to the ceremony.

Maud'huy liked the Englishman, telling Spears that he gave 'them all gaiety here' and insisting on his having his meals with him as often as possible.[7] Together with three other generals, they went into Arras where the shelling of the town terrified Spears: 'really stupidly danger- ous & if they had all been hit it would have been a disaster'. They wandered through the barricades and ruined streets in a mist, Maud'huy moving 'desperately slowly' under the pretext that 'the bon dieu guided all shells'.[8]

He went often to St Omer, the British headquarters, and here, after the first battle of Ypres, Sir John French, still looking to the huge Russian armies in the east, said that the Germans were bluffing and would soon fall back 'as they have had a biff in Poland'. Spears answered, much more accurately, that 'they are not going yet & that their position in Russia is not yet dangerous'.[9] The German skill at attack and counter-attack was formidable. On 27 November they took some trenches near Arras which were not recaptured: 'always the same this, and sickening', he wrote.[10]

Feverish and chilled until 'I thought I would die' he moved with Maud'huy to Cambligneul, 'a tiny horrid village', on the day he heard of the German naval bombardment of civilians in Scarborough; 'it will do them good', he thought.[11] In Cambligneul there were rats and a 'most damnable letter' from Jessie: 'she accuses me of not wanting to marry her & saying that if I won't she will marry someone else! I nearly dotty with rage & pain. Wrote her about half what I thought. Can't understand. Tried hard to put it all out of my mind without much success.' He expected to be shelled 'in this dirty hole any moment'.[12] The next day he was calmer and wrote again: 'if she is not mad she will appreciate it.'[13] Foch came to lunch and told Spears that at Ypres Sir John had shouted at him: 'You want me to go & get killed with my 1st Corps!'[14] On the first Christmas Day of the war Spears was 'horribly lonely. So hurt with Jess';[15] then at last, in the gloom of Cambligneul, a sweet letter arrived from her 'that healed my heart'.[16]

The stalemate seemed complete, with the Germans in control of large areas of northern France. He went into Arras again with some French officers and stamped tickets at the empty station for Lille and other occupied towns. He visited the front often, once in the area of Mont St Eloi with Captain Le Bleu where, to his shame, he ducked to avoid the shells and rifle fire more than the Frenchman, 'being highly strung, in a constant state of tension'. The Germans were only eighty yards away and the French, he thought, 'by custom or bravado, expose themselves v unnecessarily'.[17]

He thought of religion.

> It is a great help. It is horrid to believe in nothing & just do one's duty because it is one's duty as I do. Then all Frenchmen have become v religious since the war & the priests fight best. But I thought it cowardly to change my opinions & then I felt I could not really believe what my brain did not think. So I just thought – my brain is good, I will use it to save my body as far as I can – but nothing can tell you where the next shell or bullet is coming from.[18]

He hated to think of his grandmother's loneliness, of her looking for a flat in London in the rain. He read Zola and Hardy: *L'Assommoir*, then *Tess of the d'Urbervilles* which left him 'horrorstruck'.[19]

His first wound came on 6 January 1915, by the canal at La Bassée where he was shot in the right side but carried out his mission to see Sir John French at St Omer. Taken first to Boulogne, he went back to London to convalesce under Jessie's supervision at Mandeville Place. In January and February he was mentioned in despatches, commended in an order by General de Maud'huy and awarded the Military Cross. In March he brought the first specimen of a French steel helmet to GHQ and by August the first 'battle bowlers', an adaptation of this, reached the British army. They would save many lives.

A Second Lieutenant Reece of the Royal Scots Greys was posted to work with Spears. 'I must get rid of Reece,' he noted on 17 March, worried about his own position, and on the 19th obtained a letter from Henry Wilson ordering the man's transfer.[20] The press baron Northcliffe arrived, wanting to know about the French, and told Spears he was 'very excited at a Jewish plan to stop the war & call quits, inspired by

Germany'.[21] Now he had a new general, Maud'huy having been sent to the Vosges and replaced by the opaque cavalryman General d'Urbal, who asked Wilson and Huguet if he could keep Spears.

On 21 April Winston Churchill, then First Lord of the Admiralty, came to see d'Urbal. Churchill, dressed in a khaki naval uniform, drove with Spears to the front near Notre Dame de Lorette, where the French laid on a bombardment. Spears told Churchill the French thought the Dardanelles, the attempt inspired by him to force the Straits and knock Turkey out of the war, 'a bit risky' for it would take troops away from the western front, the only place where the war could be won.[22] For Churchill, coming out of France 'was the only real rest he could get'. He said the war would last until 1916 and that the allies would dictate the terms of the peace. 'Like all the young soldiers of those days,' Spears later wrote, 'I learned rather to despise the politician Churchill who, like myself a cavalry officer, had wandered off into the unhealthy and noisome purlieus of Whitehall, there to become a noisy show-off.'[23] Now he found that he liked him for his spirit, courage and frankness and was amused to see how Churchill looked at himself in every mirror.

On 5 May, Henry Wilson's birthday, Spears had dinner with him and Huguet and noted that Wilson 'is always most amusing' but regretted his unashamedly political outlook.[24] Sir John told him on 9 May that he was not sure about the wisdom of long artillery preparatory bombardment because it 'only gave the show away'.[25] At St Omer Spears was told to pronounce French names in an English way otherwise the new Chief of Staff, General Robertson, would not understand. He advised the British to get observation balloons like the French. A king's messenger called Burne said Asquith's government would bring in conscription and 'didn't care how much the French are squeezed'.[26]

That month, at Spears's instigation, British infantry were sent to relieve a French division. The French were bearing a heavy share of the fighting and on the plateau of Notre Dame de Lorette, under remorseless German shelling, their units had been in the trenches for eighteen days without relief. He admired d'Urbal. 'He is better than General Maud'huy owing to his calm. His temper is always equable, he always smiles even when badgered by Foch to death.'[27] Spears fought against French secrecy, threatening resignation if he was restricted. D'Urbal was pessimistic. 'He does not think the German nation can be squashed now,' Spears noted, 'but like the French in 1871 they may have a revolution later if they suffer long enough.' Then the General tried to be more reassuring; 'besides they may

collapse any moment. There are rumours they are suing for peace.'
Spears added later: 'rot'.[28] On 19 June d'Urbal gave him the Croix de
Guerre. 'The most wonderful thing of all', he told his friend Wemaëre
as they watched a June sunset, 'is that we are both still alive.'[29]

Sir John was angry when the French asked him to take over more
of the line. 'Our men are so much better,' he said to Spears.[30]
Colonel Montgomery of the staff observed that the British had had
proportionately worse losses than the French, to which Spears answered
sarcastically: 'if we had only sent one man & he had been killed we
would have lost a hundred percent'. He put the French case: 'with a
larger population than theirs we had a tiny front. If we were fools &
started badly they were not going to pay for it.'[31] Macdonogh agreed.
'The only people who made an effort in England', he declared, 'are the
upper and middle classes, the south of England and Scotland.'[32]

At St Pol, French officers were despondent. 'The French civil population was tired of war & showed a v bad spirit just now,' they told
Spears. 'The men could not be sent on leave as they would not come
back. In the face of the losses an advance could not be continued
under the present circumstances.' French civilians thought England
with its greater population should do more, they said.[33] The officers
praised Pétain and denigrated Foch. On 25 June the French politicians
Barthou, Pichon, Barrès and Reinach visited St Pol and Spears thought
them 'rather worms to look at, a packet of village schoolmaster tho'
clever'. But he admired the army. 'The French soldiers are really
marvels – they fight so well.'[34]

They still would not make proper trenches and the results were
terrible in the area of the Bois en Hache: 'latrines bad or non
existent. Smell awful caused by dead bodies everywhere near the
trenches, in the parapets – under foot, in several cases dead bodies
lying in the trenches in a decomposed state whilst no one thought
of burying them or even throwing lime over them.'[35] At a trench
crossroads, a dead German's feet stuck out of the parapet and
someone chalked arrows and place names on the soles of his boots
to make a signpost.

Spears thought it was 'my duty to really offer my life' in the infantry,
but Macdonogh would not let him go. 'I really can't say I am anxious
to see the end of this war,' Spears wrote, 'feel a horrid indifference.'[36]
When peace came, he would emigrate, he thought, probably to Tasmania. On 25 August he saw Sir John and was 'v annoyed to find
they are giving up the idea of attack on Loos, protested with all my
might. Will warn d'Urbal.'[37] The French wanted a British offensive.
Eventually in September, in spite of the reluctance of Sir John and

Haig, the British attacked and there were 60,000 casualties for a gain of 8,000 yards.

A wound in the arm on 12 August had taken him back to London, where he saw a French officer who had travelled through England and had been 'disgusted with the general slackness of employers and workmen'.[38] On his return, Haig (in command of the British First Army) and d'Urbal were 'at loggerheads'.[39] With the failed offensives of September, the British at Loos and the French in Champagne and Artois, each ally had disappointed the other. Robertson, Sir John French's new chief of staff, was abrupt, Haig was stiffly inarticulate and Sir John still distrusted the French; it was Spears's duty to smooth the relationship. 'V fed up,' he wrote on 29 September. 'Wish I could be relieved of this job.'[40] On 9 October, when he put the French point of view, Haig lost his temper. 'We do all the work,' he declared and said it was bad for the young liaison officer to live too much 'in a French atmosphere'.[41] Spears felt sure now that 'I will be killed' and almost wished for it.[42] As a contrast to Anglo-French discord, he reported the unofficial truces on Vimy Ridge when the Germans and French working parties repaired their trenches in the open without firing at each other, even exchanging shouts of greeting.

Then on 5 December Winston Churchill turned up at St Pol, looking for a command on the western front. Out of office after the failure of the Dardanelles, Churchill was at one of the low points of his life. The huge amphibious expedition had ended in disaster, with a consequent questioning of his judgement and apparent vindication of his many critics. In Spears he saw a similar spirit to his own: a man of courage, the possessor of an aggressive questioning intelligence, an adventurer outside conformist and traditionalist circles. The young officer was not yet harnessed to a leader or a cause. Winston Churchill's appraisals could be cool as well as emotional. On both sides the friendship was founded on affection, even love, but also on the sense each had of how useful the other might be.

Churchill confided in Spears, saying how close he believed the Dardanelles had come to success. Britain would win the war, he said, because the British people preferred ruin to 'a bad peace'. He told Spears how highly Sir John French spoke of him. If Churchill were offered a brigade, would Spears come as his brigade major? Sir John had said, Spears noted, that 'I had been wounded twice & was it right to expect more, further that I could ill be spared.' He added, 'I was anxious enough to fight, & because it was put to me that it was a come down to accept, would not say no. Flattered in a way but anxious & can't quite think it right.'[43] D'Urbal said he would be sorry to lose him but would not oppose his transfer because 'one could not remain liaison officer for ever'. To Spears this was too lukewarm; 'I wonder if he realized how much I have done for this army & how much I have championed the French!' Macdonogh advised against it because of Spears's lack of experience and the 'tremendous risk'.[44] But Spears told Churchill he would go.

On 7 December Winston Churchill took him in a Rolls-Royce from St Omer to La Panne, Ostend and Nieuport. It was an interlude from the war and they talked of politics and religion, Spears making a case for the House of Lords which Churchill 'downed'. Churchill said he believed he was 'a spirit which will live on without the memory of the present in the future'. From an observation post near Nieuport, with General Bridges and Prince Alexander of Teck, Queen Mary's brother, they saw the artillery exchanging fire, then went to a barge on the canal where the American actress Maxine Elliot was looking after Belgian refugees: 'a nice, clever woman, must have been very beautiful'. After tea, Bridges and Teck having left, they played three-handed bridge and Churchill talked, 'full of stories', for he has 'one for every event'.[45] The politician's brilliance seemed dazzling and at the end of the evening, overcome by exhaustion, Spears could hardly climb the ladder that led into the night.

Churchill wrote to his wife about the young liaison officer: 'I like him very much and he is entirely captivated.'[46] Spears, out of the glare, was more thoughtful, disagreeing with 'every word' of a pamphlet Churchill had written on the war. The odds were now against him going, for d'Urbal had at last objected, Macdonogh was against and Jessie Gordon wrote to say 'she is dead against W.C. & does not want me to go to him, says he is not nice'. He still found himself 'sick of being for ever a spectator'.[47] On 16 December, when dining with him at St Omer, he heard that Winston Churchill would not get a brigade after all, merely a battalion. That evening Churchill was 'brilliant, really fascinating', speaking of Asquith as 'a man of warm friendship' who 'never let it interfere with duty or even comfort'. He told Spears that, while still in government, he had thought of going to Russia and of taking him. 'He is of course selfish, likes me but wants to make use of me,' Spears wrote. 'He is all right.'[48] Churchill now wanted Spears to be second-in-command of his battalion.

Sir John French, Spears's supporter in high places, was replaced by Haig, and Macdonogh left to be director of military intelligence at the War Office: 'an awful loss to me'. Macdonogh's advice now was to leave liaison work, for it was thankless. Spears noted what he said: 'Having no proper chief you were never recognised, that my good work was in part wasted & often made me run counter of big men – that I had done better than anyone during the retreat & had had nothing for it, in fact it was quite forgotten.'[49] At least Henry Wilson wanted him on his staff; soon this would change. Macdonogh offered Spears a job at the War Office any time he wanted. On 22 December these changes gave him a sleepless night. The second Christmas of the war passed badly.

Winston Churchill was back at St Omer on 28 December, prophesying a political crisis over conscription. He hinted he might be offered the Ministry of Munitions and would ask for Spears, who noted, 'W.C. really clever, opening out new fields of thought'. Churchill declared characteristically: 'the reason for yesterday's failure is not the key of tomorrow's success.'[50]

On the 29th Spears took him up to the French front line, to Vimy Ridge, looking down on to the plain of Douai, then to Notre Dame de Lorette. They were, Churchill told his wife, 'the only Englishmen who have ever been on this battle-torn ground' and saw the huge rats that ate the corpses. Churchill was surprised at the quietness and the way the German and French sentries looked at each other over the top of the parapet, unlike in the British sector where there was constant sniping. The Germans advised the French to take cover because their officer was about to order some shelling. Churchill bombarded Spears with questions and spoke of new schemes like bullet-proof raincoats or overcoats. On one of these trips, his revolver started firing wildly into the ground at his feet and he and Spears leapt to avoid the bullets. When Churchill mentioned tanks, the French, who did not take him seriously, said: 'Wouldn't it be simpler to flood Artois and get your fleet here?'[51]

On 7 January 1916 Spears saw General Tavish Davidson at St Omer, who said the authorities would not hear of his move to Churchill's battalion. Six days later he saw General Kiggell to urge tact with the French: 'how our people constantly hurt their feelings, how Sir Douglas was rude to d'Urbal'. Kiggell also said he would not be moved for he was 'the right man in the right place'.[52] Promoted to General Staff Officer 2nd Grade, he retained his temporary rank of captain and still felt the lack of recognition.

What depressed Spears was 'to see how a line can still be taken and kept by the Germans whereas we can't do it. The French are very tired.'[53] He dreaded a posting to the French headquarters, where he would be even further from the line. The French newspapers were full of the battle at Verdun, praising Pétain, who was in command there.

'I like Pétain whom I know well,' Spears wrote, '– cold but humorous. He stands up to anyone.'[54] Colonel des Vallières said that neither Haig nor Robertson seemed to see what was happening at Verdun; 'nothing is asked of the British excepting to understand & to realize what a great battle is going on & that it may be wiser to be ready to undertake an offensive earlier than had been anticipated. The German depots are full of men.'[55] Spears blamed Charteris, the new intelligence chief, for hypnotising Haig and telling him that Verdun had not absorbed all the enemy, that the British might be attacked at Ypres or elsewhere: 'desperately annoying'. On 10 March Charteris said that the methods used by the French to try to get the British to take over more of the line showed 'they were a rotten people' for 'they had plenty of reserves if they would only hang on'; in any case 'French troops were no better than they ought to be'.[56]

Spears heard that his sister Kathleen's husband Christian Beck had died of tuberculosis. He feared for the child Béatrix: 'a poor delicate creature I used to wish dead'. Then he had a wild idea of adopting her, for he was, he thought, 'unlikely ever to have children of my own and with a child, for a few years at least one has something to care for and which looks up to one'.[57] Jessie Gordon's letters were often 'out of spirits & so depressing' and took 'all the life out of me'.[58] In March he left d'Urbal and the Tenth Army, with a testimonial of praise, to join General Fayolle and the Sixth Army at Boves. Fayolle was 'one of the very sweetest and wisest old men I have ever met'.[59] Gentle, rather scholarly, he lacked the authority and energy of Franchet d'Esperey, Maud'huy or d'Urbal.

Fear for his position began to obsess him, particularly in relation to that of Eric Fitzgerald Dillon, who was liaison officer with General Foch and later succeeded to the Dillon Viscountcy. Ordered to send copies of his reports to Dillon, who worked easily with GHQ, Spears would not accept that he was under his command. Certainly their attitudes were different, Dillon noting casually: 'I am really getting on better with the French tongue & consequently better with Foch who is as quick as the devil &, I think, a good old thing.'[60] Dillon's view of the French was simple: 'they are dear things but of course awfully vain and occasionally want firmly putting in their place'.[61] It annoyed him that Spears refused 'to play the game'.[62] To Dillon and Sidney Clive, the British representative at the French headquarters, Spears was conceited, talked 'awful nonsense' about matters that were 'not our business' and ought to be 'restricted' in his work.[63] At least he had an ally in Winston Churchill, also not noted for self-effacement or humility. 'What a wonderful record you have gained,' he wrote after Spears had been wounded for the third time. 'Thank God that so far you are safe from serious injury.'[64] But Churchill was distrusted and out of office. On 17 June Spears, disappointed not to have been mentioned in despatches again, wrote: 'beginning to think my being asked for by Churchill did me no good'.[65]

He watched the preparations for the Somme, the great British offensive planned to take the pressure off the French at Verdun. The French would not be ready to attack until July, he reported, so the British must wait until then. Dillon and Davidson tried to restrain him; how difficult it was, Dillon noted, 'to have to deal with swollen headed & ignorant people'.[66] The French were pushing the British. 'I often notice in Frenchmen that failure to understand the whole theatre as one army & to forever try to drive a bargain,' Spears wrote, 'looking upon us as a kind of enemy or rival at the least provocation.'[67]

Fayolle had his command at Méricourt and from here on 1 July Spears saw the first day of the battle, full of hope that he would no longer have to face French criticism of the British. A massive artillery barrage was said to have flattened the enemy front line, to allow the infantry to walk through the defenceless German positions. But the barrage had not done its work well enough, leaving the enemy machine guns to wreak terrible damage. 'French news very good, ours uncertain but sounded good.' Spears noted early on, then, after a trip to the British Fourth Army under General Rawlinson: 'when I saw how badly our left had got on I felt bitterly disappointed'. It was heartbreaking. The French gained ground south of the Somme while 'we have lost heavily'.[68] The difference in tactics was marked. Spears saw the French self-contained platoons move forward with agile speed, 'illusive as quicksilver', overrunning the German defences while the British walked slowly into the terrifying fire.[69] The courage was undeniable but what an 'irreparable waste'.[70] A French officer said that he was reminded of the Crimea.

By 7 July, still at Méricourt, he was in despair. 'We don't seem to be able to hold a place we capture,' and 'the Germans are digging, digging and bringing up guns'. The slaughter seemed inexcusable; 'some English general wants an English victory, never mind 200 thousand more men killed. Hell.'[71] His French comrades did not spare him. One called Phillipot, 'a little shit', tried 'to give advice to the British army'; others compared it to 'a second rate Italian force perpetually on the point of giving trouble'. He could not understand: 'what is the matter I don't know, but it is something damned serious. Probably our artillery.' The French hinted that the British could not stand shell fire. Perhaps this generation of his fellow countrymen lacked the vigour and courage of their forebears: 'the pride of race'. The 'bitter shame' made him 'sick unto death'.[72]

Spears sent an account of French tactics to GHQ, emphasising how they were quicker, more subtle, than the slow British bludgeoning. At last, on 15 July, Spears conveyed General Fayolle's congratulations to Haig on better progress. The slaughter made him desperate to get a battalion at the front. On the 29th General Davidson rounded on him furiously, threatening a court martial if Spears did not put himself wholeheartedly into his liaison work. He took some comfort from hearing an enemy prisoner say that the German infantry was 'thoroughly weary and demoralised and would surrender freely were they not terrified by their own machine gunners, picked men sworn to fight to the last'.[73]

At the British headquarters the mood was still truculent, Charteris complaining that the French 'were not up to our level'. Here one evening at dinner Spears caused a furore. More British cavalry officers should volunteer to replace infantry casualties, he said, for in the French army 'the best officers in the infantry came from the cavalry'.[74] Another cavalry officer present, believing this to be a slur on his colleagues' courage, left the room in a state of fury. Always on edge, Spears felt he might break. 'Think I will shoot myself,' he wrote on 9 August, overcome by loneliness.[75]

In August, French morale fell as the weather worsened, the bombardment increased and the mud held everything up. The German 'was fast becoming a superman again, when 3 weeks before he was but a despicable knavish clown'.[76] At Verdun the battle went on, with terrible casualties. The French believed the worst, officers telling Spears that the British 'have had enormous losses' and 'have finished' the offensive and 'are simply keeping up appearances by the attack of a battalion now and then'.[77] On 24 August General de Fonclare, a French divisional commander, sent for Spears. Why could the British not learn from the French mistakes and prepare more thoroughly for an attack and follow it through? he asked. An attack was only the beginning. 'The difficult task is to hold the ground', which the British often failed to do, with a resulting 'loss of human material, which is the only one which cannot be replaced'. The British left too much to the initiative of individual commanders; 'in this war it is essential certain vital points should be understood by all and constantly reiterated by the command'.[78]

In September he saw the first tanks; 'a pity we did not wait until we had 500 of them'.[79] Churchill wrote to him about his schemes for a great 'mechanical offensive'; 'I should like you to see these; but they are printed as a cabinet document and I fear it might embarrass you.' He wanted Spears to come back to England 'to plunge into theoretical investigations' of this kind, for Churchill felt sure that 'machinery not men is the agent today', but he must have known that GHQ would never let him go.[80]

The British offensive continued, with 15 September 'a great day' because of ground gained and some 3,000 prisoners.[81] Then on the 24th Spears was wounded for the fourth time, in the arm by falling shrapnel.

Winston Churchill had been writing to him since their time together at the front. 'I wish it were in my power to reward your merit & services as they deserve,' he had said on 11 August. Now, in October, he wrote a letter of heartfelt encouragement, partly also of thanks for a French helmet that Spears had sent him, which shows his feelings for his younger friend:

> I read your name this morning in the casualty list for the fourth time with keen emotion ... I cannot tell you how much I admire and reverence the brilliant and noble service you are doing and have done for the country. You are indeed a Paladin worthy to rank with the truest knights of the great days of romance. Thank God you are alive. Some good angel has guarded you amid such innumerable perils, and brought you safely thus far along this terrible and never ending road ... Thank you so much for the helmet that you sent me. It is a fine trophy. But my dear why don't you write. I should so value your letters and it would be such a pleasure to receive them.[82]

Spears had little time to reply. Fever set in but he could not leave his work. On 20 October he saw the twenty-two-year-old Prince of Wales shivering in the cold: 'nice boy, but such a boy'.[83] Fayolle mentioned him in his orders, praising his courage. His leave, beginning on 22 November, lasted only two days for he was recalled to assist with the taking over of more of the French line by the British. This time Davidson was more understanding, saying that Spears must have three weeks' leave as soon as the relief had been carried out and that he would be allowed to go to a battalion if he could find a capable replacement. At British headquarters he and General Shea spoke of British training and tactics: 'the French formations are ideally simple and supple, our own far too rigid.'[84]

Changes took place in the French high command. Joffre was replaced by Nivelle, who had proved dashing and effective at Verdun and spoke fluent English. Spears wanted Pétain but felt he would not get the job because of his bluntness with politicians. He went for a short time to the Tenth Army of General Micheler, whom he liked, and then to General Duchêne at Moreuil; then to replace Dillon at the Grandes Armées du Nord, where Franchet d'Esperey had taken over from Foch. Apparently there was no chance of a command at the front: 'the battalion business is apparently bitched. V disappointed.'[85]

The end of 1916 found him very despondent, with no sign of relief from the difficult job of liaison officer. In England his grandmother was fragile and alone, dependent on his frequent letters, and Jessie Gordon appeared distant and capricious. To the outside world he seemed unplaceable: the tall, thin French Englishman perpetually driving between the two armies. So far he had survived, clutching when in danger the small brass leopard said to have come from the gauntlet of the Black Prince.

For companionship he had his new French friends. But French messes were different from English ones, where the relationships seemed easier, although not always to Spears's advantage, because of the narrow class from which most British officers were recruited; also the British were regimental brothers, whereas Frenchmen changed regiments far more often, their only link being tedious reminiscences about their time at St Cyr. Then he had constantly to answer the charge that the British were not doing enough fighting. There was, however, a good omen, had he but known it. On 25 October from Méricourt, on a 'beastly day', he went to see a Mrs Borden-Turner at Bray hospital, 'who is in trouble with her nurses'. Arriving covered in mud with an Alsatian dog called Rex, his one faithful companion at that time, he was 'very astonished' to find women so near the front.[86]

In January 1917 at Moreuil, the French Tenth Army headquarters, General Micheler was replaced by General Duchêne. Spears found Duchêne 'not fit to lick Micheler's boots', fell ill with a fever and was shocked to find that he had been leading such an independent life that neither the British nor the French command seemed to notice his absence.[87]

At Beauvais he saw Dillon and 'Caviar' Cavendish, another British liaison officer. The French, said Cavendish, were 'not to be relied upon' for they were 'like vainglorious children who require humouring' and would keep the British as 'second fiddles'. Spears disagreed, saying there was more jealousy on the British side; 'amongst the best Frenchmen there is much more single purpose to win the war', but he admitted they were 'chauvinistic' with 'an old distrust of England'.[88] He felt that French senior officers were better than their British equivalents but French subalterns were not so good, lacking the powers of leadership that the British had acquired 'on the playing fields of their school and universities'.[89] By 1917 most French young regular officers had either been promoted or were dead and the new ones from the ranks had not yet learnt how to command.

He met the new French Commander-in-Chief, Nivelle, at Moreuil: 'very earnest and straightforward, exposing his ideas very clearly and well, a fluent talker even for a Frenchman'.[90] This fatal fluency would seduce the allies into a disastrous offensive. Colonel Armitage, a staff officer, told Spears, 'you are a bit of a tiger – quite different from the other liaison officers – be very careful'. 'His advice is excellent,' thought Spears, 'and I will follow it.'[91] Just before Spears's departure, General Duchêne sent for him to have a final talk. It was flattering that 'this rough diamond' had taken to him.[92] He saw Mrs Borden-Turner again at Amiens, only briefly. At the end of January, still feverish, he moved to the headquarters of the French northern army group under General Franchet d'Esperey at Clermont.

Although still weak, Spears went to Paris on 15 February for the christening of his goddaughter Geneviève Poulhot, the child of a French officer. At the family lunch before the service all the women were dressed in mourning because seven brothers and brothers-in-law had been killed. The experience increased his frustration and sense of shame, and his anger returned. At Montreuil, the British headquarters, he saw Philip Sassoon, the millionaire Conservative Member of Parliament and Private Secretary to Sir Douglas Haig, on 18 February and pleaded for a post as liaison officer between the two war cabinets; almost immediately he regretted this, for 'these things are better implied'. Philip Sassoon, he noted, was 'very down on Lloyd George', who had succeeded Asquith as prime minister in December 1916.[93]

Great changes would soon take place in the Anglo-French relationship. After the slaughter of the Somme, Lloyd George had lost faith in the British generals. At the Calais conference on 26 and 27 February 1917 he accepted Nivelle's plan for an early offensive and, to the dismay of Haig and Robertson, put the British forces at the disposal of the French Commander. Then there was a strange new development. In March, the Germans fell back to what became known as the Hindenburg line, ostensibly abandoning swathes of northern France to reveal a terrible desolation.

Nivelle stuck to his plan for a mass attack, whereas Franchet d'Esperey and other commanders wished to harry the Germans as they retreated. The British too could not agree on the German intentions; at GHQ Charteris thought the enemy was not withdrawing, whereas Tavish Davison and the operations sector thought they were. On 12

March Spears met Painlevé, the former professor of mathematics who would become the French War Minister a week later. Nivelle, Painlevé said, 'considered it essential the British should not take part in the victorious battle' because of 'the necessity in keeping up French morale'.[94] On the 17th, in the zone of the First Army, Spears had his last conversation with Nivelle, who asked why the British progress south of the Somme was slower than that of the French.

On the 19th, at the allied conference at Beauvais, Spears learnt of the Russian revolution and the abdication of the Tsar; the eastern front was now in danger. At lunch with Charteris they both agreed that liaison with Paris was bad, with too many disparate elements: the Ambassador Lord Bertie of Thame, the Military Attaché Colonel LeRoy-Lewis and various other channels including the mysterious Lord Esher, who had no apparent official military or diplomatic position. Spears's friend Captain Helbronner was *chef de cabinet* to Painlevé, the new Minister of War, and said Painlevé would ask Lloyd George and Haig for Spears to be liaison between the two war cabinets. That Pétain was to be the new French Chief of Staff would help because, as Spears noted, 'he is a friend of mine.'[95]

On 6 April at Compiègne there was a last conference of the allies before the Nivelle offensive. Henry Wilson joked to Spears about the doubts of the French politicians, pointing out that they could not delay the attack 'as the consent of the British cabinet was necessary'; he put his cap on the wrong way round and said he would walk in to the conference as a German and terrify everyone.[96] The British and the Canadians would go first, in the north round Arras, followed by a huge French assault further south on a front twenty-five miles long in the area of Laon and the Chemin des Dames across high ground above the River Aisne. On the 8th, Easter Sunday, the day before the British attack, the weather was good, only to change the next day to sleet and mist.

As the British and the Canadians surged forward, Spears suffered one of those bouts of loneliness and self-doubt to which he was prone all his life. On the 15th, the day before the French attack, he went with a guide along the observation posts at the front line, near the Chemin des Dames. Suddenly the terrifying obstacles facing the French on the hills above the Aisne valley made him foresee disaster; then came the news that before the offensive the enemy had captured the plan of attack. From the outset it was clear that the French were not going to get through and a terrible slaughter followed.

Haig saw Spears on 21 April. He spoke of the French failure and the young liaison officer's future. Haig thought the French offensive should not be called off because then 'the Germans would concentrate on submarines and starve England'; he said also that Painlevé had asked for Spears to do liaison in Paris but Haig did not want him to go during active operations. Spears answered: 'I had never asked for anything save a battalion and would do what I was told.' The Commander-in-Chief smiled. 'You get on so well with these politicians,' he said, to which Spears replied: 'I knew none before the war.'[97]

The French failure and British and Canadian successes at Arras and Vimy Ridge changed the nature of the alliance. Franchet d'Esperey asked about British plans; even Nivelle, now in disgrace, was in favour of French reserves being brought in to exploit the British advance. 'We are cock of the walk & can put Nivelle in our pockets,' Spears wrote on the 27th. 'We are the dominant partner.'[98]

On 2 May Lord Derby, the British Secretary of State for War, wrote to Arthur Balfour, the Foreign Secretary, about Spears's new appointment. Spears was given the rank of major and promoted to General Staff Officer 1st Grade. The idea had come from the French that 'there should be a direct service of liaison between the French Ministry of War and the War Office,' and Lord Derby was 'in agreement with M. Painlevé as to this'.[99] The Frenchman in London, Spears's equivalent, would be his old friend Fagalde. On the 3rd Spears was told to go to Paris. The next morning, a very hot day, amid excitement and sad farewells, he left Vic-sur-Aisne, the headquarters of Franchet d'Esperey's northern army group, for the French capital. The car was loaded down with luggage and the driver drove slowly, but the way ahead showed an apparently illimitable prospect.

'Nowadays thank God I meet intelligent people and talk freely to all whatever their rank,' he wrote in his journal. 'When I was in a regiment there was such a hide of stupidity all powerful over and round me, I sometimes despaired of ever fighting through.'[100] The war had given him the chance he had often dreamed of during those dull days at Aldershot.

4

'The Most Dangerous Job in Europe'

Spears came to a city where the British were divided by personality as well as by ideas.

At the British embassy, Lord Bertie of Thame had doubts about Spears's appointment. Known because of his formidable manner as 'the bull', Bertie had been ambassador in Paris since 1905. Distinguished in appearance, with a white moustache and long white hair, the last envoy to have a state coach, he combined dignity with a taste for exceptionally dirty jokes. But in 1917, when he and Spears first met, Bertie was ill and tired, plagued also by Lord Esher, an *éminence grise* close to the King and Haig, who thought the Ambassador old-fashioned and out of touch. His relations with his military attaché had almost entirely broken down, which was why he objected to Spears being given the official title of assistant to this officer, Colonel Herman LeRoy-Lewis, who was among Esher's conspirators. The Colonel lived in the Ritz hotel and was involved with a Frenchwoman who had been married to a German. Bertie disapproved intensely of this liaison, believing it to be a possible security risk.[1]

Esher proposed that Henry Wilson should run the military side of the embassy while Bertie should be sent home on sick leave and LeRoy-Lewis promoted to first secretary and put in charge of political matters. Wilson baulked at this, doubting that he could work with LeRoy-Lewis. The confusion suited Spears, who carved out an independent position for himself.

On 4 May he was pitched into this new world at a dinner at the French War Ministry with Lloyd George, Pétain, Robertson, Jellicoe and Painlevé and Major-General Frederick Maurice, the British Director of Military Operations. 'Interesting on the whole,' he noted, 'and specially as a study in men. No one very striking. Pétain rather trying to strike individual note & overbearing Painlevé. L. G. asked me many questions.' LeRoy-Lewis tried to use him as a glorified cypher clerk; 'determined to put my foot down about this at once', Spears wrote in his journal.[2]

As a result of Bertie's objections, General Sir William Robertson, the Chief of the Imperial General Staff, agreed that Spears should not have the title of assistant military attaché but should report to General Maurice at the War Office in London. His office was in the boulevard des Invalides and his staff a mixture of French and British. Maurice told him that 'there are many things I must watch,' and Spears would be independent of GHQ, Henry Wilson and the embassy. Spears felt the 'bitter' hostility of others towards him in this new, undefined role but did not control his tendency to boast. On 7 May Sidney Clive and Dillon found him 'much swollen-headed and saying silly things'.[3]

'Wully' Robertson, a huge, blunt man who had risen from the ranks, gave further advice. He wished to know the truth, he said, yet 'not be bothered with details' for 'there never was such a bloody place as Paris for rumours'.[4] Lord Esher thrilled Spears by saying that the job was the most difficult and dangerous in Europe. 'I warned him', Bertie wrote, 'not to allow himself to be drawn into association with the gang whom the French distrust,' in other words Bertie's enemies.[5]

The first test came quickly. On 17 May, Philippe Pétain, who had replaced Nivelle as the French Commander-in-Chief, called Spears into his office in the Invalides. About to leave for Compiègne, the French headquarters, Pétain asked Spears to see that Henry Wilson, then the chief British liaison officer, was out of there by the time he arrived. Wilson, Pétain said, was an intriguer: a supporter of the ousted Nivelle, too close to Foch and therefore no friend of his. Spears protested; this was 'the equivalent of tying a stone round my neck and jumping into a well'.[6] He knew that if he did as he was asked Wilson would become his enemy. Pétain looked coldly at the Englishman. Surely, he said, the orders of the new head of the British Military Mission were to convey to his chiefs the views of the French command. Spears sent the message. Wilson left, furious, for 'the job had suited him admirably'.[7]

Worse followed. Soon after his appointment to Paris, Spears was travelling as a passenger in a car that had a slight accident in the Faubourg St Antoine. A crowd, which included several soldiers, gathered and became hostile on seeing his uniform. This surprised him for he had always been treated courteously in France. At the beginning of June the girls employed by the great Parisian dressmakers went on strike for more pay and their demonstrations were joined by soldiers on leave.

On the morning of 5 June, on his way to his office, Spears saw that the guard of Annamite soldiers at the Eiffel Tower had been replaced by French territorials. His staff reported that there had been trouble in Paris the previous night when the Annamites had opened fire on an angry crowd of civilians and French soldiers. One woman had been killed and several people wounded. By chance he ran into General de Maud'huy, who said he had been quelling wholesale mutinies in the army, using cavalry which had remained loyal. Maud'huy believed the revolts had been organised by socialist agitators. Spears asked Weygand, Foch's chief of staff, whom he disliked and distrusted, what was happening, to be told that there had been trouble in the French army but it was not too serious; 'the men were in no way dissatisfied with their Military chiefs but were profoundly dissatisfied with the political direction of the war.'[8] On 6 June Spears told General Maurice that he thought the position in France was serious.

The tragic spring offensive and the slaughter at Verdun had led to despair. Since the outbreak of war, nearly a million Frenchmen had been killed, and another two million wounded, out of a population of military age of about 10 million. Spears had told Bertie on 22 May that the French had cut off all direct communications between the front and the British military and diplomatic representatives in Paris. They hoped to conceal the extent of the trouble from their ally; not until 2 June did Pétain send a message about it to Haig.

Spears went to the front to see for himself. He drove to Vic-sur-Aisne, which had been the advance headquarters of General Franchet d'Esperey, with whom he had been working only a month before. He found the place deserted, then came upon a battalion wearing red rosettes. The men had confined their officers to one section of the village but were not molesting them; elsewhere a mutinous unit was besieged by artillery and some cavalry. There was, however, no obvious disorder and specialised units such as the machine gunners were standing by their commanders.

The revolt seemed to have occurred not among troops in the line but in units which had been ordered to move up. Some of these said they would hold their positions but not attack; others had baaed in imitation of sheep on the way to a slaughterhouse. Only in a few cases had the officers been threatened; 'on the whole the attitude had been more that of strikers than of revolutionaries.'[9] The officers told him they believed the revolt had been organised from the interior with distributions of tracts invoking the recent Russian revolution. Spears went back to Paris, where at the main railway stations crowds of soldiers who had been sent on leave were smashing windows and singing the Internationale. The tension was exacerbated by rumours that Senegalese troops would be sent against the strikers. Spears warned General Maurice of the possibility of public feeling against an ally if British troops were used to quell the disorder. Then a message came that General Sir William Robertson wished to see him at Abbeville.

Spears saw Robertson in a room at the officers' club. As he listened, the General slowly took off his boots and gaiters, and the sight of this deliberate process transfixed the much younger man, Robertson's huge frame instilling in him a sense of an 'immense, vital strength'.[10] The General told Spears that he had heard nothing about the mutinies from the other British missions to the French. Spears must return to the front, find out more and be prepared to go to London in two days' time.

He went back to Franchet d'Esperey's area and saw the Commander. It transpired that in the first three days of June sixteen divisions had been in open revolt. Franchet d'Esperey had allowed the mutineers to board trains, which they believed would take them to Paris; then the trains were divided up, each section going to a different destination deep in the countryside. The same method had been applied to motor convoys. Franchet d'Esperey said that as soon as the men had lost touch with their leaders they calmed down and the leaders were being 'pounced upon and segregated'. He and other commanders thought that order could be re-established and had faith in Pétain, their new Commander-in-Chief.

Returning to Paris, Spears was summoned to London, to report to the war cabinet. He sailed from Boulogne at low tide, despite the danger of mines, and on the way thought of what Colonel Repington, the war correspondent, had told him a few days earlier: that some 'in the highest authority' feared that Lloyd George was tempted by the idea of making peace.[11] He must try to convince the Prime Minister that it was possible to fight on. He arrived in London on 11 June, in time to shave and have a bath at the Cavalry Club before Robertson accompanied him to Downing Street. 'Say what you have to say,' said the CIGS, who profoundly distrusted Lloyd George. 'Answer questions and keep to the facts you are sure of.'[12]

Much intimidated, Spears was taken into the cabinet room to face the War Policy Cabinet Committee; the chairman was Lloyd George, the members Curzon, Milner and Smuts, and on 11 June Lord Robert Cecil seems also to have been there. The Prime Minister appeared at first to be assessing Spears, with a look that was not particularly friendly, perhaps because Robertson was breathing heavily at his elbow. He took the young officer to a window, away from the other ministers, and asked: 'Is the French Army going to recover?' Spears answered that he believed it would. He had faith in the troops who had carried 'so uncomplainingly their crushing, bloody cross along the three years long *via dolorosa* of the war'.[13]

He gave the facts as he knew them. Two regiments had mutinied; there had been unrest in an unspecified number of others and four men had been shot. It was serious 'since a comparatively small incident might lead to very serious trouble and possibly even to a revolution'. Spears believed the British were 'now the mainstay of the French nation'; a German offensive against the French might have 'serious results'. His recommendation was that although French morale was already improving the British should not remain inactive, because 'stagnation would be bad for the French army'.[14] It was vital also that Ribot's government did not collapse, for the alternative was one led by the anglophobe Caillaux, who would start separate peace negotiations with the Germans.

Lloyd George's tone softened deceptively. 'Will you give me your word of honour as an officer and a gentleman that the French Army will recover?' he asked. It was a terrible demand to put to a young officer and impossible to answer; the responsibility placed upon Spears was immense. The future of the alliance, even the continuation of the war itself, seemed to depend upon him. He blurted out that he could not give his word of honour but would stake his life on his conviction. Turning towards the cabinet Secretary, Maurice Hankey, he declared: 'You can get him to put down that you can shoot me if I am wrong – I know how important it is and will stake my life on it.'[15]

He and Robertson left the cabinet room. On the way back to the War Office Spears found it difficult to walk, almost having to grasp the railings for support. General Maurice was waiting and looked at them both enquiringly through his eyeglass. 'Spears did quite well,' Robertson said.[16]

It was Pétain who saved France. The key points in his restoration of morale were personal visits to disaffected units, more frequent leave, better food and the setting up of courts martial to try the offenders. There seem to have been only forty-nine executions out of 23,385 verdicts of guilty; considerable numbers of men were deported to Indo-China and Africa. On 29 June Spears told Maurice that 'the morale of the French army is certainly improving'; by July the worst of the trouble seemed to be over.[17] Spears was in no doubt of the vital role of the French Commander-in-Chief. But the most miraculous aspect of the affair was the failure of the Germans to discover the true state of their enemy in the early summer of 1917.

The French army was a damaged force. The third battle of Ypres, or Passchendaele, in September and October was launched by the British and took some pressure off their ally's beleaguered troops, although Haig persuaded Pétain to send French support. The slaughter there further eroded Lloyd George's trust in the generals. The resentment between the allies continued. On 7 July Spears told General Maurice of a secret French parliamentary session when orators of the left, applauded by the whole Chamber, declared that the British had lost 300,000 men as against 1,300,000 French and held 138 kilometres of front as against the French 475 kilometres.[18] Pétain may have calmed the army but it was not until Clemenceau came to power in November that the political will to fight returned.

Soon after his arrival in Paris in May, Spears leased from a Belgian prince a penthouse flat at the Trocadéro, looking out on the Seine and the Eiffel Tower. On the walls were elaborate murals and there was a small artificial lake on the roof containing goldfish; he added some water tortoises but had to get rid of them when they started to jump into the street below, endangering pedestrians. Occasionally he saw his mother, who had become proud of him but was still neurotic, more pathetic now than dangerous, and preoccupied with his widowed sister Kathleen and her child. He went out in Paris, where people were interested in, and slightly suspicious of, this apparently self-confident, rather brash, bilingual young Englishman. By the end of June Lord Bertie was telling Lord Derby that Spears 'will be a great success here. He gets on very well with the French.'[19]

Then there was another person in his life: Mrs Borden-Turner, May, whom he had met first in the shadow of battle, at Bray-sur-Somme in 1916.

At Bray, Spears had seen a small woman in a bloodstained apron, opening the door of a room that reeked of gangrene. May gave him tea and he left, to enter her life again in 1917 behind the Chemin des Dames during the Nivelle offensive. Later she spoke often of her memory of Bray, of the young English officer searching for a lost British company and the way he had walked into her hospital accompanied by his Alsatian dog, apparently isolated from the rest of the war. He had seemed in a great hurry, anxious, his position indefinable and strange.

The experiences of 1914 in the converted casino at Malo-les-Bains had led May to write to Joffre to suggest that she should use her fortune to equip a field hospital of a hundred beds for the French army. The high command agreed and early in 1915 the huts of l'Hôpital Chirurgical Mobile No. 1 went up in a field in Flanders, outside the village of Rousbrugge. May imposed several conditions. She would pay for the hospital if the French army took it over as a military unit, provided the officers and orderlies and appointed her as *directrice* with complete authority over the women on the staff; she also had the right to recruit her own nurses. The result was a French commanding officer, a British *directrice* (for May had taken her husband Douglas Turner's nationality), French surgeons and doctors, and British and American nurses, who were soon joined by some French as well. Volunteers came to the unit; the beautiful heiress from Chicago began to be spoken of as a heroine. Often during a battle there were as many as 800 wounded or dying in the hospital, stretched out side by side under the shed's peaked roof. The orderlies were men too old to fight; May formed a profound attachment to these and to the French soldiers with their simple piety and courage: 'dogged, patient, steady men, plodding to death in defence of their native land'.[20]

She was a romantic with a longing for experience, an intense admiration for courage and a wish for passionate love. These Turner could not give. Later she claimed to have been distressed by his lack of interest in the war; certainly there was no obvious heroism, as opposed to usefulness, in his record. In 1914 May had followed him to Orléans, where he was working as an interpreter with the Indian Cavalry Corps; his next appointment, as an officer at a remount depot over seventy miles from the front, was scarcely more dashing, and in 1915 he moved to the Intelligence Department, again out of the firing line. He visited May at her hospital, a spruce, gentle figure among the suffering, and they met sometimes in Paris where in 1915 they decided to make their home because of the advantageous French tax laws. The children came across from London and were installed in a series of rented houses. In January 1917, May found a place she liked, 13 rue Monsieur, on the left bank, which became her home for the rest of the war.

During the winter of 1916 she met Gertrude Stein, who remembered the warmth of May's drawing room when coal was scarce and her habit of taking the works of Stein and Flaubert to and from the front. Stein liked Turner, admiring his modesty; after the war, he told her, he would be a customs officer for the British in Düsseldorf or go out to Canada and live simply. To Stein, May was 'very Chicago' because 'Chicagoans spend so much energy losing Chicago that often it is difficult to know what they are'. She felt May was in search of a new identity.[21]

At the end of 1916 the London firm of Constable published her third novel, *The Romantic Woman*, a story told in the first person by an American girl, Joan Fairfax. Like May, Joan is the daughter of a millionaire from a mid-western city, obviously Chicago. Her mother dies and she travels to Europe and India with her father and marries Captain Gilbert Humphrey Fitzgerald Dawkins (known as 'Binky'), the heir to an English dukedom. Binky is in debt, needs Joan's money and has a child by another woman whom he still sees.

There are autobiographical echoes in *The Romantic Woman*: childhood in a privileged enclave of Chicago surrounded by the immigrant ghettos; Joan's mother's fundamentalist beliefs; the freezing winters when the children test their courage on Lake Michigan's ice; Joan's discovery of cool British manners in the silence of the dull, slightly sadistic Binky which she confuses with depth; then the character of Joseph, the Vorticist painter to whom Joan turns when her marriage fails, as May had done with Wyndham Lewis. Unlike poor Turner, Binky arouses the 'delight' of her senses. Naturally he hates the 'greasy and dirty' poet, who is Jewish as well, but for Joan this taste of bohemian life, of 'the love making in the gutter', brings a momentary fascination before she pays Joseph off with a thousand pounds. Binky inherits the dukedom and the novel ends with the war and tragedy.[22]

May's themes are the corruption of American innocence not so much by European guile as by the New World's own romantic wishes: also the crushing of puritan hope by arrogant English ennui. The novel mixes Henry James and Edith Wharton with Ouida. If the writing strives too hard and too self-consciously for sophistication, what lingers is the huge, changeful city of Joan's childhood on the edge of an apparently endless lake: a symbol for the narrator and for May too, who tried always to look 'beyond the horizon'.

By April 1917 May and Spears were meeting as often as possible, whenever he could come to her hospital or for the odd day at Amiens away from the front. Soon she was calling him 'B', the abbreviation of Beaucaire, his pre-war nickname in the regiment. She sent him a poem: 'it is a long time since anyone drew poetry out of me.' The danger and the war seemed to heighten her feelings; May knew, she wrote, that 'for you and me' there is 'no other place under the sun':

> And our very day is bounded by a night
> Impenetrably dark, boundlessly deep
> Let this our fearful day be full of light
> Let this our day be sweet,
> Let us be glad for this our little time
> More glad than ever lovers were before
> And let us dare to fashion the sublime
> Within the ghostly charm of war ...[23]

Both of them felt that they were caught up in events simultaneously awful and magnificent. It seems strange now that anyone could find the First World War anything other than an earthly version of hell, but to May and Spears the war had revealed worlds and opportunities they could never have hoped to know in peacetime. Trapped in a disappointing marriage, she had wanted to live as an artist or writer, but Wyndham Lewis had warned that her social position and money would make this difficult to achieve; Spears in 1914 could expect little stimulation from his life as a cavalry subaltern. Both he and May felt the war's suffering and horror; both also knew its sharp sense of exhilaration, a complete confidence in the worth of what they were doing, the intense shared danger, the thrill of risk at an age when 'love and friendship and adventure call more persistently than at any later time'.[24]

After he came to Paris in May 1917, they saw much more of each other. May would arrive from her hospital, which had now moved back to Dunkirk, and come to Spears's flat near the Trocadéro. They became lovers and on 26 May she wrote: 'Dearest, of course I am coming back to you – and that very soon. If I can arrange to come alone I think I will go to a Hotel and spend the night. You could stay with me longer there perhaps than at home. I long to be with you as I was before and sleep with you & wake up with you there beside me.'[25]

Spears was quick to doubt. He needed constant reassurance of her feelings for him, as he had with Jessie Gordon, whose failure to write had made him despair two years earlier. 'I have an idea,' she wrote,

> however, dear B – that you have an idea that I am staying away because I do not want to be near you, so very much. Is that true? If so, it's a very 'bête' idea – & I don't think you would really like me to give up working. If I clothed myself in idleness, lay in a perfumed bath half the day and anointed my toes with sweet smelling oil – would you find more pleasure in me? I wonder. It is true that I am spoiling my looks. That is stupid. I regret that – but after all you want me to be myself don't you B – and that self is an active creature.[26]

On 18 June Pétain came to May's hospital to add a palm to the Croix de Guerre that the French had already given her for her war work, and the Commander-in-Chief's aide said that she ran 'l'hôpital le plus chic sur tout le front'. In July she told Spears: 'Only my compassion for my children & the respect & pity I have for D [Douglas] keep me – but can they always keep me from you?'[27] At the end of her trips to Paris he would come to the station to say goodbye and put her on to the train; then meet her again on her return, saying: 'You have the same voice, May.'[28] He spoke about his family and dislocated childhood in France and Ireland. 'Do you know,' she wrote on 7

August, 'when you were drawing that absurdly bad plan of Donadea you looked rather like Peter Pan – the boy who never would grow up – and sometimes you look like a wild man – a Viking – and sometimes like the future King of Europe. I don't know when I like you best. Sometimes you make me gurgle with delight and sometimes you frighten me – and sometimes the sweetness of your tenderness makes me feel quite weak and helplessly happy.'[29]

From the rain of Flanders, where 'mutilated men continue to come in and die', she wrote of how easy she found their time together.[30] 'Surprises may be delightful,' she declared,

> but the deep comfort of perfect knowledge – of accustomedness – is the greatest joy in the world. For this is a bog world and a lonely world and it is surrounded by eternal darkness, and the most wonderful thing one can hope for is to find a companion – who will stay close beside us – close enough to keep us brave and warm our hearts ... I remember so well the day I arrived in Paris from Dunkerque and how we lay down silently side by side, in each other's arms, mouth to mouth. All the relief. The exquisite recognition of our bodies. That finding each other again. So it will always be, my darling. Will it not?[31]

They spoke about the future, of how they would have a son called Michael, 'the Prince of joy'. May was working on a book about the war, *The Forbidden Zone*, which had already been bought by the publishers Collins; from London she heard that a theatrical producer had shown interest in one of her plays. She tried to overcome Spears's anxiety. 'You are worried sometimes because you think I love you less. It's not that. It's that loving you is only partly giving you kisses – and that my mind actually rebels at giving up too much time to emotion & sentiment & caresses', for 'a word from your soul to mine, a word from the distilled essence of your thought to mine, thrills me more than a kiss, B – and if our minds were not in tune, I wouldn't want to kiss you at all. Perhaps you've never known a woman just quite like me B – but there you are. You must hold my mind, by understanding – & respecting it. Otherwise you'll lose me. But you won't lose me B, nor I you ...'[32]

She chided Spears about his friends and earlier flirtations: 'Paris seems such a feverish irrational place.'[33] She advised him to 'keep a certain proportion of other people in view – more conservative people'. Of Henri de Mun, a friend from 1915 who was now on Spears's staff, May said disdainfully: 'nothing matters for him. He has no worlds to conquer.' It was the same for Charles Mendl, the son of a Bohemian Jew who had emigrated to England; 'things matter even less for him'.

Mendl had been wounded at the front and transferred to the navy as an intelligence officer in Paris. In 1918 he joined the British embassy there and became head of the news department. He and Spears were sometimes compared to each other because of their knowledge of France, slightly mysterious backgrounds and reputation as rootless adventurers. For May, however, Spears was different; 'you are to be a great man. You know what you are. And besides my heart is set on it.'[34]

He must be careful.

> There is about you an element of uncertainty too, even of danger. You frighten me sometimes and sometimes I am afraid for you. And it is all so very worthwhile ... I sometimes watch the play of your mind with bated breath. It is such a swift, daring mind. It races ahead – sometimes it runs away, just breaks away. Mostly it goes straight to the point – but sometimes it slips. Ah then I hold my breath. And sometimes you play tricks with it. That you should not do. It may be fun. I've no doubt it is. You let your imagination get away with you. You allow yourself excesses of spirit – do you know what I mean? Am I wrong? It's fun, it's amusing. But sometimes I wish you took things more quietly – in a more matter of fact way. For your own sake I mean. You are in such a hurry to get the poor old world into your hand and squeeze life and meaning out of it. You are in an almighty hurry and are nervous lest you don't get it – everything – me included quick. This I should almost think was due to lack of self-confidence. Take things more easily B – and have more faith.[35]

A voice from the past was raised suddenly against them. In August 1917 Spears went to London with the French war cabinet. While there he called on Jessie Gordon and, in an act of almost unbelievable casualness, left some papers in her flat. Among these was a love poem written to him by May, and Jessie, in a fit of jealousy, sent the poem to Douglas Turner, with an anonymous note: 'It may interest you to know that your wife is the mistress of Col Louis Spiers. Ask her about the enclosed erotic outburst given to him, written on Hotel de Crillon paper & dated July 13th.'[36] Turner showed the letter and the poem to May, thinking that they were not genuine. 'How could you have left the poem and your papers – papers sacred to me – in another woman's room?' May asked Spears. She began to doubt him. 'Tell me that what frightens me is not true – but if it should be true – that you forgot us – so there – then say nothing. Do not explain.' The affair seemed to be threatened. 'Surely all this is a nightmare.'[37]

He explained that the action had been that of a furious, abandoned woman whom he had visited as a friend, and May told him of her relief; 'for one terrible moment, I was afraid that out of compassion you had been drawn back to her. And my own realization of the terrible suffering she must have gone through made this seem all the more possible.' She would say nothing to Turner 'until I tell him the truth' for he had not asked her, although she suspected that he knew. 'I will tell him very soon.'[38]

Soon they were back in their old happiness. The drama of his work thrilled her; 'you're there, at the heart of the struggle & I'm with you – and if there's one thing I care for more than others, it's just that, the feeling that one's in it, that one's at the hub of the universe where things are spinning fastest. It's not the same as being at the top. It's got very little to do with success, tho' I suppose it means incidentally that one's succeeded. It's just the sensation of having one's hand on the pulse and feeling it throb, falter, flicker, leap again. And that's what you do to me ... If by some weird chance, you should ever fail – I'd love you – only more.'[39]

In October May went to London to see Douglas Turner. From the Carlton Hotel she wrote to Spears: 'London reminds me of how unhappy I used to be. I have never been happy, except with you.' To Turner she wrote a letter preparing the way. 'I have never lied to you and never pretended,' she told him. 'You know how it has been with us. You know. Since the day we married there has been something – a want. Now I have found out what it all means and is.' She still liked him; 'I can't bear to hurt you. It hurts me so to hurt you that it has made me ill.' To Spears she said she knew she had hurt 'that man whom I admire profoundly & who has been true to me from the day he first saw me'.[40]

On 8 October Turner came to the hotel and they had dinner together before going upstairs to May's room. She shook 'all over' and wept and said that she loved Spears. Turner sat 'quite still' and asked: 'What do you wish to do about it?' Her answer was that she wished him to set her free so that she could marry again. To her question about the children, he said he would keep them and try to begin a new life 'to compensate for the loss of their mother'. Afterwards she wrote to Spears: 'I lose the children. I have not quite taken that in. I shall realize it later and suffer but you will understand that suffering ... You will fill all the void.'[41]

In fact Turner was 'phenomenally unselfish'. He told her that 'the worst thing in the world to him was my being unhappy. That he wanted my happiness but that he couldn't believe I would be happy in taking this step. He said I would lose everything – my family, my reputation, my world. That it was a horror to him to think I was going into the world of divorced women. He said he would be one of the few who would think kindly of me.' He would divorce her but not until after the war because 'he could never live it down in the army' and had 'taken such an immense almost childish pride in his wife – that he couldn't bear people's sympathy'. Such pathetic dignity 'broke me up for a moment' but she said she did not want to wait. Then they parted for the night. The talk had been 'very strange and quiet'. It seemed unspeakably sad; 'if only I could have had some other relationship with him – but marriage.'[42]

In October 1917 May and Spears began to keep a diary together; this and the other papers of the time reveal the scope of his work.

First there was the question of the future of the alliance, not only in France but, since the Russian revolution, on the eastern front as well. On 18 August Spears saw a Captain de Maleissye, who had left Russia on 5 July, having been there since the beginning of the year. The Captain believed that within eight months the Tsar would be restored and in the meantime the best answer might be a military dictatorship. The whole nation wanted peace and there were three million deserters at large in the country. What Kerensky and the provisional government needed was strong intervention on the part of the allies so that they could be seen 'to have their hands tied'. The Cossacks were a stable element because they terrified all Russians; 'a strong Government which made use of them could re-establish order in a fairly short time'.[43] In all this lay the genesis of the allied intervention in the Russian civil war, after the Bolshevik coup in October, which was urged by Winston Churchill. In Paris Spears worked to promote this and saw it end in ignominious failure.

Then it seemed as if Bulgaria might leave the German alliance, and Spears met Bulgarian representatives in secret. The best way forward seemed to be to offer bribes from clandestine funds but the British and French Foreign Offices thought that Bulgaria could never be detached, Bertie saying angrily that King Ferdinand was 'entirely in Germany's hands and would at once inform Germany'.[44] The talks had no result. Spears still felt threatened. On 5 October Sidney Clive listened to his complaints about interference from Dillon, and Spears persuaded Colonel Repington, the influential military correspondent of *The Times*, to write to Robertson to suggest Dillon's transfer. But there could be no doubt about his usefulness, and on the 21st Spears was put in liaison with the Polish army in addition to his other duties.

He observed the French political scene. Although the mutinies at the front had died out, the uncertainty lingered with Malvy, the

Minister of the Interior, in touch with pacifist agitators in German pay; waiting in the wings was the former minister Joseph Caillaux, who favoured a negotiated peace. There was a sense of despondency, of faltering will, in Paris. Then in November this changed when Georges Clemenceau became prime minister of France.

For Spears Clemenceau was 'probably the most difficult person, the most dangerous, that I have ever met'.[45] Aged seventy-six in 1917, the old man had been in politics since the days of the Commune. Irascible and brave, he had fought several duels and was at one time accused of being in the pay of the British. As prime minister from 1906 to 1909 he had been detested by the left for his supposedly militaristic outlook and use of troops against strikers and by the right for his strong republican and anticlerical views. After this he went back to opposition and campaigning journalism, watching the conduct of the war with dismay.

On 23 November, after their first official meeting, Spears wrote to Lord Derby about the new Prime Minister, who was also Minister of War. In common with most French politicians Clemenceau had had a questionable career, 'but one is used to that sort of thing over here for, if you remember, M. Briand was at one time Minister of Justice having some years previously been indicted for indecent behaviour'. To Spears, Clemenceau had 'an admirable faith in the ultimate victory of the Allies'; he spoke English fluently, having been briefly married to an American, was 'markedly pro-English' and felt certain that 'France will last out to the bitter end.'[46] The new Prime Minister told the young Englishman that he could come to see him whenever he wanted. Spears took Winston Churchill, now Minister of Munitions, to meet Clemenceau. The conversation was difficult because Churchill insisted on speaking in French and the Frenchman in English.

Spears watched Clemenceau with awe.[47] Served by a sinister but utterly loyal *chef de cabinet* Georges Mandel, the son of a Jewish tailor, 'always cold' but as alert as 'an adder', and a military aide General Jean Mordacq, he became a wartime dictator.[48] Tight censorship was imposed upon pamphlets or newspapers, although latitude was allowed to the trade unions and their publications; Clemenceau often found that an impression of ruthlessness was enough. Caillaux and Malvy, the leaders of the peace party, were arrested and there were executions of traitors in the moat at Vincennes. Clemenceau's oratory was unyielding; 'I wage war,' he declared. To his small band of ministers, selected to appease parliament, he was openly insulting, ruling through Mandel and Mordacq.

The old man would receive Spears seated at an enormous table strewn with papers. On his head was a small black skull cap, covering a few grey hairs, and he wore grey thread gloves because of a skin complaint. Prominent among the documents at his elbow were the police reports; once Spears glimpsed a list of the people who had dined with him the night before. Often Mandel would be summoned to provide information from an immense store of incriminating evidence on influential figures in French life. Once the Prime Minister asked Spears for information from the British secret service on Caillaux, whom he wished to have shot, but this proved to be impossible to find. 'You are less bright than I thought you were,' Clemenceau said icily. 'As for your Intelligence Services, I always thought them overrated.'[49]

Spears made good use of his closeness to the French leaders. On 27 November he reported Clemenceau's views to Hankey, the Secretary to the British war cabinet. The French Prime Minister, he said, was 'out to wreck' the Supreme War Council, set up at the allies' conference at Rapallo earlier that month, and wanted a single commander-in-chief who of course must be a Frenchman.[50] Clemenceau wanted Foch to be chief of staff as well as the French military adviser to the new War Council, which was to have its headquarters at Versailles. Hankey took this news to Lloyd George.

Clemenceau felt that the danger called for ruthlessness. On 12 December he told Spears of the prospect of a huge German offensive and his wish that the British should extend their front. Spears noted: 'M. Clemenceau was most cordial thro'out, he is brutally frank but is sincerely well disposed towards the British; he is the first man I have met in French politics.' But Spears warned of the French domination of Versailles, where the British permanent representative was to be Sir Henry Wilson, with Foch and his chief of staff Weygand for the French. 'Generals Foch, Wilson and Weygand are working in the closest touch with M. Clemenceau,' he told General Maurice, 'whereas it appears to me that the British Government and the War Office are to a certain extent out of it. What it amounts to is that all the soldiers in Paris and Versailles are under the direct influence of the French Government.'[51]

To Wilson, Spears was 'one to make mischief'.[52] On 25 December Lord Milner saw Spears for over an hour and tactfully told him to do everything he could to help the British Military Adviser at Versailles. He explained the problem between Lloyd George and Clemenceau: 'both men were little Gods in their own countries, intent on having their way'. Spears suggested that Lloyd George should trust Clemenceau and treat him as a member of his own cabinet. 'A little better than that perhaps,' said Milner.[53]

*

On 30 November May wrote in her diary of a 'dreadful day' of accusations brought by Douglas Turner.[54] On this same day Robertson, Macdonogh and Foch sent for Spears; the strain made him ill. But May was able to convince Turner to go ahead with the divorce, and he even apologised to Spears for having spoken badly of him.

The new Supreme War Council met at Versailles on 1 December; May described Spears's role as the 'master of ceremonies' because of his work as interpreter and general go-between.[55] Robertson was said to be 'cross as a bear' at the council's existence. On 15 December Foch told Spears that he was 'furious with Haig' and that the British Commander-in-Chief's campaigns of 1917 had been 'a complete failure'. Why was Haig not sacked? It seemed odd to Foch also that Lloyd George had sent a note to Pétain asking about a new French method of attacking 'without casualties'. May noted: 'Lloyd George occasionally appears a most appalling fool.'[56] Henry Wilson seemed to be scheming against Haig and Robertson in alliance with Foch and Clemenceau.

May felt sick and exhausted. She had her lungs X-rayed and was told she should go to bed for a month. They spent their first Christmas together; he gave her 'a wonderful present – the loveliest watch and chain ever was seen'. After dinner they 'saw ghosts', an expression that denoted anxiety, and 'were unhappy'. On 2 January 1918 he was gazetted a lieutenant-colonel. Macdonogh wrote to congratulate him: 'you needn't think of Tasmania after the war now.'[57]

General Sir William Robertson was the new father-figure, the latest in a line that had begun with Macdonogh and Sir John French and passed through Joffre, who had cast a distant glow, and Maud'huy. They all share a rather gruff inarticulacy, breaking occasionally into a wise smile, and treat Spears with the indulgence of a parent towards a clever but mischievous son. Often he describes their aura of physical power, their distrust of words and a silent dependability very different from the weakness of the often absent Charlie Spiers or the slippery Francis Bennett-Goldney, the substitute parent of his young manhood.

But eventually Sir William Robertson went, in the way that Sir John French had gone also: moved aside by the politicians. As an opponent of Lloyd George, particularly of the Prime Minister's search for sideshows, or alternatives to the western front, he had become increasingly at risk. While he was Chief of the Imperial General Staff, Robertson seemed encouraging. On 14 January, on the way back from a conference at Compiègne, he told Spears that he was to be made a brigadier-general. 'I thought he was pulling my leg,' Spears wrote to May. 'Aren't you pleased, my May?'[58]

The divorce had come through on 8 January, by the decree of the Tribunal Civil de la Seine. In Paris, the gossips got to work. LeRoy-Lewis told Spears of stories in which May was the victim and he the villain. 'I am accused', Spears told May, 'of 1. breaking up a happy home, 2. forcing you to give up the children, 3. receiving large sums of money from you (you told a friend you had given me large sums), 4. You pay for my flat. 5. I force you to drug!' Her reputation as a writer who moved among bohemians inspired such talk. It would not be the last time that her name was linked with drugs.[59]

Under French law, she was not allowed to marry him for ten months. The wait would be impossible to bear. 'Marriage for us is essential,' she told him, '– not only because we must share everything, including name, house, friends, bed and breakfast, but because marriage for us has a special and beautiful significance. I want above all things to call you my husband, and be your wife, in privacy and before the world. Our marriage is going to be one of those perfect poems that will make people wonder and desire God in their hearts.' What a contrast he would be to the gentle, submissive Turner. 'All the bustling about will be your affair. I expect to do nothing but obey you – and love you. I shall ask you to settle for me all difficulties – make all arrangements – and ask me nothing but the service and slavery of loving.'[60]

Spears proposed a settlement: 'you should make a will leaving £20,000 to each girl, the sum to be at my disposal during my life time to make them allowances as I think fit, I to have the power to leave the money of one to the other in case of need.'[61] He would be rich beyond anything he had ever imagined. They thought of the children they would have and she became worried for her own three daughters:

> I find my heart goes out to them – but with an 'élan' of sadness and self reproach, because I know I do not love them as I shall love our children. It is Michael that I dream of – Michael who tugs at my heart strings – and around whose image I build castles in Spain. It is your little girl who thrills me. I see you with her. I see her clinging to you. I see you tucking her up for the night – and my eyes fill with tears of pure joy. Let us have them both, B my darling. Let us be complete. Let our lives be perfectly rounded. Let us have all the joys. Every kind of joy.[62]

Towards the end of 1917 May contracted an infection in her hospital, possibly from the gangrene that was prevalent among the wounded. In the new year she went to St Jean de Luz near the Spanish border to recover, on the advice of Dr Gaston Rafinesque, Spears's relation. At first her rest seemed to go well and Spears noted: 'Little May is happy playing in the sun. I am so at peace.' But on 27 January he had a telegram to say that she needed him and on 1 February he wrote, 'V worried about May. She not at all well.'[63]

It came at a time when he was very busy, seeing Clemenceau often three times a day about the extension of the British line and the creation of a general reserve from the two allied armies. He had also to guard his flank against the council at Versailles; both Foch and Henry Wilson were suspicious of him and jealous of his constant contact with the French Prime Minister. Sir William Robertson, his protector, could do nothing, for Wilson was answerable not to the CIGS or the War Office but directly to the politicians.

On 3 February Spears wrote: 'only five weeks until divorce made absolute'.[64] Earlier in the day a telegram had come from May at St Jean de Luz. Something had happened which she had feared, she was suffering and he should come to her as soon as possible. He caught a night train, thought it 'would never arrive'; then on the morning of the 4th 'the sweet smell of this country' lifted his heart on the approach to the southern town. But May was not at the station to meet him; Spears was 'horribly frightened'. Arriving at her hotel he found her in bed, having had a miscarriage of two months. She had been told not to move for a fortnight. He spent the day with her; 'happiness can only be felt by me in her sweet presence.' He felt he could heal her; 'my little May. She will be well now.' Her doctor had looked after his mother in 1914 when she had come to St Jean de Luz and he remembered Spears from the retreat of August in which he too had taken part. He said May would recover if she took care.[65]

That evening he read the letter which she had written to him when the miscarriage had made her fear for her life. 'I thought it would break my heart,' he wrote. 'It made me realise I might have lost her, how much she loved me, the wonderful quality of her love. I don't think I will ever get over that impression and I pray I never shall. I feel she is far too good and sweet for me. I felt at last that her life before she met me was an unreality, a bad dream. My little May. May God help me to be worthy of her and never disappoint her.'[66]

It was settled that he would leave in two days' time and return when she was able to get up. She was upset, but he felt that 'we have been happier than we ever were – we always are but this was v special. No more ghosts. Am much stronger.' On the way back thoughts of her never left him 'for a moment'.[67] There were obstacles in the way of them getting married in Paris, in spite of the support of Francis Bennett-Goldney, who was now in the embassy as assistant military attaché. Goldney also advised on the redecoration of May's house in the rue Monsieur, taking commissions from various antique dealers.

Later Spears found that he had been dishonest with them over these transactions.

On 12 February Goldney wrote to Lord Robert Cecil at the Foreign Office, bending the truth by saying that, in the question of the divorce, 'the lady is absolutely innocent.' Although the marriage could be performed in England, the ten-month rule made it impossible in France. Spears could not get away from Paris because of his work. Could they be married at the British consulate in Paris, which was technically British territory? There was no question of any religious difficulty, because both parties, the oleaginous Goldney assured the pious Lord Robert, 'are as thoroughly and devotedly Christian as you or I'. The Foreign Office officials thought that the delay required by French law must take place. Lord Robert Cecil, however, held out some hope of getting round the bureaucratic objections but 'I am afraid some little delay in settling the matter will be inevitable.'[68]

The Bishop of London, under whose jurisdiction the clergymen in Paris came, was also being obstructive. Goldney, Spears told May, had seen Blunt, one of these, 'who won't marry us either as he is under that fool the Bishop of London, the devil in hell burn his narrow brain'.[69] Goldney threatened Blunt, saying that he would make a speech in the House of Commons on the disestablishment of the Church of England when he returned to parliament.

On 16 February Spears's anxiety flared up when he went to see Elizabeth Craven, one of May's hospital assistants, and she said that May had told her that she wanted to stop Douglas Turner going into the infantry where he would be in greater danger.

Suddenly an abyss opened. Did she still love her former husband? Elizabeth Craven hinted that there was a lingering attachment. 'Unutterably unhappy', he sent May a telegram.[70] On the telephone the next day she explained that she had thought of this only because it might harm them if Turner was killed. Relieved, he tried to enjoy a dinner that he gave at his apartment to which Lord Bertie came. An air-raid alarm interrupted it; the guests fled but the Ambassador went out into the roof garden and beat a tin tray with a ladle in defiance of the Germans. Spears admired 'this old gentleman, the breeze blowing through his white locks', a survivor from a more predictable world.[71]

From St Jean de Luz, May wrote to contradict Elizabeth Craven and the foolish talk. 'They all need husbands or lovers,' she wrote of these gossips, '– or if they can't have them, any man who will give them normal sensations and children.' He should not worry but must be sensitive to her condition. 'You are nervous about the possibility of my not wanting you physically. There will be days, perhaps, when I do not. I don't know – but this should not worry you. It must be true, that you love me and need me in so many ways, that you will feel no less tenderly towards me, and no less happy.' She knew his impetuousness; 'you are just a little boy, my B': also his need for constant reassurance. 'Believe that I am consecrated to you – that I was born for you and that Heaven has made me fit to make you the strongest and happiest of men.'[72]

On 17 February he told her of a hard blow. 'My head is so heavy I cannot think. Wully has gone, Wilson is in his place. I can't think what it means.'[73] Sir William Robertson, his latest mentor, had been pushed out and given a command at home. Henry Wilson, Spears's enemy, took his place. Whoever succeeded Wilson at Versailles would now come under the new Chief of Imperial General Staff – so, as Spears noted, 'although Robertson falls the principle for which he fought survives.'[74]

5

'The Honour of One's Country Is a Costly Thing'

At first Spears thought Henry Wilson's appointment would not affect him. Then he heard that Foch, Wilson's friend and ally, suspected that the friendship between Spears and Georges, an officer on Foch's staff who would have an important role in 1940, enabled the Englishman to know too much. On 19 February 1918 Foch said that Spears could no longer see the diplomatic despatches; Spears retorted that he would complain to Clemenceau, and his position remained unchanged.

He took the train to St Jean de Luz a day later, to find May 'so much better', and the next day they went for a drive along the coast. As they watched the sea from the top of big slanting rocks, he was 'perfectly happy', although May seemed 'a little weak yet'.[1] Two days later, though, she was listless and despondent. Henri de Mun telephoned to say that Henry Wilson was coming over from London to raise the question of liaison; May said Spears must return. They had a bad evening and quarrelled – 'our first and I hope last scene', he wrote – and he began to see ghosts again. The next morning they drove to Biarritz for lunch and then on to Bayonne, but turned back because May was tired and 'v nervous'. Spears realised that 'we have been doing far too much. We sat on the beach afterwards. Sweet May. She is just too tired.'[2]

On the 25th, May saw him off at the station. He did not sleep on the journey to Paris because of anxiety for her and for his own position. In the office the rumour was that Wilson would sack him because of his reputation as Robertson's man. This was an affront to his professionalism; 'whatever I may think personally I am a soldier and absolutely loyal to my chief.' Then another supporter arrived in Paris. Winston Churchill sent for Spears, congratulated him on his marriage, which had not yet taken place ('how he knew I can't think,' Spears noted), and wanted to meet May. He also said how pleased he was that Spears had become a general and this seemed to be the chance to speak about the threat of Henry Wilson. Churchill said he would take a strong and personal line about and 'could not imagine' Wilson touching Spears.[3]

Spears wondered who else would speak up for him. They were an eclectic bunch: Arthur 'Boy' Capel, an English businessman long resident in Paris, confidant of Clemenceau and the lover of Coco Chanel; Maurice Hankey, the cabinet Secretary; General Rawlinson, whom he had seen often during the battle of the Somme; Northcliffe; Colonel Repington and Clemenceau himself. He feared above all Foch and his chief of staff, Weygand; 'I am too strong to please them and too well informed.' Capel spoke to Wilson on 26 February, saying that Spears was 'indispensable' with an 'exceptional' knowledge of Paris. Capel repeated this to Lord Duncannon, Henry Wilson's staff officer. Duncannon spoke of Wilson's worry that Spears was Robertson's man.[4]

Spears then had the first of his two interviews with the new CIGS. Initially Henry Wilson was encouraging and said he knew that Spears would be loyal to him, but Foch must be consulted. Foch's advice, however, as Wilson wrote in his diary, was 'to get rid' of Spears, 'who he said plotted against me, & who was always creeping about' with Clemenceau, Painlevé and Helbronner. Sackville-West, another aide, said that 'he knew for certain that Pétain was plotting the downfall of Foch.' Wilson thought Clemenceau was in this plot and also 'indirectly' Spears.[5]

A message came on the evening of the 27th. Spears must see Henry Wilson after dinner at the Ritz. Here he found Wilson, Winston Churchill, Churchill's brother Jack and the Duke of Westminster. He was told to accompany them to the station and, on the platform, moving away from Churchill, Wilson spoke to Spears. Foch, he said, wanted him replaced. Wilson found it hard not to agree, because if, he reasoned, he put himself in Foch's position and thought of Fagalde, Spears's equivalent in London, seeing Lloyd George and sending independent reports he would not allow this. Spears argued that Lloyd George, unlike Clemenceau, was not Minister of War and that Foch's hostility came from resentment. These reports had always been welcomed in London; if Wilson wished, he would stop sending them. Wilson assured him he would do nothing in a hurry. Before leaving, Spears just had time to ask Churchill to 'get at him hard'.[6] In fact, as he guessed, the CIGS had not told him 'the whole truth'. 'I don't propose to move him,' Wilson wrote, 'but the fright will do him good. Winston, in the train, interceded for him . . .'[7]

Spears went to the Opéra Comique for relief, to find that the show was over. Some friends came round to his apartment: Henri de Mun, Charles Mendl, two girls and a Swedish nurse. They stayed late discussing the threat. He dreaded being taken away from May, for if he went back to the front 'I may be killed and I so want to be happy with her.'[8] He spoke again to Capel and asked him to intercede again with Clemenceau, then he spoke to Rawlinson. To May he wrote, 'I am fighting this to be with you,' for 'I don't want you to have the anxiety of having me in the trenches. The whole thing is you, you.' He even boasted to her that through his contacts with Northcliffe, the press baron, and Repington he could push Foch out 'if I had half a chance or rather if I had the time, which I have not'.[9] Clemenceau told Capel that he would not allow the young Englishman to go, and Mordacq, the Prime Minister's military aide, offered to help. Spears argued that he was attached to Clemenceau and not to Foch, therefore the latter could not ask for his dismissal. At last, on 6 March, May wrote in her diary: 'B had had a letter from H.W. saying he is to stay here.'[10]

Paris still teemed with conspiracies and rumours. A Polish count called Horodyski, whom Hankey thought was a German spy, told Spears of an anarchist organisation called the Bund which was run by the head of German espionage in Stockholm. Nominally a Polish-Jewish group it had 'ramifications all over the world', and was powerful in America and England, where Milner might be involved because of supposed 'pacifist' leanings: also Steed of *The Times* through 'his mistress Madame Rose'. Horodyski suggested that Spears might be made British minister to the Vatican; Spears doubted this but he would undoubtedly get 'priceless information' there.[11] It was his information that he thought made him indispensable and therefore safe. Horodyski prophesied a German attack on 22 March.

He had heard that Turner had been writing to May and this gave him 'the acutest distress'.[12] May's answer shows her exasperation.

> B, can't you see that this nervousness of yours, this lack of confidence, will kill me if it goes on. You say you are so disappointed that I don't look so well for our marriage ... I am doing my best to get well ... What will become of us if this goes on? You will lose me – before our life is half fulfilled. Read those verses in the *Ballad of Reading Gaol* ... And for the first time I receive a letter from you (written in bed) in which there is no word of affection – not even my name – just a telegraphic account of what you have been doing ... All this makes me feel that your love is a tyrant, your tyrant.[13]

He went again to St Jean de Luz, found that his telegram announcing his arrival had not been delivered and that May had already left for

Paris, so he came back immediately to be met by her at the station. 'She rather thought I would scold her,' he noted, 'as if I could.'[14]

On 21 March, all the scheming in Paris suddenly seemed irrelevant when the Germans attacked, the day before the date suggested by Count Horodyski. Over ninety divisions surged forward on a fifty-mile front. The British Fifth Army under General Gough reeled back; the weather, a dense fog, was in the attackers' favour and they overran the machine-gun posts almost unseen. Pétain fulfilled his promise to Haig and sent up reserves, but inevitably the main French wish was to protect the capital. The bombardment of Paris began.

Spears thought Foch should take command of the allied troops and wanted General Rawlinson to suggest this. May saw the effect on him; that he considered it 'a catastrophe – quite possible that the Germans will break through and get to Paris'. He wanted to telegraph to London for permission to get married 'at once' because then 'he could provide for me more easily in case of panic and getting me away'; in Paris the British Consul refused to marry them, because the divorce was still not settled. If the British army was beaten, Spears told her, he would bear the mark of it to his grave. 'If it were not for me,' May wrote, 'he would want to go and get killed there. The honor of one's country is a costly thing.'[15]

He faced a critical ally. 'The French rather sarcastic about the British collapse,' May wrote on 24 March.[16] Foch asked Spears why the British did not put machine guns behind the forces who were holding on 'to shoot them if they move. Such measures have to be taken.'[17] Then on the 26th, at a meeting at Doullens, with Lord Milner representing the British cabinet, unity of command was created under Foch. The confusion over liaison, and Spears's sense of a threat, grew when Brigadier-General Grant, a former associate of Wilson, was appointed to Foch's staff. Grant's only qualifications, Spears noted icily, were 'amiability and good family connections'.[18]

On 30 March they were married to the sound of the bombardment. May spent the morning of the wedding lying flat in the bath, hoping that no splinters would disfigure her if the rue Monsieur were hit. The ceremony took place at the British consulate. Her brother John Borden, then a lieutenant-commander in the United States Navy, to which he had presented his huge steam yacht, gave May away and Lord Bertie and the American Ambassador were witnesses. Both bride and groom were about to be 32: she in May, he in August. Spears wrote to his grandmother, his other great love, who could not come across from London: 'I am going to be married today and all my thoughts go out to you, my only regret is that you will not be there. But I know I have your blessing on this, the most solemn day of my life, & so it is as if you were with me my darling grandmother, the companion & love of all my life ...' The German offensive gave him no chance of leave or a break of any kind.[19]

Of the French morale Spears wrote, 'Paris is confident – perhaps over confident', although many people were leaving the city. The provinces seemed more nervous; 'what is undoubtedly keeping the whole country together is the magnificent attitude of M. Clemenceau, whose morale is superb; he is certainly worth a couple of armies to the allies.'[20]

Henry Wilson still loomed. On 6 April, in London, the CIGS saw Spears and Capel and said Foch trusted neither of them. General Maurice told Spears that Wilson wanted to get rid of him but he (Maurice), Hankey, Milner and Churchill had said that his information was indispensable. It was settled that he would stay but have nothing to do with Foch's headquarters at Beauvais. On the way back to Paris the roads were crowded with British troops 'all singing and merry as can be'. The railway through Amiens was blocked, so the journey from Boulogne to Paris took thirty-six hours.[21]

The French thought that the British might have to retire to the Channel ports and break their link with the French armies. On 17 April Clemenceau said furiously to Spears that if Sir Douglas Haig asked for the whole of the British army to be relieved it 'might as well go back to England, that the French could not relieve the English army indefinitely, that each must hold its own ground and that he had told Sir Douglas Haig that he was tired of finding the British Army continually retiring'. 'I naturally objected to this statement,' Spears told General Maurice, 'but there was no possibility of arguing with the French Premier ... The above will show you how difficult it sometimes is to place the English point of view before the authorities here, but you can be assured that it is being done.'[22]

Milner came across to Paris and showed his 'ignorance'. To Spears he said, 'but if we do retire, can't we join the French again by sea?' Capel nearly fainted after he left. There seemed to be 'no head – not a man anywhere in the British Government or Army to take a line'. Spears complained: 'No one has any plan. Lloyd George afraid to assume responsibility. H.W. [Wilson] non existent, does nothing, sits in London – won't commit himself. All Wully's prophecies coming true.' Haig raged 'because the French don't help more', while the French could not understand 'why the British can't hold'. 'If we win, it will be in the same old way, little groups of British workmen led by gentlemen holding on here & there and being massacred while the rest walk away and re-establish themselves.'[23] He asked Mandel to stop the anti-British tone of the French press. Sympathetic headlines appeared almost immediately.

On 20 April an ally left. Lord Bertie, sick and old, was replaced by Lord Derby, whom Lloyd George wished to change for Milner at the War Office. Derby, a figure of immense territorial power from huge estates in Lancashire and the north-west, was known for the inconstancy of his loyalties, although this sprang more from a tendency to listen to persuasive colleagues than from self-serving treachery. Esher briefed the new Ambassador on the military in Paris, describing Spears as 'a clever young fellow, with a good deal of charm. He is an ambitious youth, and small blame to him. He has not, of course, an experienced judgement.'[24] By 27 July, Derby was telling Hardinge of the Foreign Office that he found Colonel LeRoy-Lewis useless as a source of military information and got all this 'direct' from the Spears Mission.[25]

Both sides were now wary of Spears. On 24 April Charles Sackville-West, on the staff of the Supreme War Council at Versailles, wrote to him: 'Now you no doubt know the reason why communication between you & Clive & you & Foch has practically been closed? You are said to be "in" with too many Ministers & deputies & as a result the French soldiers won't give any information on military matters to you. I don't say it isn't your business owing to the post you hold with Clemenceau to know all these people ...'[26] From the French came another warning, from Paul Cambon, the Ambassador in London, to his brother Jules. There was, Cambon wrote, in the Ministry of War in Paris a very dangerous person, General Spears, 'who is no more a general than you or I'.[27] A Jew and an intriguer who had insinuated his way into his position by winning the trust of Painlevé, Spears read high-level correspondence and passed secret information to the British, or so Cambon thought. Spears also looked out for spies. He claimed that the French Professor Alfred Mantoux, who interpreted at many of the top-level conferences, fed information to the French socialist politician Albert Thomas and sought the confidence of the British so as to be able to spy on them for Clemenceau. Hankey noted on 1 May: 'Spears is jealous of Mantoux, who is his successful rival as interpreter.'[28]

On the 9th Lloyd George scored a debating triumph in the Commons on Asquith's motion of censure, brought because of Major-General Sir Frederick Maurice's letter to *The Times* about the shortage of manpower at the front. 'At present we are well on the road to defeat,' Maurice wrote to Spears, 'and it appeared to me that the only thing to be done was to spring a mine in the way and try and head our governors on to the right path. I was defeated by a House of Commons which thinks more of politics than the safety of the country.'[29] But now the American troops were coming across at the rate of 200,000 a month.

On 30 May the Germans reached the Marne. To May, the 'affair seems to have been a complete rout'; she heard that some of the staff of her hospital had been captured.[30] Derby felt that Spears, now ill with mumps, was indispensable, because of his links to Clemenceau. 'I do not know', he wrote, 'that there is anybody, except perhaps Capel, who would be able to do that part of your work.'[31] May nursed her husband and he told his grandmother: 'May has been perfect to me. She has not left the house once since I was taken ill. She sleeps on a couch at the foot of my bed & is sweetness itself.'[32]

Now Clemenceau had turned against him, lining up with Foch, Wilson and even Pétain. This, Derby thought, was because Spears 'finds out and tells our government a great many things which he (Clemenceau) does not wish them to know'. The Ambassador was in no doubt of his usefulness: 'he has done such invaluable service that I hope nothing will be done to hurt his feelings.'[33] For once Henry Wilson was sympathetic: 'Clemenceau is trying to grab more & more power & is trying to brush to one side anybody who gets in his way.'[34] To Spears, Clemenceau said: 'I used to treat the English as allies & friends. Now I treat them as allies only.'[35] The Germans were held on the Marne, but not until 15 August could May write: 'All Allies full of hope. Turning point in war.'[36]

In July Francis Bennett-Goldney was killed in a car crash in Brittany. Mrs Hack, Spears's grandmother, was distraught, in spite of his past attempts to swindle her. 'I cannot get over Frank's death,' she told Spears. 'I cannot bear people to speak about it, and all the letters that come speak of it, it has made me so nervous about you and May.'[37] Derby saw Spears's distress at this loss of a 'second father'.[38]

Spears took Winston Churchill to dinner with Pétain, where they spoke of the future: of the conversion of the cavalry into tanks and the need for 'vast numbers' of light lorries to carry the infantry forward. Churchill wanted a pooling of the material of war, with each country producing what it was best at to supply the others.[39] In August Spears reported that British successes had made 'an enormous difference in the attitude of the French people', apart from a statement in *Le Temps* that there were as many American troops as British.[40]

Now he annoyed Derby. The trouble came from Spears's belief that he should be made military attaché when LeRoy-Lewis left in September. The job went to General David Henderson, who, like Derby, was monosyllabic in French. Spears threatened resignation, which the

Ambassador thought absurd, writing of his 'swollen head'.[41] 'He has got so high and so quickly', Derby thought, 'that he would make a great mistake if he chucked it as he says he is going to do. He would simply go back to be a Junior Captain in a Cavalry Regiment.'[42] Invitations to the embassy, where Lord and Lady Derby kept great state, ceased to be issued to Spears and May. Derby knew there would be agitation about Spears: 'he is a great friend of Winston and Winston will try to influence the Prime Minister.'[43] On 3 September a notice appeared in the *London Gazette* that he had changed his name from Spiers to Spears. 'Nothing matters,' May noted a month later. 'We're too happy to be bothered by anybody.'[44]

The enemy was now in retreat. The French press hailed President Wilson's reply to German armistice proposals, although the allied leaders were furious that he had not consulted them. The French papers gave little credit to the British army, in spite of Foch's praise, but there was a whiff of victory with the Place de la Concorde full of captured German guns. On a visit to London, May thought that people seemed stupefied at the speed of the collapse of the Central powers. She was frightened of the political future: 'one feels already the stirring of class hatred. After all war was simpler. Things are going to be an awful mess.'[45]

On 11 November, the armistice came at last. Clemenceau made no mention of the British in his victory speech to the Chamber of Deputies, which Spears thought 'calculated rudeness'.[46] In London the crowd cheered the French Ambassador, and Lloyd George and Balfour paid tributes to the French in parliament. The British army finished at Mons where it had begun: the French at Sedan, the scene of the humiliation of 1870. 'On the whole we miss the significance of the great day,' May wrote. 'We feel nothing.' It was the revolution in Germany, and the flight of the Kaiser, that seemed so dramatic.[47]

May was sure of their love, safe with her daughters in the rue Monsieur for Turner had relented and allowed her custody as long as he could see them for at least two months a year. But after the divorce and difficulties about the children, she felt dislike for him rather than pity and, as for Spears, she did not doubt his difficult nature yet even after a quarrel 'nothing could change me – or separate me from you but your ceasing to love me – and I know it is the same with you – so we can face life in all its fullness with confidence in eternity'.[48] Now the prospect of peace and freedom was wonderful: 'full of possibilities, of beauty, of adventure'.[49]

6

'Winston's Spy'

On 25 November 1918 Spears and May were with Pétain and the French high command for the victory parade in Strasbourg to mark the return of the lost provinces of Alsace and Lorraine. Mass was said in French in the cathedral for the first time in forty-five years and the preacher excused himself for having forgotten much of the language. General Gouraud reviewed the troops and, as the fanfares sounded through the city, it was hard to remember that just over a year before the army had faced mutiny and collapse. Afterwards Spears told Gouraud he thought of this resurrection as a miracle and imagined the dead watching with delighted realisation that their sacrifice had not been in vain. May and he washed their hands in the Rhine and saw the statue of the German Emperor overturned, its head torn off and placed at the foot of a statue of Kléber. They went to Nancy and to Metz, where General de Maud'huy had returned as governor of the town of his birth.

Spears reported to Sir Henry Wilson on his journey, which took him also into the German Rhineland. The welcome for the French was much more enthusiastic in Alsace than in Lorraine; in Metz, the capital of Lorraine, the population had to be ordered to put out more French flags. He ascribed this to the greater level of German propaganda in Lorraine, which was closer to France than Alsace, and to the fact that more of the original French population had left. In Metz, he heard that four French sentries had been murdered. One surprise was that there seemed to be no real shortage of food, in spite of the blockade. Coal was cheap, partly because the Germans controlled the huge French and Belgian coalfields, and many articles difficult to obtain in France and England were found easily in Alsace, Lorraine and parts of the Rhineland.

Spears feared that the German revolution might reach the provinces; two days before the entry of the French into Strasbourg there had been rioting, with six people killed. But the German Reichstag deputy for Alsace told Spears that 'the German revolution was a vast hoax' and spoke of the enthusiasm in Strasbourg when war had been declared in 1914. The Germans he saw in Germany itself expressed surprise at the revolution, because they thought the nation was devoted to the Kaiser. The attitude of the population struck him as being 'remarkably dignified'. M. Marainger, the new French Commissioner for Alsace, said that the German behaviour at the hand-over had been impeccable, the German servants in his residence waiting for him in two rows, each wearing a tricolour cockade.[1]

In Paris, Derby asked them to the embassy again, and on 29 November Spears and May dined there to meet King George V. Foch was given the Order of Merit and the King complimented Spears on his work, saying that 'he saw his papers every day'.[2]

The royal visit seemed to please the French. 'People looking back over the four years of the war', Spears told Henry Wilson, 'realise the enormous effect of the British, by which, in comparison, the American effort seems very small indeed.'[3] The French were beginning to fear President Wilson's idealism, particularly over imperial questions, and his forgiving attitude towards Germany. Sometimes Spears sent Henry Wilson news of more particular incidents, and one reported to him by Capel shows his tendency to dwell on the macabre. A wounded British officer in a German hospital had been suspected of using dum-dum bullets and the German surgeon, in retaliation, had cut a piece of flesh from his thigh 'as large as the palm of one's hand', and left him to suffer for five weeks before operating. 'I thought', Spears wrote, 'this story might interest you'; it probably turned Wilson's stomach.[4] But the Peace Conference opened with evidence of old French suspicion and jealousy. There were no Union Jacks flying but plenty of stars and stripes.

With May's great fortune and her house in the rue Monsieur, she and Spears embarked upon tremendous social activity. They gave receptions and dinners and musical parties, and the guests included Paul Valéry, T. E. Lawrence, Maynard Keynes, Lloyd George, Jean Cocteau and Marie Laurencin. Paris, May wrote later, 'opened its doors' to them; if her French was not as perfect or as elaborate as Spears's she had learnt enough to make conversation easily. Later she recalled these days as the happiest of her life and at night would hear the nuns in a nearby convent chanting the hours with heartbreaking sweetness. The house stayed in her memory as the scene of those first years of her marriage: the panelled drawing room, a small winding staircase at the top of which stood Houdon's bust of Voltaire, pieces of antique furniture bought in Paris. The rue Monsieur seemed always to be 'full of colour and music and laughter'.[5]

But she showed the strain left by her wartime work and the divorce. On 2 December Spears and May gave a dinner at the rue Monsieur. The Derbys came, as if to mark a rapprochement; other guests included the Duc de Guiche, Comte and Comtesse Etienne de Beaumont, Baron and Baronne de Rothschild, Princesse de Polignac, Sir Eyre Crowe, head of the British Foreign Office, the Polish Minister and Spears's wartime comrade Comte Henri de Mun and his wife. Lord Derby wrote of his hostess: 'I never saw a woman so nervous in my life as she was. She was trembling all through dinner.' She told him that she wanted to write a novel about the Peace Conference in which fictional characters would mix with real figures like Clemenceau, Lloyd George and Balfour. Derby begged her not to publish it.[6]

Spears could not forget the tenuousness of his position. The old insecurity, a certainty of nothing except his own intelligence, meant that he watched always for threats or slights. His enemy Dillon, in a reference to Spears's brief time with the German army before the First War, had supposedly told two officers on Foch's staff that Spears was not trusted by the British owing to his former friendship with the Crown Prince. When Lord Derby said that a French officer 'of high rank' had told him that Spears had served in the German army, Spears complained furiously and on 7 December Dillon denied having started the rumour.[7] The furore died down but this curious magnification of what had possibly been a joke cannot have done Spears any good with his superiors.

In January 1919 Winston Churchill was made secretary of state for war, and Spears became, in effect, his man in Paris; in Whitehall, and in the French capital, he was certainly looked upon as 'Winston's spy'.[8] In spite of Lloyd George's doubts, Churchill urged allied armed intervention on the side of the White Russians against the Bolsheviks and Spears worked hard to promote this as if to counteract suggestions from Henry Wilson and others at the War Office that his mission should be disbanded.

Bolshevism was Churchill's new obsession. When the Bolsheviks signed the Treaty of Brest-Litovsk with the Germans in March 1918, allied troops stayed to support those Russian forces that had continued to fight, and after the armistice of November these remained to help the anti-Bolshevik forces in the civil war. At the end of 1918 there were some 30,000 allied troops, half of which were British, at Murmansk and Archangel, 70,000 Czech troops in Siberia and French forces in the Ukraine. In Siberia Admiral Kolchak of the provisional government in

Omsk challenged the Bolsheviks and in the south General Denikin led a White army of over 30,000 men. British warships steamed to the Baltic to aid the Whites.

Spears was a wholehearted supporter of intervention. 'More and more of the people whose opinions count in France are realising the prime importance of the Russian question,' he told Churchill on 6 March, 'and it is thought that Clemenceau himself is a partisan of intervention'; certainly 'civilisation is gravely menaced.'[9] M. Diamandi, the Rumanian diplomat, told two officers on Spears's staff that Bolshevism threatened Rumania, Slovakia, Hungary and Poland as well. 'The basic fact is', Spears wrote to Churchill, 'that the Eastern European States are at war with the Bolsheviks.' The French Minister of War told Spears of the danger to Rumania; 'if she goes, the Yugoslav lands will rapidly follow.'[10]

The French were disappointed with the Peace Conference. Foch wanted a permanent occupation of the Rhineland, whereas Clemenceau held that an Anglo-American guarantee of France's eastern frontier would be enough. The two giants faced each other: the Marshal representing clerical, pre-revolutionary France, the Prime Minister standing for the anti-clerical, radical tradition. It seemed that Foch might resign, and Spears thought that this would lead to bad feeling against Britain and especially America. The French newspapers wrote again about the huge scale of French losses as compared to the British. The American General Bliss complained that British policy seemed to be 'to bolster up for ever the decadent races (the French) against the most efficient race in Europe (the Germans)'.[11]

May caught the atmosphere of disillusion. Clemenceau's government was weakening. Lloyd George came under vicious attack from the Northcliffe press and there was 'a very deep & general depression throughout the British delegation'.[12] Hungary went Bolshevik and British forces aiding the Whites were ice-bound. On 11 March the cabinet decided to withdraw from north Russia, a process not completed until the end of the year; it was followed by the defeat of the Whites. The Germans refused to allow the Poles to have Danzig. In France, opinion was 'desperate' over indemnities and security with an increasing distrust of President Wilson.[13] Clemenceau and Foch quarrelled publicly about the occupation of the Rhineland, and Italy was said to be about to break off relations with the allies if she did not get what she wanted. At a reception for the Polish President Paderewski, May said that the last time she had seen the great pianist had been at Carnegie Hall before the war, and Madame Paderewski whispered sadly: 'my dear child – what a different world.'[14]

Russian refugees had terrifying stories. A Princess Kotschouby, recently escaped from the Caucasus, told Spears about people being buried alive and Red guards cutting steaks off live cattle and pouring petrol over the beasts before setting them alight. Women who were caught with more than two shirts and one sheet were shot. She spoke of Bolsheviks throwing live babies off trains and the regime fighting disease in Kiev by sending out gangs of Chinese to kill the sick with hatchets. 'One curious fact is that people, even in the position of the Princess, feared the Anti-Bolshevik army almost as much as the Bolsheviks,' Spears wrote, 'as they appear to have been quite as cruel.'[15]

A May Day demonstration in Paris was badly handled. 'The population, although in some cases carrying red flags in the processions,' Spears told Churchill, 'were quite good tempered, and if they had been allowed to walk the streets it is very unlikely that there would have been any trouble of any kind.' But the police and cavalry charged the crowd 'in the roughest possible manner', with women suffering particularly. 'It is evident that in Paris they have no idea of handling a mob.'[16]

The anti-Bolshevik cause was hopeless. Lloyd George had never been an enthusiast and the forces committed had been far too small, for it was thought that public opinion in Britain would not tolerate more. The Reds used allied interference as a patriotic card. 'Practically all Russians, non-Bolsheviks as well as Bolsheviks, have become profoundly anti-Entente,' Spears told Churchill on 8 May.[17] He found himself dealing with a strange gallery of revolutionaries and counter-revolutionaries. In the latter camp was Sazonov, once the Foreign Minister of the Tsar, who wanted a restoration of the monarchy. On one occasion Spears introduced Sazonov as Savinkov, thus committing 'the worst gaffe' of his life, since Savinkov was a former terrorist who had been involved in the assassinations of the Interior Minister Plehve and the Grand Duke Serge before the war.[18] It was Boris Savinkov whom Spears saw the most, because Churchill admired this anti-Bolshevik revolutionary who had been twice imprisoned by the Czar, and condemned to death. Eventually duped into returning to Russia, Savinkov disappeared, presumably murdered.

Savinkov introduced Spears to the spy Sidney Reilly. Born Rosenblum of Jewish ancestry in Odessa, Reilly had worked as a businessman in St Petersburg. After the revolution, he showed courage on behalf of his British paymasters even if some of his ideas were impractical; one of these was to debag Lenin and Trotsky and parade the humiliated pair through the streets. Reilly worshipped Napoleon and was both intensely secretive and wildly boastful. He had been with Denikin's forces in south Russia and, when Spears first met him, supported Savinkov. Spears became cautious about believing a man who claimed to have been attached to the German staff during the war.

Winston Churchill wrote on one of Spears's letters about Russia, for Henry Wilson's eyes: 'C.I.G.S. This is a very good specimen of the admirable reports and sagacious outlook of General Spears. I do not find this grasp of the true situation in many others who are so readily accepted as fit to fill quasi-military positions. It is a great criticism of a department that it prefers blunt tools.'[19] To Spears he said: 'My dear Louis, I am really very much obliged to you for the numerous excellent reports with which you are furnishing me. I read them with great attention and with much appreciation of your insight and industry.'[20] Such praise encouraged him to try once more for the post of military attaché in Paris. Pressing his case to Churchill, Spears told the War Minister: 'the fact is the better I get on with the French, and the more work I do for you, the less Derby likes it.' His letter ended: 'we dined with the P.M. alone the other night, he was most kind and appreciative of my work.'[21]

Lord Derby was against the appointment, telling Churchill of Spears's unpopularity in certain circles in Paris. But Spears had another ally in Sir John French, who had just published his book *1914* in which he praised the young liaison officer. At a meeting with Lloyd George and Derby, Churchill, in an effort to promote Spears's cause, produced an extract from this which Derby had to read aloud because the Prime Minister and the Secretary of State for War had not brought their spectacles. The Ambassador told Henry Wilson: 'I must say French does slobber people. He attributes every virtue to Spears and there is only one which he really possesses and that is bravery. He is undoubt-edly brave but to say that he is tactful and popular with French and English Staffs seems to me to be the absolute limit of inaccuracy.'[22]

The two sides lined up. For Spears were Churchill and Macdonogh, now the Adjutant-General; against were Wilson, Derby and Henderson, the departing Military Attaché. Clemenceau had turned against him, distrusting the way he got his information, and Foch too disliked his unorthodox habits. Another enemy came forward, Major Cecil Higgins, whom Spears later claimed he had sacked for negligence and gambling while on duty. Higgins accused Spears of opening a letter from Cle-menceau to Winston Churchill. Captain Elsworthy and Captain Gielgud, also in the Military Mission, said that this practice, sometimes carried out by prising open the envelope, sometimes by steaming, had been quite common. Spears claimed that it was understood that he should see every communication that passed through his office in order to be able to give accurate information to London. He denied looking at the letter from Clemenceau. 'The reason I did not do so', he said, 'was because I thought this letter might contain some reference to me.'[23]

Lloyd George, whose methods were often unscrupulous, did not seem worried. Henry Wilson noted on 29 May in Paris, 'I had a long talk with L.G. about Spears but I was not able to make much impression on him. Very curious and unaccountable.'[24] Meanwhile Spears deluged Churchill with memoranda about Russia and the Bolshevik threat to eastern Europe, which was exactly what the Minister wanted to hear. Henry Wilson intensely disliked this officer's unique access to his political master. There was further sign of official displeasure. On 12 June neither Spears nor any of his officers was asked by Lord Derby to the embassy to celebrate the King's birthday.

Higgins was to bring 'the documentary evidence', a statement signed by three officers that Spears had got them to open letters, to Henry Wilson on 15 June, but the paper had disappeared from the safe in the embassy.[25] Wilson then decided to hand the case over to General Asser, the Commander-in-Chief in France, for an official investigation and Brigadier-General Wroughton took charge of this. New statements were made by Higgins, Gielgud and Elsworthy. Meanwhile one of Wilson's staff officers had seen Weygand, formerly Foch's chief of staff, who detested Spears. Weygand said that Spears 'sold military information to French politicians & in exchange received French political news which he gave to our politicians'.[26] Wroughton thought these unorthodox methods, for which there is no evidence, worthy of a court martial. Wilson, worried about the harm it might do to Franco-British relations, said he wished Spears 'to be given every chance'.[27]

Spears moved fast. On 22 and 23 June he obtained written statements from other members of his staff to say that they had never opened, or been ordered by Spears to open, 'any letter addressed to any person other than General Spears or a member of his staff'. Gielgud retracted his earlier charge, as did Lieutenant Alan Brodrick, the French interpreter Stagiaire and the file clerk Roland Wilde, who declared: 'I worked in the room occupied by Capt Elsworthy & later by Major Higgins, during the time the latter formed part of this Mission ... I wish to certify that I have never once seen the Mission correspondence opened otherwise than by tearing or with a knife.'[28] Winston Churchill was satisfied. On the 29th his aide Colonel Scott told Spears that the Minister regarded the defence as 'quite conclusive and occupies himself now only with the pursuit of your enemies'.[29] It is significant that the high-principled, dour Macdonogh, his early patron, supported Spears vigorously, feeling perhaps that whatever short cuts his protégé might take they were likely to be in the cause of improving his work.

The row showed how Spears's methods could divide his superiors and those who worked with him. It also harmed his reputation at the War Office, where he already had an enemy in Henry Wilson. He knew he would have to leave Paris. The American General Bliss, at Spears's instigation, wrote to Lloyd George to suggest that he might be 'Allied Representative at Danzig'. Spears asked Churchill to support this, but Henry Wilson now wanted his dismissal. The strain was terrible. 'One reason for my being anxious to know what you intend doing with me', he told Churchill on 22 July, 'is that I have been rather ill lately, fainting fits, and the doctors say I should have some leave or else run a very good chance of a complete breakdown.'[30]

An unpleasant interview took place in the War Office in London on 6 August. Ranged against him were Sir Henry Wilson, the Chief of the Imperial General Staff; Thwaites, the Director of Military Intelligence; and Radcliffe, the Director of Military Operations. Spears once more denied opening letters he had not been meant to see, and Wilson wrote in his diary: 'The man is a liar. He pretended he did not know how the letters were opened & whether they were shut up again.'[31] Spears knew Wilson detested him. 'Speaking absolutely unofficially,' General Macdonogh told him on the 15th, '& merely as an old friend I should say it would be much better for you to take up some diplomatic or semi-diplomatic employment than remain under your present masters.'[32]

Wilson proposed that the mission, now consisting of four officers and eleven other ranks, should be closed down, but Churchill said that its information 'is incomparably superior to any other source open to me' and 'I cannot consent to deprive myself of this during these critical & disturbed times.'[33] Radcliffe, the DMO, took up the fight, saying the work could be done by the Military Attaché. Then Churchill proposed sending Spears to the Baltic as a member of an allied mission, but Wilson said he could not agree to Spears remaining on the General Staff. The CIGS was near despair: 'I told Winston some of the things that were said about his association with Spears, & also what the unanimous opinion of Paris & WO was about it, also that neither Foch nor Clemenceau would like the appointment.'[34] Both Radcliffe and Thwaites said they refused 'to have any dealings with Spears'.[35] But Churchill pushed the Baltic posting. The mission would be commanded by a French general and Spears should set out immediately from Paris for the headquarters of General Yudenich, who seemed poised to take St Petersburg from the Bolsheviks. Spears, however, had collapsed. 'Spears is now going to resign owing to ill health,' Henry Wilson wrote, after speaking to Churchill again.[36]

At the end of October Marcel Rafinesque, now a qualified doctor, said that Spears was suffering from nervous depression and a fear of responsibility brought on by the fatigue of war; a long rest was essential. On 1 November, May thanked Churchill, in a letter drafted by Spears. 'They've done better than they knew,' she said of his enemies. 'Their persecutions have borne fruit. Thanks to you – he has pulled thro', but he's a sick man now ... Thank you for all you've done & been to my husband. I shall not forget it. It's been a horrid six months – but it's over now.'[37]

To Lord Derby she wrote also, again following a draft by Spears. 'His health is gone now & his one desire is to leave the service. He gave all his strength to his work – & has nothing left now – but the feeling that he did his best for his country during five terrible years. You can, I am sure, understand how I personally have suffered while all the world attacked my husband. That is all over now. He is young & I am sure will do great things...'[38]

Winston Churchill answered on 18 November. 'I grieve to hear that Louis' health has been so seriously affected by his hard work and by the harassing time he has gone through, but I am glad to think that as soon as he has completed his work in Paris, which is now drawing to a close, he can retire from the Army and obtain a well earned rest.'[39]

On 5 December, Spears saw Henry Wilson in Paris, who asked why he had not resigned. He answered that he was waiting for his mission to be abolished; 'I promised to fix a date,' Wilson wrote.[40] The CIGS had won over the question of who was to be the military attaché, Churchill having finally agreed to Charles Sackville-West taking the post, stating on 13 February 1919, however, that he would not have Spears 'interfered with'. The resignation was further delayed.[41]

May was ill again, a recurrence of the old infection picked up in her hospital during the war. On 4 March, from a hotel in Fontainebleau where she was convalescing, she told Spears: 'We've been married nearly two years. And I love you much more.' But she felt physically and emotionally exhausted: 'I wish I were more loving. Sometimes I'm loving you deeply when you think I'm not. It's got something to do with the difference between emotions and feelings. I get emotionally tired but my love for you is never tired.'[42]

He prepared for life after the army, thinking of possible involvement in trade with eastern Europe. On 1 June he wrote to Prince John Callimachi in Bucharest about investing money in Rumania, and Callimachi bought Spears shares in a bank and an oil company. Then there was further official anxiety when the French government asked

Lord Hardinge, the head of the British Foreign Office, about Spears's position in Paris. On the 11th Curzon, the Foreign Secretary, said that he too had been approached on this subject by the French Ambassador in London.

Research by the Foreign Office produced an astonishing collection of wrong information, giving Spears the DSO as well as the MC. It mentioned his work for Macdonogh and his time with the French Fifth Army but added: 'later he appears to have served in England and run away with the wife of an officer serving at the War Office.' As Head of the British Military Mission in Paris he was not answerable to the Military Attaché or the British Military Mission to Versailles; nor was he 'in charge of the British Military Secret Service'. The note added: 'with none of the above mentioned bodies is he believed to be persona grata.' It said Spears knew many French politicians, 'whose methods he would not be above imitating', and that his French equivalent in London ('I unfortunately forget his name') was, unlike Spears, under the direct orders of the French Military Attaché. The note ended: 'General Spears's position in Paris was always anomalous and nobody ever seemed to know what precisely his duties were.'[43] His determination to have an independent existence had led to a mystery in official circles about his identity and work that would last all his life.

On 15 June Spears wrote to the War Office to resign his commission and was told he could keep the honorary rank of brigadier-general, which he had held since January of the previous year. His first business appointment came on 28 June, when he was made a director of the British Corporation of Mine and Steamship Owners in Russia.

In August May went to Deauville with her daughters and Spears's widowed sister Kathleen and Kathleen's infant daughter Béatrix. Kathleen was 'too nice', May told Spears; 'she makes my heart ache' for 'her face is worn & lined' from poverty and anxiety. The child was precocious, very intelligent but 'impertinent'. May, still weak and unsettled, wrote: 'I have horrible dreams about you.' In these he was often harsh: 'you say you don't care for me any more – & are sometimes unspeakably cruel. Why? Why? I think of you all day & watch the changing lights & expressions on your face – and love you constantly – & tenderly – with such longing – and then at night these awful dreams. What are you doing while I dream these horrible things? Are you thinking of me? Or have you forgotten to think of me?'[44] She hated Deauville, felt lonely after Kathleen left and dreamt of him making advances to the American heiress Daisy Fellows.

Their wish for a child of their own surfaced again. It must be a boy, the longed-for Michael. 'Darling, I adore you,' she told Spears from

Paris on 14 October, while he was in London. 'I'm somewhat troubled however by the idea that when Michael has arrived you will no longer be so angelique to me. You must think about this.' In Paris her life was sybaritic, 'shopping all afternoon & drinking a divine ice cream soda' with her friend Constance Leveson-Gower and seeing Elsie de Wolfe, the hostess and interior decorator who would marry Charles Mendl, and Henri de Mun and his wife Annie.[45] But, like many who had been caught up in the war, she could not find peace. 'Sometimes I get very frightened thinking of the end of life – and our not being together anymore,' she wrote. 'I would – ah what wouldn't I give – to keep just that one thing – permanent forever.' Joy seemed always to have its price; 'the horror of the inevitable end is there to make one suffer,' although 'nothing matters but you and me being together without misunderstanding.'[46] In the autumn of 1920 his business took him to London and eastern Europe; this she hated. Could they go for the winter to the south of France, where Michael could be born? 'I can't go on being separated from you. I simply can't. It's an anguish. My darling, darling B. I love you all the time, more than I ever did before – and it all frightens me.'[47]

In October the French President Millerand made him a Commander of the Legion of Honour. The war and its aftermath slipped away and on 21 December Macdonogh wrote of the distant world of 1914 when Spears had saved an army. 'What an age it seems since Le Cateau.' His courage then had been 'amazing', but 'I fear nobody ever appreciated what we owed to you.'[48]

Then Sir Frederick Maurice, now out of the army since the failure of his challenge to Lloyd George in 1918, wrote to say that he would be passing through Paris in October on his way to Italy with his daughter Nancy and wanted to call on Spears at the rue Monsieur.

Maurice had only a meagre pension, supplemented by his writing on military subjects, so his children had to make their own way in the world. Nancy had been educated well for a girl of her generation at Queen's College, Harley Street, founded by her grandfather, the Victorian social reformer Frederick Denison Maurice. Born in 1900, the eldest of a family of four girls and one boy, she trained as a secretary and worked for a Harley Street specialist who, to the General's dismay, had turned out to be a slavedriver. Nancy Maurice had a phenomenal memory, a quick grasp of figures, a sharp, hard view of the world and was determined and ruthless. Handsome rather than beautiful when young, very tall and slim as a stoat, she soon showed herself to be capable of an absolute and very useful devotion to a person or a cause.

Whether or not Spears and she had met before is hard to say;

certainly they might have seen each other in Paris during the Peace Conference, which General Maurice had reported for the *Morning Post*. Now Spears needed a secretary. Nancy impressed him by her obvious ability and he admired her father. Might she take the job? She agreed to try it on a temporary basis, and stayed with him for forty-two years, slowly invading almost every aspect of his life.

7

Post-War and Parliament

They were poised on the brink of civilian life: a retired British brigadier-general and his American wife, both aged 34, with a house in Paris and an income of at least £10,000 a year.

The omens seemed good. A baby was due in March 1921, their first child, perhaps Michael, the longed-for son. In January Spears was made a Commander of the Order of the Bath. From the French War Ministry, Paul Keller, a former colleague, wrote admiringly of his unique combination of artistic and military qualities, of his feeling for beauty and poetry as well as his courage.[1] His contacts, particularly those in central and eastern Europe, would help in his new life as a businessman; he did not want to be entirely dependent on his wife's money.

But there were also signs of a darker world. The row with the War Office had left its mark; Spears could not sleep and had crippling attacks of anxiety that led him to see a psychiatrist in London. His beloved grandmother fell ill and his mother grew increasingly irrational and vindictive, railing at her second husband for his dishonesty and unfaithfulness. Ton Ton Rafinesque, Spears's closest childhood friend, killed himself in Paris after a series of failed business ventures; and his sister Kathleen, penniless and pathetic, looked to him for help as she struggled to bring up her daughter Béatrix. Then Douglas Turner, who had previously been generous with May about the custody of their daughters, struck back at his former wife and her new husband.

After his demobilisation in 1920, Turner worked in London for the League of Nations Union. Conscious of his duties to his children, he found a house in Oxford, near the Radcliffe Observatory, the home of Hugh Sturge Gretton, a fellow and tutor at Keble College and the extremely respectable nephew of the Dean of Canterbury. The puritanical Turner had heard that the rue Monsieur was shunned by the more conventional members of the Paris *monde*, partly because May and Spears had married after a divorce. May's boast of the eclectic nature of her parties, with T. E. Lawrence, Paul Valéry, Misia Sert,

Lloyd George, Gertrude Stein and Winston Churchill among the guests, did not impress Turner, who believed his daughters were not only being neglected but meeting people of dubious morals as well. It rankled also that much of the activity there was angled towards the promotion of the prospects and career of Brigadier-General Spears.

In December 1920 the children came to Turner at Oxford and he arranged for them to go to schools in the town. On 5 January 1921 May, now seven months pregnant, arrived at Hugh Gretton's house accompanied by a German governess and furious that the children had not been returned to her earlier. There was a dramatic meeting in the drawing room, first between May and Turner, who was later joined by Mr and Mrs Gretton. May demanded to see the children, Turner refused and Gretton called a solicitor, who ordered her off the premises. On leaving the house she took a taxi to the station and from the taxi saw Mr Gretton walking near by with her youngest child Mary Borden-Turner, known as Emmy. May called to the little girl, tried to get out of the cab, but stumbled and nearly fell. Gretton ran off with the child into his house.[2]

Later she claimed that this incident, and the consequent emotional turmoil, affected her physically. On the afternoon of 2 March 1921, Michael Spears was born at 11 Portman Square, rented so that the child might arrive in England. The birth was very difficult, May's life was despaired of for several hours and Spears did not feel confident about her until four days later. The baby was healthy, although the doctors thought May too weak to feed him, and Spears and she set about finding suitable godparents. Lord (formerly Sir John) French, Winston Churchill, Lady Millicent Hawes (formerly the Duchess of Sutherland), May's sister Joyce and General Macdonogh were approached and the christening took place at St Martin-in-the-Fields on 11 April with a somewhat bare line-up, Lord French being detained in Ireland (where he was now lord lieutenant), Lady Millicent in Paris (her home since the war) and Churchill away on political business. Other guests were caught up in a railway strike. The post-war age was not to be as golden as many had hoped.

Delight at the arrival of his son was clouded for Spears by May's weakness and the lawsuit over the custody of her daughters. Both sides collected supporters and the affidavits show how unpleasant the quarrel became. May depicted Turner as inadequate in almost every way, especially as a man; in the war he had been far from the front line and before that had lived unashamedly off her fortune. Turner said that May had gone astray as a result of her liaison with Spears and that she stopped at nothing to get what she wanted. He cast doubt on the validity in Britain of their marriage and the French divorce and claimed that the children were neglected at the rue Monsieur.

Each side called witnesses to support its case. For Turner, the novelist John Buchan spoke of the good character of the Grettons and how he had seen the children obviously happy on a holiday with their father in Scotland. Paul Maze, the French artist and former liaison officer with the British army, said there had been talk in wartime France of May's fast way of life, cruel treatment of her first husband and indiscreet romance with Spears. The Grettons spoke well of Turner and his love for his daughters.

May fought back. Paul Maze, she said, was not French but of Dutch descent and had a reputation in her hospital for malingering. The governess Miss Fischer spoke of how much the children missed their mother and disliked Mrs Gretton. Spears persuaded the army surgeon who had treated his wounds to testify to his courage as a contrast to May's depiction of Turner. Lady Millicent Hawes gave a touching account of the domestic felicities of the rue Monsieur.

Turner's lawyers concentrated on the inappropriateness for children of the life led by May and Spears. Lady Millicent Hawes gave an opening here; as the Duchess of Sutherland she had been a celebrated Edwardian beauty, and a novelist in the style of Ouida, but a loveless marriage led to several affairs and, after the death of the Duke, a second husband almost half her age whom she later divorced. Her latest husband, Colonel Hawes, was a homosexual. Her courage during the war, when like May she had nursed in France, was not in doubt, but she could not be described as an example of wholesome living. In his affidavit Turner mentioned her as someone from whom his children should be protected.[3]

May had one solace. Her mother, Mrs Borden, who had previously sympathised with the devout Turner, now supported her daughter. But the court's decision would not be known until the end of the year and this hung over them with dreadful menace. Meanwhile Spears observed, not always with approval, May's relations with her children, noting how the eldest daughter Joyce, a girl of great intelligence, was 'tyrannised over by her mother who won't let her do anything'. 'Little Joyce is sad,' he wrote in unconscious anticipation of tragedy.[4]

In the spring of 1921, May and he took Ightham Mote, a medieval house in Kent. Here they brought Michael, or 'the Peti', later shortened to 'Peti' and pronounced 'Pea-Tie' – a Scottish nanny's corruption of 'Le Petit'; but people seemed reluctant to see them, perhaps because of the divorce and the court case. Phyllis Maurice, the little sister of Spears's new secretary Nancy, came to stay but he thought this was a 'mistake' for 'she had absorbed the children away from us'. He liked always to be in charge, to control, otherwise he felt helpless, abandoned. He and May lacked a 'position such as we had in France'.[5] Only the visit of Henri de Mun brought a hint of the old days.

Not even Michael could give him pleasure when May was not there. One evening he drove down from London to Ightham while she was away in Paris, past roadblocks put up by police to stop Irish terrorists. The loneliness overwhelmed him and he felt 'panic stricken' because 'I just can't do without her.' He read the wartime letters from St Jean de Luz again and knelt by his bed and wept. 'We should give more time to being happy together,' he wrote. 'Life is so short.'[6]

There were other reminders of the past. May and he stayed with some friends near Huntingdon and found Cecil Higgins there. Spears spoke to Higgins as if nothing was wrong and May avoided him. Spears felt: 'it did me good to face it & have done with it & it was he who had the rotten time.'[7] He was still not sure of how he was regarded in the army but at an 8th Hussar regimental dinner in June everyone was 'v nice'.[8]

The Americans withdrew from Europe, the Senate having refused to ratify the Treaty of Versailles or permit United States membership of the League of Nations. France, without an international guarantee of her security, faced a resentful Germany. Winston Churchill, now Colonial Secretary, asked Spears to find out more about how the French thought.

He consulted Fagalde, who spoke of strong anti-British feeling and said also that the French Ambassador in London was useless, being inclined to make chauvinistic speeches which were no help to the entente. Clemenceau had declared of this diplomat: 'I should have had him shot when he was at Bucharest.'[9] But Churchill confirmed British lack of interest: 'public opinion here not in state for being worked up re France.'[10]

The Churchills visited Ightham Mote. Spears found 'Clemmie a little difficile' at first; then on the next day the local clergyman came to lunch and Churchill was 'delicious with him & put him posers' like 'Should the clergy be patriotic? Jesus Christ wd not have taken sides in this war.' They played tennis and Churchill painted 'a nice picture' which he later sold for fifty pounds. May fascinated him by talking of her hospital and he was 'wonderful' and 'Clemmie was v nice.'[11]

Spears, mindful perhaps of May's feelings about the way Turner had not earned money of his own, launched himself into business. He had a partner, a Finnish banker called Brunstrom who had links with Russia; and Sidney Reilly, his old colleague in espionage, worked with them. Brunstrom seems to have guaranteed Spears £1,000 a year, but his own position was by no means secure; on 2 July Spears noted that the Finn was 'living on capital'.[12] They both felt unsure of the mysterious Reilly, whom Spears thought 'a clever but not a very pleasant individual, speaking English but with an awful accent'.[13]

Paris was the base for their operations. May might think that the world of the French capital was 'v small' but he loved 'our house, our home', where they had first lived together. The bills were mounting, too much even for her fortune. He knew the place should be let but did not worry as he might have done in the past, 'as I am so happy with M, she only counts, everything else is trifles'.[14]

In July he went to Prague with Reilly. May came to the station to say goodbye; 'how I adore her. It is hard to leave her.' The journey took them through Germany ('v unpleasant') and they arrived at Prague to find 'a wonderful town, so animated and v beautiful'. At the Czech Finance Ministry the officials were 'extraordinary' in their efficiency; he discussed radium and the national loan with them and had lunch with Robert Bruce Lockhart, once a British agent in Russia and now trying to make money in business; 'I do pity these exiles,' Spears wrote. The next day he drove out to meet Eduard Beneš, the Prime Minister, at a castle that had belonged to the Archduke Franz Ferdinand, and sensed the character of the old Habsburg aristocracy: 'proud, simple and stupid' with 'houses razed for miles to make shooting'. Beneš told him that everything depended on the Franco-British alliance. The Czechs believed that Russia and Germany would become allies, for Russia would be forced to 'accept offers from those who offer most'. He prophesied more Russian revolutions. The west should not interfere; 'to have Russia on our hands would be a bore, we can manage without her.'

Beneš had dinner with Spears, Reilly and Lockhart in Prague and talked late into the night. Germany he wished to see 'down for ten years to give Central Europe a chance'; the treaties should be applied, with 'a relaxation after every time Germany does something good', but the 'defiance' of the Germans was worrying. The next day Spears had lunch with Jan Masaryk, the son of the Czech President, and liked him 'immensely'.[15] May had written to say she had food poisoning and was lonely in the unusual English heat. He missed her dreadfully, especially in the evenings when Reilly took him out to night clubs and doled out huge tips to the cabaret performers, who included ex-officers of the Russian imperial army. It was a relief to get back. He found May 'not looking bad but v nervy & tired & in absolute need of rest'.[16]

They left Ightham for a house in Rye. From here May's daughters set out again for a visit to Turner which had been postponed; Comfort in particular was miserable at going and Spears's 'heart bled for the poor child'.[17] The eldest, Joyce, wanted to stop the journey, but May felt they should stick to the agreement with the court's decision imminent. May and Spears were going to Venice in August for a holiday; then Comfort wrote, describing what sounded like 'moral torture' by Turner; a telegram arrived from the lawyers which reassured May. In Venice she cried often about the children but in Paris on their way back, where they stopped to see Brunstrom, the rue Monsieur exercised its healing powers and Spears noted, 'we have been so happy these last two days.'[18] He stayed on in Paris alone but felt vulnerable and during dinner at the Jockey Club thought that Charles Mendl and Henri de Mun were ignoring him. Even after his return to Rye in October, he found himself 'v depressed in the evening'.[19] He missed the sense of doing an important job.

A dinner party in London on 18 October showed how some people felt. It was given by Major-General Sir Frederick and Lady Maurice and among the guests, in addition to Spears and May, were General Sir Ian Hamilton, once the commander in the Dardanelles, and Eddie Marsh, Winston Churchill's private secretary, patron of the arts and friend of Rupert Brooke. The talk turned to Germany, Hamilton expressing anger at Silesia being given to Poland and Marsh observing: 'I am feeling pro Boche.' Maurice declared with approval that 'Wully' Robertson had said to him in 1916: 'the trouble with this war is that we are on the wrong side.'[20] Hamilton was fascinated by Spears's stories of the retreat of August 1914 and said he should write a book about it. He described Spears and May as 'the alert General and the languid beauty'.[21] Spears's fitful social confidence flared up, only to be doused the next day at lunch with the Churchills because May had not been asked; 'v unkind of Clemmy & M hurt', especially as 'we have been v kind and hospitable to her.'[22]

Sidney Reilly was a difficult associate. Spears now had an office in London which the spy used when he was there; in October the telephone was cut off because Reilly had not paid the bill, there were exorbitant claims for expenses and the spy was rude when these were challenged. 'I won't stand cheek,' Spears said.[23] He warned Reilly of 'the danger of dealing with shady people & mixing politics with business'. Reilly had damaged his position in Prague by identifying himself with Savinkov, 'who is now out of favour there'. The disadvantage of the spy, he decided, was the company he kept: 'he is not careful enough.'[24]

He found the atmosphere in London 'depressing' even in the Cavalry

Club, for 'I don't know a soul there now & occasionally people I dislike'.[25] He was cut by an officer, a friend of Dillon's; another old army adversary did not know what to do on seeing him. One social engagement had omens for the future; on 22 November he 'gave Miss Maurice dinner late and then went to film of N.W. Australia. Most interesting.'[26]

They took a house at Guisborough in the Northamptonshire hunting country and Spears taught May and the children to ride. Then Colonel Scott, once Winston Churchill's private secretary at the Air Ministry, came to stay and suggested that he should go into parliament. Again Spears turned to Churchill, who seemed 'delighted'.[27] Churchill spoke to his secretary Archie Sinclair, who took Spears down to the head-quarters of the National Liberal party, Lloyd George's group in the coalition. Here Jarrow or Loughborough were suggested by Scovell, the party organiser; Spears did not like the idea of the former and the latter depended on the departure of Oscar Guest, who was in the midst of a nasty divorce. Again he saw Churchill, who was grumbling about the French, this time because they were building submarines. A phrase of Briand's had infuriated him: 'if the English want capital ships to fish for sardines, the French want submarines to examine the submarine fauna.' Sinclair seemed to think there was still a chance of a guarantee to France that Britain would not tolerate threats to her wartime ally's security. 'Nothing Winston could do would mean much as it had no weight behind it, the Foreign Office pursuing a line of its own...'[28]

Guest decided not to stand again at Loughborough and suggested Spears as his successor, possibly a disadvantage because of the retiring member's unpopularity. Scovell said Spears must move quickly. Suddenly he felt desperately lonely, for 'like everything else it is evident I must work it mostly myself in spite of powerful backing.' These sloughs of self-doubt were terrible, 'suicidal in tendency. It is awful and makes life a burden.'[29] On 10 December he spoke to the full executive committee at Loughborough and was adopted unanimously.

There was still the ordeal of the legal battle with Turner. On 19 December May appeared in court; the decision went in her favour but had worn her out. Spears found Turner's hypocrisy 'nauseous'.[30] The three girls went to their father for Christmas and Spears, May and Michael set out for Paris and the rue Monsieur. On the 31st Scovell telegraphed to say that he must return soon for a probable February election. That night he looked back on 1921. 'Thank God this year ends better than it began. We could not have stood the strain, as it is we have both been profoundly affected. Our nerves have been strained so that they will ever carry the marks & our characters have been changed. We are less lighthearted than we were. It was almost too much after the War Office row which had affected me terribly.'[31]

In Paris, the French felt deserted by Britain and the United States: 'much bitterer than I had imagined and even quite good friends of mine have proved very difficult to argue with', Spears told Churchill.[32] The press was anti-British; only Painlevé seemed reasonable. At a dinner and ball at the rue Monsieur May looked lovely but the cabaret of clowns 'fell v flat' and 'there were less people than there used to be and none from the embassy.'[33] His return to London on 12 January was, as usual, sad. 'I adore her,' he wrote of May and hated 'being separated'.[34]

His nerves were still bad, he had insomnia and the increasingly important Nancy Maurice was away, which made his work difficult. Reilly said that Lockhart in Prague was broke and he had advanced him £500 out of a prospective tobacco-trading contract; there was a chance still of a deal with the Czechs over radium. Brunstrom and he had ambitious schemes for exploiting the iron and coal reserves of the Donetz basin and the oil in the Russian Caucasus, but these hinged on Savinkov's prophecies of a transformation of the Bolshevik government and now look wildly optimistic. On 20 January he heard Churchill make 'a magnificent speech' to the Liberal conference and spoke to May in Paris on the telephone when she shocked him slightly by saying she had been to a fancy-dress ball on her own dressed as Mistinguette.[35]

In Paris, where he returned at the end of the month, his eighty-one-year-old grandmother, the adored icon of his childhood, was seriously ill. He rushed to her apartment and saw her sleeping, but the next day, the 29th, she was worse. Her breathing became laboured; one night, in Spears's presence, the old lady said, clutching a photograph of her husband: 'Give me my shoes & stick, I want to start across the water towards the bright star in the east.' She died on the 31st at 3 a.m., apparently without pain, with Spears and his sister Kathleen at her bedside.[36]

He was devastated. 'I had thought I had made up my mind the old lady I knew died long ago, but it is my old lady I miss & mourn. All my childhood has gone with her,' and 'the long years of devotion' with 'the little boy & the old lady adoring each other'; the silent, reassuring presence of someone who was 'always to be counted on to make a sacrifice – always true & fundamentally honest & brave'. She had shaped him more than anyone; 'her trust in me, her belief & her indulgence – for she wd ever pardon – were my very soul until May.' Now the end had come: 'the nightmare that often awoke me in agony when the fear of her dying made me want to die too.'[37]

Obviously feeling no sadness, his mother and her husband Raymond de Maratray suggested that people close to them should be asked to see the body; Spears snapped that 'this was not a social function.' His mother mentioned the inheritance and was furious when he refused to discuss this. Kathleen at least was 'wonderful'. May returned from London, where she had been involved in the final settlement of the dispute with Turner, desperate at not having been there; 'the darling', Spears wrote, 'it was such a relief to tell her my sorrows.'[38]

He would not allow the Maratrays to ask anyone to the funeral in the British embassy church; there was just himself, May, the old lady's two devoted servants and the Rafinesques. May arranged for the coffin to be covered with a sheet of violets and the church was filled with the scent of these, the old lady's favourite flowers. In April she was buried in the cemetery at Voutenay in the rain and Spears read the burial service.

After the funeral, the quarrel about the old lady's possessions began in earnest. The Maratrays tried to seize the contents of her flat, lawyers were called in and on 5 February Spears thought all day 'of the fiendishness of Madame de Maratray'.[39] The rows lasted until his mother's death in 1927. She challenged her daughter's right to anything of her grandmother's, and Kathleen was left almost destitute again.

At Loughborough he was feeling his way. May told him he had spoken badly at a meeting there because he had gone 'into far too much detail' and been 'quite unconvincing'.[40] In March Churchill came and the Town Hall was packed. This time Spears's speech went down well, although his hand trembled and he felt he had stuck too closely to his notes. When people asked him to intercede for them with Churchill, Spears saw how much he was linked in the public eye to his patron. Others imagined his riches, as the husband of an heiress; 'I suppose your income is now in six figures,' wrote Major Geiger, his old colleague in the British Military Mission.[41] They took a flat in London, at 3 Cleveland Row, St James's Street. Elsie de Wolfe, the decorator, came to tea and criticised the furnishings, so Syrie Maugham, her rival, was called in to transform the place.

He still lived on the edge. General Macdonogh warned him that two copies of the papers on the Higgins incident were missing from Spears's dossier at the War Office. Churchill had one but the other had been taken by Sir Henry Wilson, perhaps to use against him in his public life. This worried Spears; then on 22 June Wilson was assassinated by two Sinn Fein gunmen on the doorstep of his London house. In 1927, to Spears's unconcealed delight, extracts from Wilson's diaries were published in a biography and their revelation of a scheming nature and intemperate opinions sent the Field Marshal's reputation into a decline from which it never recovered.

He would gaze at his beloved Michael, or Peti, and feel overwhelmed; 'I can hardly realize he is my very own little son.'[42] When on 12 June the baby left London for a house they had rented near Loughborough, he wrote, 'I can't express how much I have dreaded this moment. He means so much to us & it was wonderful seeing something of him each day.'[43] London still seemed foreign. He wanted May to be presented at Court but was told this would be difficult because of her position as a divorced woman. They found a literary party in July dreary, 'so much duller than Paris'; he hated a dance the same summer because they knew no one.[44]

Expenditure was still a worry; 'there is an awful waste of money.'[45] On 2 August Brunstrom and he broke their connection with Reilly 'v pleasantly'; the spy's methods had proven too outlandish.[46] One piece of good news was General Macdonogh's departure from the army to work for Shell, where Spears hoped 'we can help him and he can help us.'[47] He saw the Rumanian Prime Minister in Paris about a maize contract but, as so often with his deals with eastern Europe, the promises did not meet the reality.

In September he accompanied Sir John French, now the Earl of Ypres, to France to act as his ADC for the celebrations commemorating the victory of the Marne. There was a service in Meaux cathedral, followed by lunch at the Hôtel de Ville and visits to the battlefield and local cemeteries. Lord Ypres praised the French commanders in his speech, but in the sermon by the Archbishop of Rouen there was only one mention of the British and that was to say that 'Field Marshal French' had crossed the Marne with three army corps: 'c'était tout!'[48] The Archbishop said that the allies should be grateful to France for the great victory won for them in the name of civilisation. Spears complained to Fagalde about this discourteous chauvinism.

In Loughborough, during the election campaign in October, there were rumours about May's divorce, casting doubt on the legality of her marriage to Spears. He convinced his supporters that these were false and Lord Ypres sent a letter of support, declaring that 'any constituency should be proud to be represented in parliament by a man of such tried indomitable courage and with so fine a military record.'[49] On nomination day he handed in his papers, only to find later that his Labour opponent had arrived two minutes after nomination time and therefore was not permitted to stand. As the Conservatives had agreed not to put up a candidate against him, Spears was elected unopposed.

Hearing of this, Winston Churchill, in a London nursing home with appendicitis, asked Spears to campaign for him in Dundee, where he was standing also as a Lloyd George coalition Liberal with Conservative support. He and Nancy Maurice set off to have 'eighteen days pure hell' in 'the dreariest and most revolting town I have ever visited'. Never, he recalled later, had he met in Britain 'before or since anything to match the virulence and brutality of a section of the Dundee mob'.[50]

This industrial city with its huge jute mills and black rain falling from a heavily polluted sky was utterly foreign to Spears. After work, the men were 'rarely' sober and 'always hostile'; the Seamen's Union, supporters of Churchill, guarded Spears, who had to be locked in the lavatories at the end of the meetings for his own safety. Speaking was almost impossible, for 'no one got a hearing.' Lord Birkenhead came up by the night train, on which he had been drinking heavily, went straight to a Turkish bath to recuperate, reorganised the constituency workers and made a 'magnificent' speech, making fun of the French origins of E. D. Morel, Churchill's Labour opponent, which may have sent a slight shiver through Spears.[51]

Clementine Churchill sat on the platform 'like an aristocrat going to the guillotine in a tumbril', but she too was howled down and spat upon. A few days before polling day Churchill himself appeared, against doctors' orders, with the stitches still in his stomach, and addressed a huge meeting, able to stand only by gripping a chair. His obvious courage 'cowed the mob into silence for a few seconds', but then, overcome by weakness, he had to sit down and the uproar started again. Every time the cork popped from one of the many bottles of champagne that had been distributed to Churchill's supporters Spears feared 'it was Winston being shot'.[52]

Churchill was defeated and, in a move that shows his immense admiration, Spears offered to resign his seat at Loughborough and allow him to stand for it in a by-election. Churchill wrote to him of this 'extreme kindness' and 'splendid proof of your friendship', but added, 'I could not accept it from you.' He wanted Spears 'to enjoy your seat in parliament'; in any case he liked to feel 'I have one or two friends there' and 'what I want now is a rest.'[53]

Spears was now a member of parliament, a National Liberal who had relied on Conservative support. As such he stood against the Asquithian rump of the old Liberal party and looked to Lloyd George as his leader. In 1923 the Prime Minister and leader of the Conservative party was Andrew Bonar Law, a presbyterian Canadian-born Scot of dour aspect and gritty determination. In May, Bonar Law resigned with incurable cancer of the throat, to be replaced by Stanley Baldwin.

From the start Spears showed independence. He took an interest in the forgotten and the pathetic, taking up the cause of P. G. Spackman, a Royal Engineers officer who had been unfairly dismissed from the army at Salonika on charges of indecency, and persisted with an attempt to get this man a pension until 1952 when Spackman was living in poverty in Venice and dying of tuberculosis.

Another case was the extraordinary story of Trooper Fowler. A French family had sheltered a Trooper Fowler of the 11th Hussars behind the German lines from 1914 until the end of the war, hiding him in cupboards in their small house during the constant coming and going of enemy troops and an ever present possibility of betrayal; another family who sheltered a Corporal Hull under similar circumstances was informed upon by a neighbour and tortured vilely by the Germans.

Fowler survived, thanks to his protectors. The King gave the mother and her daughter the OBE, but the British government offered them only Fowler's extra messing allowance, a miserable sum worked out to the last centime by the War Office. The couple wrote to Spears, having heard that he had taken an interest in the case, to say that they were destitute. He started an appeal among the officers of his old regiment, who subscribed generously. The money raised, however, gave only temporary relief and in 1928 Spears approached Lord Burnham, proprietor of the *Daily Telegraph*, who published the story. As a result of this the women were brought to London, met the King and Queen and the Lord Mayor and were given money raised by another collection on their behalf. At last, Spears felt, 'the whole French nation' could see 'that England knows how to recognise and honour heroism and self-sacrifice'.[54]

He also took up penal reform, became honorary secretary of the House of Commons Penal Reform Committee and tried to repeal the law against suicide. A supporter of free trade, he opposed the Baldwin government's protectionist plans. Winston Churchill remained the politician he admired most.

In February 1923 Spears made his maiden speech, criticising the Foreign Office and the Paris embassy for being out of touch with French opinion. Charles Mendl, to whom he sent a copy, defended the diplomats; 'remember what I told you once about attacking a certain institution being like attacking the Roman Catholic church. Take it as friendly advice from a man much older than yourself: you are saving up for yourself the bitterest of enemies if you go on doing this.'[55] Spears ignored this and would often be in conflict with the Foreign Office. On 7 March, in a letter to *The Times*, he proposed the permanent demilitarisation of the Rhineland, supervised by an international force. A month later he saw Bonar Law, who encouraged Spears to bring this forward at the Inter-Parliamentary Conference at Copenhagen in August.

The occasion was marred, he reported to Lloyd George, by the bitterness of the Germans and the fact that France was badly represented; the air had been 'full of thunder' whenever the Germans met the French and France's new allies of the Little Entente of Czechoslovakia, Rumania, Yugoslavia and Poland, to which she had turned in the absence of guarantees from Britain or the United States.[56] His demilitarisation scheme was criticised in Germany and in France. On 30 May 1925 Professor Ludwig Quidde described it in the *Frankfurter Zeitung* as a 'quite monstrous' attack on German sovereignty and another commentator wrote of 'the extent to which Spears and with him the whole of Europe outside Germany had lost all sense of justice'. In the 1930s he would return to this theme, again in vain.[57]

In the December general election, Baldwin's gamble of advocating protection failed and the Tories lost. Spears, challenged this time by a protectionist Conservative as well as a socialist, was returned with a 'sound' majority as 'a Liberal and a Free Trader', with the Conservative bottom of the poll.[58]

It was around this time that he returned to France, as a civilian, to Montreuil, once the British headquarters during the war. Here he found almost no trace of his compatriots and little interest in them. Apparently the great armies of their allies had left only a small impression on the French. Once more the Channel had resumed its position as an extraordinarily effective barrier.

8

A Loss of Faith

Success came also to May. Her first two novels had not received much attention and the reviews of *The Romantic Woman*, her third, were respectful but few. In 1921 she wrote the draft of a long comic work provisionally called *The Diary of Sir Peter Pottle, Serious Snob, being a Faithful Rendering of Paris Gossip during the Peace Conference*. Too unwieldy to be published, its humour depending on topical allusions now obscure, this was probably written mostly for her own amusement; it may also have been the result of the idea with which she had shocked Lord Derby.

In 1923 May brought out her first work under her own name instead of the pen name of Bridget Maclagan. *Jane Our Stranger*, published by Alfred A. Knopf in the United States in October and by William Heinemann in London two months later, proved to be her greatest success. Again the theme is of the new world clashing with the old, this time through the person of Jane Carpenter, an American heiress. Jane is married off by her scheming mother to a French aristocrat, Philibert Marquis de Joigny, a monster of over-refinement and cynicism, utterly inhuman except in his feelings for the wild Bianca, a girl of Provençal exoticism and mystery.

Narrated by Philibert's crippled brother Blaize, the novel contrasts Parisian brilliance with American seriousness and tells how Jane with her magnificent body and awkward looks ('confused, intimidated, glowing') falls victim to the artful, selfish French aristocrats who take such pride in their 'gift for living'. Its background is the Paris of 1913 and 1914, when the rich enjoyed 'a season of delirium, of fever, of madness' before the war tarnished their hedonism for ever. Some of the book's best scenes are incidental to its main plot: the bohemian friends of Blaize who educate Jane, the artless cosiness of her old home in the American mid-west, the portrait of Philibert's sly mother who seems not so much evil as a figure of anthropological interest, typical of her tribe. Philibert and Bianca are figures of melodrama, Jane a symbol more than a character. But May knew the Paris of the *gratin*

well and her descriptive touch is sure. The novel begins in the rue
Monsieur where Blaize hears the distant singing of the nuns in the
convent.[1]

Gossip swirled around the book. It was said that Philibert and Jane
resembled the Marquis de Castellane and his American heiress wife
Anna Gould, another cynical and ultimately unsuccessful union of
breeding and money, although, unlike Jane, Miss Gould was notoriously
ugly. Like Philibert, 'Boni' de Castellane built a huge palace in Paris
with his wife's fortune and challenged colourless, republican France
with his aristocratic ostentation. Like Philibert, Boni was obsessed with
taste and style; like Philibert he joked openly about his wife, referring
to the marital bedroom as 'La chapelle expiatoire'. Spears knew Boni
and laughed with and at him. But May, as *Jane Our Stranger* shows,
retained her puritan scorn for idleness and display. Jane's nursing
during the war sets her free from 'too much brilliance', which had, for
her, 'the effect of darkness'.[2]

The book had an instant success, being widely reviewed and praised
with only a few reservations (*Punch* called parts of it 'crude'). The
Manchester Guardian admired 'its serene poise' and another critic
thought this 'admirable novel' to be 'not unworthy of the pen of
Charlotte Bronte'.[3] The book had gone through six reprints by October
1924. On the back of *Jane*'s popularity Heinemann reprinted *The
Romantic Woman* in the spring of 1924 and critics discovered this as
well, Arthur Waugh (father of Evelyn and Alec) writing in the *Daily
Telegraph* that Mary Borden was 'one of the most vivid and engrossing
figures that have dazzled the English book-world for many years'.[4] Her
prose may now seem mannered but conveys a sense of repression,
of hysteria hidden beneath stultifying convention. She echoes Edith
Wharton in her portrayal of the power of an unexpressed or inex-
pressible sexuality, the desperation of trapped desire: also that silence
which makes possible redemption so threatening and strange.

In 1924 the writer A. P. Herbert came to interview May for the
Queen magazine. By this time Spears and she had moved from Cleveland
Row to 8 Little College Street, a house built by Lutyens in Westminster,
conveniently close to the House of Commons. Little College Street was
both modern and grand; the dining room had a steel floor and there
was a marble staircase in the entrance hall. Some of the furniture and
pictures had been left to May by her father, Spears had inherited
several pieces from his grandmother and other items were bought by
them in Paris: French nineteenth-century pictures, etchings by Van
Dyck, eighteenth-century French furniture and Houdon's bust of Voltaire. To A. P. Herbert she seemed at ease in London; unlike Edward

Marsh, who had recently stayed at Ightham Mote, he did not comment on her voice, which Marsh compared to the sound of a screeching peacock. At lunch, Herbert noted the excellence of the food and dismissed as incredible her claim that her heart was still in the American mid-west, noting that by the time the coffee arrived it seemed to be in Westminster, where he thought 'it truly resides'. She told him of her next book, which would be about English country life. He hoped she would put in 'more conversation' for 'she is a good talker' and this was 'what one missed in *Jane*'.[5]

In October 1924 this next book came out in Britain and the United States, where it had been reprinted before publication. *Three Pilgrims and a Tinker* is about Marion, who has married Jim as her third husband (the first two died) and come to settle with him in 'middle England' to hunt and bring up her children: three daughters from previous marriages (the three pilgrims) and a baby boy with Jim (the tinker). Much is clearly autobiographical: the passionless life with an earlier husband in India, her later years in France, the winter bleakness of the English midlands. Unlike Spears, Jim is a simple soul, chronically inarticulate, occasionally muttering a few pregnant monosyllables through teeth battened on to an unlit pipe. Like Spears he was brave in the war and has immense physical energy.

It is the women who rule the world of the hunt, partly because the men speak scarcely at all except in curses or grunts. The contrast with the fluency and elaborate manners of the French aristocrats in *Jane* could not be greater, but the silence in *Three Pilgrims* is that of self-confidence arising out of the solid certainty of position. Into this comes Captain Waring, redolent of Mr Rochester with his opaque character, legendary bad luck and mysterious past. Marion falls in love with him, strangely reflecting an incident in May's marriage in 1924 which showed how careful she had to be with Spears.

In August 1924 she took baby Michael, the Peti, to America. She wrote to Spears from the boat of how 'I am incomplete – I am empty when away from you,' for 'I adore you' and 'it's you, you and your true heart that I love.' She felt guilty that she had not helped him more in the Loughborough constituency. This year her books had taken up much of her time; next year would be his for he must know 'how much I believe in you'. May knew that she could be moody and short-tempered and apologised to him for being 'disagreeable'. She had, she said, been 'worrying all day'.[6]

Spears was still inclined to fits of jealousy and doubt; in August 1923 he wrote resentfully of his year-old son that 'he adores his mother' but 'me he accepts without remark or comment.' When her husband was busy in parliament or with his business interests, May went out independently and among the people whom she met were Colonel and Mrs Claude Rome. Suddenly Spears erupted about Rome (who was in his old regiment, the 11th Hussars), having found a letter or declaration of love. From America May wrote in explanation, hurt because Spears was also in the United States on business but had not been able to meet up with her and Michael.

'I did not lie to you,' she said. 'I told you I liked Rome – I was not frank however, because I didn't dare be. Your nervous jealousy terrified me. You were suspicious of so much, of so many little things. Sometimes you were cruel. You did not know how you looked and spoke.' That year he had become a different man. 'You were ill, maladive, I loving you so with all my heat, with a deep exclusive devotion, felt at times an absolute need of relief.' She liked dancing and knew few people in London. The Romes provided relaxation. 'You seldom talked to me except about difficulties,' so 'I had to go without you if I was to go out at all.'

May had visited Paris and been fêted in the Faubourg St Germain; the Princesse de Polignac declared herself to be fascinated by *Jane*. Here it was the old mix of the artistic and the smart: the world of Charles Mendl, who was involved with an 'insane woman', and Millicent Duchess of Sutherland, now Lady Millicent Hawes and regretting her marriage to a homosexual. In London May still felt 'depaysée' and this was her excuse for Rome. What is more he looked like her father and reminded her of her happy childhood.

'It exasperated me to think I had to give an account of my every action,' she told Spears. 'I was yours body and soul. I was loyal. I had given you my self, my life, my love, everything.' In fact she had seldom been alone with Claude Rome; now in America she recovered the sense of her father's world and did not need him. But her family suspected a rift between her and Spears and she and he would have to meet up at least at the end of her time in her homeland. May recalled all that she had suffered for him: the miscarriage, the divorce, her near death at the time of Michael's birth, his conflict with Henry Wilson and the War Office, his nervous breakdown. 'It seems to me again and again I have been crucified for you – for my love.' She asked: 'what was the point of it all if you now have lost your faith in me?'[7]

The trouble had been there for some time; her every snubbing word of irritation or complaint had struck deep into his fragile self-esteem. 'Don't you understand', she declared, 'that however cross and irritable I am when you are with me, the minute you have left me, I am beside myself with remorse and can only think of getting you back and am incapable of any interest in anyone?' She wanted 'only to live for you and the children'; but all this sounded so cold. 'I cannot express what I feel.' He must come to her and they would return to England together. 'How could I have been so blind, so stupid? Forgive me B. Let me try to prove to you how I love you.'[8]

Spears sent her the draft of a letter she might write to Rome, who had gone on military business to India. The tone is vigorous if unsubtle. 'I cannot conceal from you that the idea of seeing you would be absolutely repugnant to me now owing to the fact that you were connected with an incident that upset my husband, the only individual who ever counted with me,' May told her admirer. 'The only result of your attempting to see me would be your getting kicked downstairs.' Spears, however, wanted the incident kept secret. 'Louis has decided that should we meet socially the usual greetings are to be observed so as to avoid comment from all sources.'[9]

Claude Rome was Captain Waring of *Three Pilgrims and a Tinker*: the melancholy, silent intruder on her marriage. May had spoken to Rome before he left for India when he had seemed 'so depressed' about his life; if only he could marry her 'all would be different'. In a letter to Spears, she recalled the summer in London and a matinée at the Hippodrome when Rome had declared himself to her and she had felt sorry for him; what a mistake it had been. Now she had 'no other desire' but 'to forget' and wished that they had never met.[10] Spears, however, could not forget the affair. To him, used to the unquestioning idolatry of his grandmother, it showed how far May's independence of spirit might take her, at least in his imagination. Years later, he claimed this had been the reason for his increasing intimacy with Nancy Maurice, the loyal and single-minded secretary who had no life outside her work and her ceaseless attempts to further his cause.

In parliament, France and Germany and the effect of Versailles occupied Spears most in foreign affairs. The French should be saved from themselves, as their occupation of the Ruhr and the Saarland showed. 'Are the French going to advance more and more, until 39,000,000 Frenchmen spend their lives guarding 60,000,000 Germans?' he asked in the House of Commons in February 1923.[11] The French risked an explosion of Germans in the Ruhr: a 'Sicilian Vespers on a scale unheard of in this country'.[12] He admired the League of Nations and spoke against Curzon's Treaty of Lausanne with Turkey, a nation that had cost Britain 'millions of money to defeat', because it involved giving guarantees to the Turks outside the auspices of the League.[13] He praised the French army, 'the most efficient' in Europe, and deprecated the bloated bureaucracy of the British. France needed to feel she had international support against Germany.[14] The French nation, contrary to what many people thought, was 'profoundly pacific', Spears declared.[15] But Anglo-French imperial competition and distrust rose again. He criticised expenditure on the Singapore naval base. What threat could there be to it? Certainly none from our 'ex ally' Japan.[16]

Spears's compassion for the wretched, for those who had fallen into the abyss, came from a part of him buried beneath his own comfort and the apparent absolute financial security provided by May. In his speech on the introduction of his bill to abolish the charge of murder for a survivor of a suicide pact he spoke of human despair, consciously or unconsciously echoing his own dread of failure, abandonment and loneliness. This 'cruel law', he declared, left Britain 'so far behind other nations'.[17]

How much of a mark did Spears make politically? Later, after his return as the Conservative member for Carlisle in 1931, he was to be labelled a crook by some of his colleagues, who mistrusted his business connections. Certainly from 1922 to 1924 he did not hesitate to ask parliamentary questions about the problems of foreign investment in Rumania, where he and his partner Brunstrom were involved, without declaring a personal interest. Hankey deprecated his scheme for demilitarisation, reminding him that Luxembourg had been technically in a demilitarised state, guaranteed by the great powers, in 1914 and this had not stopped the German invasion. But to be a member of parliament made Spears a figure, even if the old sense of exclusion could still rear up; at the Court ball at Buckingham Palace for the King and Queen of Rumania he had the sensation of being completely invisible. The French War Ministry sent him private information, recognising that France now had an ally at Westminster, and in the United States, where he and May finally met up, the Bordens welcomed him as a British statesman.

In October 1924 he and May returned to England, the Claude Rome imbroglio hidden from view: a brilliant young couple with their infant son. Ahead of them went the story of their involvement in a rail crash in California; Spears had apparently flung himself in front of May to protect her and she had helped the injured, using her wartime experience of nursing. From the liner *Homeric* Spears cabled the Liberal association in Loughborough: 'Greetings from mid-Atlantic. Everything points to fine weather and smooth course to victory.'[18] On the 18th, after docking at Southampton, Spears and May chartered an aeroplane to fly to Loughborough, scattering leaflets from the air as they came in to land; the local papers recorded this dramatic arrival. But it was Stanley Baldwin's hour. Spears, opposed by Tory and Labour candidates, was beaten into third place, the Conservative being elected with a majority of 1,363. Among the unfinished business in parliament was the suicide bill, which got no further without his support.

Winston Churchill was back in the House of Commons, having left the Liberals for the Conservatives. A rumour started that Spears would do the same and he told Brunstrom: 'I am not going to be out of it for long.' He felt he could make a difference. 'The mere thought' of the war 'gives me nerves', he wrote and he wished 'to do all in my power to prevent such an abomination ever taking place again'.[19]

But Joynson-Hicks, the Conservative Home Secretary, said that the chances of getting an early seat were not good, and a Loughborough dignitary, Sir Edward Packe, warned him not to be 'too impetuous'. Churchill recommended him to the Conservative party organisation and at an interview Spears made 'no conditions whatsoever'; he had never been much attached to Liberal dogma. Then on 18 December he left once more on business for the United States, apprehensive 'owing to the stormy weather in the Atlantic'.[20] From Paris, May wrote to show how wrong he was to doubt her loyalty. 'I love you so, more, much more than ever before. I had the same little thrill and shiver in my heart at the station today that I had in 1918 when you met me coming from the front.' He seemed 'such an attractive man' in defeat. In Paris 'people are all buying & talking about The Pilgrims', but she was quick to assure him of her love, of his own importance: 'darling I adore you. You were never so absorbing to me as now.'[21]

Some of his connections in central and eastern Europe were potentially embarrassing, perhaps even worse. In May 1925 it became clear that Sidney Reilly had committed Spears to a complicated commission arrangement with a Polish financier for tobacco sales to Czechoslovakia. Now Reilly could not be found and the Pole threatened Spears with a writ. This was more squalid, and more dangerous, than the Palace of Westminster. He longed to return there.

In April he had joined the Conservative party. 'Once more I have nailed my colours to your mast,' he told Churchill, now Chancellor of the Exchequer in Baldwin's new government, and in May asked for help finding a seat.[22] He told Eddie Marsh how 'utterly weary and miserable' he was at having nothing to do.[23] Some ventures he thought of were a possible involvement in Brendan Bracken's magazine *English Life*, a colonial governorship, work with Hankey in the Cabinet Office or at Geneva with the League of Nations. But Hankey said he was full up and too many former Liberals had been made governors. The Foreign Office did not like his demilitarised-zone scheme and Austen Chamberlain, the Foreign Secretary, begged Spears 'before everything else' not to venture into discussions on the German–Polish frontier.[24]

May and he rented Bisham Abbey at Marlow in Buckinghamshire for weekends from London and in the summer took houses in France, sometimes in the south, once at his beloved Voutenay which the Rafinesques were finding expensive to keep up. At Bisham, a notoriously haunted house, he was almost suffocated one night in his ground-floor bedroom by 'some earthy, elemental Thing from the garden' and during a weekend party a table reared up and, followed by astonished guests, hurled itself into a corner, smashing a china vase. One weekend a young woman came down from London, bringing a poodle, which habitually slept on the end of her bed. In the middle of the night the dog began to growl, and when its mistress reached down to pat it, a horny hand seized hers, pulling hard. With a loud scream, she resisted the pressure; her hand closed on air, and she fell back on the pillow. When she switched on a light, there was nothing to be seen, but she was so terrified that she insisted on leaving the house there and then. Spears kept his childhood belief in ghosts.[25]

In 1927 he stood for parliament as a Conservative in a by-election at Bosworth, an industrial and mining seat in the Midlands. Winston Churchill sent a letter of support about 'British reds' but Spears was handicapped by the fact that he had been beaten as a Liberal in the neighbouring constituency of Loughborough. The Conservative party chairman J. C. C. Davidson said no cabinet minister could come down, not even Churchill, who had begged not to be pressed 'to take anything for a while'.[26] Cuthbert Headlam, then the Parliamentary and Financial Secretary to the Admiralty, was sent to speak in a cinema in Coalville and commented severely on Spears's own oratory ('a feebler performance I have seldom heard') and May's speech of twenty minutes in 'an outrageous American accent'.[27]

A Tory majority of 358 was transformed into a Liberal victory of 271 over Labour with Spears trailing in third place. He claimed this was not a bad result because half the electorate were miners. 'The formidable hold the extremists have in the Midlands' shocked him, for many people seemed 'really disaffected', the young in particular being 'devoid of patriotism' and given to ripping up Union Jacks. The result encouraged hopes of a Liberal revival and cost Spears some £1,153 in expenses.[28]

In June 1929 he was beaten at Carlisle and accused of being a carpet-bagger in another campaign vitiated by class warfare and memories of the General Strike. 'Who starved the miners?' was a cry at his meetings; the socialist candidate was elected on a minority vote. Winston Churchill encouraged him in the aftermath of defeat. 'Your course now seems clear,' he wrote. 'You must win Carlisle and in less than three years, possibly less than two, you will have your chance.'[29]

Having taken Ian Hamilton's advice, Spears had embarked upon work of a different kind. By 1926 he was sending out draft chapters of a book about 1914, and an editor from the American firm of Houghton Mifflin wrote: 'I don't recall anything in the field of war literature that I have recently read that has held me more completely.'[30] Churchill and others urged him to cut the manuscript, make the narrative move faster and concentrate on his personal experiences rather than general history. Macdonogh said the text reminded him of 'the most extraordinary week's work – Charleroi to St Quentin – that any British subaltern has ever done'.[31]

In 1927 his mother died, worn out by drugs and bitterness. Her behaviour after his grandmother's death had made Spears implacable and he thought once of putting her into an asylum. His sister Kathleen had gone to live in Grenoble with her daughter Béatrix; Spears tried to help but their worlds were far apart. Old landmarks were falling; at Voutenay the Rafinesques were trying to stave off a sale and at Donadea the Aylmers struggled with the huge, unmanageable castle. His immediate family now consisted of May, her three daughters and Michael.

Joyce, the eldest, was a brilliant and imaginative girl. She went to Somerville College, Oxford, spoke French, German and Italian and taught herself Russian by reading the Bible in that language. Passionate and serious, she fell in love with an artist and when her affection was not returned became overwrought and unstable. Joyce found Spears fascinating. To her he seemed exotic in spite of his military bearing, immaculate tailoring and smart appearance; in him 'a certain gaiety of step, a tilt of the hat and gallantry of manner' reminded her of 'periwigs and cutaway brocades, monocles and long canes'. It was of course his 'courtly ways' that had led to him being 'much chaffed' in the army and nicknamed Beaucaire. At home, however, he was charming and easy among the dogs, horses and children, always ready with stories that might last for two or three years without repetition; his enjoyment in the telling of these was 'earnest and often so absorbed as to be funny'. He knew history well and poetry, particularly French poetry. Then there were the lively and pathetic Irish and French songs which he taught the children. They sang these to him, wishing to please, reciting also his favourite passages from de Vigny's stories of the Napoleonic Wars.

How easily he could be carried away, how 'easily illusioned and often terribly disillusioned': capable also of 'great depth of feeling and enthusiasm'. The children played up to him; in truth he found them a mystery, not liking them to grow up and shutting his eyes and ears to their precocities. His childhood in Ireland and France still loomed large for him, a source of remembered happiness, resentment and perplexity, for he had never really grown up. Human beings he did not really understand; nations, crowds and regiments seemed much easier. Only the poetry of his disposition saved him from 'complete disillusionment'.[32]

In the summer of 1928 Spears and May took a villa near Villefranche in the south of France. Cyril Connolly came to stay as Joyce's guest and marked the company out of ten for various attributes; Spears got 1 for charm, 6 for sex appeal (Connolly was not generous with his points), 4 for intelligence, 1 for virtue and 7 for guts. May's scores were respectively 4, 4, 6, 6 and 6; Nancy Maurices's, 0, 0, 3, 8 and 6. Bernard Shaw, rather out of place amid the 'Café Society', came last in all categories.[33]

Spears had a yacht, *The Bittern*, which he kept on the south coast and took to the Channel Islands, Normandy, Brittany and Holland. May's daughters came, as did Michael, who for Spears was now the perfect child, settling in at day school in London where he did well ('he despises meanness') at work and games. In a charity boxing match he was, to his father's delight, the only boy to knock his opponent down.[34]

In 1929 guests came on *The Bittern*: A. P. Herbert; old friends from the 11th Hussars like Roger Lumley and Luke Annaly; Lieutenant-Commander Reginald Fletcher, a former Liberal colleague in parliament and a journalist who in the early 1930s worked in intelligence before becoming a Labour MP. Spears's book, to be called *Liaison 1914*, was moving forward. Fletcher read the manuscript, advised cuts and, like others, suggested giving it a more personal slant. A ruddy-faced clubbable man who had joined the navy at fourteen, 'Matelot' (as Spears called Fletcher) became a close but not always admiring friend. Then came news from the United States of a catastrophe on Wall Street with the Borden fortune at risk. In November Spears and May crossed the Atlantic to find the worst. John Borden, her brother, had lost the family's money through rash speculation. All May's capital had been wiped out.

May had followed *Jane Our Stranger* and *Three Pilgrims and a Tinker* with other successes, building upon her position as a popular and serious writer. In 1925 came the novel *Jericho Sands*, in 1926 a book of ten short stories called *Four O'Clock*, in 1927 and 1928 the novels *Flamingo* and *Jehovah's Day*, in 1929 *The Forbidden Zone*, sketches of her nursing work with the French army, in 1930 and 1931 the novels *A Woman with White Eyes* and *Sarah Gay*.

Jericho Sands has Priscilla as its heroine, a woman with a religious mother, a decent clergyman for a husband and a vigorous war-hero soldier lover called 'Crab' Willing. One can identify these people as May, Turner and Spears, although Willing's only symptom of sensitivity is his love of gardening. Hunting, shooting and the English countryside are once again the background to life in a small isolated village where Priscilla's husband is the vicar and Crab's father the squire. It is not an idyll; eventually Crab and Priscilla go to a ranch in New Mexico to find extra-marital happiness and have a child. May could not be regarded as a respectable writer.

The stories of *Four O'Clock* have an atmosphere of 1920s sophistication with the world of Michael Arlen and *The Green Hat* satirised only gently, as if the author cannot quite keep her tongue in her cheek; the women drive Hispano-Suizas, the villains are cosmopolitan, often Jewish, and an Anglo-Saxon falsely accused of fraud kicks his heels in Italy longing for a proper breakfast. There are para-normal features in two of them: one about a medium, the other a send-up of a Lady Colefax type of London hostess who introduces her ghostly guest Jesus Christ as 'having been born in dear Bethlehem'. Another comes directly out of Spears's parliamentary attempt to abolish the charge of murder for the survivor of a suicide pact; 'No Verdict' tells of a weak young clerk on trial for this offence.[35]

Differences between the old and new worlds continue to be a theme, as in *Flamingo* (praised by Cyril Connolly in the *New Statesman*), where a group of characters cross the Atlantic on the *Mauretania* to the New York of the Jazz Age; it is the world of big business, 'coon' cabarets, Jewish financiers and the unimaginative Victor Joyce, a British member of parliament ('taller and more massive than most men') accompanied by his devoted private secretary and loving but exasperated wife. For Maurice Baring, *Flamingo* was 'a wonderful work of art' that made him conscious of his own 'creative poverty'. *Jehovah's Day* is more ambitious, a 'Darwinian' account of evolution from 'primeval slime' to the General Strike. To its author 'human beings were the only animals in the whole scheme of creation who were depraved'. A disappointed Connolly thought May should stick to 'the cosmopolitan world'.[36]

She returned to this in *A Woman with White Eyes*, in which Caroline

Merryweather, an American approaching sixty, looks back on a life of much money, many love affairs, a loveless marriage and her present involvement with Tawaska, a huge albino Finn, 'a cross between Sheikh and Rochester', 'a great sensual brute secretly vowed to chastity'. The book ranges from the United States to life among the English upper classes ('I know no people in the world so lapped in luxury, so spoiled, so pampered, so stupefied with every kind of pleasure'), then Paris and Monte Carlo and villas on Cap Ferrat, leaving Edith Wharton for Michael Arlen's cocktails and chic. Caroline becomes 'an old man's mistress', having seduced Hugo, an English sporting peer. Pregnancy follows, then marriage to Jock ('a pathetic man off a horse'). The tone is outwardly cynical, inwardly tragic: an Arlen with morality in spite of the promiscuity, abortions and hints of sado-masochism. *Sarah Gay* has a calmer heroine: Sarah, Lady Howick, married at the start to a stuffy general who is relieved of his command. She nurses at the front and falls in love with the young, unmarried, wounded officer Johnnie Gay. Her work in the hospital is a fictionalised version of May's account of her own experiences, *The Forbidden Zone*, published in 1929.[37]

The Forbidden Zone is much more *A Farewell to Arms* than *The Green Hat*. Squalor, pain ('the harlot in the pay of war'), courage and pathetic attempts to ease physical suffering give an elemental effect to these eight sketches, the most powerful of which is the struggle of a priest for the soul of a dying Apache. At times the hospital made May feel 'dead, past resurrection', with 'the familiar damp smell of blood' on her apron and agony strangling the dreams of the wounded. As a peasant has his leg amputated and cries out about his farm, the surgeon, his pity frozen by experience, speaks of oysters from Amiens, and a man's brain comes away in May's hands. She recalls the steel-blue eyes of the inspecting General Pétain and how different the talkative French patients were to the silent agonies of the British. *The Forbidden Zone* is a significant Great War text, a feminine reaction to the limitations and the importance of what a woman could do near the front line of battle.[38]

In December 1929 Spears and May returned from the United States in the aftermath of her financial disaster. Only Joyce, May's sister, married to a Yugoslav violinist called Zlatko Balokovich, had kept her share of the Borden fortune, and that by chance rather than design. Henceforth they would be entirely dependent on what they could earn but May never complained about the loss. Her strength of character, which Spears thought was a legacy of her puritan ancestors, saw her through.

The children were growing up, sometimes uneasily. Douglas Turner had married again, to another American novelist, Margaret Wilson. After leaving the League of Nations Union, he taught at Oxford before becoming a prison governor and eventually an inspector of prisons. Happy with his second wife, he remained gentle and unassuming, utterly removed from the world of May and Spears, and his daughters spent more time with their mother. The brilliant Joyce was prone to depression, and Emmy, May's youngest daughter, had to leave her school at West Malvern for a term because of severe 'nervous debility'. Comfort, the middle daughter, seemed more stable and went to study agriculture at Oxford.

Then in May 1930 came the day of Michael's departure for his first boarding school, West Downs in Winchester. To Spears, with his continental upbringing, the patrician English habit of sending a child off at eight cut deep. But this was the world which he and May had chosen for themselves.

At Waterloo station they said goodbye to the boy, who was to catch the school train. To Spears it was 'unendurable'; 'I feel I have lost him forever & that although only 44 I am a very lonely old man.' The first chance to visit Michael a fortnight later brought disappointment, for in the dormitory Spears's photograph had been 'relegated' out of sight; this was relieved by 'a spontaneous hug' when they left. Although Michael seemed well, the melancholy persisted and he and May felt 'like two very lonely people drifting in a very small boat towards the twilight'. Subsequent visits showed Michael to be distant and Spears wondered if he had succeeded in making his son feel 'he should look up to me'. He said, 'I would be glad if my boy were half as glad to see his Dad as his dad is to see him,' to which Michael answered, 'he is more.' May thought the boy worried too much; Spears noted, 'he has got that from me.'[39]

On 22 September 1930 *Liaison 1914* was published by William Heinemann, dedicated to 'my son Michael', with a foreword by Winston Churchill (who found its pages 'so captivating that I could scarcely lay them down') and bound in the colours of the 11th Hussars.[40]

Two years earlier, General Huguet, former French Military Attaché in London, had brought out an anglophobic study, written under the influence of Britain's failure to guarantee French security in the treaty of 1919, called *Great Britain and the War: A French Indictment*. It was part of Spears's wish in his own book to argue the British case. He said later that he had also been inspired to write it after a lunch at the French Senate when several senators had told him that Britain had played no part in the war until 1916.

The book begins with the author's arrival in Paris in July 1914 and ends on 14 September as the allies' advance dies out on the banks of the Aisne. The story of the retreat is recounted largely from Spears's own point of view, too full of prejudice and opinion to be objective history, but it is a bravura performance: a work of vigour, powerful description and sudden illumination of human endeavour and frailty in which the occasional piece of overwriting does not diminish the undoubted triumph of the whole. In *Liaison* Spears let loose that hidden part of him: his sense of fantasy, wonder and poetic imagination, the deep, occasionally uncontrollable, emotion. The chief actors come alive through the oddly compelling, rather jerky rhythm of an idiosyncratic prose brilliant with metaphors and similes of light and movement: the preposterous, blundering Lanrezac, by turns tragic and absurd; Sir John French, honest, limited and emotional; Maud'huy, the epitome of simple heroism; Franchet d'Esperey, the hard man who rallies an army; Joffre, the imperturbable victor of the Marne. Nor are the minor participants neglected, with Huguet 'suave and friendly, professing the greatest admiration for England and all things English'.[41]

Towards the allies, Britain and France, Spears, unlike Huguet, is fair in the distribution of praise and blame, tending perhaps to be too generous to Sir John French when describing the Field Marshal's undoubted loss of nerve. Of the young French officers, his former colleagues, he writes with undisguised emotion, reviving the dead in his evocations of their courage and humanity, and he depicts the countryside, villages and towns of northern France, inanimate behind the chaos, with the skill of a painter of landscape. But it is the sense of early confidence crumbling into desperation in the scorching heat of that terrible August which gives an epic quality to the narrative.

Spears had his heroes, especially Macdonogh, Sir John French, Joffre and Franchet d'Esperey. Lanrezac is the most criticised character, with only a faint shadow of dislike falling on Sir Henry Wilson, perhaps because the author knew that irreparable damage had already been done by the extracts from the diaries in the 1927 biography. Brilliant as his pen portraits are, there is also the sense of the horror of war not so much in the movements of huge armies as in particular tragedies: the shoeless refugees, a devastated landscape, the loss of comrades, the dependence of thousands of lives on the overwhelmed Sir John French, the stubborn arrogance of Lanrezac or centuries of Anglo-French distrust.

Liaison is a sensual book, alive with sounds, feelings, sights and atmosphere: the thrill of fear, then leaden exhaustion, the glimpses of horizons lit by burning villages, the flash of bursting shells, the view of columns of field-grey German troops pressing forward; or the jangle of the bridles of French cavalry waiting to move off, the odd sense of calm at British headquarters in the palace of Compiègne. Poets like Sassoon, Blunden, Graves and Owen wrote of the collision of pastoral pre-war innocence with the horror of the trenches; for Spears, trained for battle and longing to escape from peacetime soldiering, the disillusion was also great, not least because he would never lead fighting men in the way that, for him, marked the highest of wartime's possibilities. *Liaison* is a brave display; only occasionally does one glimpse the young officer who thought he might kill himself in 1916 and who broke down completely in 1920.

The reviewers were overwhelmingly favourable. Some of them knew Spears; in the *Morning Post* Macdonogh had reservations only about the fairness of the indictment of Lanrezac and in the *News Chronicle* Sir Frederick Maurice praised the vindication of the BEF, hoping this would be read 'as widely in France as it deserves to be in England'. In the *Daily Express* Harold Nicolson wrote of *Liaison*'s 'literary quality', which other war books lacked, noticing also the 'crushing criticism of war as a method of settling international disputes' and 'the vanity of human temperament' which showed how 'conceit in a man such as Lanrezac can kill ten thousand men'. Nicolson found 'the picture of that obese and arrogant general one of the most striking satirical portraits I have read for years' and was thankful that 'General Huguet's cruel attack on the British Army' had been answered. Even writers who detested militarism were impressed, the poet Richard Aldington describing *Liaison* as being 'so well written that it deserves to become a military classic' and Osbert Sitwell hoping only that this 'delightful and interesting book' would not persuade the next generation that 'war was a glorious thing'.[42]

By 24 October a second edition was ready and the printing of a third under way. In Carlisle, where he was to stand again at the next general election, Spears's reputation was boosted by a very favourable review by Field Marshal Lord Allenby in the *Cumberland News*. Desmond MacCarthy praised *Liaison* in a BBC talk in December; by the 22nd of that month it had sold 3,423 copies and by August 1932 it was out of print. A dissenting note came from Basil Liddell Hart in the *Daily Telegraph*, who championed Gallieni against Joffre as the architect of the victory of the Marne. To Liddell Hart the book was magnificent in its vivid descriptions of personal experience but less convincing on larger historical questions, and Spears and Maurice answered him in the correspondence columns of the paper. *The Times Literary Supplement* also thought *Liaison* too partisan and disliked the photographs, many of which had been taken by Spears, and the descriptions of the atrocities; 'the horrible pages on the shooting of spies, with photographs, might well have been omitted.'[43]

Success made people want to hear from him. In October he wrote in the *Spectator* on 'The War of the Future' and in November in the Armistice Day edition of *Everyman* to advertise the plight of unemployed ex-soldiers, worse in urbanised Britain than among the peasant population of a still overwhelmingly rural France supported by the land and the strength of French family life.

In October and November, May and he were in the United States. From Chicago on 4 November he wrote to Nancy Maurice and the letter shows how close they had become.

> My dear, a v curious thing is happening to me. Really & sincerely I am turning Bolshevik. I see this civilisation, its drabness, hopelessness as far as the mass is concerned & I think of what is going on in Russia & suddenly communism seems lighted by a great light, a hope, for it is at least an unselfish effort towards the betterment of the people as a whole ... I send you the nicest thoughts.[44]

9

'The Greatest Possible Anxiety'

Winston Churchill wrote in February 1931: 'everyone continues to praise *Liaison*,' and Edith Wharton admired its 'extraordinary human quality': 'I closed the book under an impression of grave tranquillity which, in remembering those days, & the greatness they called forth in men, is as it should be.'[1] In May the book was published by Doubleday in the United States to high praise.

He had become an authority on the war. Foch's memoirs had been serialised in the *Morning Post* and Spears was asked for his comments by several papers. He criticised the book, particularly for its harsh view of British conduct during the first battle of Ypres in 1914; whereupon Weygand, once Foch's chief of staff, wrote a letter of furious protest, refusing to answer Spears's riposte. *Liaison* brought the chance of earning money from writing, now useful after the Borden family crash. To Brunstrom, his old business associate, Spears wrote of 'very heavy' loans and how he could not raise 'even £100 more'; 'I am living through a period of the greatest possible anxiety.'[2] They sold the lease of Little College Street and moved into a more modest house in John Street, Mayfair.

May weathered the financial disaster but her eldest daughter's depressions were potentially much more tragic. While in New York, Joyce had tried to take an overdose of veronal. Cyril Connolly, her great friend, wrote of her as someone 'condemned by excess of sensibility, courage, distinction of heart to suffer a perpetual kind of adolescent brainstorm of passion and disappointment'. She had, he thought, 'a neurotic missionary side', unexpected in the Spears family, who seemed to Connolly sometimes to be 'hard American socialite success worshippers'. But May he admired as a 'woman of exquisite elegance and chic, simple, cordial, ironic, a flower of capitalism'.[3]

At least there was the adored Michael, doing well at West Downs preparatory school in Winchester. When he had 'flu there, Spears sat by his bed, having 'one of the happiest days of my life'. The headmaster was 'astounded' at the maturity of the boy's mind; to Spears he seemed 'a perfect child'.[4] But May's adoration could take the form of nagging, as it did in her relationship with her husband, and occasional harsh, frank criticism. Her children's failure to find happiness shows perhaps that she could not give them a sense of that ultimately unquestioning love in childhood which is the foundation of a secure adult life. Domesticity was not what she wanted or enjoyed.

In October 1931 there was another general election. Spears stood at Carlisle as a National Conservative, pledged to support MacDonald's national government. His meetings were broken up by gangs singing the Red Flag but on 28 October he was elected with a majority of 4,634, hailed in the local press as a 'great victory'. He chided Charles Mendl for not sending congratulations from Paris; perhaps Mendl was 'in a coma' or absorbed by 'some lady'. The new cabinet pleased him; 'I have ten personal friends in it.' Mendl's reply was mocking; 'how ridiculously touchy you are.' Spears must see that 'lip service or pen service' should not count in friendship. In any case he had never written about Mendl's knighthood. The letter ended with advice: 'cut all that out my lad if you wish to succeed even more than you have!'[5]

In the House of Commons, Spears became known, not always affectionately, as the member for Paris. Soon after the election he went over to the French capital and saw, among others, Pétain, Pierre Laval and Pierre-Etienne Flandin, all of whom declared themselves anxious to be on good terms with Britain. Spears, in a report to the Foreign Secretary Sir John Simon, wrote of the peculiarity of this sudden anglophilia and put it down to fear of France's 'increasing isolation'. On the principle of German reparations, Flandin in particular was firm, declaring them to be worth 'five army corps' to France.[6] In January 1932 Spears wrote an article in the *Daily Telegraph* stressing the importance of Anglo-French relations. Sir William Tyrrell, the British Ambassador in Paris, attested to his 'remarkable position' with the French.[7]

Again he thought of international solutions, advocating an International Air Police Force to be used under the auspices of the League of Nations. In parliament he criticised waste in the defence departments, comparing the low administrative costs of the French army to the much higher ones of the British and Liddell Hart wrote to congratulate him on this. In a speech in Carlisle in April, he advocated equal pay for men and women.

A friend helped him find a French translator and publisher for *Liaison 1914*. This was Yvonne de Lestrange, an heiress to huge properties in

Belgium and France, who had worked as a nurse in Paris during the First War, where she had met Spears. Yvonne had married a French duke who turned out to be impotent and she left him to pursue scientific studies at the Pasteur Institute. In her apartment on the quai Malaquais, and later in the rue de Rivoli, intellectuals gathered in an atmosphere that mixed informality and grandeur. A patron of writers and artists, she fostered the genius of her young cousin Antoine de Saint-Exupéry and was an intimate friend of André Gide. Yvonne intrigued Spears, perhaps because she stayed always a little beyond his reach.

It was to Gide that she turned with *Liaison* and his enthusiasm was immediate. He persuaded Gallimard to publish it in what Spears thought an indifferent translation. Pétain refused to write a foreword, saying he had enjoyed the book, particularly the portrait of Maud'huy, but could not be seen to condone Spears's judgement of certain generals.

The French edition of *Liaison* went well. In the *Figaro*, Pierre Hael admired the book's judgement and described its author as a good friend of France; Yvonne de Lestrange said that Gide was praising the book all over Paris. Colonel Gillot, an old colleague from the war, said he could hear the author's voice through his prose and was reminded of Spears's appearance of indifference that disguised a lively passion; he longed for a sequel. The French right-wing paper *L'Action Française* carried a favourable review by Hubert de Lagarde. But the son of Lanrezac, who had died in 1925, wrote to *Le Temps* to deny the details of the General's rudeness to Sir John French at their first meeting. *Mercure de France* also saw spite in this portrait, its reviewer comparing the conceit of Spears, the 'so fashionable and so perfect gentleman', to the more modest Lanrezac, a marquis who did not use his title. The French politician Paul Reynaud in *La Liberté* took the book as an illustration of how France must not allow herself to be separated from Britain. Spears with his Parisian-accented French, Reynaud declared, had been the most intelligent and the most sensitive of the liaison officers and in his brilliant picture of Paris on the eve of war in 1914 showed how completely mistaken both the British and the French had been about German strength. Surely now British opinion must see the need for the two countries to face a common enemy together.[8]

The success of *Liaison* encouraged Doubleday to suggest a biography of Talleyrand. But it was still the First War that interested Spears, in particular the disastrous Nivelle offensive of 1917. He interviewed Pétain, Robertson, Franchet d'Esperey, Painlevé, Sidney Clive and others; again the theme would be the strains of the Anglo-French alliance. From Pétain he received an extraordinary gift: that of the

Marshal's own account of the mutinies of 1917, which Pétain said Spears could publish after his death.

Spears and May bought a house of Tudor origins, a cross between a farmhouse and a large cottage, called the Old Gables at Warfield near Bracknell in Berkshire. This would be their country home until his death; later he changed the name to the more pretentious St Michael's Grange, after his son. When visiting his constituency of Carlisle he stayed at Naworth Castle, the home of Lord and Lady Carlisle. With the handsome, tough 'Biddy' Carlisle, who later left her husband for the lawyer and politician Walter Monckton, he struck up a close friendship; her daughter Carolyn remembered 'a lot of fun at Naworth' when he was there, also 'a few good rows'.[9] Then, in the spring of 1933, May's mother died, reviving for her the memories of a happy childhood unspoilt even by the religious crusade, and Spears saw 'an irreparable loss'.[10] She became more independent: always loyal but not the constantly adoring presence he craved to relieve his sense of isolation.

In parliament he kept on with his work on behalf of the dispossessed, taking up the case of Thomas Parker, a vagrant who had been picked up by the police and had later died in prison. 'This man's crime', Spears said in the House of Commons, 'was his extreme poverty. I say to myself, "This man Parker was an ex-soldier, just as I am. He may have been a better soldier than I was, for all I know. In any case, he volunteered to go to the war, whereas I was sent. He did his duty, he was honest, and, but for the mercy of God, it is Louis Spears, not Thomas Parker, who might have been standing in the dock." '[11]

Spears introduced a private member's bill to amend the Vagrancy Act so that it would not be a crime to sleep out with 'no visible means of subsistence'. For a suspect in another case, a Flying Officer Fitzpatrick who had been stopped in the street for no apparent reason by plain-clothes policemen, taken in for questioning and beaten up, he obtained a personal apology from the Commissioner of the Metropolitan Police, Lord Trenchard. The *Cumberland News* reported on 5 August 1933 that 'a parliamentary commentator' had said that because of these two interventions alone 'in the last session General Spears was the member who had most strengthened his position'.[12]

In January 1933 Adolf Hitler became Chancellor of Germany. Winston Churchill, now out of office, suggested that Spears should write to the French Ambassador on 27 April that year to put Churchill's views: those of an individual who had 'so much authority, although very much free lance at the moment'. Churchill thought the French should take advantage of the momentary swing of opinion against Germany and her brutal new rulers to demand compliance with the post-war treaty. Churchill believed, and Spears agreed, that British anti-German feeling would subside once 'the Jewish persecution' ceased, for in Britain German hysteria was attributed 'largely to French action' and demands.[13]

In the House of Commons, Spears warned of a possible German move into Austria. From Paris the British Ambassador Sir William Tyrrell congratulated him on his speeches: 'our pacifists à outrance and intellectuals trade on the short memories of ill informed people. Never forget that if we refuse to shoulder responsibilities as a continental power this winter we shall be assisting sooner or later at a repetition of 1914.'[14]

At the end of November Spears dined at the German embassy and suggested to the Ambassador that he might call on Hitler in Berlin to discuss an international scheme for peace and security, possibly a zone of demilitarisation or the Air Police. The Ambassador said he thought it unwise to raise the subject of a visit until matters at issue between Paris and Berlin had become clearer.[15]

Spears was criticised for his views on the European crisis. Visiting Carlisle in November, Lord Beaverbrook poured scorn on its member's apparent wish for foreign entanglements. On 17 December, his newspaper, the *Sunday Express*, attacked the way Spears concealed his origins in *Who's Who* ('he says nothing of a birthplace. French visitors to Parliament always assume that the birthplace was France'). The paper mocked his perfect French ('He talks just like a Frenchman'), change of allegiance from the Liberals to the Conservatives and the way he praised Jimmy Thomas, once leader of their trades union, to the railways workers of Carlisle: 'I am a General. Jimmy Thomas was a railway cleaner. I would be proud to serve under that man's orders.' The *Express* said that Spears spoke 'very well in Parliament (in English) in defence of freedom for the individual at home, not necessarily so well in favour of entangling the nation abroad'. A week later the paper raged against 'foreign-born' MPs: 'the danger of an alliance with France is overwhelming. It means another war like 1914.'[16]

In March 1934, a cross-party group which included Robert Boothby, Josiah Wedgwood and Clement Attlee met at Spears's house. Out of this grew the European study group, of which Spears was hurt not to be made the first chairman (it was thought he would give the gathering too francophile an air). In 1936 he took the chair and in the next three years the group became a focus for members of parliament who were suspicious of the European policies of the Chamberlain government. By 1939 it included Harold Nicolson, the Duchess of Atholl, Victor Cazalet, Harold Macmillan, Ronald Cartland, Duff Cooper, Leo Amery, Hugh Dalton, Arthur Greenwood and Ronald Tree.

In May 1934 he went on a trip that gave a glimpse of a role in which he would find comfort, satisfaction and escape after the Second World War. Kenya, Spears believed, might have prospects for business and he flew there to speak to the white settlers, whose way of life and freedom he admired. On his way to Africa he passed through Italy and, like others at this time, announced that, although no supporter of fascism, he was impressed by what Mussolini was doing for the country.

Then his life fell apart. In June 1934 Michael took the scholarship examination for Eton and narrowly failed. Soon afterwards, at the beginning of July, he was struck down by osteomyelitis in his thigh, a disease in which the bone marrow becomes dangerously inflamed. One of the symptoms was a high fever and the condition could be fatal, particularly in the young.

Spears was in Kenya when he had a letter from his son, then still healthy and happy at West Downs. On his way home to London he stopped in Paris, to be given a message at the airport from May about Michael's collapse. From Paris he managed to telephone twice and May's halting response showed how desperate the position was. 'I have never gone through such hell as on the plane to London,' he recalled. He read Michael's last letter again and wept. May's note showed her love: 'when you come, our little triangle will be complete and strong again – dear B.' From the airport, he went straight to the nursing home at Winchester, saw Michael and went down with a severe attack of malaria himself.

To Spears the agonies of the following months were 'beyond description'. Michael's disease had taken an acute form and the surgeon did not want to operate until August, when the boy would be stronger. May took a room in a nearby hotel, but as soon as his malaria cleared up Spears had to return to the House of Commons. He came every weekend to Winchester and during the week kept in touch by telephone: 'I shall never forget the phone calls & especially the last one at night, to know how he was last thing and what the temperature was.' The wife of Michael's headmaster suggested that the nuns of the League of Health should pray for the boy. Spears was grateful: 'May thinks & so do I that the prayers arranged by Mrs T. made all the difference.'

He could scarcely believe the disaster; 'why should this have happened to us who have had so many blows and to whom our boy means everything?' To lose Michael would be worse than death: 'death without hope – & everything that had ever happened wiped out'. There was also the worry of the medical bills. In her hotel room and in the hall of the nursing home, May worked desperately on her novel *The King of the Jews* to deliver the manuscript in time to get the advance.

Michael came home for the winter of 1934. While his son was under an anaesthetic following another operation, Spears had to telephone the doctor to ask him to tell May that her eldest daughter Joyce had killed herself at the age of 23 while in a fit of acute depression.

In August 1935 they took a house at Ullswater in Cumberland and on the first day there Michael fell and broke his bad thigh. It seemed as if the whole nightmare might start again but by October he was fit enough to go to Eton for the first time, joining the school at half-term on crutches: a 'heartrending' sight for Spears. In 1938 the boy left Eton, having won school prizes in history and English verse and an Exhibition to Magdalen College, Oxford. But a silence had come upon him, a withdrawal into a passion for chess and solitude, as if he felt apart from the world. Its origins seem to have been partly in the debilitating illness, partly in an enduring adolescent rebellion brought about by the obviously high expectations and constant attention of his parents. Henceforth he was no longer the darling boy on whom his father had poured so much demanding love and hope.[17]

To make money May turned her hand to what Cyril Connolly described as 'potboilers about the Holy Family'.[18] *Mary of Nazareth*, published in 1933, was a study of the Virgin's human dilemma, in particular when her sweetness of temper is forced to confront her bigoted, Pharisaical other son James, who wishes to restrain the 'mad' Jesus; the story goes up to the Crucifixion, when she shares the last vigil with Mary Magdalen. Two years later came *The King of the Jews*, about the experiences of the disciples after the Crucifixion: 'the adoring, bewildered love of the boys John and Mark', 'the flaming fidelity of Mary Magdalen', Peter and those at Emmaus who speak with the risen Jesus, the disillusion of the disciples when there is no second coming, then the dawn of Christianity itself.[19]

On the whole clergymen approved. Only the *Catholic Herald* protested publicly, declaring in 1933 that May had blasphemously traduced the idea of Mary's virginity. She sued the paper but allowed the case to lapse when the editor died. Critics were divided. Peter Quennell said that May's reliance on the gospels made it hard for her to fit 'something at once too large, too misty and too inhuman' into her 'charmingly human background'; whereas to Rupert Hart-Davis, her publisher son-in-law who married Comfort that year, *The King of the Jews* was 'excellent', 'beautifully written and enthralling to read'. Korda thought of making it into a film but saw difficulties with the censor. Both books sold well, in Britain and the United States.[20]

In *Action for Slander*, published in 1936, May returned to the world of her earlier books but with a less literary slant, perhaps because she needed a bestseller. In an atmosphere redolent of Sapper or E. Phillips Oppenheim, the vicious Captain Bradford accuses his superior officer Major Daviot, who is having an affair with Bradford's wife, of cheating at poker and Daviot is ruined at the subsequent trial. The background is that of the very rich: Cannes, Deauville, English country houses, polo, shooting and the threat of expulsion from 'society'. *Action for Slander* is a thriller with stock characters and chic settings. Winston Churchill liked it; 'I offer your wife my sincere congratulations on her brilliant book,' he wrote to Spears. Algernon Blackwood told her the book 'must sell in its thousands' and it was made into a play with the help of Felix Felton. In 1938 May earned £1,663 17s 1d in literary income, whereas Spears's writings made him only £396. In 1939 the figures were surprisingly similar: £1,662 4s 1d for May and £504 10s for Spears.[21]

In 1937 May published *Black Virgin*, about a politician's unfaithful wife, again with a country-house background. In 1939 came her last pre-war book, *Passport for a Girl*, a melodrama set in Austria after the Anschluss. The narrator's daughter has a Jewish boyfriend called Hans Hartmann; another character is the press tycoon Sir Gregory Trumpet, a mixture perhaps of Rothermere and Beaverbrook. The book is anti-Nazi, and has lurid descriptions of Hitler's victims: Hans's grandmother is murdered; his mother tortured and compulsorily divorced, and dies in a cow shed. One passage on Trumpet makes one think of Spears, or Spears after 1945; 'he had never liked Jews and for some reason that he didn't trouble to investigate, he had begun, during the past year ... to dislike them with increasing intensity. Some people said that it was because he had a streak of Jewish blood himself...'[22]

May seemed modern. This was the secret of her appeal, combined with a narrative gift and a sure touch with the lives of the rich; she gave a literary gloss to palaces, villas in the south of France, country houses, foxhunting and cocktails. In 1933 she took an ostensibly cool 'modern' look at marriage in *The Technique of Marriage*. Described as 'somewhat advanced', the book details the perils of romantic love ('young people should awake from the fairy tale of cheap fiction') and the advantages of the French example and not being swayed by 'any such emotional reason as jealousy of any crime, if it is a crime, of infidelity'. There was, she thought, much to be said for parents arranging marriages, as in France, on the supposition that love will come later.

Honeymoons were 'traps' and 'unreal, dangerous'; the double bed also should go. A 'normal man' needs a room of his own.

> I live with one. A mass of his paraphernalia in a small house. And all the stuff he needs for a week-end, of fishing or shooting or golf ... boots, guns. And his pipes ... dozens, all over the place ... disgusting things. Too many ties. Too many suits. I, the loving and adoring wife, like to ride with him, fish, play golf, trail across a grouse moor or a turnip field. But I do not want to see him shave, or fuss with hair oil. I do not want to see him in his bath. I am not his mother. And I do not want him to see me doing my face, however small the house is.

Wives also need financial freedom. May told how angry she had been when Douglas Turner paid her fine after she had thrown stones at the Treasury windows in 1913; 'he had paid without consulting me.'

Passion fades but happiness can last. Married life is not natural, whereas desire and 'fornication' are. Marriage, however, is civilised, like friendship. Divorce should be made easier, not only on grounds of adultery, and May suggested 'partial divorce' in which the law would allow a couple to separate, 'forbid them, in fact, to live together, but refuse to grant them the right to re-marry'.

One vignette is reminiscent of Spears and Nancy Maurice: that of 'John Lovejoy and his wife Jane'. John is a man whose business means everything to him. 'He went at it snarling. The only woman who was any good to him was an employee of his, a sexless creature, who wrote all his letters for him and always understood exactly what he was driving at. He came to depend on her as he might on a maiden aunt, and he let her bully him. He enjoyed it ... it was somehow comforting.' Perhaps this was a shaft, perhaps a tease, for by 1933 Nancy Maurice's power had grown, with Spears back in parliament and trying desperately to build up his business interests as well because of the loss of May's fortune. Then there was Joyce, her brilliant daughter. 'I have a Bohemian in my own family' who was 'translating a verse by Dante' and 'writing an essay on Kant ... I love her, but she should not marry.' The tragedy was that Joyce went beyond the reach of May's power to help.[23]

May denied that she put her experience into her writing and would complain later that a crowded life had made her work less good than it should have been. The novelist Elizabeth Russell, author of *Elizabeth and Her German Garden,* came to see May in London between the wars and, observing the clutter and noise in the house of children, frequent entertaining and Spears's demanding, aggressive presence, suggested that she should seek greater isolation and desert her family for weeks on end to write. May answered that life meant too much to her: 'I didn't write, I lived.' It was, she said later, with her hospital unit in the two wars that she lived with the greatest 'intensity'.[24]

She was also restricted and influenced by her time and position in a way that a more solitary or dedicated author would not have been. From the beginning, writing had been an assertion of independence, a wish to make a mark, in one of the few worlds open to her sex, rather than the itch of an undeniable vocation. In the novels, women, often ostensibly strong women, strive for freedom, for that 'intensity' of life, yet fall back into uneasy domesticity or unsatisfactory love. Jane, the descendant of pioneers, the troubled Marion in *Three Pilgrims*, a cynical but tragic Caroline Merryweather in *A Woman with White Eyes* or Joan in *The Romantic Woman* coolly experimenting with bohemianism but trapped by the dreadful Binky: all these reflect the ultimate fragility of a woman alone and the often perilous journey of her heart.

May loved Spears. She was transfixed by his energy, his domineering egoism, the brilliance of his mind and his strange mix of integrity and ambition. But she kept a section of herself apart from him: her writing, her hospital work in the two wars, her own integrity that refused to stifle criticism or irritation. The 1930s were a difficult decade for her. Michael's near-fatal illness and the death of Joyce brought terrible unhappiness. She began to drink more and to smoke heavily and people saw a change, the misery coming out in her ravaged face and increasing irritability and impatience. Her hands shook, reviving rumours of drugs, she put on weight and began to lose her looks. The difficult birth of Michael had nearly killed her and after it she found sex difficult, needing patience and a sympathy that Spears seems to have been unable to give. Looked upon as being un-English in his habit of touching and making physical contact with people whom he was with, he began to acquire a reputation for making passes at women, one of whom had to engage in a steeplechase across the various chairs and sofas of her drawing room to escape him.

May knew of her husband's behaviour and did not mind because she thought, rightly, that it was not serious. With Nancy Maurice, however, he went further, visiting her in her studio flat in Battersea (known to them both as 'the stud') where their relationship developed during these years into a love affair. Nancy's loyalty was unshakeable, her involvement in his personal and political life and business career without any other distraction or interest; to Spears, who felt he could depend upon no one, she became an essential confidante and aide. He had three serious love affairs in his life: one with her, one earlier on with Jessie Gordon, the other with May. Ruthless, and with nothing outside her time with him, Nancy pushed hard, greedy for his attention. May stayed by her husband, knowing now that there was another presence in her marriage. Her loneliness grew, for she never ceased to love and admire Spears, however cruelly he might seem to treat her. It was this apparent cruelty that shocked some who saw and judged him harshly over the years.[25]

In 1933 the British had refused to give a military guarantee to France. In October of that year Hitler withdrew from the disarmament conference and left the League of Nations.

In February 1934 Spears criticised the government for only paying 'lip service' to the cause of Austrian independence. 'If Austria falls to the Nazis,' he told Lady Violet Bonham Carter, who had written to say how much she agreed with his views on the European scene, 'there is nothing in the world to prevent Germany's pursuing the same tactics with the three million Germans in Czecho-Slovakia.' The problem was that many Austrians wanted to join Germany; Hitler, Spears thought, had been 'extremely clever' to exploit this with such skill.[26]

In March 1935 MacDonald resigned as prime minister of the national government, to be succeeded by Stanley Baldwin, the Conservative and leader of its largest constituent group. On 29 October Spears was adopted again as National Conservative candidate for Carlisle, to fight a Labour and a Liberal. Again his meetings were often disrupted. A rumour spread that he was about to accept an appointment abroad 'to govern some place', which he denied vehemently. He would, he said, rather represent Carlisle than 'all the wealth and fashion of Mayfair'. He was elected with a majority of 2,635; Labour came second and the Liberal third, losing his deposit.[27]

Other dictators were on the march. On 3 October Mussolini had invaded Abyssinia; the League of Nations imposed economic sanctions but weakened these by allowing Italy to import oil. In December the British Foreign Secretary, Sir Samuel Hoare, concluded a pact with Pierre Laval, his French counterpart, to buy Mussolini off. Italy obtained most of Abyssinia in return for the Emperor Haile Selassi being allowed to rule over the remaining small area, approximately one-third of the country, and keep an outlet on the sea.

In the House of Commons, Spears introduced an amendment, signed also by Victor Cazalet, Robert Boothby and Harold Nicolson among others, supporting Attlee's motion against the proposals. Hoare was replaced by Anthony Eden and the Hoare–Laval pact buried. Ineffective sanctions continued until the Italians entered Addis Ababa in May 1936. The League, in which Spears had put such trust, would never recover.

Michael was not the only family sadness at this time. In 1935 Miss Aylmer of Donadea had left her entire estate to the Church of Ireland, with the castle and everything in it to be sold. 'You were very keen on Donadea once,' a cousin wrote to Spears. 'By any chance would you like to buy it?' Before the loss of the Borden fortune he might have considered this; now it was impossible and after 400 years the property left the Aylmer family.[28]

A year later came a worse blow, and one that may have led to feelings of guilt. Kathleen, his widowed sister, had always been vulnerable, tormented by poverty and by her vindictive mother. She had lived in France, at St Germain en Laye outside Paris and later at Grenoble, where she had thought the climate would suit her child. She had hoped to translate *Jane Our Stranger* into French, but May's agent advised against such work being done by an untried hand. Then in 1936 Kathleen committed suicide.

Could Spears have done more? He had tried to keep in touch with Kathleen, had asked her daughter Béatrix to stay in England and had offered financial help; but, when the Borden fortune was still intact, had insisted on keeping all his grandmother's jewellery as a memento of her love.

Now he felt mortified, remembering their childhood together and the brave, isolated girl among the boys at Voutenay. In the same year Béatrix married Naum Szapiro, a Polish communist, and had a daughter of her own: Bernadette.

The abortive Hoare–Laval pact had brought about the greatest furore over foreign policy for years. In February 1936 Spears was one of the founders of the December Club of members of parliament, named after the month in which the pact had been negotiated. He took the chair at the first meeting at the House of Commons on 27 February and membership began at thirty-five, increasing later to forty; among these were Harold Macmillan, Harold Nicolson, A. P. Herbert, Robert Boothby, Victor Cazalet, Ronald Tree, Kenneth Pickthorn, Ronald Cartland and Sidney Herbert. To Spears, the group's purpose was to show that there were 'quite a number of us who are perfectly prepared in a real emergency to take action independent of the Whips should we deem it in the national interest'.[29] His vociferous opposition to the pact put him at the forefront of those Conservatives who were against attempts to appease the dictators.

Winston Churchill, his eye on Germany, moved less positively on the Italian action in Abyssinia, which was a startling illustration of international inability to contain fascism. In March Hitler introduced conscription in Germany and the following year marched into the Rhineland, breaking the treaties of Versailles and Locarno.

The will to resist this move into Germany's 'own back garden' was weak in Britain and France. It suited French politicians to blame the British for refusing to act with them. Harold Macmillan remembered listening to Pierre-Etienne Flandin, who had replaced Laval as foreign minister, at a dinner arranged by Spears. This 'large and powerful figure' spoke aggressively of how France would certainly follow if Britain took the initiative to resist Hitler; but, to Macmillan, Flandin seemed 'not unwilling to escape' by putting the blame on the British.[30]

Flandin was, with Spears, the joint chairman of the Anglo-French parliamentary group. He came from the Morvan, near Voutenay, and he and Spears had met with the Rafinesques. Tall and aggressive, inclined towards blackmailing techniques of negotiation, Flandin was tainted with financial scandal and had avoided military service in the First World War. May remembered this exponent of false bellicosity pushing back his chair at her dinner table and saying through clenched teeth: 'Very well, if you refuse to build up your armaments, France must come to an understanding with Germany.'[31] Once in Spears's house, he hinted to Churchill that France, by use of her deposits at the Bank of England, could bring down the British financial system; Churchill's response was an eruption of 'burning phrases' about the 'power and resources of the British Empire'.[32] Flandin's congratulatory telegram to Hitler after the Munich agreement showed his opportunism, as did his later role at Vichy. After Munich, the Frenchman tried to use his contacts in the Conservative party to oust Spears from the joint chairmanship; but the Labour members rallied and it was Flandin who went. More straightforward was Paul Reynaud, whom Spears also entertained.

Pétain warned Spears, whom he saw on visits to London or in France, that the poisonous divisions in internal French politics prevented the French public from having a true and objective understanding of international affairs. One form of international intervention Spears opposed was any involvement in the Spanish Civil War. A Cumberland newspaper carried a report that May had decided not to send her son to Cambridge because some undergraduates there had gone to fight against Franco.

Winston Churchill and he disagreed about the abdication. Spears and May had met Mrs Simpson at the American embassy, where she seemed alert and chic, with a wide jaw like the mandibles of an insect, and had expressed admiration for one of May's books. In November Spears glimpsed the unattractive side of Edward VIII when one of his courtiers, Louis Greig, declared himself to be 'violent' against the King, who was trying to sack him. Spears, with Greig's support, urged the editor of the *Daily Telegraph* to break the press silence and tell the King that public opinion would not stand for the marriage. But it was not until December 1936 that the Bishop of Bradford uttered the first public criticism.

When the news broke, Spears found the gloom in the country and parliament 'indescribable'. He conjured up a comparison which he repeated often, an example of that occasional pomposity which he may have felt appropriate in a member of a ruling caste: 'the position of the country was very much like that of a man who, having struggled for years to recover his position and at last seeing daylight, came home rather cheered, to be told his daughter was in the family way by the chauffeur.' Robert Boothby said he thought soon 'there will be no monarchy to bother about'. In fact Baldwin settled the matter quietly. Spears had offered to mobilise the December Club to support the Prime Minister, but the Chief Whip, David Margesson, told him it was better not to put public pressure on the King.

In the lobby of the House of Commons, a week before the abdication, he saw Churchill, who had foolishly tried to rally support for Edward. His old patron, now in the wilderness, said to him: 'we have often thought differently though on other occasions we have thought alike, and I never forget what you did in the war, but next week you will be singing "God save our other King".' Then, to the amazement of those standing near by, he sang this variation on the national anthem.

Spears was not optimistic about King George VI. He felt himself to be 'playing' at loyalty and his true feeling 'though one of great pity' was 'certainly not one of esteem'.[33]

He had his business interests alongside his political career. In 1934 the Czech shoe manufacturer Tommy Bata, head of a world-wide empire, made Spears chairman of his British company, which had a large factory at Tilbury in the East End of London. In 1936 he joined the West End board of the Commercial Union Insurance Company and in 1937 negotiated a link with the stockbrokers Schwab and Snelling at a fee of £500 a year and a commission on business that he brought in.

The central European connection endured, especially that with Czechoslovakia. In 1938 he joined the board of the merchants J. Fisher of Holborn, which had a strong trade link with that country, and became a local English director of the Czech Witkowitz steel works, where the Rothschilds had a large interest. In November 1938 he featured in the *Sunday Referee* series 'Men in the City', primarily as chairman of Unit Investments and Selective Fixed Investments, both offshoots of the unit trust movement. His other directorships mentioned were those of Associated Portland Cement, British Portland Cement and the Ritz and Carlton hotels. Most significant of all was the start, in 1937, of his association with the Ashanti and Bibiani gold mines on the Gold Coast, or Ghana as it later became. After 1945 this would dominate his professional life.[34]

Spears's involvement in business did him no good with the Conservative party. One of the representatives of its country-gentleman tradition, still strong at that time, Captain Charles Waterhouse, thought him 'shifty and unreliable', and certainly his mysterious, supposedly foreign or Jewish origins perpetuated his position as an outsider in public life, especially among anti-semitic Tories, and drew him naturally to buccaneers like Winston Churchill.[35] Estranged also from the prosaic world of Baldwin and Chamberlain, both of whom came from more orthodox, and inherited, business backgrounds, Spears inspired dislike by his quick aggressive manner brought on by his belief that his brain and sharp wits were ultimately his only weapons. When Rupert Hart-Davis fell in love with May's daughter Comfort in 1932, he asked his uncle Duff Cooper about Comfort's stepfather. Cooper answered: 'if he had the word SHIT written on his forehead in letters of fire it wouldn't be more apparent than it is now. He's the most unpopular man in the House. Don't trust him: he'll let you down in the end.' It was a formidable indictment.[36]

His French contacts were unique among members of parliament. There must, however, be doubts about the accuracy of the picture of French opinion and capability that these and his own temperament gave him. Perhaps the most prominent politician whom he knew at this time was Pierre-Etienne Flandin. More dependable were Paul Reynaud and the nationalistic Henri de Kérillis, who berated the pacifists at the time of the Rhineland invasion. Then there was the military hierarchy: Gamelin, a pessimistic bureaucrat; Weygand, the dour former assistant to Foch; and, behind them, Marshal Pétain, still the hero of his people. Spears's view of these men and their country was distorted by his own emotion and recollected glory. He thought still of the troops entering Strasbourg, of the heroes of the Marne, Notre Dame de Lorette and the Chemin des Dames: of the extraordinary, almost miraculous changes that had led to an eventual victory.

He had wanted a continuation of the wartime alliance. In the House of Commons in 1933 he attacked Lloyd George, 'the only survivor of the powerful triumvirate' of Versailles, for 'the clever clause' inserted that the guarantee to France should operate only if it were ratified by the United States. The failure of this ratification led to the failure of the treaty and the rise of a warlike Germany. To disarm and not to engage in a commitment to stand by any nation if she was attacked seemed to be folly; the covenant of the League of Nations provided the means to fight aggression. If Germany had known that the British would come into a war against her in 1914 'she would not have taken it on'. The lesson should be applied in 1933. 'If we act as we did in 1914, the events of 1914 will be repeated and, this time, there will be no excuse'.[37]

Spears stood by the League, that hope of the inter-war years. When the Japanese marched into Manchuria in 1932, he called for united action and indulged in one of his strange bouts of public sentimentality. 'There are in this country a lot of small boys, growing up, little chaps whom we tend and look after, who mean everything to us because they are our sons. Let us do everything that within us lies so that at least they shall be spared from going through what we ourselves went through.'[38] He knew of the charges against him. 'I am often accused of being pro-French,' he said on 21 December 1933, but he believed that 'our democracy and the French democracy can, if they stand united, maintain peace in Europe'.[39] He understood French fears and remembered how in March 1917, when the Germans had withdrawn to the Hindenburg line, they had left 'not a single house' or 'a single fruit tree'. He abominated the Nazi persecution of the Jews and asked the Home Office to allow more immigration from Germany. 'This country has always afforded a refuge for the persecuted' and would benefit from 'the many distinguished men who at present are forced to fly from their homes'.[40]

In September 1937 he went to Germany in a delegation of 224 people, including 57 members of parliament, who were guests of the German government on a tour of the new autobahns. As chairman of the newly formed House of Commons Motoring Club, he was impressed, but still feared Hitler's territorial ambitions. In October Sir Robert

Vansittart of the Foreign Office brought the Czech Sudeten German leader Henlein to London. Spears attended a meeting of MPs in Harold Nicolson's rooms in the Temple to try to impress upon Henlein that the British and the French would go to war against Germany if Hitler attempted an annexation of the Sudetenland.

In 1938, the year of Munich, rebel Tories, Spears among them, formed a group: a successor to the December Club. Winston Churchill, although with them on most of the essentials of foreign policy, was not its leader. His intemperate opposition to more self-government for India and open support for the doomed Edward VIII had ruled him out; he was thought already to be a man of the past. Instead they looked to Anthony Eden, who had resigned as foreign secretary in February 1938. Spears thought this 'a poor commentary on the politicians of that period'.[41]

In March he was in Czechoslovakia. On 14 March, the day Hitler entered Vienna to be acclaimed by huge crowds in the Heldenplatz, Spears saw the Czech President Dr Eduard Beneš. The Germans, Spears advised, must be given no excuse to invade the Sudetenland, the predominantly German-speaking area of the country. Beneš replied that 'under no circumstances' could the German-speaking districts be given autonomy; he was prepared to offer only cultural concessions. He put his trust in the treaties the Czechs had with France and Russia. He thought that only 25 per cent of the Czech Germans were Nazis, 'and these can be dealt with'.

Beneš showed wild optimism, comparing the position of the western powers in 1938 with that of 1914. Now he thought the prospects for Germany were much worse, particularly as, unlike the Kaiser, Hitler lacked the full resources of the former Austro-Hungarian empire. 'Today France is relatively much stronger,' the Czechs barred the way to the east, and the small countries would rally if given a lead by the western powers. Beneš thought that Mussolini would be 'somewhat of a liability' to whichever side he joined.

Beneš said the only way, 'a remote one', of maintaining peace was for Britain to declare that she would support France if the latter went to war to save Czechoslovakia. If Czechoslovakia surrendered because the other powers abandoned her, Hitler would turn against France; 'but this situation cannot arise because the French will stand by us.' Spears found a 'quite dreadful' feeling of isolation in Czechoslovakia, also 'a stubborn determination' and 'a pathetic faith in France'.[42]

Since the war he had come to know the newly independent nation well, partly through business contacts. He saw much of Jan Masaryk, the Czech Minister in London from 1925 and son of the first President:

a man who oscillated between ebullience and melancholy. May and he had stayed at Lany, the President's hunting lodge in the Bohemian forests, where she thought of Turgenev. This time, on his return to London, Spears called on Chamberlain, who showed impatience, even distaste. 'These Czechs are a queer lot,' the Prime Minister observed.[43]

Beneš and Henlein, the leader of the Sudeten Germans, faced each other with unrealistic demands. Spears, equally unrealistically, wanted a united front with France against Germany and in May he wrote to *The Times* calling for a British commitment. He tried to persuade Churchill to go with him to Czechoslovakia. In July, in Paris for the state visit of the King and Queen, he spoke at a lunch of French and British businessmen and, near to tears, remembered the young French soldiers who had gone laughingly into battle in 1914. Now the Czech people, he said, were showing a similar courage.

In July Lord Runciman, sent as a mediator to Prague, failed to get an agreement. Hitler stood behind the demands of the Czech Germans. Chamberlain saw Hitler at Berchtesgaden on 15 September and proposed the separation of the Sudeten Germans from Czechoslovakia. Runciman's report recommended self-determination for them as well. Daladier, the French Prime Minister, and Bonnet, the Foreign Minister, came to London on the 18th and asked Chamberlain to guarantee the new, smaller Czechoslovakia; Chamberlain agreed and Beneš accepted the loss of territory. Chamberlain flew to Godesberg on the 22nd to find Hitler demanding immediate cession of the German-speaking areas. The Poles and the Hungarians were also claiming parts of Czechoslovakia.

That day Spears telephoned Georges Mandel in Paris, who told him that Daladier and Bonnet were returning to London with 'a definite mandate' to declare their backing for the Czechs. In Britain the atmosphere was one of imminent war. From Brussels, where they now lived, the Jewish son and daughter-in law of Spears's old First War colleague Helbronner telephoned May to say that they were sending their children to England for safety. At lunch on 26 September Spears and May quarrelled. She felt a 'curious sense of loneliness and isolation. Very different from 1914.'

Her daughter Comfort was miserable, because Rupert Hart-Davis, her husband, would be called up in the event of war. 'This is her tragedy,' May wrote. 'I feel nothing. Have lived too long. It means nothing to me personally.' There were anti-aircraft guns and men digging trenches in Hyde Park. On the 26th the Foreign Office issued a warning that Britain and Russia would stand by France if she went to war for Czechoslovakia. In Paris Bonnet, desperate for peace, repudiated this. Chamberlain sent Horace Wilson to plead once more with Hitler. Spears told May to take all their good pictures and valuables from London to Warfield. 'I don't want to as I've got to live here,' she wrote. 'But I shall.'[44]

The next day Spears was shocked by the tone of Chamberlain's radio address to the nation: 'the speech of a man who is going to make concessions'.[45] He telephoned Corbin, the French Ambassador, who could not say if Daladier and Bonnet had a mandate to fight from a united cabinet. The British fleet mobilised. Churchill asked Spears to tell Paul Reynaud that Chamberlain's speech did not reflect feeling in the country. On the 28th, in front of a recalled House of Commons, Chamberlain said he was convinced that the Sudetenland was Hitler's last territorial demand. Then John Simon handed him the message to say that Hitler had asked to meet him at Munich. Cheering broke out, but Spears felt only dismay. Jan Masaryk rang that evening, lamenting that his country was not to be represented at the talks.[46]

The household, like many at that time, was divided, Rupert Hart-Davis declaring, 'Chamberlain's a great gentleman. I'd always vote for him.' News came through of the Munich agreement. Over ten days Hitler would occupy the Sudeten territories and the Czechs were told of the terms. Hearing this on the radio Spears wept openly and declared he had never been so ashamed, so heartbroken. That evening he saw Churchill, who said it was too late to do anything; this Spears denied, saying it was never too late. To May he declared that if he could afford to, he would leave the country.[47]

Neville Chamberlain returned to a hero's reception, appearing before ecstatic crowds on the balcony of Buckingham Palace with the King and Queen. The feeling of resolution crumbled. Only Duff Cooper resigned from the government and the newspapers were full of praise for the Prime Minister. Spears had been told by the French diplomat Léger that the French ministers had capitulated because they could not depend upon British support.

His personal position was threatened. Although he had written to Lord Halifax, the Foreign Secretary, to say that his constituents in Carlisle supported a firm line, Spears knew that most Conservatives were strongly in favour of Munich. If Czechoslovakia broke up he would lose his business connections there and an income of about £2,000 a year. 'No ray of light anywhere,' May noted. 'No way of undoing what has been done. He is admirable.'[48] Tommy Bata, the Czech shoe magnate, declared that he would leave Britain. Churchill said in the House of Commons: 'we have sustained a total and unmitigated defeat.'[49] On 6 October Spears abstained in the vote of confidence that followed the debate on the Munich agreement, along with thirty or forty other supporters of the government.

Beneš resigned and Spears wrote to him of the shame he felt at the betrayal of Czechoslovakia. In Carlisle he explained his views to a packed meeting in County Hall with May and Biddy Carlisle sitting alongside him on the platform. The pro-Chamberlain President of the Carlisle Conservative Association resigned after his executive committee approved of Spears's stance. In France, Flandin declared his support for the agreement, produced a manifesto against war and sent a congratulatory telegram to Hitler. On 2 November Boothby wrote to Spears with an alternative view: 'After Munich I was given certain information by two people who knew the facts which led me to the conclusion that in the event of war we should probably have been defeated within three weeks. In these circumstances I don't think Chamberlain had any alternative but to come to terms.'[50]

Spears continued to infuriate some of his fellow Conservatives. In November he sent certain MPs a memorandum by territorial anti-aircraft officers on the deficiencies of London's air defences. Waldron Smithers thought this circulation of a confidential document, 'to say the least of it, un-English'; Patrick Donner said that such unpreparedness showed how right Chamberlain's search for peace was; Sir Patrick Hannon declared himself 'shocked to think that an officer of your rank' should publicise 'the alleged defects'.[51]

In November some Germans who had helped with his 1937 tour of autobahns came to London, but Spears refused to meet them; 'in the present circumstances I do not wish to meet any Germans socially.' He spoke in Carlisle about Hitler's persecution of the Jews: 'we feel, and it seems almost impossible to take in, that we are flung back thousands of years to the days when the Jews were in slavery and bondage in Egypt.'[52]

He was never much of a success in parliament. Perhaps it was those mispronounced *r*s or the 'un-English' tone mentioned by Smithers, not to mention his failure to act as a party man. What he could do was to help Winston Churchill, and Spears can partly be blamed for Churchill's unrealistically high opinion of the French army during these years. Others watched his influence with irritation. In September 1938 Sir Eric Phipps, the British Ambassador to France, reported angrily that Spears and Churchill were in Paris trying to stir up opposition to any agreement with Hitler over Czechoslovakia. In March Spears's worst fears came about when Czechoslovakia disintegrated and Hitler marched into Prague. The Skoda arms factories and the Witkowitz steel works came under German control.

Munich brought Spears close again to Winston Churchill. On 31 May 1939, in a speech at Carlisle, he called, like Churchill, for an alliance with Soviet Russia and in July sent him the proofs of *Prelude to Victory*, an account of the doomed spring offensive of 1917. Churchill read the book carefully, marking the pages as he went along, and judged it 'one of the finest I have read in the literature of the war', certainly a text that should be studied 'by all British and French field officers and upwards – especially upwards!'[53]

He asked Spears to arrange a trip to the Maginot line and General Gamelin, the French Commander-in-Chief, issued an invitation for August. On the 1st of that month Spears was at Churchill's house Chartwell to discuss the proofs of *Prelude*. Churchill and he lamented the poor condition of the French air force, yet remembered the magnificent review the French army had put on at Versailles in honour of the visit of the King and Queen.

In France itself, where he went with May a few days later, he found a febrile atmosphere. In Normandy, staying with Henri de Mun, he was told that England was once again using France as a shield and the 'gens du monde' expressed a far greater detestation for Léon Blum and the Front Populaire than for Hitler. France was too weak to defend herself, they argued; what foolishness to go to war for the Czechs, 'upstart successors of a great power', or for the Poles.[54]

He felt better on the Maginot line with Churchill and General Georges. This was the France that he loved: the pretty villages of Alsace, the receptions in Paris and Strasbourg, the deference accorded to him by the French army. Churchill doubted the impregnability of the Ardennes against armour in great strength. At Strasbourg the French and German sentries stood within a pistol shot of each other. Spears suggested the mining of the Rhine if war was declared, but Churchill dismissed the idea; Spears later claimed it was the genesis of the operation known as Royal Marine. He was astonished by Churchill's vitality but did not approve of his habit of ordering a whole chicken for breakfast.

Then he went alone to Chitré, near Poitiers, a medieval château owned by Yvonne de Lestrange, to find Yvonne, her son Michel (whose father was possibly Marc Allegret, the film director and friend of André Gide) and an English governess, Miss Adams. The atmosphere was calmer than it had been with his Norman friends: less bitter against Britain but regretful that the British had not stood with France against Germany during the previous decade, uncertain also of the need to go to war for Poland. Spears and Yvonne planned a trip south, to the valleys of the Dordogne and the Lot. On the morning of 22 August, she came into his bedroom, pale with anxiety, to show him the newspaper headlines about the Nazi–Soviet pact. 'This is very bad news, isn't it?' she said.[55]

They set out on their journey, reaching Châteauroux in time for dinner. Here they heard on the wireless that the British parliament had been recalled for 24 August. All night long Spears heard the sounds of men and horses in the street as the local regiment mobilised. He knew he must go back. Early the next day they returned to Chitré and he drove on alone across France, reaching Dieppe just in time for the nine o'clock boat.

On 1 September the Germans crossed the Polish frontier. The next day Spears telephoned the diplomat Roland de Margerie at the French embassy to say how essential it was that France should stand by Poland, for there were rumours of the French government's vacillation. The Foreign Minister, Georges Bonnet, a veteran of appeasement, had reputedly spoken to the Polish Ambassador about possible German retaliation if the French gave the Poles air support: 'You don't expect us to have a massacre of women and children in Paris.'[56]

On the 3rd, after Chamberlain's apparent delay in honouring the commitment to Poland, Spears saw hostility and dismay among the Conservative members of parliament. One pro-Chamberlain member was in tears, two others were sick. The socialist A. V. Alexander said: 'Well, Spears, are you still proud of being an Englishman?'[57] He went to a meeting of the Eden group in Ronald Tree's house in Queen Anne's Gate, aware that the sun shining through the windows might mark the last few hours of peace. A message came; Corbin, the French Ambassador, wished to see Brigadier-General Spears immediately.

At the embassy in Albert Gate, Hugh Dalton was with the Ambassador, so it was de Margerie who told Spears that the French had delayed sending their ultimatum to Germany because the French General Staff insisted on more time to complete mobilisation. 'The obvious answer was that they should have started mobilising earlier,' Spears thought. 'But then so should we.'[58] Corbin was reassuring; Spears should tell his colleagues that France would be at war by 5 p.m. that afternoon. He believed the Ambassador, whom he found likeable if reserved. Later Corbin, like many others, failed the moral test after the fall of France.

Returning to Tree's house, Spears found the members of parliament leaving to return to the House of Commons and gave several, including

Eden and Harold Nicolson, a lift. Then the air-raid sirens wailed and people began to run to nearby shelters. In the Chamber, at six minutes past noon, Chamberlain announced that the country was at war; 'it seemed simple and inevitable.'[59] After speeches by Arthur Greenwood for Labour, the Liberal Archie Sinclair, Churchill and, 'best of all', Lloyd George, MPs were herded into gas-proof rooms near the terrace. Spears, easily bored, went outside with others. He told them what General Ironside, the CIGS, had said to him earlier: that if you were hit by a bomb the plane would probably be seven miles away and out of hearing. Soon he was left alone in the perfect September morning to listen to the low sound of a passing barge on the Thames, apparently the only break in the silence.

10

'If the Real Thing Begins'

Mᵃʸ got a job with an ambulance unit parked in an ARP garage in Fulham, rather different from 1914 when she had embarked for France to set up her own hospital. In 1939 the atmosphere seemed much more subdued as she and Spears sat in the blackout discussing the political and diplomatic blunders of the last decade.

She stayed at her post in Fulham, in Munster Road, sometimes for eight hours at a stretch. At fifty-three, they both felt useless, also unwanted: he because of an apparent military prejudice against retired men, particularly members of parliament who might prove obstreperous. Michael was in the United States, staying with May's family during the Oxford vacation. She went to lunch at the Carlton and saw Noël Coward, an admirer of her books, full of a mysterious intelligence job in Paris. May wondered 'nastily' why he didn't 'do a little man's work with a rifle'.[1]

On 17 September, while at Warfield, they heard that Russia had invaded Poland. 'Matelot' Fletcher, now a Labour MP, came to lunch and said that Britain was beaten already; after all last time she had taken four years to defeat Germany with Russia, Japan and Italy as her allies and now they were either out of it or against Britain. He was for capitulation when the first peace offer came, but Spears was much 'more fiery'. May thought also that it must end soon with Hitler victorious, partly because the spirit of the country seemed bad, 'not a cheer anywhere nor a military band', and no demonstrations outside Buckingham Palace, where the crowds had been jubilant after Munich. Instead there were muddles over rationing and the blackout. The Information Ministry was useless.[2]

Henri de Kérillis told Spears that the morale of the French army was better than that of the people. The trouble was that the huge defensive systems on the Franco-German frontier made it impossible for either side to break through. The stalemate might be resolved if Germany invaded France through Belgium; 'that is perhaps the answer.'[3]

May wanted to go back to France, and Lady Hadfield said that her husband Sir Robert, a steel tycoon, would pay for an ambulance unit. The French seemed inclined to accept the offer, remembering May's work in the last war. Spears was 'very sweet' when she told him, 'but depressed at the idea that he is the one to stay at home'. In Fulham her gloom deepened when a Hungarian woman married to an Englishman told her in the canteen that Hitler was 'a very great man'; the odd thing was that the other 'young nitwits' in the unit agreed. There seemed to be no hatred for or even fear of the Nazis, no realisation either of German brutality towards the Poles. She was shocked by the defeatism of Lloyd George as reported in the *Daily Express*; at least the French appeared to be stalwart. Spears found French radio much more imaginative and stirring than the BBC.[4]

General Gamelin told Spears that he would give instructions to his chief of staff to help May's unit in every possible way. At Warfield, the borders were full of colour and the leaves beginning to turn. Spears bought some hens, to ensure a supply of eggs, and congratulated himself when the price went up by half a crown soon afterwards. 'All is peaceful here,' May wrote. 'No feeling of being at war. No sign or sense of tragedy.'[5] Then in the middle of October she and Lady Hadfield left for Paris.

In parliament Spears urged the bombing of German airfields and communications to relieve the pressure on Poland. He wrote to Winston Churchill, now back in the cabinet as First Lord of the Admiralty, and suggested in the House that the call-up should be accelerated to encourage the French. 'France and France alone appears to be bearing the main brunt of the fighting,' he said of the limited French activity on the eastern frontier. He warned of the resentful attitude of the French public towards the British; 'the spirit of the French Army, on the other hand, is splendid.'[6]

Hankey told him that the French must see the reality of the shared effort. 'They knew they were strong on land (defensively, at any rate), and that we were strong on the sea and would have to hold it. And that we were stronger than they in the air. They knew that we have a great potential strength but that, as in 1914–18, it would take us a long time to mobilize it.' To Spears's hopes of some sort of liaison work, Hankey offered only the bland response that contacts were being built up; 'I think at least we can say that we are miles ahead of 1914 or 1915.' There might, however, be an opening later; 'it is a pity that as yet your unrivalled experience in these matters has not been utilized.'[7]

On 28 October he led a mission to France of eight backbench members of parliament, including Hugh Dalton, Harold Nicolson and

Leo Amery. They were fêted by their hosts and seen by Paul Reynaud, then Minister of Finance, and Daladier, the Prime Minister and Minister of Defence, for whom Spears felt contempt as a man of Munich. As they left Daladier's room, where Spears had talked often with Clemenceau during the last war, a figure in a wheelchair hailed him: 'ce sacré Spears!' It was Marshal Franchet d'Esperey, the old hero of 1914.[8]

Dalton had written in September 1938 that the French army was 'still the best in Europe' and the responses of others on this visit were similarly ecstatic.[9] Harold Nicolson wrote a tremendously francophile article for the *Spectator*, praising the 'knowledge, thought, certitude, and resolution' of the French ministers he had met and 'the quality of the discipline' and 'virility of the French' on the Maginot line. 'How comes it that they are so disciplined as soldiers and so subversive as civilians?'[10]

Spears found the French soldiers poorly clad and bored with the phoney war. He saw General Georges, in command of both the British and French armies in the field, at his headquarters in the north, and General Gamelin, the Chief of Staff to the Minister of Defence, at Vincennes. Georges, apparently stern and uncompromising, he preferred to Gamelin, a competent, academic soldier who had become enmeshed in the intrigues of the politicians with whom he had to work; Spears's public praise of Gamelin was based more on hope than on real enthusiasm. In certain circles in France, as in Britain, Spears had a bad reputation. Yvonne de Lestrange said that a member of the French naval mission in London had been told not to see him by some person in authority because of his connection with Churchill and 'des affaires louches'.[11]

Henri de Kérillis, although a deputy of the right, declared that there was a much greater danger of defeatism and subversion from the extreme right than from the extreme left. Georges Mandel, now Minister for the Colonies, observed that the politicians of 1914 had been poor creatures but giants compared to the present team. The British, preferably Winston Churchill, should take over direction of the war. Mandel wanted to see Churchill alone.

On 2 November Winston Churchill came to Paris while Spears was still having meetings with the French. A dinner took place at the Ritz for Mandel, Campinchi, the Corsican Minister of Marine, and Admiral Darlan, a squat, burly, pipe-smoking figure who had a reputation as a 'political' sailor. Darlan told Spears that his great-grandfather had been a petty officer in a privateer during the revolution and at the time of Napoleon, which could only mean an hereditary conviction that Britain was the true enemy, a sentiment traditionally strong in the French navy.

Other French politicians were pessimistic. Giradoux, the Minister of Information, said that, as in 1914, only an invasion would unite France and mentioned German propaganda that the British were sheltering behind French soldiers. Dautry, the Armaments Minister, spoke of the chaotic conditions of French production brought about by the mobilisation of thousands of key men from the factories.

In London, Spears approached Lord Halifax, the Foreign Secretary, and Corbin, the French Ambassador, with the idea that France and Britain should declare that neither would sign a separate peace. Halifax agreed with this and Corbin said he would approach his superiors.

On the way back from the Maginot line during the parliamentary trip to France, Spears saw that Harold Nicolson was reading the recently published *Prelude to Victory*.

In the story of the doomed Nivelle offensive of 1917, Spears resurrected an earlier example of Anglo-French suspicion and mutual misunderstanding. As with *Liaison 1914*, vitality and narrative power drive the book forward. If there is nothing quite to compare with the extraordinary pen portraits of Lanrezac and Maud'huy, the depiction of Sir William Robertson, whom Spears makes into a hero, and the evocation of the shattered areas of France after the German withdrawal are powerful and moving. On battle he is always strong but occasionally prone to overwriting, as if anxious to exalt the martial spirit, for the book was written when its author wanted a tougher stand against Hitler's Germany. In his account of Lloyd George's devious treatment of the British generals, he sought revenge for the politician's scathing remarks in his memoirs about Sir Frederick Maurice, Nancy's father and a former superior who had been kind to Spears. He may also have recalled the former Prime Minister's attempt to thrust a terrifying degree of responsibility on to him when he had reported to the cabinet about the French mutinies.

The reviews of *Prelude to Victory* were as good as those of *Liaison 1914*. Nicolson, in the *Daily Telegraph*, compared it to Thomas Hardy's *The Dynasts* as a drama and conflict between destiny and human endurance; like Hardy, Spears had taken this to the 'higher levels of creative art'. Harold Laski in the *New Statesman* declared *Prelude* to be 'one of the most illuminating and exciting books of its kind that I have ever read', evidence that neither cabinet ministers nor generals can rise to 'the drama of war'. Hugh Walpole proclaimed himself 'obsessed' by it, and John Buchan, who eight years before had given evidence against May in the battle over custody of her children, praised 'perhaps the best book yet written on the last war', also 'the fine spirit behind that brilliant writing'.[12]

Margot Asquith was particularly pleased. 'I don't care what Winston says in his preface,' she wrote, 'you are not at all hard on Ll.G., he is a treacherous untruthful little brute.' For George Orwell, reviewing the book in *Horizon*, it was 'less controversial' than the 'outstanding' *Liaison 1914* but with 'the same vivid quality'. Again the photographs were criticised, Orwell calling them as 'bad' as those in the earlier book but with 'a certain amount of documentary interest'. This time there was nothing comparable to the shot spies in *Liaison*. Criticism came only for some purple passages, as when A. G. Macdonnell in the *Observer* suggested that the author should have confined himself more to accurate, plain reporting.[13]

Among the military, the book became required reading. Gort, the commander of the British Expeditionary Force in France, wrote to Spears from his headquarters to say that *Prelude* 'will be a most valuable reinforcement to all my private notes on the lessons of the last war which I have with me'.[14] Edmund Ironside, the Chief of the Imperial General Staff, believed that 'it is a masterpiece'; 'I feel that my work with Gamelin will be a lot easier than similar work was in 1914, but similar difficulties may arise in any adversity that comes.' He wrote with greater prescience than he knew.[15]

Sales went well: over 2,000 by the end of 1939, a further reprint of 2,000 in March 1940, and the French rights sold to Gallimard in the same month. By April Jonathan Cape had embarked on a third reprint and Spears's literary reputation soared. In May Cyril Connolly asked him to write on 'strategical' matters for *Horizon*, but by this time he had work of a different kind.

Spears still had no official job, apart from being a member of parliament. Worried about subversion, he wrote to Sir Vernon Kell of British counter-intelligence about a Sudeten German, Victor Schmidt, the Managing Director of the British Bata Shoe Company. A letter from Cuthbert Headlam, an old parliamentary colleague, struck home: 'the last war was bad enough, but, at any rate, one had a job of work: but to be without a job of any kind, as I now am, is infinitely worse.'[16]

He had a low opinion of the head of the British mission attached to General Gamelin: an amiable aristocrat called Howard-Vyse whose command of French was distinctly shaky. Others shared this, Major-General Sir Ernest Swinton writing: 'why they did not appoint you, with your knowledge of the French and your previous association with the French Army, God only knows.'[17] At least the Germans thought he had influence; their propaganda broadcasts called him a warmonger whose defence of the Czechs had been influenced by his business connection with Tommy Bata. By 1940 he was on the Gestapo blacklist of 3,000 people who would be arrested after a German conquest of Britain.

At the end of January, twelve French deputies came over as guests of the Anglo-French parliamentary committee. At first it was feared that communists might be included, thereby restricting what the group could be shown because of the Nazi–Soviet Pact, but none came. This encouragement of the Anglo-French entente was, Spears thought, the most he could do without any official position. In response to his broadcasts on French radio, emphasising Britain's commitment to her ally, he received letters from all over France: 'never have I felt I was doing something more worthwhile.'[18] In February one British correspondent wrote that she felt 'safer about the war' after hearing the eulogy of General Gamelin on the BBC.[19] With Lord Crewe and Lord Tyrrell (former ambassadors to France) he started the Friends of the French Forces Fund. By launching an appeal in *The Times* for money to pay for parcels of food and clothing to be sent to French soldiers, they hoped to show British gratitude for the large French army supposedly holding the front line against a German attack in the west. By 11 March, £2,500 had been collected, one contribution arriving in the form of a postal order made out to the Marquess of Spears. German propaganda raised the total to £2,800 but ridiculed it as representing only 25 centimes for each French soldier.[20]

In February he was back in France, on a mission for Churchill to work for the launch of Royal Marine, the scheme of mining the river Rhine. In Paris he learnt of opposition to this, notably from Daladier, who feared enemy retaliation and suggested mining Norwegian waters instead. Spears lectured on the British war effort at the Théâtre Marigny in the Champs Elysées; among the audience were Paul Reynaud and several other ministers, and a laudatory article appeared in *Paris-Soir* by the academician Louis Gillet under the heading 'Ce Cher Général Spears'. He saw both General Georges and General Gamelin. Spears asked Gamelin if the BEF came under his command or that of Georges, the commander of the north-east army group. 'Mais le Général Georges,' answered Gamelin; then added: 'And of course I give General Georges his instructions.' This put Gort and his troops under the French Prime Minister Daladier, the man of Munich from whom Gamelin took his orders. It seemed a bad omen.[21]

Georges lent him his car to visit the army in the north. At St Omer he spent the night with his old friend Fagalde, now a general commanding IV Corps. Fagalde had two poets in his mess, and an artist who painted a Croix de Guerre with Three Palms, the number to which Spears was entitled, on the English visitor's dinner-menu card: evidence, he thought, of a characteristic French elegance. Fagalde, an anglophile, said that he thought the officers of the BEF unimpressive and told how the Duke of Windsor had said to him: 'moi, j'aime les Allemands.'[22]

Back in Paris Spears dined at the Ministry of Finance with the Minister, Paul Reynaud, who said that Daladier, with whom he had clashed over Munich, would like to get him out of the government. He showed Spears a poster of a map of the world, much mocked during the German occupation, with the immense British and French empires clearly delineated. Printed on it were the words: 'Nous nous vaincrons parce que nous sommes les plus forts.' One name Spears had not heard before came up in the conversation: that of a Colonel de Gaulle, an advocate of the use of tanks as an attacking force. A meeting with Henri de Kérillis was more disquieting. De Kérillis said he had tried to persuade Daladier to lock up supporters of the extreme right as well as the communists, but the Prime Minister had hinted that the rot went too deep.

While in Lorraine Spears visited May. The Hadfield–Spears ambulance unit, with British nurses and French doctors, was installed in a convent in the zone of the French Fourth Army, whose commander, General Réquin, had known him in the last war. 'We never see our British allies in this part of the front,' Réquin said. 'My men keep asking me "Where are the English?"'[23]

Here in the front line, among the Maginot forts, Spears felt 'everything was perfect,' with 'fine troops and fine officers': at last 'a land of men and a manly spirit'. On the German bank of the Rhine was a huge hoarding, 200 feet long, with 'Ein Volk, Ein Reich, Ein Führer' written in red letters against a blue background. The French, on their side, had put up a similar construction, this time in blue letters against a red background; it read 'Liberté, Egalité, Fraternité'. He returned to London to report to Churchill.

On 12 March the Finns, after an heroic resistance, were forced by Russia to sign peace. The repercussions were felt in France and the Daladier government fell, to be replaced by one led by Paul Reynaud. Daladier stayed on as minister of defence; and Spears noted the hatred of the two politicians for each other.

Spears complained to Sir Ronald Campbell, the British Ambassador in Paris, that French friends had told him of defeatist talk among the embassy staff. Campbell asked stiffly for evidence of this, saying he believed the rumour came from some of the 'very many' French people who held similar views.[24] At least a meeting of the Supreme War Council in London on 28 March led to the declaration that neither the French nor the British would sign a separate armistice. Reynaud said he must seek the approval of the French cabinet for Royal Marine. Significantly, Daladier had not come to London.

On 4 April, while having lunch at the Ritz with the French Assistant Military Attaché and his wife, Spears was called to the telephone. He should be at the Admiralty in thirty-five minutes with a bag packed for a few days' journey.

From here Churchill took him to Paris again. At the embassy, Reynaud came to dinner but Daladier refused; Churchill would have to call on him the next morning. Spears had to eat separately with naval staff at the Ritz. 'Bitterly disappointed and annoyed,' he wrote in his diary. 'Not to be included in his dinner with Reynaud was to diminish my own value & importance. This I told Winston next morning over the telephone and asked to be sent back to London.' Churchill told him 'not to be so susceptible about not being asked to this function or that'. Spears was only partly mollified. 'I explained to him that that was not the point at all. I was thinking of my value, and that to be relegated to the rank of some sort of expert was reducing that value enormously, going back in fact to a worse position than I had in 1917.' The First Lord asked Spears to summon General Georges to Paris from Lorraine for a meeting after the appointment with Daladier. 'I have never known of a commander-in-chief being conjured up like this. Only you could have done it,' Churchill said later, trying to soothe the wounded pride.[25]

Daladier turned down Royal Marine, fearing reprisals on 'the defence-less French factories'. His antipathy towards Reynaud was clear. Afterwards at the restaurant La Peyrouse, with Georges and Spears, Churchill said of the confusion: 'Nous allons perdre l'omnibus': a translation of the phrase used by Chamberlain on the same day about Hitler. Georges spoke of his worries about the morale of the older French troops.[26]

On 8 April the allies laid mines off Narvik. That evening German convoys were reported to be crossing the North Sea. News came on the 9th of the German invasion of Denmark and Norway, and Gamelin told Reynaud it was all the fault of the British. That evening Spears had dinner with Jan Masaryk in London, who said he felt that Norway was already lost.

Spears felt impotent. Almost his only parliamentary power came from his membership of Lord Salisbury's Watching Committee, a group of peers and members of parliament who met weekly until the fall of Chamberlain. The committee's tone was that of doubt about the Prime Minister's capacity as a war leader; among its members were Lords Swinton, Lloyd and Trenchard and, from the Commons, Lord Cranborne (Salisbury's son), Leo Amery, Harold Macmillan, Harold Nicolson, Richard Law and Paul Emrys-Evans.

Spears understood the French objections to the bombing of targets within Germany and remembered how even Clemenceau had opposed this for fear of retaliation. Could the French fix a date ('say four months') after which the bombing of military objectives would begin? On 7 May he told a correspondent: 'I have been clamouring for Air Force action against military objectives in Germany for months but I am beginning to despair of the present government.'[27]

He watched the fiasco in Norway, dreading that it might threaten the position of his patron Churchill, who had been involved in some of the disastrous decisions. On the 7th, in the House of Commons, Admiral of the Fleet Sir Roger Keyes attacked the conduct of the campaign but, to Spears's delight, said the country looked to Churchill for leadership. Oliver Stanley, the Secretary of State for War, advised Lady Astor, who had praised Lloyd George's war cabinet, to read the critique of its methods in *Prelude to Victory*. The loftiness of his tone led Spears to think that 'this was the severest punishment he could devise for her on the spur of the moment.'[28]

Churchill wound up the debate the next day, and Spears thought that the First Lord, by not glossing over errors, impressed the House. Chamberlain's private secretary, Alec Douglas-Home (then Lord Dunglass), told Spears and others that if they supported the government in the vote the Prime Minister would meet them the next morning to hear their suggestions for reshaping the ministry.

At the end of the debate, Spears followed Duff Cooper into the Opposition lobby. The Conservative Chief Whip, David Margesson, an old brother officer, was the teller and called out the figures: '151,' he said for Cooper; '152,' for Spears, who saw his expression of 'implacable resentment'. The Government's majority fell from a nominal 200 to 81. There was a roar from the Labour benches: 'Resign! Resign!' Suddenly Chamberlain seemed 'a truly sad and pathetic figure'. This was the last time that Spears saw him in the House of Commons.

On 10 May the Germans invaded Belgium, Holland and Luxembourg. That evening Spears, listening to Berlin radio, heard that the King had asked Winston Churchill, 'the man whose hateful face is well known to all Germans', to form a government.[29]

*

In Lorraine, May heard of the German attack on the Low Countries, and that Churchill had become prime minister. Her unit was in a convent alongside German-speaking nuns and she felt oddly safe. Even when the wounded came in it seemed that 'our little world is complete – as if on its own planet'.[30]

They had arrived in the village of St Jean-Le-Bassel on a cold February day, having driven from Paris over roads like glass. Spears's contacts in the French War Office had been helpful, providing four French surgeons, a doctor, an X-ray specialist, an escort of fifty 'soldats de IIième Classe' and twelve military drivers for the heavy trucks. Chief of the medical team was the efficient Jean Gosset, a surgeon with a ruthless, polished charm.

Lady Hadfield stayed with them briefly before leaving for her villa in the south of France. The recruitment in London had gone well; a team of twenty-five women (ten nurses and fifteen drivers) made up the British contingent. The tone was elevated, even grand, among the drivers in particular, with names such as Dorea Stanhope, Elaine Bodley, Alexandra Forbes, Rosaleen Forbes, Kit Tatham-Walker, Barbara Graham and Pip Scott-Ellis. Elaine Bodley quickly became 'Boddles', Alexandra Forbes 'the Strawberry Queen' because of her taste for uniforms of strawberry pink. Dorea Stanhope dominated the group. 'Big physically, big mentally and big hearted', she teamed up with an equally large American woman and they called themselves 'Mr and Mrs Rubens'. May, in charge, was 'Madame la Générale'.

The local commander in Lorraine was the kindly General Réquin and he helped them settle into the convent, where the wounded began to come in. The 200 nuns went quietly about their business, one taking time off to look after May and bring her coffee in the morning. The Mother Superior was dying and some weeks after their arrival May visited her for the first time to find the nun lying in bed, her dark yellow masculine face propped up on white pillows. Around her the sisters were praying. May fetched Gosset, who could do nothing, and two days later the Mother Superior died, murmuring her gratitude. 'Why', May wondered, 'did this stranger thank me at the very end?'[31]

Visitors came: the fussy, timid Médecin Général Wörms and General de Lattre de Tassigny. De Lattre, with his heavy good looks, fanciful talk and effusive admiration for the English, fascinated her, but she found him too good to be true. To May the soldiers seemed softer, frailer than the *poilus* she remembered in the last war, pathetically grateful for the spring lilac she and the nurses put in their wards. Michael came out for a part of his Easter holiday from Oxford. 'Our surgeons are all boys,' May wrote. 'They know nothing of war, are doing good work. I wonder if the real thing begins ...' Lady Hadfield came on another visit, then went back to Vichy and the south.[32]

On 2 May, May and two girls from the unit went to Sarreguemines, a town on the front line, evacuated by civilians on 3 September. The River Saar wound through the centre and on the opposite bank were the Germans. Houses were empty, rotting bread in bins in a bakery, the remains of lunch served eight months before still on the table in an abandoned private home. At the empty china factory she chose a dinner service, taking a plate as a sample. The Commandant would have the rest packed for them, their escort said, and the owners would be paid by the government at the war's end. In the evening French soldiers fished in the river. One told May that the Germans were 'good chaps' and did not fire.[33]

The 15th was her birthday and she spoke to Spears on the telephone from Réquin's office. The news from the north depressed her. 'I am frightened,' she wrote two days later. 'I wasn't ever in the last war. I don't think it is fear for my life. Fear for France – for England – for everyone and everything I know.' She had heard of Gamelin's order to his troops to die rather than give away a foot of soil. The imagined horror of war haunted her. 'If I let down I would weep. As it is I feel just a little sick all the time.' She was appalled by the fanaticism of some German prisoners in the hospital: 'huge, magnificent specimens who made noises like brute beasts'. One refused a blood transfusion, saying he would rather die than have French blood in his veins.[34]

On the 18th she told Spears of her anxiety. 'It is a strain. I have moments when I envisage the possibilities of the Germans winning – cracking through – then I wish I were with you – think to myself how good it would be to hide behind you. But the moments are rare – pass quickly. I find I really am indifferent to what happens to me personally.'[35]

On 19 May Gosset told her that in the north every unit similar to theirs had either been wiped out or evacuated. He had heard of nurses who drowned while trying to cross a river under fire. In the chapel of the convent there was an evening service and members of the unit sang 'Nearer My God to Thee', reminding May of childhood worship in Chicago. 'I am 54,' she wrote. 'The greatest battle in history is raging to the north of us. I still worry about the length of my aprons. Make up carefully. But that last is part of my plan. To be immaculate and look as nice as possible – part vanity, part policy.' She heard that the Germans had reached Landreçy. How would she get her girls out? Which port should they make for? Probably Cherbourg, for the Germans surely would not reach there.[36]

On 20 May Réquin told her that Spears had been made a major-general and on the 23rd she heard on the wireless that he had spoken on French radio, recalling 1914. So Churchill must have used him at last; 'would have been so glad to have heard B's voice.' A nurse, Miss Pearce, learnt that her fiancé, an airman, had been drowned off the Dutch coast and asked if she could nurse the German prisoners that night because she thought if her fiancé had been captured 'some nice German girl would have been kind to him'. May noted, 'I have forbidden it,' believing she should be hard: 'one sign from me and half the female staff would get sentimental about these brutes.'[37] She wrote to Spears, 'darling little B, so you've got the job you wanted.' Although at that stage she did not know precisely what he was doing, she felt it might be like 1917 with the two of them elated by the sense of fighting for a good cause, of being at the centre.[38]

On 28 May she heard of the Belgian surrender. Réquin had been ordered to leave in the morning. How could the French and the British have allowed the Germans to become so strong? he asked her. Weygand, the new French Commander, had ordered his troops to die in their positions. May decided to try to stick with Réquin, whom she trusted. Spears came on the telephone from Paris. He could not tell her what he was doing but gave news of the German bombing of a hospital in Ostend. She must stay where she was and not follow Réquin. They quarrelled and she felt better. Here was B 'so natural and cantankerous', which 'restored my sanity'. That evening she and some of the unit drank brandy together; 'one must be stupefied at night so as to sleep.'[39]

The mixture of outward calm and inner dread disturbed her. 'How could I know that France was crumbling under our feet? Our part of France was utterly peaceful. Never had she been more beautiful.' Her unit yielded strange titbits of information, some of which she passed on to Spears. An American woman had once been married to Lord Lymington, a right-wing British member of parliament and later the Earl of Portsmouth; upset, she showed May a letter from her son in which the boy described Winston Churchill as 'That bloody little man' and wrote: 'I hope we lose this battle then we can get the Government out.' To May it looked like the influence of the father, who had links with Mosley. 'I don't see why he hasn't been locked up before this,' she said.[40]

Spears telephoned regularly, urging her to come to Paris. He was astounded to hear that she had had time to do some painting. Gosset said she should not go in case the road was cut and it became impossible for her to get back. On 6 June, with the German armour closing on Rouen, she went, driven by Barbara Graham in a big Buick, thinking that if the unit was ordered to move in her absence she could join it again the next day.

At half-past six in the evening she arrived at the Ritz, where Spears was staying, to be told that he was at the British embassy. The hotel's telephones had been cut off so she went round there. A secretary said he was with the Ambassador and went to fetch him. When he entered, one look at his exhausted face dispelled her illusions; 'I had been thinking of him as he was in 1918. Realised suddenly that he was 22 years older.'[41]

Barbara Graham crashed the Buick on the Champs Elysées and Spears arranged with General Colson's office for May to be driven back to her unit in the east. They covered the 250 miles in five hours: 'wonderful driving, blazing heat'. After finding the unit with difficulty, May embarked upon a desperate journey south in the company of thirty French orderlies, the doctors and surgeons and the twenty-five girls who had been recruited in London. The flight took them away from the approaching Germans, through towns and villages either crammed with refugees or eerily silent.

Incidents interrupted the onward rush: the loss of her washing in Rosnay, when the only solution was for the town crier to march through the streets shouting, 'Qui a la linge de Madame la Générale?', the abandonment of the weighty Sarreguemines dinner service at Amance, a meeting at the Duc de Clermont-Tonnerre's renaissance château of Ançy-le-Franc (where May and Spears had stayed before the war) with the exhausted General Huntziger who would observe after signing the armistice at Compiègne: 'If Britain is not brought to her knees in three months, we are the greatest criminals in history.' They hoped to hear of a stand by the French, perhaps on the Loire; but no news came.[42]

Twice they met up with Réquin, who vaguely agreed with May's idea that they might make for Voutenay in the east. Once she managed to speak on the telephone to the British consulate in Lyon, which promised to try to get a message to Spears. She became separated from her unit and when she found it again heard that Maureen Schreiber, her second-in-command, was planning to take them all off without her, with little petrol and no maps, on a dash for the coast. May faced down the potential rebellion.

They heard about the armistice. Almost immediately the attitude of the French authorities changed to one of cold dislike, as the British were no longer their allies. May had to turn to Gosset, and this strange, icily efficient man saw them through, for now her command counted for nothing. Towards the end of the journey, when the French members of the party separated from the British, who were to go to Bordeaux and a hoped-for rescue by sea, he said savagely: 'It will do France good to live under the German yoke.'[43]

Some of the British girls wanted to stay, having embarked upon romances with the French. The Jewish Dr Bernard was apprehensive about his fate. A Sergeant Altenbach asked for a souvenir and May gave him a blue enamelled cigarette case that had been a present from Michael. Altenbach promised that he would destroy the trucks and equipment given by Lady Hadfield before the Germans could capture them; later May heard that he had not, although it was hard to tell where they had ended up. In any case after the war only one of the French party, who later joined General Leclerc's Free French division, kept in touch. Two joined the resistance, others (like Gosset) could not be traced, none joined de Gaulle until after the liberation of Paris, when his movement grew at an astonishing pace, and several (Bernard included) refused to have anything to do with the wife of the then infamous General Spears.

There was a rumour that Bordeaux had been closed but they got in and were greeted at the British consulate by Lord Malise Graham, the Military Attaché, and grates full of burning papers. The Ambassador, also still there, could not see them. Spears, May was told, had left two days before by air. The heat was terrific and Graham and his secretary gave the unit their rooms for the night. They were told to drive to Arcachon, where, on 20 June, they met the writer Ian Fleming, then a naval lieutenant: 'the complete man of the world and perfect host but not very forthcoming'. Fleming sent them to a restaurant for supper where, almost unbelievably, a feast of cold food appeared; before they could eat it a summons came for them to go the harbour for immediate embarkation. On the jetty, after an hour's wait, they were told they would be put up for the night in an empty hospital near by.[44]

The next morning the girls bathed from the beach, where French people lay in the sun. A woman approached May and asked if she would take her lover to England. Shocked by the idleness of the sun worshippers, May attended to five wounded British soldiers whom she found in a truck at the gates of Fleming's villa. Not until half-past three the morning after did they embark in two sardine boats on a rough sea, with the fishermen saying they were mad to go in such conditions; many of the girls were sick. They went on board the cruiser *Galatea*, were taken down to St Jean de Luz and transferred to the transport ship *Etric* because the Admiral in command said that he could not risk an engagement with a fighting ship while carrying twenty-five women.

The *Etric*, the last British transport ship to leave France, had 3,000 people on board. All the first-class cabins were taken by rich old women and their maids from villas in the south of France, and it seemed as if the only place to sleep was on deck underneath the hammocks of a battalion of Poles. Eventually one officer gave May his cabin at night and the twenty-five girls were put in the third-class dining room. No first-class passenger would allow any of the unit to use his or her cabin for even a part of the day, although May had met several in London before the war. Among them was Mrs Keppel, once the mistress of King Edward VII, who said she hoped notice would be taken of the magnificent way she had coped with the discomfort.

On 26 June they docked at Plymouth. At the foot of the gangway was a Military Police sergeant. 'Mrs Spears?' he asked. 'But you are the lost unit we've been worrying about.' May answered: 'Are we? Well you needn't worry any more. I've lost none of the girls.'[45]

In France Reynaud had reshuffled his government, riven by disputes, after the German attack on the Low Countries; Gamelin and Daladier, the Commander-in-Chief and the Minister of Defence, remained. The Germans occupied Liège, raced through Holland and advanced across the reputedly impenetrable Ardennes. They crossed the Meuse and on 15 May the French evacuated Sedan. The next day the great Belgian fort of Eben-Emael surrendered. Spears pored gloomily over the maps of *Liaison 1914*.

That same day Léon Blum, who had been addressing the Labour party conference at Bournemouth, had dinner with him at the Ritz in London. Blum, like Hugh Dalton, was a man of the left whom Spears admired: 'a great orator, very courageous and with a truly international outlook that many French politicians lacked'. He spoke with foreboding of the attack through the Ardennes, where the French, believing such an assault to be impossible, had placed their worst troops.[46]

News came in that they were burning secret papers at the Quai d'Orsay. A strike of Belgian railway workers impeded the movement of troops. Again, as in 1914, there was fighting at Guise, and Brussels and Antwerp were lost. Reynaud changed his cabinet, taking over the Defence portfolio himself, moving Daladier to Foreign Affairs and Mandel to the Ministry of the Interior, bringing in Pétain, symbol of resistance, as vice-president of the Council. Weygand, aged seventy-three, took over from Gamelin, Spears remembering him from the First War as a staff officer who had seen little fighting, Foch's man.

Apparently an Egyptian doctor had examined Weygand recently in Cairo and said the General was a rare case of a body that had remained young while the mind had aged according to its years.

On 20 May Spears broadcast again to France, speaking of how courage had saved the allies in 1914. News came of the fall of Laon, then Arras and Amiens. On the 21st, in the lobby of the House of Commons, he met Brendan Bracken, who said he knew Churchill wanted to use him. The next day, Bracken was more definite. 'Winston,' he said as he shot past, 'expects you at 10.30 tonight at the Admiralty.'[47]

Spears arrived at the appointed hour and waited in the dark in the long gallery, surrounded by the famous dolphin furniture. His presence was not reported and his house, 10 Downing Street and Scotland Yard were telephoned. Had he been kidnapped? At last someone walked in and saw him.

Winston Churchill sat in his office, apparently relaxed. He offered Spears a cigar, seemed distant for a moment, then smiled before becoming serious again. 'I have decided to send you as my personal representative to Paul Reynaud,' he said. 'You will have the rank of major-general.' Spears should see 'Pug' Ismay, Churchill's chief military staff officer, the next day. Then the Prime Minister called to someone to offer Spears a drink, made a movement at which Spears also stood, and Ismay, who knew the howls of protest that this unprecedented appointment had aroused in Whitehall, entered with a telegram. Spears left to walk out into an unlit London.[48]

Ismay briefed him the next day. It was a story of French losses: two armies out of the three between Sedan and Antwerp had disappeared, the Germans had bridgeheads south of the Somme. Georges was still at his post but the French generals were being reshuffled by Weygand in a move reminiscent of Joffre's purge before the Marne.

Then there was the British Expeditionary Force under Lord Gort, whom Spears remembered as 'fat boy', a young Grenadier Guards officer who had won the Victoria Cross in the First War. A theme emerged that would be constantly repeated in the days ahead, that of the French plea for more air support from the RAF. 'But what on earth has happened to the French?' Spears asked. Ismay's answer was reluctantly scathing: bad generalship, indifferent troops, the effect of surprise, a weak air force, inability to cope with a heavy attack by armour. The French told the British nothing. Spears would report through the Paris embassy, where the Ambassador, Sir Ronald Campbell, had been informed of his appointment. He would have to fix his own position with Campbell.

At least the genial, tough Ismay would be an ally. 'There are not many men I can say I love,' Spears wrote of him later, but this former Indian Army cavalry officer was one of them. He had qualities Spears always admired: ruthlessness when necessary, also 'a bon viveur in excelsis, a collector of good cigars, a connoisseur of wine, and a real man if ever there was one'.[49]

On the afternoon of 24 May he was back at the Admiralty to be questioned by Churchill about the terrain of northern France and the French high command.

What about General Billotte? Churchill asked. Once a man of vitality, Spears answered, but this had evaporated in over-heated offices; at their last meeting he had looked soft, worried, a big flat-footed man. 'Well, he is dead,' said Churchill. 'What of Blanchard?' Spears admitted he did not know him but had heard of a shy, charming, professorial type, more suited to the lecture hall than the battlefield. 'What is the condition of the roads in the Somme basin?' Perfect for the invader, Spears replied: 'for motorised traffic on a big scale'. Churchill trusted Weygand's plan of attacks in the north and south of the Somme and was beginning to accept the French complaints that Gort was not doing enough. The Prime Minister seized another point; there was simply no command, no co-ordination between Belgians, French and British. This would be one of the principal matters for Spears in Paris, where he must go the next day.[50]

Whitehall proved to be incapable of providing him with maps or briefing papers. His uniform, dating from the First War, had to be rapidly adapted to his new rank. That evening he again saw Ismay, who said Paul Reynaud had telegraphed Churchill about Weygand's shock at the reported evacuation of Arras by Gort, against French wishes, and the apparent British decision to move out of Le Havre. Ismay told Spears he was in for a tough time. Unless Weygand could break through the German ring from the south, the BEF would have to leave from Dunkirk.

To Churchill, whom he saw again in the evening, Spears mentioned his critical review of the memoirs of Foch, Weygand's old master, and Weygand's fury at it; also his clashes with Sir Henry Wilson, whom Foch had liked and admired. Churchill said this did not matter. 'They always said you were a bit of a tiger in the last war,' he added indulgently. Reynaud and Weygand had welcomed the news of Spears's appointment. Then Spears returned to his office to find a message that he should see Ismay again, who told him that Blanchard had been replaced by his old friend Fagalde. In France the encircled armies were to try to break out to the south. Churchill had told Reynaud that the

British wanted to stick to the principle of a single command under Weygand.[51]

At 10 p.m. he saw Churchill for the last time. The Prime Minister proclaimed his belief in four Frenchmen: Reynaud, Mandel, Pétain (now in the government) and Weygand, who seemed to be 'fighting hard'. 'I shall expect you to report from midday tomorrow onwards,' he said. 'In the present circumstances you can hardly report too much or too often.'[52] On the same day Spears published an article, presumably written before his appointment, in which he praised Weygand and the French army, saying it was better than it had been in 1914.

At 2 a.m. on 25 May, the day of his departure, he was woken by a banging at his front door. Turning on the light, he heard shouts from passers-by of 'Put out that light' and 'Send for the police'. It was a messenger with a secret exchange of telegrams between Reynaud and Churchill. The French were complaining of a further retreat by Gort towards the Channel ports, in a repetition of 1918. Churchill had replied that Gort must protect his line to Dunkirk, if only to ensure the arrival of supplies. The Germans were at Abbeville, Boulogne and St Omer and threatening Calais and Dunkirk. 'General Spears', Churchill told his French counterpart, 'will be with you tomorrow.'[53]

11

'A Crack in the Crystal Cup'

On the morning of 25 May Spears was flown across the Channel on a brilliant day; from the airport at Villacoublay a car took him to the British embassy in Paris. The Ambassador, Sir Ronald Campbell, was out, so he told the driver to go to Paul Reynaud's office in the Ministry of War; on the way there they saw Campbell walking with the Military Attaché, Lord Malise Graham. The Ambassador warned that Reynaud's theme of the moment was that of British generals always making for harbours. Spears found the diplomat 'wizened up', apparently not understanding military messages from Churchill and 'brow-beaten by Paul Reynaud', but 'genuinely glad' at his arrival.[1]

He drove near the rue Monsieur, 'my first married home, the best beloved house I have had or shall ever know', then to the War Ministry in the rue St Dominique.[2] Here Paul Reynaud showed Spears the letter Winston Churchill had written about the newly created post of liaison officer between the two Ministers of Defence who were also the Prime Ministers of their respective countries. The Frenchman then remarked on how British generals always made for harbours before taking him to meet the War Committee. The first to rise in greeting was Pétain, pale and melancholy; then Weygand, oriental of aspect and unexpectedly cordial; Darlan the sailor; the urbane Baudouin, a protégé of Reynaud's mistress, the defeatist Madame de Portes.

Spears tried to prevent blame being pinned on the British. Weygand expressed his confidence in his own generals, then Reynaud took a telephone call from someone asking that his son-in-law should be transferred to a quiet part of the front. Commandant Fauvelle, a staff officer from the French army group in the north, came in, 'the very embodiment of catastrophe,' and declared that air bombardment, the constricting flow of refugees, lack of ammunition and disastrous losses of equipment must lead to an early capitulation.[3] Weygand blamed the politicians; 'we have gone to war with an 1918 army against a German Army of 1939.' Spears tried to sound optimistic to Churchill later, at least with regard to his own usefulness. 'Incidentally I made up my old feud with General Weygand quite easily,' Spears told the British Prime Minister later, 'and he has been very helpful and welcoming to me.' In his diary he wrote: 'I should say Weygand all right, unrattled but hardly up to frightful situation. He is efficient, astonishingly alive and precise, all there, but the spirit is missing. He is very wizened and dried up.'[4] Pétain, Darlan and Baudouin had spoken no more than a few sentences and, when all stood as Spears departed, the old Marshal stayed in his seat, staring at the carpet.

At lunch at the embassy, the Ambassador's second-in-command, Oliver Harvey, the Minister, was horrified by Spears's depressing report of the meeting. Gort, Spears told Harvey, should make for the coast because this was his only chance. Campbell, although now obviously wary of the interloper, provided a large room giving on to the courtyard of the embassy, near the Ambassador's office. It seemed a gesture of trust. Spears would sleep at the Ritz, where messages were already piling up, but there were no telephones at the hotel, for every private line in the city had been cut off because of the crisis. He contacted Georges Mandel, the Minister of the Interior and Clemenceau's former aide. Within an hour a telephone was installed.

He went to see Mandel, who spoke frankly of the poor morale of the army, the lack of reserves, then of the men at the top: Georges, who had never got over being wounded when the King of Yugoslavia had been assassinated in Marseilles in 1934, the vain Pétain, and Weygand, who thought himself the incarnation of Foch. If Paris had to be abandoned, the government should make for Bordeaux as in 1914; it would be easy to embark from there to North Africa. But in August 1914 the people had hurled themselves at the Germans, whereas now the factionalism of the last decade was reflected in the army. France had felt abandoned by her allies. Then Mandel raised the question of Gort's apparent break with the French armies in the north.

Spears telephoned May in Lorraine and she spoke of how few wounded they had to look after and the joys of picnics in the beautiful spring weather; really, the pink villages of the Vosges were lovely. He could not believe her ignorance and lost his temper. Maps told him of the crisis, the names a horrible replica of twenty-five years ago: the Lorette ridge, Béthune, Arras, the marshes of the Somme.

On the morning of the next day, Sunday, 26 May, Spears heard that Reynaud had flown to London. His old fear of being excluded flared up but not even Campinchi, the French Minister of Marine, whom he called on, knew why the Prime Minister had suddenly left. Suddenly Spears thought Reynaud might have gone to propose an armistice. But Campinchi reassured him: 'England can be sure we shall honour our signature.'[5] When Spears telephoned Ismay from the embassy, Reynaud was within five minutes of leaving London. Then Ismay said, 'decision taken not to link hands', and Spears knew that the attempt of the northern armies to break out to the south had been abandoned. It was to be an evacuation at Dunkirk.[6]

What of Pétain, symbol of resistance? Spears went to the Marshal's office at the back of the Invalides to find the atmosphere 'as dead, as somnolent, as the chambers of a provincial lawyer's office on a Sunday afternoon'. Pétain was welcoming and spoke of his memories of the Lorette ridge, now in the news again. Spears must come and see him whenever he liked. Unlike Weygand he seemed to accept catastrophe as if detached from the present, even from the world. But why had the RAF committed only some thirty-five fighters to the battle in France while keeping 600 in England? he asked. To Spears's denial, the Marshal said that this was what he had been told by Vuillemin, the French air force commander.[7]

At the embassy, Major Archdale, the British liaison officer with General Blanchard and the French northern command, spoke of bad liaison, indecision, German mastery of the air, French lack of transport, a shortage of ammunition and supplies, the terrifying Stuka dive bombers. The morale of the British was better, partly because they had had an easier time of it than the French.

Spears thought Archdale could answer French criticism of Gort and took him to see Pétain. The Englishman declared Blanchard to be tired, incapable of inspiring his troops, who had fought well against overwhelming odds; then Pétain asked a question that stunned Spears, who was used to French assumptions of omniscience. Would General Gort take command of all the northern armies? Archdale reacted strongly. The BEF was more than enough for Gort without involving him in chaos elsewhere.[8] At the end of the meeting Pétain said that Weygand feared a revolutionary movement in Paris and that sixteen French generals had been relieved of their commands by 25 May. Spears remembered that half the divisional leaders of the French army had been sacked before the Germans were checked in 1914. The Marshal responded that this time the news had been made public, which was bad for morale.

Spears discovered that there was another defeatist in Paul Reynaud's entourage, apart from the anglophobic Madame de Portes: his military adviser Colonel de Villelume, 'fat and sly, pouring defeatism into his ears'. He told Churchill: 'if Colonel de Villelume is half as dishonest as he looks, he has Fagin beaten by furlongs.' On Weygand he was realistic. 'I have seen him twice in three days. He is not the heaven-sent saviour of our dreams but a good, conscientious and honest workman.'[9]

Later that day he saw Reynaud, who seemed worried about a possible Italian attack on France. Spears said the Italians, if they came in, would be easily beaten. 'It would be wonderful for morale.' He held Reynaud's shoulders; 'I shook the little man,' he told Churchill afterwards, 'in a quite friendly way of course. Somehow it all worked. He gained in confidence visibly as I spoke.'[10] There were further sweet words for the British Prime Minister. 'The one real factor that worked with Reynaud was your opinion of him. He can't bear to think you might believe he lacked resolution.'[11]

The atmosphere in Paris was strange: not excited as in 1914 but bewildered, even apathetic, although the rich like Charles Mendl were already leaving for the south. That evening, at 7.30, Spears was summoned, with the Ambassador, to Reynaud's office at the Ministry of War, where they also found Pétain and Weygand.

The King of the Belgians had surrendered. 'There never has been such a betrayal in history,' Reynaud said furiously. 'To think that this is the man to whose succour we flew is unbelievable.' Pétain said not a word; and Spears thought of Admiral Keyes, who was King Leopold's British liaison officer: 'Had I been Keyes, I would have shot him.'[12] As he and Campbell stood up to leave, Weygand said to Pétain that if Gort had counter-attacked more vigorously the Belgians might have resisted longer and Spears broke in to deny this. But the next morning, 28 May, Reynaud's speech on the radio, in which he castigated the King of the Belgians, was, he thought, 'the old, authentic voice of France'.[13]

Disappointment followed when the French Prime Minister told Campbell and Spears that he might appeal directly to President Roosevelt for the United States to join the war. What did Campbell think? Sir Ronald said he would have to refer such an important matter to the British government, but Spears declared that the obviously useless appeal would affect British morale by its apparent acceptance of defeat. Angry, Reynaud said the French would think it right. How did Spears know that the Americans would not declare war? Reynaud spoke again of concessions to Italy involving French North Africa, and perhaps Suez and Gibraltar, to keep Mussolini out of the war. To this, Campbell gave a very discouraging answer with Spears's silent agreement.

The evening of 28 May he had another meeting with Paul Reynaud. The French, to deflect attention from their own disaster, had heaped public scorn on the wretched King of the Belgians and Reynaud was angry about the generous statements made by Churchill and Duff

Cooper with regard to the Belgian surrender. The French Prime Minister thought that the reports of the Germans blowing up Somme bridges, perhaps to take up defensive positions, meant a respite for Paris. Spears wondered if it might be a prelude to an invasion of England. At this the Frenchman could not conceal 'a smile of satisfaction'.[14]

The next day, 29 May, Reynaud asked for figures for the British war production. He was worried that Britain was holding back her forces, particularly in the air, and seemed 'very worked up'. Spears said he was sure General Vuillemin had the wrong figures. The French Prime Minister declared aggressively that he hoped French troops would be given the same chance of evacuation at Dunkirk as the British. Spears answered that the commanders on the spot would see to this; if not, Churchill would intervene.[15]

'Spears is being very useful after all,' Oliver Harvey wrote in his diary. 'He bucks up the French and is a useful contact to have with the P.M. He feels, as we all do, that French morale is the important thing now.'[16] To Ismay, Spears said that the excuses made for the King of the Belgians by Roger Keyes in particular were 'completely contrary to French policy and a very great deal depends upon making him out to be the villain he certainly appears to be'. The diplomat de Margerie thought that the Baroness von Thyssen, an intimate of the King's, had been planted on him by the Nazis. 'This may or may not be true,' Spears told Ismay, 'but even de Margerie, just because he is French, will always tend to think out an explanation of that kind.'[17]

He had dinner that night in a small restaurant in the avenue de la Grande Armée with Yvonne de Lestrange and her cousin, the writer and pilot Antoine de Saint-Exupéry, then serving in the French air force, whose account of his aerial view of the German columns pushing through the countryside recalled the relentless enemy of 1914. The youngish man, animated, a swarthy 'Creole' face above a bulky body, his slightly protruding eyes wide apart, transfixed the Englishman with his extraordinarily imaginative if rather wild intelligence. It was almost possible to forget that the Germans were at Amiens, less than a hundred miles away.

Could quick-firing anti-tank guns be mounted on aircraft, Saint-Exupéry suggested, or a long steel cable be dragged from the air over advancing troops? The blackout was a waste of time, he declared: much better would be the use of powerful headlights to throw up a sheet of light over the whole country and thus blind the bombers. Of his own long-range reconnaissance group he was scathing; there were only fifty teams for the whole of France and half had already been lost. In any case the French infantry fired at them quite as frequently as the Germans. Spears found little to console him apart from the company of his friends, but he reported Saint-Exupéry's ideas to Ismay.[18]

At 4.00 a.m. the next morning, 30 May, he was called to the embassy to take an urgent telegram from Churchill to Reynaud. At his flat in the place du Palais Bourbon, an irritated Prime Minister opened the door himself, wearing a kimono, for he had been doing his physical exercises. Churchill described the Dunkirk evacuation which had begun on the 27th and said that French forces should share fully in this. It was hoped to build up a new BEF at St Nazaire after a reorganisation of forces to meet the threatened invasion. Regular troops were arriving from the empire as reinforcements.

Reynaud said that French opinion would be mortified if French forces were not also evacuated and repeated his anger at Churchill's attitude towards the King of the Belgians. Spears shot back that it was only Churchill's refusal to utter blame in public that had stopped British opinion from turning against the French and their commanders. As for the King of the Belgians, Reynaud should remember that France was a republic and Britain a monarchy, which might mean a difference of approach to the matter.

Reynaud seemed to calm down. He had, he said, passed on a notably pessimistic report by Weygand to Sir Ronald Campbell. He himself was thinking of resistance in Brittany. Spears felt annoyed that the diplomats had not informed him of Weygand's views but was relieved by Reynaud's mention of Brittany and its suggestion of the will to fight on. Worse news was the shortage of weapons and uniforms for the latest conscripts and the Prime Minister's blustering demand that the British should put men evacuated from Dunkirk straight into boats to be returned to fight in France.

At a morning meeting of the French War Committee, Weygand gave a very pessimistic report. In the afternoon the British Air Attaché, Air Commodore Douglas Colyer, told Spears of the poor tactics and morale of the French air force, and Colonel Redman, a liaison officer, brought reports from the countryside of heaps of abandoned French weapons ignored by a confident enemy, of French officers on parole making no effort to escape from their German captors, of unburied bodies of refugees shot from the air. There were rumours of German fifth-column activity which he passed on to Ismay and Churchill. France seemed like 'the body of a loved creature dissolving in death'.[19]

The next morning, 31 May, the Military Attaché told him that Churchill would arrive by air at Villacoublay at 10 a.m. The signal announcing this had come the night before and Spears thought again that the diplomats were trying to exclude him. The Prime Minister was delayed by the need to avoid German fighters north of Paris but seemed stimulated by the danger. With him were Attlee, whom Spears liked, Dill, the CIGS and Ismay. Over lunch at the embassy Churchill questioned Spears, who saw he had no illusions about the worth of the French command in the north.

The Supreme War Council met at 2 p.m. in the French Ministry of War. Spears joined the British team, with the Ambassador and an interpreter, Captain Berkeley. For the French, Reynaud came with Pétain and Darlan; Baudouin took notes. Weygand wore uniform, with spurs on his huge riding boots. De Margerie was the French interpreter. Churchill tried to inspire with his language and his spirit. The French and British, he declared, should leave Dunkirk 'bras dessus, bras dessous' on equal terms. Spears grew worried that in the emotion of the moment he might commit the British too much. The French called for more RAF help and, inevitably, Reynaud wanted vigorous public condemnation of the King of the Belgians.

Pétain seemed morose. At the end of the meeting, Churchill moved over to him, taking Spears, and a group formed. A French voice spoke smoothly of military reverses perhaps leading to a change of policy: a hint at a separate surrender. Spears spoke quickly addressing Pétain. 'I suppose you understand, M. le Maréchal, that that would mean blockade?' Another voice said: 'That would be inevitable.' Spears went on, again to Pétain: 'That would mean not only blockade but bombardment of all French ports in German hands.' Churchill added that Britain would fight on, whatever happened.[20]

Mandel, Reynaud and Dautry came to dinner at the embassy and the talk was desultory. After the French had left, Churchill said to Attlee: 'What a pity Louis has not been here a long time.' The diplomats were also aware of his worth, Harvey noting: 'Spears is most useful as A.D.C. and nurse to P.M. on these occasions. He packs him off to rest before dinner.' Spears realised now that the French were beaten and that they knew it. He felt that Churchill knew it too.[21]

At 6 a.m. the next morning, 1 June, he went out to Villacoublay to see Churchill off, passing hundreds of labourers apparently engaged in widening the road on the far side of the Bois de Boulogne. He recalled the complaints that lack of workers south of the Somme hampered the laying of minefields, yet here were these men engaged in an activity of little use to the war effort.

Churchill commented dismissively on the small enemy air raids of the previous night. At the airfield he spoke to the pilots of his fighter escort and as each one's face smiled up at the Prime Minister Spears thought of the angels of his childhood: serene, protective creatures from the prints in his nursery, more beautiful in his memory than any study by Michelangelo, Giotto or Botticelli. It was a glimpse of lost certainty, a fugitive vision.

He saw Reynaud several times that day. The French Admiral Abrial was sending reports of British perfidy from Dunkirk and Reynaud had news of nine German panzer units withdrawn from fighting to be overhauled. Could the panzers be bombed by the British? Spears passed on the messages to Ismay, who, in an effort to thwart French surveillance, asked: 'Can you speak Urdu?' Spears said no, to which the answer came: 'A pity. Redman can.'[22]

Churchill telephoned to say that the end was near at Dunkirk. Reynaud spoke angrily of the French being left to defend the perimeter while the British rushed for the ships, and Spears complained about Weygand's determination to blame the British for the French defeat. But at the end of the talk they shook hands, Spears having promised to remind Churchill of the importance of getting every Frenchman out of Dunkirk. At the embassy a further message arrived from Churchill to say that the embarkation might go on through the night and into the next day. Some 225,000 had left already, but there were few French troops at the bridgehead.

The next day, 2 June, when Spears saw Darlan at the Ministry of War, the Admiral had embarkation figures of 194,000 British and 22,000 French. The British had concentrated on getting away, whereas by forming a rearguard, and defending the perimeter, the French had put themselves further from the beaches. At eleven o'clock that morning the War Committee was dominated by Dunkirk and the quarrel about the numbers taken off rumbled on, as did the call for British troops to be returned immediately to France. Spears was asked to pass on to Churchill the request for more troops and for British fighters to operate from French airfields.

That evening he saw Pétain. The Marshal was tired, having been with Reynaud to the front beyond Compiègne, once his headquarters in the last war. He spoke peevishly of the British, who he said gave Weygand a convenient scapegoat. Churchill was a fine speech-maker but did not fulfil his promises. Spears argued that the difficulties in the north came from incompetent French command; he would not accept Weygand's sneers, particularly those at Churchill, 'the best friend the French ever had'. Pétain said perhaps he should not have raised it but Spears should know 'how things appear to us'. Spears recalled an earlier joint British–French victory at Dunkirk, the battle of the Dunes, and Pétain astonished him with a feat of memory. Yes, he said, 14

June 1658, when Turenne beat Condé and Don Juan of Austria. But
why had the puritan Cromwell sent help to Louis XIV, persecutor of
the French protestants? The English of course were always skilful
politicians. The sarcastic tone showed the old French charge that
British policies were formed solely by self-interest. Spears thought the
old man had enjoyed teasing him.[23]

That evening the Ambassador told Spears that Italy would enter the
war in a matter of days, perhaps hours, and that Eden had broadcast
to say that four-fifths of the BEF had been taken off from Dunkirk. Of
the 25,000 French troops defending the perimeter, neither Campbell
nor Spears said anything.

The next morning, Churchill sent him a telegram for Reynaud and
Weygand to say that ships would be there that night to pick up more
Frenchmen. At the same time, at the French War Committee, this time
without Spears, Weygand declared that Churchill had disgracefully
abandoned France by the British rush to harbours. When Reynaud
said he would tell this to General Spears, Weygand protested, saying
he was on the coldest terms with the Englishman, who in the last war
had been a double agent working for Lloyd George.

Spears had lunch with Count Horodyski, 'whom I don't trust a yard',
the Pole who had reputedly once worked for British intelligence,[24] and
in the Count's flat on the top of a high building near the Champs
Elysées, the sharp guests 'du monde' all disappeared when an air raid
began. That afternoon Reynaud gave him the answer to Churchill's
telegram, expressing thanks for the ships ordered to Dunkirk and
adding, in English, that Paris had just been bombed by 300 planes and
'similar treatment inflicted on the Berlin region would be greatly
appreciated.'[25] Later Mandel asked to see Spears and spoke of his
contempt for the Belgian King, also of treachery and defeatism.
Frenchmen of the 'monde' were dangerous, Mandel thought,
because they saw Hitler as a bulwark against communism; of the
pro-German politicians he named Laval, Flandin and Bonnet, saying
that Laval was worse than the others.

The next morning, 4 June, Spears arrived at the Ministry of War to
find Sir Ronald Campbell delivering a telegram from Churchill addressed
to Spears for onward transmission to Reynaud. His old fears of being
cut out were only partly soothed by Campbell's assurances that he had
tried to reach him. Churchill's telegram said that the BEF would be
reconstructed as soon as possible, but the request for more aeroplanes
had to be considered by the cabinet and the decision would probably
come that day. A note that Spears saw later at the embassy, addressed
personally to him, said he should prepare the French for a favourable

response as regards the army and a disappointing one for the air force.

Later, at Reynaud's military cabinet, one item annoyed him; in spite of their pleas to the British, the French were not to employ their own troops taken off from Dunkirk for at least a month. He told Ismay, asking that Churchill should not be informed for it could only hurt him. That evening, on the radio, he heard of Winston Churchill's speech made earlier in the day in the House of Commons: 'We shall fight on the beaches, we shall fight on the landing grounds, we shall fight in the fields and in the streets, we shall fight in the hills; we shall never surrender ...' Dining with some old French friends, he felt a sense of estrangement in spite of the beautiful and familiar setting, 'a slight crack in the crystal cup sufficient to change its sound when touched'. Perhaps Churchill's words, potent in their appeal to Spears's courage and patriotism, had partly caused this, especially when heard in the desolation of a collapsing France; 'a life steeped in French feeling, sentiment and affection was falling from me'. He realised that the Germans were making for the Oise valley, the traditional invader's route to Paris.[26]

At the French War Committee the following morning, 5 June, the atmosphere worsened. Churchill refused the French demand that virtually every RAF fighter should be thrown into the battle and Spears read out parts of the Prime Minister's House of Commons speech, including the reference to a remark supposedly made to Napoleon when he threatened invasion: 'there are bitter weeds in England.' Admiral Darlan was angry that the British were shipping back anti-aircraft defences from Le Havre. Spears feared that Churchill might lose patience with the French, particularly when he heard that a tactless, demanding letter from Vuillemin to Weygand about the performance of the RAF had reached London.[27]

From General Héring, the Governor of Paris, he heard stories of French military successes at last, against German armour and infantry, and momentarily forgot Weygand's barbs. At half-past ten in the evening Spears called on Reynaud at the French Prime Minister's flat with messages from London. The anti-aircraft defences of Le Havre would not be weakened and the provision of these for other harbours was being urgently considered. But to the French suggestion of a single Anglo-French air command, the answer was short. The British said they would consider unity of bomber forces, under a British air force officer, but not a united fighter command.

Reynaud took this philosophically and repeated his disapproval of Vuillemin's attitude towards the RAF. He then said he was in the process of reconstructing his government and Spears saw some of the members of the new cabinet. Baudouin was to be under secretary of state for foreign affairs and kept his position as secretary of the War Committee. Another defeatist, Prouvost, a textile tycoon and owner of the newspaper *Paris-Soir*, took the Ministry of Propaganda. The most significant new addition was not there: a Colonel de Gaulle, advocate of tank warfare and the Brittany redoubt and leader of the 4th Armoured Division in its spirited resistance to the Germans at Abbeville. Professional, dour of manner and devoid of social aspirations, de Gaulle had once been on Pétain's staff. Spears knew also that he and the Marshal had fallen out, partly over the Colonel's views on the tactical importance of armour.

Late that night he spoke to May. General Réquin, she said, had left. Spears knew she was worried when she said she wanted to see him. Should she make for Switzerland or the Mediterranean if the Germans broke through? His memory of her courage reassured him, but he said she would have to come soon for he might be called to London at any minute. As if to echo this, Churchill rang in the early hours. Communication by telephone or telegram was not enough, the Prime Minister said. Could Spears come back to explain what was happening? What about tomorrow, Thursday? Spears answered that he had the French War Committee meeting the next morning. Would Friday be all right? Churchill agreed.

At the War Committee the next day Reynaud said Roosevelt had promised to go as far as American law allowed in helping the allies, 'and even a little further'. Then Weygand began a tirade against the British, demanding that the RAF fighter force should be sent to France and placed under the command of Vuillemin. To Reynaud's question 'What are you really doing for us?' Spears said that almost certainly two RAF fighter squadrons would refuel at French aerodromes that day to give them longer over their targets on the Abbeville front. Two British fighter squadrons operated from Seine bases on 6 and 7 June and it was planned that the number should be increased to four. But on the 8th when three were flying from the French airfields, the British decided that the threat was too great and no more home-based fighters were refuelled in France.[28] The damage to the trust between the two countries had reached an almost irreparable state, perhaps exacerbated by Spears's sharp responses to French criticism. 'One of my most notable failures in life', he wrote later, 'has been to earn the reputation of being long suffering.'[29]

Spears went to the boulevard des Invalides to ask Pétain to persuade Weygand not to blackguard the British. Together he and the Marshal looked at the map. 'This is like old times,' Pétain said, 'but we have never looked at anything like this.' His stronger forefinger traced the German attack. 'You cannot even help us in the air,' said Pétain, and Spears, far more than with Weygand, felt ashamed. In the last war, Pétain observed, the allies always had time, but now there were no reserves and too few weapons. He blamed the policies of the last decade; 'the country has been rotted by politics.' The arrogant, vain, friendless de Gaulle would be no help. He had published a book with the Marshal and claimed all the credit.

Spears asked about the French lack of resistance. Why had the great forests of France not been cut down and trees heaped in the path of the invader, and bridges and culverts blown up? 'And aeroplanes,' Pétain interjected. The Americans could supply those, Spears said, given time and a renewal of French fighting spirit. He thought of the Marshal and himself as two witnesses of a previous transformation of defeat into victory, living symbols of Verlaine's melancholy lines:

> Dans le vieux parc solitaire et glacé
> Deux ombres ont évoqué le passé.

Pétain spoke as if isolated by the fog of old age. The attack at Abbeville could take the Germans through to the Seine, at Rouen. At the mention of Rouen, Spears said: 'What France needs today, Monsieur le Maréchal, is another Joan of Arc.' Suddenly the animation returned. Did Spears know his speech on Joan of Arc, delivered at Rouen in 1937 or 1938? Pétain asked. He would read it to him. Pétain's ancient chief of staff, General Bineau, was summoned to fetch the text and the Marshal settled into a stiff armchair and began to read in a monotone to the astonished Englishman. Joan of Arc was a peasant, Pétain declared at the end. Peasants were the backbone of France. He had spoken on the French peasant as well. Bineau was called, this time to give Spears the text of the speech to read for himself.

Too dejected, he could not concentrate and, abandoning the type-script, stood up. He tried to raise Weygand's attitude to the British, and the certainty that Britain would fight on and attack France if she sided with the Germans. Pétain did not respond; again the fog had fallen and probably deafness had blocked out the words. Instead he took Spears into another room to look at a small bronze sculpture: a tender representation of the Marshal on a horse bending forward to two *poilus* of the last war who smiled up at him in affection and trust.

'This is the epitome of the 1917 mutinies,' Spears said, much moved. 'It is the story of the whole way you handled them.' Pétain heard him immediately. 'You are right,' he said and recalled how he had given Spears his own account of the mutinies for eventual publication. The group, he hoped, would one day be a commemoration of him to the French people. Spears saw that the Marshal believed the quelling of the mutinies had been far more of an achievement than Verdun.[30]

On the way back to the embassy, Spears thought there had been an unspoken message in the way Pétain had shown him the sculpture. The Marshal would never abandon his children, for this was how he saw the First War soldiers and their descendants, and his pessimism had made him already accept defeat. But the interview had shown also the reserves of his cunning. Spears knew that Pétain the man of Picardy, old rival of Foch, hated Weygand the Belgian and Foch's former disciple. Perhaps the deafness and the recitation of old speeches had been a deliberate distraction, to avoid having to criticise a man with whom Pétain suspected he would soon have to work in a defeated France.

12

Flight

In the late afternoon of 6 June, May arrived at the British embassy in Paris. Dressed in her nurse's uniform, a long grey cape lined in blue, and with her hair in a coif, she looked 'like a small girl' intending to brazen out an anticipated scolding. Spears remembered his first sight of her in similar clothes during the First War and as they spoke of the possible dangers he thought, 'my wife would not lose her head, or fail to fulfil the task assigned to her,' which he knew must be back with the hospital. She went to the Ritz, tired after her journey, and he said he would join her there later.[1]

Georges Mandel rang to ask him to dinner. Because of May, he refused but went round to the Ministry of the Interior instead where Mandel was doubtful about a last-ditch stand in Brittany. Was it realistic to govern France from there? Spears suggesting holding out on the Plateau Central and defending the Mediterranean harbours, to which Mandel answered that Weygand thought this would be futile after the loss of the industrial north and the Paris region, which produced 70 per cent of the war material. The French commander was also against fighting on in Africa. Pétain had accepted defeat, agreeing with Weygand's pessimism. Spears should not be in London for long, Mandel advised; 'events are moving very fast.'[2]

A French friend telephoned him, a rich woman with two sons at the front. Could he get news of them for her? Then her tone became one of hatred as she castigated England and Churchill for getting France involved in this terrible war. It was not the only call of this kind that he received during those days.

Spears got back to the Ritz at ten o'clock to find May optimistic and remembered that she had never experienced the chaos of the retreat of 1914, which he imagined must be repeated now. Then Barbara Graham, May's driver, came in to announce that she had crashed their vehicle on the Champs Elysées. Now the military reports were even worse, for the Germans had gained ground in the north and were within reach of Rouen. The next morning May woke her husband to remind him of his promise to arrange transport back to the unit. His friend General Colson produced a car with two drivers and when she left May waved to Spears, who was on the telephone. Apart from one message, he had no more news of her until she landed at Plymouth twenty days later.

'So you are abandoning the sinking ship,' Sir Ronald Campbell said at the embassy, smiling wryly.[3] He lent Spears the ambassadorial Rolls-Royce for his journey to the airport, where Churchill's plane was waiting to take him through a cloudless sky on a circuitous route to London. In the garden of 10 Downing Street, Winston Churchill was waiting, with Archibald Sinclair, now Secretary of State for Air, Air Chief Marshal Sir Cyril Newall and Sir Edward Bridges, the Secretary to the cabinet. His haggard appearance shocked them; 'you look as if you had not slept for a week,' the Prime Minister said.[4]

That night he dined with the Churchills at the Admiralty. The only other guest was the Prime Minister's intimate adviser, Major Desmond Morton, and Churchill spoke of individual feats of bravery he had heard of during the war, showing that physical courage in a good cause was what he admired more than anything else. At the end Spears made his way home through the blackout, having given Mrs Churchill some presents from Paris that included a pair of earrings for her youngest daughter Mary.

The following day, 8 June, was a Saturday. After seeing Ismay, Sinclair and Eden, he went to Warfield and slept. Nancy Maurice was there, and on Sunday Michael came over from Oxford with a friend, but Spears missed May, of whose whereabouts he knew nothing. That day de Gaulle saw Churchill in London and acknowledged that the British were right not to commit their entire force of fighters to the battle for France.

On Monday the 10th, Lord Lloyd, the energetic Secretary of State for the Colonies, who knew Reynaud and was going to Paris the next day to encourage his resolve, asked Spears if the French would fight in and around Paris, as Clemenceau had said they would in 1918. Spears knew they would not, given the present malaise, and urged Winston Churchill to call a meeting of the Supreme War Council to show British support for Reynaud. 'We will go to Paris this afternoon,' the Prime Minister said, but this was impossible. The latest news had the Germans possibly in the French capital in two hours.[5]

That night at dinner with the Churchills, the CIGS Dill seemed 'a very tired man'. Spears argued with him when Dill spoke of the strain a last ditch resistance in Brittany, the Breton redoubt, would put on the RAF, whose fighter bases in England were too far away to cover the peninsula. 'The attitude of the War Office seems to be to fasten all responsibility on to the French,' Spears thought.[6] Churchill worked on after dinner and Spears stayed with him as bad news poured in: losses, sinkings, marooned units, the Italian declaration of war. After listening to Dill, he despaired of the British war machine; 'it is true that everyone on this side is terribly amateurish.'[7] Churchill asked him about the French navy and Spears spoke of unsophisticated sailors and officers whose motto should have been 'love God and hate the English'.[8] Spears was unimpressed by what he had seen in London. 'So worried' was he about Whitehall's lack of coherent organisation that he went to see Mrs Churchill, who advised him to write to her husband.[9]

It was half-past two the next afternoon, 11 June, when the Prime Minister's Flamingo took off for France with an escort of twelve Hurricane fighters and a party that included Ismay, Eden, Dill and Spears. They landed at Briare near Orléans on the Loire and were taken to Weygand's temporary headquarters, an ugly red-brick building inappropriately called Le Château de Muguet or Lily of the Valley Castle. Their cold welcome at the airport by a stiff French colonel was reflected in the atmosphere of the château where, in spite of the quick appearance of tea, Spears felt 'our presence was not really desired'. The conference began almost immediately in a large dining room. For the French there were Weygand, Pétain, de Margerie, Colonel de Villelume (Reynaud's defeatist military adviser) and, for the first time, de Gaulle.[10]

Spears sat between Ismay and de Gaulle. The Frenchmen were white-faced, 'for all the world like prisoners hauled up from some deep dungeon to hear an inevitable verdict'.[11] He observed de Gaulle's strange looks, great height, lack of chin, shrewd hooded eyes, assertive manner, a secret face that would not have been out of place in the council chamber of Catherine de Medici but with a frank smile: likeable. 'V good impression,' Spears wrote in his diary. He thought later that this was the best aspect of de Gaulle: the direct, clear-headed soldier rather than the suspicious, aloof politician.[12]

The news was bleak; the sweat poured off Spears's face as he listened to Weygand. The French Commander, 'very calm', demanded every available British fighter. Churchill refused, mindful of the coming defence of Britain, countering that Paris should be defended. He promised twenty to twenty-five British divisions if the French could hold on until the spring of 1941; at this offer Reynaud could scarcely suppress his irritation. General Georges entered to give another account of the collapse. Pétain dismissed any comparison with the last war, saying that in 1918, when Gough's British army had been overrun by the Germans, he, as the French commander, had sent twenty divisions immediately, followed later by another twenty. Now there was no such help at hand for the French; 'to make Paris into a city of ruins will not affect the issue.'[13]

'Winston was understanding and kind to the French yet very firm,' Spears wrote in his diary. The British Prime Minister spoke again of guerrilla warfare, invoking in Spears a twinge of shame. Was this all that the British could offer? Then Churchill's rhetoric rose. 'I have never seen anything to approach it, especially as he was under stress, great emotion,' Spears wrote,[14] recalling the lines of Victor Hugo on the invincibility of the human spirit: 'l'espoir changea de camp, le combat changea d'âme.'[15] Reynaud seemed moved but not Pétain or Weygand.

That night Spears had dinner with the French officers of the mission attached to the British GHQ and the war was not mentioned; 'courtesy shone through fatigue.' Among them was one of partly British descent, Captain de Penderill Waddington, who told him years later what had happened after Spears left. The eighteen officers declared the war to be lost. What ought they to do? Eight, while not particularly pro-German, thought the national interest dictated they should join the Germans, to which Waddington said that at least the majority were in favour of going on with the war in alliance with England. At this, the other ten protested; all they wanted was that France should remain neutral.

The story has an interesting sequel. Waddington escaped to America, got a commission in the Canadian army, came over to England with the Canadians on the eve of the Normandy landings in 1944 and went to see de Gaulle to try to join the Free French. 'I understand you are very pro-English,' de Gaulle said, to which Waddington answered that he was; whereupon the General shouted, 'I detest the English and the Americans, you understand I detest the English and the Americans. Get out!'[16]

Churchill alone of the British party slept at the Château de Muguet. The rest were put up on the French presidential train. Spears wrote his letter to Churchill about the bad organisation in London, suggesting that the Prime Minister should take on as his adviser General Sir George Macdonogh, now over seventy but still fit. Then he went to sleep thinking about the French navy.

The next morning, Wednesday, 12 June, the French provided a traditional English breakfast on the train, at which Commander Thompson, Churchill's detective, who sometimes acted as his valet, complained at being separated from the Prime Minister. Spears heard afterwards how much Thompson had been missed. Apparently Churchill, used to being constantly attended upon, had burst into the dining room dressed in a long red silk kimono, his sparse hair on end, demanding angrily of two French officers: 'Uh ay ma bain?'[17]

Spears found the Prime Minister in his bedroom. 'Don't point that revolver at me!' he barked as Spears adjusted his own weapon; then, ashamed at this bad-tempered greeting, referred to an incident during the First War. 'Do you remember when I let mine off?' Churchill had been angered by the news that the French, frightened of retaliation on their own cities, had driven lorries on to the airfield near Marseilles to prevent British bombers from making raids on Genoa and industrial centres in northern Italy. They spoke of the French fleet, and Spears imagined German threats to burn the great cities of France one by one until the ships were surrendered. Then, remembering May, he said: 'The one thing I simply can neither face nor think about is that my wife should fall into German hands and be tortured to bring pressure on me.'[18]

Pétain, Georges and de Gaulle were not at the conference that followed; nor were de Margerie and Captain Berkeley, probably because they were working on the minutes of the previous meeting. Spears had to do the interpreting, a task he disliked. Vuillemin was present, and Darlan 'rubicund and nautical'.[19]

Weygand spoke again of catastrophe. 'It is I who read out the armistice terms to the Germans twenty two years ago,' he said. 'You can imagine what I feel.'[20] Again he called for help in the air and, in response, Churchill raised mildly the sabotaged British bombing attacks. Vuillemin did not respond, but Reynaud apologised. Paris, Weygand said, would not be held. Reynaud said the only hope seemed to be the United States. Churchill declared that he must emphasise one matter, 'the importance of which overshadows all others'; the British government must know about any fundamental change in the French circumstances. He would come immediately to discuss such a change at any convenient place. He spoke slowly and repeated his words. Reynaud said that he understood. 'Weygand's hostility to us is potent,' Spears wrote.[21]

At the end of the conference, Spears was summoned by Dill to interpret in a discussion with Weygand and saw Churchill in the hall talking to General Georges. As the Prime Minister got into his car to leave he told Spears that Georges had said that an armistice was inevitable, but Darlan had promised to keep the French fleet out of German hands. 'W.C. told me to stay,' Spears wrote in his diary. 'Felt very naked and alone:' also 'dreadfully anxious about May.'[22]

Marshal Pétain came up to him to say again that France and Britain were paying for the policies of the last decade. 'You have left us to fight alone,' he said. When Spears protested that Britain would never surrender, the Marshal added that he was referring to the years between the wars. 'We have both been very blind,' said Spears. Suddenly the Marshal seemed to rally. 'You have no army,' he declared. 'What could you achieve where the French army has failed?' To Spears's reminder of Churchill's eloquence the old man said: 'Words are very fine but you cannot beat Hitler with words.' He gave Britain no more than a month after the collapse of France and raised again the withheld fighters. Spears urged that France must fight on through her empire. But the Marshal spoke as if joyful in defeat. Shocked, Spears saluted Pétain but did not shake his hand.[23]

Rumours swirled round the château. Pétain was in touch with the Spanish Ambassador, someone said, to ask Hitler for an armistice, and someone else spoke of Weygand and de Gaulle being at daggers drawn. Spears searched for a telephone, remembering how in August 1914 signallers had rapidly laid lines all over the French temporary head-quarters at Compiègne. Now there was one machine on the wall of the pantry outside the only lavatory in the building and dependent on a village operator who took two hours off for lunch and went home at 6.00 p.m.

He wanted to find the British embassy, reported to be somewhere in Touraine. As he chatted to the operator, listening to her unsuccessful attempts to put him through, he became aware that by standing there he was preventing Weygand from reaching the lavatory, but he persisted in his search, learning every detail of life in Briare from the girl in the process, until the French Commander pushed past in fury, slamming the lavatory door. Then the operator said it was twelve and she must go to lunch.

Weygand and Pétain were at lunch with Reynaud but mutual suspicions made conversation almost impossible. The Marshal spoke of his memories of the high Alps as a young soldier, at ease in the past. Spears, who now had a car and a driver, left as soon as he could, saying goodbye to Reynaud, who seemed overcome by gloom. 'Do not forget the aviation,' the French Prime Minister said, returning again to the fighters.[24]

The main roads were packed with refugee traffic but there seemed to be no panic: only resignation, even in the queues for petrol or food.

The absence of big limousines meant that the rich were already at Nice or Biarritz. At the Post Office at Tours, 150 miles from Briare, Spears discovered that the British were installed in the Château de Champchévrier only a few miles from the town. He arrived at the vast seventeenth-century stone castle to find Sir Ronald Campbell and his staff and the Baroness de Champchévrier and her family living side by side.

At breakfast the next morning, Thursday, 13 June, the Champchévrier family ate apart, at a tactful distance from the diplomats, apparently more at ease than the British, although they must have known that defeat was near. On his way to see Paul Reynaud, with the Ambassador and Oliver Harvey in another car, Spears passed Langeais, where Ann of Brittany had married Charles VIII, and Cinq-Mars and thought of the present humiliation of France, then of her powers of recovery. Only a few generations before these huge châteaux had been built, the English had occupied most of the ancient French kingdom. May and he had once contemplated renting Azay-le-Rideau, the renaissance castle that stretched out over water, and another memory revived the sensual side of France, always important to him: how once in a quayside restaurant at Amboise the trees had cast islands of shade on to a sunlit river.

Reynaud was now at the Château de Chissay high above the Cher. Here the past vanished for Spears when he saw the ridiculous figure of Madame de Portes, the Prime Minister's mistress, wearing a dressing gown over red pyjamas and apparently directing the traffic in the courtyard. Inside, de Margerie and Reynaud's secretary were in the owner's 'den', a dusty room hung with hunting trophies and dark pictures, attempting to keep in touch with other ministers housed in châteaux near by. De Gaulle was in the hall, on a circular sofa, and told Spears that he thought Brittany could be held, but Weygand lacked the will.

Reynaud sent for Spears. Campbell was already with him and the French Prime Minister seemed more optimistic than at Briare. The cabinet, he said, supported his resolution to fight on in Africa, in spite of the doubt of some of its members. He seemed unenthusiastic about any move to Brittany. Weygand and Pétain, he said, wanted an immediate armistice, believing that the army must be saved to prevent outbreaks of civilian unrest, but Reynaud thought he had triumphed over the defeatism of the two soldiers. Spears asked if troops from the Maginot line might be moved to Brittany, and Reynaud suggested he should take this up with de Gaulle.

Spears could not find de Gaulle. He asked de Margerie for a telegram from the French embassy in London; eventually it was found in Madame de Portes' bed. Several times Madame de Portes came into the room where Spears and Campbell were talking to de Margerie, exuding hatred for the Englishmen. Spears thought her very unattractive.

He took Campbell and Harvey to lunch in a restaurant at Chenonceaux. The place was deserted, apart from the family of the millionaire chocolate-maker Menier, who owned the huge château near by and again Spears saw another France in the beauty of Madame Menier and her pearls and the 1929 Vouvray that they drank. Afterwards the diplomats left for Champchévrier and Spears for Chissay in the hope of catching de Gaulle. That evening, now completely won round, Oliver Harvey wrote in his diary: 'I must say Spears is very good.'[25]

At Chissay, Spears was astonished to hear that Reynaud had gone to Tours, where Churchill was expected. His driver took him off again on the crowded roads, past a refugee camp on the outskirts of Tours to the Préfecture, where he found the British party: Churchill, Ismay, Lord Beaverbrook, Lord Halifax (the Foreign Secretary), Sir Alexander Cadogan (the permanent head of the Foreign Office), the Ambassador and Captain Berkeley, the interpreter. Churchill, looking stern, asked Spears about Paul Baudouin and was told of his defeatism. In a small room on the first floor, presumably the Préfet's office, they found Georges Mandel talking on the telephone and eating a chicken with his fingers. Churchill was pleased to see this opponent of surrender, but Mandel left and Reynaud and Baudouin entered. The meeting began: nine British facing two French ministers. Again Spears found himself asked to translate, this time from English into French, as de Margerie was not there.

Reynaud had changed from resolution to acceptance of defeat. He explained the terrible state of the French armies. Would Britain release France from the joint declaration and allow her to make a separate peace? Now there was no talk of carrying on the fight from North Africa. In spite of Churchill's show of sympathy, particularly in his use of the phrase, 'je comprends', which was misinterpreted by Baudouin, he did not agree to the release of France from her pledge. In the middle of one of Churchill's orations de Margerie took over the interpreting from Spears. Churchill urged a last appeal to Roosevelt and raised once more the prospect of a blockade being imposed on France if she stood between the British and their enemy. Reynaud spoke of the need to show that Britain would not prolong the suffering of France.[26]

Remembering how, when faced with a deadlock at the Peace Conference, Lloyd George would call for an adjournment in order to consult his colleagues, Spears passed a note to Churchill to suggest that he should do the same. The Prime Minister made the request of Reynaud; then took the British into the drab garden of the Préfecture.

Spears recalled that everyone was too stunned to speak at first: 'I certainly was.' He wondered if Reynaud had been playing the defeatist to see how the British would react. To Churchill's questions about de Gaulle, he said he thought the young Minister was completely staunch and that fundamentally Reynaud also wished to fight on. Beaverbrook, in a sudden shaft of realism, said there was no point in staying because nothing could be done until Roosevelt answered the proposed French and British messages.[27]

The conference reconvened. This time de Gaulle was there but stayed silent, and Reynaud seemed more confident. They would each send a message to Roosevelt and meet again when the answer had been received. Churchill repeated that Hitler would eventually be smashed and Reynaud, 'showing emotion for the first time', said rather pathetically that he too had that faith. At 5.50 p.m. they walked downstairs into the courtyard.[28]

De Gaulle told Spears of a new rumour. Apparently Baudouin claimed that the British Prime Minister had said he would understand if France signed a separate peace. Was this true? Spears denied it. He rushed to catch Churchill and found he had left for the airfield. Here, on a bomb-pitted runway against a background of smashed buildings, Spears told the Prime Minister of Baudouin's claim. Churchill denied it; 'je comprends' had meant 'I understand': no more. Then the roar of engines drowned his words and he boarded the Flamingo to return to London.[29]

Spears drove to Tours and found that the French had left. He battled through the refugee columns to Chissay in the twilight to be told by de Margerie that Reynaud had gone to a cabinet meeting at the château of the President of the Republic at Congé near Tours. Spears arrived at Congé to hear that the ministers had left, the President had retired for the night and Mandel was in the Préfecture at Tours.

In the Préfet's office, Mandel spoke coolly of Weygand's passionate wish to accept defeat, of the anger of some ministers that Reynaud had not brought Churchill to discuss the crisis with the French cabinet. He mentioned Pétain's immense prestige; the Marshal's support for an armistice was much more telling than Weygand's hysteria. Now Churchill's departure without seeing the cabinet had added to the impression of abandonment.

Then the door opened, to reveal Reynaud. The Frenchman looked ghastly. 'Have you any orders?' he asked Mandel, after a moment's agonised silence. 'No.' 'And Paris?' 'No.' Spears offered to leave, but it was Reynaud who walked out.

Five minutes later Madame de Portes came in, hostile and aggressive; not finding Reynaud, she left. Mandel observed that 'her influence has been sinister this day.' The Minister of the Interior then listed the defeatist ministers and those who were prepared to fight, seeming almost to delight in these odd human antics. He said the government would move to Bordeaux the next day. Spears should tell the Ambassador that embassy staff should also leave by ten o'clock in the morning.[30]

At Champchévrier, he reported this to Sir Ronald Campbell and suggested that the Ambassador should ask for a British destroyer to be sent to the mouth of the Gironde river, within reach of Bordeaux.

The next morning, Friday, 14 June, Madame de Champchévrier and one of her daughters, dressed in black, stood at the door to say goodbye to the diplomats, for she and her family were staying to face the Germans. Spears went with the Ambassador in his Rolls-Royce as far as Tours, then got into his own car and was driven to Chitré, where he was greeted by Yvonne's son, who said that she had gone to another of her properties further south, at Melle. He found Chitré packed with refugee relations from Belgium and the north who spoke pathetically of fifth columnists; his sense of dislocation, brought on by memories of earlier days of happiness, was added to by an absence of maps. How would he find his way to Bordeaux? What if the car broke down?

The roads became emptier. He passed several French air force convoys with aeroplanes tied on to long trailers; surely they should have been in the air, protecting the infantry from the Luftwaffe. Soldiers were idling in the villages: several thousand of them, he thought: so different from the spirit of 1914. He remembered his friend Captain de Rose, the heroic airman killed in the First War; then the book he had wanted to write after *Prelude* about the French army's recovery from the mutinies of 1917; the way the troops at the front in 1918 had been forbidden to fall back, how Clemenceau had wept at their sacrifice. Now he saw only humiliation, lassitude. 'During this horrible, depressing journey,' he remembered, 'I endured the kind of sorrow that withers faith.'[31]

He stopped at Melle, near Niort, to see Yvonne. She had some scientists from the Pasteur Institute there and Spears encouraged them to continue their work in England but they said they could not move without orders. Yvonne did not turn back when she walked away from him as he left; 'sad,' he wrote in his diary, 'felt might never see her again'.[32]

In the towns and villages people were hostile on seeing his British uniform; near Bordeaux he was stopped by gendarmes who said all traffic was being diverted from the city. Spears explained his mission and reached the British consulate, where the embassy was installed, and the Hôtel Montré, where Harvey had got rooms. The Germans had entered Paris that morning. He tried to get news of the Hadfield–Spears unit by telephoning various points on the way south, but no one had heard of it.

Campbell, Harvey and he ate at the restaurant Chapon Fin, across from the Montré. Churchill had sent a telegram to Reynaud emphasising 'the indissoluble union of our two peoples and of our two empires', and it was this that Campbell and Spears delivered to the French Prime Minister's office at 11.00 p.m. in the rue Vital-Carles.[33]

Reynaud, de Margerie and two secretaries were eating poached eggs and were not pleased at being disturbed. Campbell, 'rather slow off the mark', translated the telegram, and Reynaud, clearly exhausted, looked angry, for Churchill obviously wanted to keep France to the agreement that she should not surrender separately.[34] He snapped at Spears that Weygand and Pétain might resign. Roosevelt had not promised to declare war but showed support for continuing the struggle from North Africa. At least Reynaud seemed still to believe in the African option and had sent de Gaulle to London to ask for help in moving troops and war materials there. Spears and Campbell despatched a joint telegram to London in which they said that the French Prime Minister was wavering under the influence of the defeatists. The British government, they advised, should stick to its opposition to a separate peace.

New arrivals poured into Bordeaux; Mandel and his mistress were at the Préfecture and Pierre Laval at the town hall as a guest of the defeatist Mayor. Spears heard of other enemies of Reynaud, advocates of a quick surrender: the limp representatives of defeat. He wrote later: 'I felt that night as if all the sewers in France had burst and that their nauseating mess was seeping into the beautiful city like a rising tide of abomination.'[35]

The next day, Sunday, 15 June, Reynaud showed Spears and Campbell the full text of his telegram from Roosevelt, which urged the French to fight on outside France. Everything, Reynaud said, depended on a later telegram he had sent to the President asking for direct American intervention. But Spears knew that Roosevelt would not declare war on Germany.

Campbell and Spears saw Reynaud several times that day, and were

cheered always by a watching crowd in the rue Vital-Carles. 'A dreadful
afternoon,' he wrote in his diary. 'One of the worst days I have ever
lived, with always the back-ground feeling we may easily be trapped
here.' The Germans had mined the mouth of the estuary. 'There is
literally nothing between us and the Germans.'[36] French citizens begged
the British for passages out of the country; many were Jews who knew
what they could expect under a Nazi occupation. He thought of May,
probably trapped.

He and Campbell were sent for at 7.00 p.m., after a cabinet meeting,
and the washed-out Prime Minister repeated Baudouin's contention
that Churchill had agreed to France seeking a separate armistice.
Spears and Campbell contradicted him but Reynaud wrote a message
to Churchill to say the French cabinet had decided to ask, through the
United States, about German and Italian terms for an armistice before
taking any decision about a move to North Africa. Then he was handed
Roosevelt's response to his last telegram and his eyes became 'just slits,
his face contracting'. 'Our appeal has failed,' he said. 'The Americans
will not declare war.' Weygand had said the army might break up at
any moment.[37]

Spears and Campbell asked why Reynaud did not resign on the
understanding that the President of the Republic would then invite
him to form a new government from which the defeatists would be
excluded. To this the Prime Minister replied: 'and Pétain?' No government could survive if it was opposed by the Marshal. Would Reynaud
come to England, Spears asked? The Frenchman answered that it had
to be North Africa or nothing.[38]

They left to see Mandel at the Préfecture, who gave a more cynical
account of the cabinet meeting. To ask for the terms of an armistice,
ministers had told themselves, was not the same as surrendering.
Mandel urged that Britain should refuse to release France from her
obligation not to make a separate peace. No one, he assured Spears
and Campbell, was in favour of giving up the French fleet. Spears
telephoned Winston Churchill to report what Mandel had said and
suggested that Churchill should come over to meet Reynaud the next
day. The Prime Minister said he would consider this. Spears saw that
metropolitan France was lost; the army was no longer fighting. The
French empire and the French fleet, however, might be saved.

If Pétain resigned, Spears and the Ambassador told Reynaud the
next day, Sunday, June 16, public opinion need not be inflamed because
the government controlled the news. Madame de Portes looked in
several times; afterwards de Margerie told Spears: 'she is ugly, mal
soignée, dirty, nasty and half-demented, and a sore trial to me.'[39] News

came that a destroyer, HMS *Berkeley*, had arrived in the Gironde but could not get close to the city because of German mines. A message came from May through the Consul-General at Lyon. Where should she make for? Would Spears send an answer to Nevers, to the Prefecture? This was 300 miles from Bordeaux and the Germans were said to be on the Loire, only a few miles north of Nevers. He sent a message but she did not receive it, for the Germans occupied the town that day. At least, he consoled himself, she knew he was in Bordeaux.

Then Churchill telegraphed Reynaud to say that the British government would agree to a French approach to ascertain the terms of an armistice as long as the French fleet sailed forthwith for British harbours. To Spears this demand seemed both a sign of weakness and an insult to the French, but Campbell felt it was his duty to carry out the instruction from London. They saw Reynaud, who, as Spears had suspected, was irritated by the reference to the fleet; he said Churchill had suggested a meeting that night or the next day, in Brittany. It was finally arranged that this should be at sea, off Concarneau.

Another message came from London, repeating the need to save the French fleet. Reynaud showed petulance at this to Spears and Campbell, who had come to see him again; then the telephone rang. Reynaud answered; it was de Gaulle, again from London. Suddenly his whole demeanour changed and he began to write with a short gold pencil. Astounded, Spears held the paper to prevent it from sliding over the desk. The conversation changed to English, for Churchill had come on the line to make the offer of a declaration of union between the two countries, which de Gaulle would bring across by air. Reynaud put the receiver down, apparently 'transfigured with joy'; now France would remain in the war. Spears wrote later: 'my friendship for him surged out in a wave of appreciation.'[40]

The French cabinet was about to meet. Quickly the offer was typed out by the secretaries and read with horror by Madame de Portes, who must have transmitted it almost immediately to her defeatist allies. But Reynaud said: 'I shall die defending these proposals.' He asked Spears and Campbell if the earlier telegrams about the French fleet had been superseded and they answered that now the fleet's future would be settled by a joint command.[41]

As he waited with Campbell at the Hôtel Montré, Spears felt optimistic at last. They tried to imagine an Anglo-French government and an Anglo-French parliament, one of them saying, employing a French expression: 'it would be a basketful of crabs.' Spears joked that he might become an actual 'Member for Paris', then, as the cabinet meeting dragged on, his hopes fell.[42]

They were sent for at 7.30. In the rue Vital-Carles, the crowd cheered again and Spears thought this a good omen. But inside de Margerie told them that Reynaud was going to resign as the proposal had been defeated. They saw Reynaud, who seemed strangely relieved: 'gaiety rippled under the surface of his manner', because he could speak with detachment at last. At the cabinet, the defeatists had voiced their horror at becoming a British dominion, Pétain saying it would be like being tied to a corpse. Spears and Campbell tried to persuade Reynaud not to resign and asked him to rest, adding that they would return at ten o'clock. Then they went back through the cheering crowd to send a message to London to stop the Prime Minister's journey to Concarneau.

Dinner at the Chapon Fin was particularly bleak, with Laval, 'dark, bloated and satisfied', again at a nearby table.[43] At ten o'clock Spears and Campbell left to see Reynaud. There was the same cheer from the small crowd at the entrance to the rue Vital-Carles and a ghostly darkness inside. A French air force major approached them to say he would take his bombing formation to England to fight on. As the Ambassador spoke to de Margerie in a corner, de Gaulle came up and asked to see them later that evening.

First they had to call on Reynaud, and the former Prime Minister told them of Pétain's new government, the origin of the Vichy regime. Baudouin was to be foreign minister, Weygand minister of defence, Darlan at Marine. Spears was shocked to hear that General Colson had taken the Ministry of War. 'Much as I had liked him, I wrote Colson off the precious list of my friends.'[44] Reynaud spoke as if he thought Lebrun might call on him again if the Pétain government failed; then remembering the planned meeting with Churchill off Concarneau he said he must ask Pétain for an aeroplane to take him there. To Spears, it was absurd to imagine that Churchill would travel across the Channel at this time of crisis to see a politician without power or office. The failure to see reality seemed unbelievably vain. The meeting, he said, had been cancelled.

Now there was de Gaulle. Spears's version of the General's departure is still controversial. It suited Vichy to claim that de Gaulle had been smuggled out of France by the British in a state of panic, and after 1945, when the name of Spears was detested in France, Gaullists in particular played down the Englishman's role in the last hours in Bordeaux, even implying that he had fled in terror because his Jewish origins were known to the Germans.[45]

Spears went to the British diplomat Henry Mack's room in the Hôtel Montré to try to speak to Churchill. First the telephone rang. It was the Duke of Windsor from Nice. Could a warship be sent there to pick up him and the Duchess? At that moment there was only a collier in the southern harbour. Mack said this was impossible and they should drive to Spain. Earlier on Spears had had his photograph taken in civilian clothes, with a view to getting a passport; he noted that 'a diplomatic visa is necessary as the Spaniards have closed the frontier.'[46]

De Gaulle came that evening to the Hôtel Montré. Spears's diary, as opposed to his later version of events in *Assignment to Catastrophe*, has a clear account of what happened; significantly there is no mention of a meeting behind a pillar at the rue Vital-Carles with de Gaulle asking to be put up for the night on a British warship. 'De Gaulle turned up at the hotel and was very afraid of either being arrested or given orders to go to some distant part by Weygand, thus making it impossible to go back to England.' The British Air Attaché, Douglas Colyer, remembers de Gaulle in Spears's bedroom at the Montré, saying he would return to England the next day. Spears's diary reads: 'he has kept the plane he came on this afternoon' bearing the offer of union, 'and [I] told him to wait till 9 o'clock.'[47]

The diary also makes clear his own thoughts. 'I took the instant decision that my work was finished here. It would seem to condone the action of this defeatist Government if I remained, besides which I cannot keep a civil tongue in my head when talking to any of these people, which would make matters worse. I decided to go with de Gaulle in the morning.'[48]

He spoke to Churchill on the telephone about his decision; 'he did not seem very enthusiastic but I am sure I am right.' The Ambassador and Oliver Harvey, both of whom stayed on, agreed with him. Churchill had wanted Spears to pursue the question of the French fleet, but eventually accepted that he should leave Bordeaux. It was decided that de Gaulle should come to the Hôtel Montré at seven o'clock the next morning. Later Gaullists and Spears in a battle of the memoirs would fight over the aeroplane and at whose disposal it had been. The diary seems to show that in June 1940 Spears accepted it as de Gaulle's.[49]

Spears returned to the Préfecture to see Mandel and asked him to come to England the next day. This was impossible, he said; he must not look as if he was running away, particularly because of his Jewishness. Perhaps he might leave in two or three days' time. A door opened to reveal Mademoiselle Bretty, his 'bland, fat' mistress, who told him that the trunks were packed. Mandel went to North Africa. He was sent back to France and murdered in 1944.[50]

Back at the Hôtel Montré, de Gaulle had gone. He and his ADC, Geoffroy de Courcel, spent the night in different hotels. Spears worked late with Campbell on despatches and then packed for his journey. The shy Ambassador said awkwardly how sorry he was to be losing him. At least he had won Campbell's trust.

The next morning de Gaulle and Geoffroy de Courcel were late and Spears rang up the Air Attaché, Air Commodore Colyer, to find out if they had been arrested. Colyer arrived but by this time the Frenchmen were there with their luggage. They drove in Spears's car, first to the temporary quarters of the Ministry of War, where de Gaulle told officials to make a series of appointments for later that morning; then to the airport, past the guard at the entrance, to find the field packed with French aeroplanes waiting to go to Morocco: 'quite frightful that they should still be there', Spears thought.[51]

They found the British plane, a De Havilland Dragon Rapide, without difficulty. The Frenchmen later denied any drama, Courcel saying that they had only two pieces of luggage each; even so, that was enough, according to Spears, for the pilot to say that 'the bags must be tied'. Courcel was sent off for a ball of string to lash down the luggage. The wait lasted ten minutes, Spears dreading the arrival of Weygand's men. Then Courcel returned and Spears said goodbye to his driver, 'the salt of the earth'. 'Finally,' Spears wrote of de Gaulle in his diary, 'as we were on the point of starting, he having stood as if he were seeing me off, he hopped in followed by his A.D.C. and off we went'.[52]

He opened a local paper and read a eulogistic article about de Gaulle. Soon they were over the sea and saw the sinking troopship, *Champlain*, with thousands of tiny figures in the water, then Brittany and smoke from burning British army dumps, and the sea again and descent into Jersey to refuel with the petrol gauge almost on empty. The airport director there remembered fifty years later how a De Havilland Dragon Rapide had landed at 11.30 a.m. and two officers, presumably Spears and de Gaulle, had come to his office. He led them to the Hôtel Saint-Pierre for lunch; perhaps it was here that de Gaulle, given a cup of coffee, said courteously that it was tea and suffered 'his first introduction to the tepid liquid which, in England, passes for either one or the other'. Spears noted: 'his martyrdom had begun.' Before leaving, they bought a case of whisky.[53]

At 2.30 the aeroplane landed near London in fine weather: at Hendon, not Heston as Spears writes in *Assignment*. For de Gaulle the break with his country, shameful in defeat, seemed simultaneously demeaning and bleak; 'there was nothing romantic or difficult about the departure,' he wrote later.[54] To Spears, however, it was a great drama for he was with the man who might keep alive the spirit of a free France. This, he hoped, would be the start of an exalted life as a link between his two countries: one defeated, the other still magnificently resisting. De Gaulle was seven years younger than he: inexperienced, no longer a minister, merely the youngest brigadier in the French army and desperately in need of help.

13

The Warrior Monk

Spears knew little about the Frenchman with whom he had flown across the Channel. Charles de Gaulle was said to be on the right but with almost no political experience, having been a professional soldier until June 1940, and free of any faction although at one time a disciple of Pétain. The son of a schoolmaster, he had been born in Lille in 1890, into a strongly Catholic family from the grande bourgeoisie of northern France.

There were undercurrents of which Spears would gradually become aware. An Irish grandmother and a childhood awareness of Fashoda, the colonial humiliation of 1898 when the French Captain Marchand had been forced by the British to abandon an attempt to set up a military post in the southern Sudan, had laid the beginnings of a distrust of Britain and de Gaulle's perception of her ancient rivalry with France. During military service in the Levant he experienced the jealousy each country had of the other's imperial ambitions. He had doubts about the British role in the First War, particularly during the German offensives in the west of 1914 and 1918, and felt that France had been deserted by her ally after 1918. The British departure from Dunkirk had reinforced his scepticism. German was his second language, not English.

Although stimulated by the arguments of Charles Maurras, who also abominated Britain's historic attitude towards France, and of the followers of Action Française, de Gaulle was not an extremist of the right. Later there would be imputations of fascism, of a dictatorial outlook, and rumours of connections with disreputable organisations. But de Gaulle's extremism lay in his patriotism, in a mystical sense of France and her past, and this embraced her democracy as well as her heroes and conquests. On 17 June 1940 his sense of humiliation was intense.

De Gaulle and Spears shared a love of France and an understanding of her history, but there were differences in their perceptions of this, conscious or unconscious. Spears's feelings for the country of his childhood had a strongly sensual side, rooted in the lush surroundings of Voutenay and the legends and songs of Brittany. These memories of fabulous sweetness evolved into an emotional admiration for the French army of the First War; then the chaos and lassitude he saw in the summer of 1940 banished much of his respect. As a British member of parliament between the wars, he had been able to contrast a stable, comparatively incorruptible Westminster with the drifting, turbulent and venal French politics of the time. Britain, however misguided, meant power and political seriousness; France, however picturesque, seemed ultimately a less considerable country.

De Gaulle never doubted France's potential power. Unlike Spears, he was an ascetic who seemed at times almost to welcome privation; he also cherished the idea of a hard, elemental side of France. In December 1947, at Colombey-les-Deux-Eglises, his home in the austere département of the Haute-Marne, de Gaulle flung open the windows to show a surprised visitor the storm of wind and rain outside, delighting in this sign of a 'terrible' rather than a 'douce' land.[1] He became particularly alert to patronising foreign attitudes towards his country after the humiliation of exile, believing that he, in every move and word, must represent to the world a great and noble national identity.

In June 1940 de Gaulle was alone and virtually destitute. As Spears and he were flying to London, Pétain had broadcast to the French people to say that he had begun the negotiations for an armistice; the change of government and his flight meant that de Gaulle would be stripped of his rank, with his wife and children lost in a defeated France where they might be held as hostages by the Germans. At Bordeaux Paul Reynaud had given him only FF100,000 with which to establish his cause.

He and Spears went first to Seamore Street in Mayfair to a flat that had been rapidly obtained for him; then to the RAC Club for lunch, before going to 10 Downing Street, where, in the garden, Winston Churchill stood up to greet his guest with a smile.

In contrast to de Gaulle's distrust and ignorance of Britain, Churchill possessed an intensely sentimental affection for a France he had visited often and whose army he had extolled between the wars. But the Prime Minister and many of the British were disappointed by the arrival of this unknown army officer, having hoped for a figure of greater repute, perhaps Reynaud or Mandel. For Spears, however, there was no point in lamenting de Gaulle's lack of reputation or standing. He was the only minister who had been prepared to make the journey from Bordeaux and must be helped as much as possible.

Winston Churchill gave de Gaulle permission to broadcast the next day and Spears secured an office for him in St Stephen's House on the floor above his own. Slowly the organisation began to take shape: the loyal Courcel; a secretary, Elizabeth de Mirabel; Reynaud's former aide, Gaston Palewski; the legal adviser Professor René Cassin; the intelligence chief Captain André Dewavrin (to be known as Passy); René Pleven; Admiral Muselier. Spears's old friend Henri de Kérillis joined de Gaulle, quarrelled with him and left for the United States; Robert Mengin stayed in Britain but not with de Gaulle. Jean Monnet and Alexis Léger also went to Washington to escape the General's domineering personality.

When the Foreign Office and Jean Monnet tried to stop the broadcasts, Spears and Duff Cooper persuaded Churchill and the cabinet to allow de Gaulle to go on the air usually at intervals of two days for the rest of June, then less frequently. Spears acted as the link between de Gaulle and the Foreign Office over the texts of the broadcasts which, to de Gaulle's fury, the British sought to see beforehand; on 22 June Nancy Maurice went with the Frenchman to 10 Downing Street and translated his text into English. Spears found Richmond Temple, a British publicity agent, and persuaded a reluctant de Gaulle to take Temple's advice on how to make his cause better known.

There was no disguising the disappointing French response. Duff Cooper and Lord Gort went to North Africa to invite Mandel and other senior military and political figures to come to London but the Vichy officials forced the British emissaries to leave. From the French empire only General Legentilhomme from Somaliland and General Catroux, the Governor-General of Indo-China, broke loose from Vichy, the latter because he had been dismissed by Pétain's government. The French Ambassador in London, Corbin, left for South America, and the staff of the various missions and consulates prepared to leave too, contriving in the meantime to thwart de Gaulle.

His aspect took on an outward hardness. When Spears told him that the flying boat sent by Churchill to search for Madame de Gaulle and their children had been lost, he did not react. On 19 June, on receiving a telephone call from his wife, who had left France on a British ship, his curt answer was: 'Oh, it's you. I'm in London. I shall be waiting for you.'[2] Spears noted how de Gaulle seemed almost to glory in suffering; later, in Africa, he would speak enviously of the Tuaregs in the Sahara, who were always thirsty and were said to enjoy their torment.

Towards the end of June, Spears was appointed head of the British government's mission to de Gaulle, now recognised as 'leader of all free Frenchmen'. He was allocated offices in Gwydyr House in Whitehall, while the Frenchman had his headquarters in Carlton House

Gardens. Almost immediately Spears began to castigate the slowness of the Foreign Office and, in particular, the committee under Sir Robert Vansittart that was responsible for liaison with the French.

The chance of organising French resistance in Britain was being frittered away. 'Since I have been back from France I have witnessed a most unbelievable vacillation and changes of policy on the French question,' Spears told Churchill. 'Everybody including de Gaulle himself has been inclined to lose heart.' There was only one answer. 'I venture to suggest that you put me in charge of the whole French question and let me be responsible to you. Under present conditions things have taken such a turn that it can hardly be deemed a Foreign Office question. I might not be able to do much but I am not afraid of taking decisions or incurring responsibility.' The Spears Mission shows that, to a certain extent, he got his way.[3]

De Gaulle, Spears felt, must visit the French soldiers and sailors then in camps throughout Britain. The French officials still in England, particularly Chartier, the Consul in London, tried to stop all recruiting, and the General, as he came increasingly to be called, could seem inflexible and cold in public. Again the response was disheartening, Colin Coote, a journalist on *The Times*, telling Spears that many of the French wounded he had visited in British hospitals were 'deeply suspicious' of de Gaulle, associating him with the morass of French politics, and fed up with being called cowards by British civilians.[4] Spears's task of resurrecting a free, fighting France seemed immensely difficult. At the end of June, Hugh Dalton noticed that he was exhausted and had a high fever.[5]

Worse was to come. On 2 July Churchill showed Spears the ultimatum that Admiral Somerville would deliver to the French Admiral Gensoul, who was in command of the French fleet at Oran and Mers-el-Kebir in North Africa. It demanded in effect the surrender of the ships to British control.

Churchill asked if he thought Gensoul would accept. Spears answered: 'I think he is bound to if he is made to realise we mean what we say.'[6] The Prime Minister said it would be better to wait until the next day before telling de Gaulle, for the decision was an entirely British one. To Spears, it was a miserable prospect. On the way from Downing Street to Strathearn Place he saw some French sailors in Hyde Park laughing with a group of English girls and wept at the thought of the possible fate of their colleagues in North Africa.

The next day he told de Gaulle. As was his custom with matters of great importance, the General was silent at first and then said he felt sure that Gensoul would accept one of the alternatives offered to him by the British. On the afternoon of the delivery of the ultimatum, Spears sat at Gwydyr House on a committee dealing with French affairs and the Admiralty's representative kept the members informed of what was happening at Mers-el-Kebir. The French did not obey the ultimatum; at 5.45 Somerville opened fire. One French battleship and five destroyers escaped to Toulon but the remainder of the fleet was put out of action and 1,300 French seamen killed. The operation was not one of which the British could be proud. Rushed and ineptly directed negotiations had failed, several of the most effective French ships had survived, the French navy's traditional anglophobia grew more hateful and, inside France and the French empire, many turned furiously against their former ally.

That evening Spears saw de Gaulle, who seemed calm. He said that if the action had been 'inevitable' from the British point of view it left him uncertain about whether he could still collaborate with Britain or instead withdraw into private life in Canada. He would let Spears know of his decision the next day. Spears tried to encourage him by saying that France still had to be saved, and he informed Churchill of de Gaulle's 'magnificent dignity'.[7] On 4 July de Gaulle told Spears he would not leave, although the position might be 'radically changed' if France declared war on Britain – which he thought unlikely.[8] Years later, after their quarrel, Spears thought: 'This decision went beyond heroism, it was that of a man prepared to face martyrdom for the sake of his country.'[9]

Spears thought war with France was possible. Recruiting became immensely more difficult for de Gaulle, and when on 18 July Duff Cooper, the Minister of Information, allowed him to speak freely on the BBC he castigated the triumphalism in the British press about Mers-el-Kebir but declared it was better for the ships to be destroyed than for them to fall into German hands.

Spears fought hard for de Gaulle. On 7 July Major Desmond Morton, an old ally of Churchill whom the Prime Minister had also put to work on liaison with the Free French movement, told him that two distinguished French scientists, M. Rapline and M. Fournier, did not want to join de Gaulle because of his reputed pro-fascist tendencies and pre-war links with Action Française. 'I am quite certain that de Gaulle is no more fascist than I am,' Spears answered, 'and, even if he were connected with the Action Française, which I do not know to be the fact, I know that his whole policy as leader of the French forces of liberation is to steer clear of all political affiliations. As you probably know, against this one accusation of his being pro-fascist, we have had dozens that he was connected with the Front Populaire affiliation and he was supposed to be associated with Léon Blum and Pierre Cot, which is completely untrue ...'[10] Vichy also had its agents. The ex-Naval Attaché in London, Denys de Rivoyre, whom de Gaulle wished to have arrested, sent men into the French camp at Olympia to distribute anti-British tracts. He lured young officers 'of very good standing and family' to his house and tried to persuade them to return to France.[11]

Colin Coote condemned the contemptuous British attitudes which had led to the ostracising of French soldiers and the change 'from the extreme of thinking all the French heroes to the extreme of thinking them all swine'.[12] Spears heard on 22 July of how the French wounded in a London hospital were asked by non-French-speaking nurses and doctors whether they wanted to stay in England or not, without any explanation of what they might expect if they did, and then were given only ten minutes to answer. His informant said that the French-speaking nurses and French visitors were barred from the wards.[13] The truth was that the British did not want the French, whom they distrusted, at a time when weapons were in very short supply and an invasion was expected.

De Gaulle began to see spies everywhere, from Vichy and the British. His defences went up and an apparatus of counter-espionage grew under the direction of the formidable 'Passy' Dewavrin, with sessions of interrogation and even torture in the cellars of Duke Street near Manchester Square. One victim sued de Gaulle in the British courts.

The General seldom relaxed, although the diplomat Henry Hopkinson remembered a lunch at the Ritz Hotel, given by de Gaulle to introduce Spears, May and the Hopkinsons to Madame de Gaulle, as 'totally delightful', with de Gaulle 'ruminating over his experiences and the affairs of the world'. 'He could', Hopkinson recalled, 'be a man of enchantment.'[14] A sense of absurdity, however, was not among his more obvious attributes. One evening in the Connaught Hotel, where he lived during his early days in London, he said suddenly: 'I really am Joan of Arc'; to which Spears declared, astounded by the ridiculous comparison, 'if I were you, mon Général, I would not recall Joan of Arc too often in England. The English adore her, but nevertheless when she is evoked here a slight smell of burning is often perceptible.'[15]

On 3 July, the same day as Somerville's bombardment at Mers-el-Kebir, British soldiers boarded French naval vessels docked at Portsmouth and Plymouth and between 10,000 and 15,000 French seamen were taken off to be interned at Aintree racecourse near Liverpool. One group was sent on a twelve-hour train journey without food or water, a senior French officer protesting that French law insisted that cattle in trucks had to be watered every four hours at least. Conditions at Aintree reached a state of near anarchy; the men wandered around Liverpool, refusing to pay bus or tram fares, terrifying the locals and demanding to be sent back to France. De Gaulle and his naval commander, Admiral Muselier, visited the camp and were met with open hostility.

Spears flew up to Aintree at the end of July to find the area surrounded by barbed wire and British soldiers, who had been pelted with stones by the French, wanting to shoot their former allies. The French cut the leads of the loudspeakers from which he had hoped to speak but, in spite of this, he entered the camp alone on a Sunday morning when most of the inmates were at mass. He addressed some 300 officers in a room under the stand of the racecourse, with two admirals sitting in state on chairs at the back, and there were shouts of 'the government of France' whenever he mentioned the 'Vichy regime'.[16] Most of the young sailors, to Spears's despair, wanted to get back to France as quickly as possible. In another infuriating example of bureaucratic timidity, returning soldiers were allowed by the British War Office to take their weapons with them, General Dill countering Spears's protests by saying that anything less might lead to a riot. Ships left British ports for France loaded with Frenchmen and their rifles and bayonets and even small tanks.

Far more to his taste was a scheme pushed by Winston Churchill for a show of strength in the French empire. On 17 August, May noted in her diary: 'B told me the night before last that he was going with General de Gaulle on the mysterious expedition of the Free French forces.' Archdale cryptically remarked to her: 'de Gaulle will have succeeded or failed within 3 months', and Spears showed himself 'so particularly sweet that I knew something was up', talking of her grey hairs and how 'pleased' he was to see them for in Paris twenty years before he had wished he was fifty so he would not be 'jealous' of May. She thought of French Somaliland, but the target was Dakar, the French naval base in Senegal.[17]

De Gaulle's movement had some success in Africa. Chad, led by its black governor Félix Eboué, rallied to him at the end of August, followed by the Cameroons. But Vichy remained strongly entrenched at Dakar, where the Governor of French West Africa, Pierre Boisson, was loyal to Pétain, whose government he saw as the rightful rulers of France.

'De Gaulle certainly did not initiate Dakar and had in fact very little say in the matter,' Spears recalled in a post-war letter to Lord Winster, 'although it would not be true that we pushed him into it.'[18] As early as 5 July Spears, at Ismay's behest, had asked de Gaulle for his reaction to an attack on Dakar by Free French forces and the General had approved the idea but was worried about landing with only a few men. 'He did not say so,' Spears wrote, 'but French people always have in mind the ridiculous figure cut by Napoleon III at Boulogne', where the future Emperor had been arrested in 1840 after a feeble attempt at invasion.[19] Spears, Morton and de Gaulle, pushed by Churchill, worked out the details, in conjunction with the Chiefs of Staff and the Joint Planning Sub-committee, who viewed with suspicion these intimates of the Prime Minister from outside the service hierarchy.

Dakar was an obvious target. As a port on the route to South Africa it threatened shipping in the Atlantic; another prize was the Polish and Belgian gold which had been diverted there when bound by sea for Canada. But Dakar was well defended and the *Richelieu*, the most heavily armed warship in the world, had taken refuge in the harbour. De Gaulle at first favoured a landing at Konakri, to the south, and an attack on Dakar from the land. Then Churchill enthused him with the idea of an approach to the port itself, where he believed a show of force would bring about an early capitulation. De Gaulle wanted to avoid Frenchmen fighting Frenchmen and hoped that a few Free French troops taken by the Royal Navy to West Africa would almost instantly succeed in rallying the French empire. The British Chiefs of Staff and the joint planners were lukewarm about the whole idea.

British commanders were appointed: Vice-Admiral Sir John Cunningham for the naval forces and Major-General Noel Irwin for the military. To Spears this joint command was a mistake, perhaps because he had wished to take charge of the expedition himself. Cunningham, a peppery, brusque man, particularly distrusted Spears and looked on him as a commissar or political figure sent by Churchill to spy on the services.

Attempts were made to put out the cover that de Gaulle and his forces were bound for Egypt. Once at Dakar, the allied force would send an emissary to the Governor inviting him to hand over the city and the colony to de Gaulle. Spears told Churchill on 26 August that they had found the ideal man: Thierry d'Argenlieu, who had left the French navy for the Carmelites but had rejoined at the start of the war. As a former monk he had 'immense prestige amongst the ardent Catholics in the French navy'.[20]

By August de Gaulle had consolidated his hold on the French who had joined his movement; Catroux, although senior in rank and years, seemed content to serve under him. The General scoffed at the notion of Weygand coming over, as Spears told Churchill on 26 August.

'General de Gaulle's reaction is that General Weygand who in his opinion takes a very personal view of events (he says at 73 one always does), feeling things are going from bad to worse, is looking for a means of avoiding complete dishonour. His plans have failed, the immensity of the mistake made is being realised in France and he is looking for a way out.' If Weygand did defect, 'his presence would be useful as a living proof of the complete failure of the policy he pursued'; yet de Gaulle 'actually thinks Weygand's most useful role is in France', where he could resist the more extreme adherents of Vichy.[21]

As for Dakar, the role envisaged by Churchill for Spears was made clear in a letter from Desmond Morton. 'For the period during which the expeditions last, your status will remain unchanged. You will continue to report to the Prime Minister in his capacity as Minister of Defence on matters within your province, but will have no jurisdiction over naval, military or air operations . . .' Spears's line to Churchill was secure. 'In carrying out your duties as liaison officer between His Majesty's government and General de Gaulle, you will have the right of direct and independent communication with His Majesty's government by telegram or despatch on matters within your province,' Morton wrote, 'but in all other matters you and your mission will act under the orders of the British naval and military commanders of the expedition . . .'[22]

'The type of men who have so far rallied to de Gaulle are magnificent,' Spears had told Churchill on 5 July.[23] They were also adventurous and spoke freely of their hopes of getting back into battle. The Inter-Service Security Board had spread the story among the French that the purpose of Operation Menace, the name given to the Dakar expedition, was to send reinforcements to the Middle East, but Colonel Hollis of the War Cabinet Offices told Spears on 25 August that 'the true destination is being freely talked about by all ranks.'

The source in this case was an officer attached to de Gaulle, a nephew of the Rothschilds, who 'stated openly that the Free French forces were earmarked for an expedition to French West Africa, where a landing would be made at Dakar. He went on to say that the expedition was due to set out about the end of August. This officer is alleged to be very free in his confidences to the opposite sex.'[24] A group of de Gaulle's men were said to have raised their glasses in a London restaurant in a toast: 'A Dakar!'[25]

May was at Aldershot with the Free French troops, acting as a general welfare officer. The first time she and Spears dined with the de Gaulles, she found the Frenchman disconcerting, for 'his face never showed the slightest change of expression as he talked. No flicker of interest lifted his hooded eyelids.' Later there were more dinner parties, usually with only two or three other guests, for Spears to introduce de Gaulle to prominent people. 'He was often biting, scathing in his criticism of England and the English,' May remembered, 'just as much or more so of France.' None of the men who had served under de Gaulle in the campaign of May and June followed him to London.

Pride seemed to be the basis of the General's character; 'his one pleasure was to hate' and 'the last thing he wanted was to be on intimate terms with anyone.' May thought that a feeling for France bound Spears and de Gaulle together: this and an acute sense of shame. When they spoke of Pétain, Weygand and Baudouin, 'B's lips would twist with the same painful bitterness and the two would look strangely alike.'[26]

A detachment of the French Foreign Legion was at Aldershot under their commander Colonel Magrin-Verneret (later to be known as Monclar) and his ADC, the tall beak-nosed Captain Koenig. Magrin-Verneret lived openly with a woman called Raymond, 'out of a brothel somewhere', and to May this warlike figure with his soft voice and snake's eyes was different to other Free French 'sweet silly officers' who were polite but would, she suspected, be useless in battle.[27] Lady Hadfield was still in her villa in the south of France even though her husband, Sir Robert, was dying in a country house near Epsom, and she could give no more money for the ambulance. Then the American–British War Relief Society produced £20,000 to secure the future of the Hadfield–Spears unit. Re-formed and re-equipped it would embark from Glasgow on 24 March 1941.

In London, Spears spent evenings with Nancy Maurice in her studio flat in Battersea. On 29 August he felt able to be open enough about his visits there to complain of the behaviour of an ARP warden who broke in to reprimand them for not observing the blackout.

The war had brought Nancy more intimately into his life. After June 1940 Spears insisted on taking her with him as his closest assistant, first into his mission to the Free French and then to the Levant. While he was away on the Dakar expedition, in West Africa or the Middle East, Nancy stayed behind as his eyes and ears in London: the only person whom he felt he could trust fully amid the suspicion and hostility shown to him as an outsider in Whitehall. Nancy was now not only his mistress but his agent, alert to plots against him or attempts to besmirch his name. All this inflated her power at the expense of May, who knew how essential her rival was to Spears's sense of personal security and to his ability to do his vital work.

Reluctantly May accepted the position, which left her even more emotionally wounded and bereft.

On 27 August the War Cabinet approved the plans for the Dakar expedition. Spears reported of de Gaulle: 'the General says Joan of Arc spilled French blood, and he is prepared to do the same.'[28]

One of the planning faults was that the British did not see the French intelligence reports, relying entirely on de Gaulle's men for details of these, and Spears remembered later the over-optimistic information passed on by them that 'the whole population of Dakar was against Vichy.'[29] The British Colonial Office emphasised the pressure that the Vichy government could exert on local officials and argued that there was no reason to believe that the Governor, Pierre Boisson, would declare for de Gaulle. Boisson, who had lost a leg in the First War, was politically on the right, naturally attracted to Vichy, and felt especially aggrieved at having been deposed as governor of the French Congo by the Free French.

The entire board of the Admiralty was against the expedition and Irwin, the Commander of the troops, had serious doubts, as did Admiral Keyes, now Director of Combined Operations. The rumours of the security leaks proliferated. De Gaulle, when buying tropical equipment at Simpson's in Piccadilly, had apparently said publicly that he was going to West Africa. At Liverpool, on the eve of departure, there were more French toasts 'A Dakar' in the Adelphi Hotel and the destination was said to be 'common talk' among French troops.[30]

To May, it was Spears's campaign: 'though de Gaulle bears the responsibility and his head is forfeit it is B's doing.' She was worried. 'The world I touch thinks of me as bravely facing all manners of dangers and horrors. Actually I have had a very good time – have led a life of luxury and great interest.' Now she faced a frightening possibility; 'I may lose B and ... I would be literally lost without him.'[31]

On 30 August Spears and de Gaulle and their staff left for Liverpool from Euston station; with them was Lieutenant John Stokes, who had answered a request from the War Office for officers with some knowledge of French. The departure time seemed to be public knowledge, and Stokes was astonished to see his father in the crowd who had come to see the force off. At Euston a case fell from a porter's barrow and burst open to reveal blue, white and red leaflets with a clear message in capital letters: 'AUX HABITANTS DE DAKAR'.[32] Yet only when they were on their way to Liverpool did Stokes himself hear the truth about their destination, although at the port even the dockers seemed aware of the force's purpose. The extraordinary aspect of all this was that Vichy appears to have had no idea of the actual target until just before the first attack, perhaps because there were so many contradictory rumours. But the obvious leaks led the British to believe that de Gaulle's men could not be trusted with secrets.

The force set out from Scapa Flow, the Clyde, Liverpool and Gibraltar: two battleships (*Barham* and *Resolution*), an aircraft carrier (*Ark Royal*), three cruisers, ten destroyers and twelve transports carrying 2,400 French and 4,270 British troops. Spears and de Gaulle were in the Dutch liner, the 16,000-ton *Westernland*: the commanders, Irwin and Cunningham, in the cruiser *Devonshire*, which sailed from the Clyde to join the Liverpool section of the convoy north of Ireland. The commanders wanted de Gaulle on the *Devonshire*, but he refused to join them, saying he would not direct French operations from a British ship.

On the eve of sailing, Spears looked back on the time since the fall of France. De Gaulle, he thought, had been magnificent and the British seemed at last to be approaching him in the right way. He liked the Frenchman and believed he had reached beyond the shyness to a sympathy that could suddenly be revealed in a look of kindness in those often obscured eyes. He recalled with pride his own work on behalf of the Free French. 'Day in, day out I have fought through the trammels of departments and fiercely torn down the network of prejudice, hesitation and procrastination.' He had made, someone told him, sixty enemies a day. Then he thought of defeated France, of his grandmother's grave at Voutenay which he might never see again and how de Gaulle's movement had revived his faith in his second country. On the journey he found again among the French some of the camaraderie that had transformed his life in the First World War. A French airman quoted from Marcel Pagnol's *Marius* in perfect Marseillais and even de Gaulle laughed, often at schoolboy jokes, repeatedly smacking the palm of one hand with the fist of the other in momentary delight.[33]

But the British were uncertain of their allies. 'The French mostly looked very unprepossessing – very poor specimens of manhood,' John Stokes told his wife, 'but when they talk all that changes. They are delightful, naturally the crème de la crème of France, otherwise they would not be doing what they are.' The men of the Foreign Legion were rumoured to have decapitated their prisoners at Narvik; often there were fights with knives, Spears once tripping over a corpse outside his cabin. Twelve women were on board and Stokes remarked that the only two 'presentable looking' ones were surrounded by the French.[34]

During the daytime Spears and de Gaulle sat on two armchairs on a part of the deck of the *Westernland* set aside for them. The General spoke of his family: the second oldest in Paris, he said. After the war he would leave public life and live in the country; to this Spears declared: 'No, mon Général, you have condemned yourself to a life sentence from which there is no reprieve.'[35] Sometimes they sat in silence, de Gaulle thrusting his hands into the wide sleeves of his tunic in the manner of a monk. Spears thought: 'there is much timidity in him, overcome by will.'[36]

Occasionally the Frenchman told stories against himself, once of the time when he had caused a stampede of terrified horses during a review at Metz by mistakenly ordering his men to start the engines of their tanks. For hours he would look at maps, then try out a plan on Spears, one idea being a raid on occupied France by small groups of light armoured cars which might capture Pétain's government at Vichy and then race to a rendezvous with submarines and other craft at points on the coast. He did not hesitate to turn down Spears's advice. 'On purely personal matters,' he said, 'I like doing things my way.'[37]

News came that the Roman Catholic authorities in West Africa had urged support for Pétain. Then on Friday, 13 September at 5 p.m. the BBC Empire News announced that a powerful Vichy squadron of six modern warships, fast and well armed, was on its way to West Africa. These ships had left Toulon on the 9th, given the Royal Navy the slip and reached the Atlantic. Their aim was to prevent colonial Free French successes. At that stage Vichy did not know of the destination of the Dakar expedition.

Spears and de Gaulle were horrified. It would be fatal, Spears noted, 'if they arrive at Dakar before we do'.[38] At 7.05 p.m. they asked to see Cunningham, who answered that he would talk to them on arrival at Freetown in Sierra Leone. They thought this too late, wanting to impress upon the Admiral the need for every available ship to be used to stop the Vichy force reaching Dakar or, if it was already there, leaving Dakar for other ports in West Africa. Shortly after midnight, Cunningham heard from the Admiralty that the French warships had left Casablanca and he should do his utmost to stop them, even using the *Ark Royal* if necessary. He signalled the *Westernland* and at 1.00 a.m. the Admiral's barge came across in the brilliant moonlight.

Irwin and Cunningham went below to the Dutch Captain's cabin where, cradling glasses of warm whisky, they talked intensely for twenty minutes with Spears and de Gaulle. Speed was vital; 'alas that so many precious hours had been lost since General de Gaulle and General Spears had first drawn the Admiral's attention to the importance of this situation.'[39] It was agreed that Cunningham should set off with a detachment of his fastest ships in search of the Vichy cruisers. At Spears's suggestion Captain Thierry d'Argenlieu accompanied him with a personal letter from de Gaulle. The rest of the force sailed on to Freetown, de Gaulle observing dryly that Friday the 13th is always a day to beware of.

On 14 September the *Westernland* arrived at Freetown. The next day Spears was given a signal which stated that three of the French warships had reached Dakar without being stopped and that Cunningham's forces would be in Freetown on the 16th. 'The intention is that the whole force should sail early on the 17th.'[40]

On 16 September the Admiralty sent a cable to say that the presence of the French warships at Dakar made Operation Menace impracticable and de Gaulle and his force should land at Duala to consolidate the Cameroons, Equatorial Africa and Chad and extend influence to Libreville. Meanwhile the British should remain at Freetown. It was feared that the warships must have brought reinforcements for Dakar. Winston Churchill, won over, wrote later: 'I had no doubt whatever that the enterprise should be abandoned.'[41]

Spears's response was to send a telegram in his most pugnacious style direct to Churchill. 'If changes in policy are often puzzling in London they are heartbreaking here,' he began. Surely the French ships 'now lying helplessly in harbour under awnings' could be dealt with by bold naval action. If de Gaulle was seen to agree to 'vegetate at Duala his power to rally any other part French Empire is gone for ever'; and if the fleet left de Gaulle behind, 'the accusation of having abandoned him to his fate will swing French opinion totally against us in France as well as in Africa.' The strategic importance of Dakar meant that every effort should be made to take it. Vichy forces 'even more hostile under enemy influence will threaten our repeat our colonies. Freetown, where over 60 ships now lying, is under an hours flight from important French aerodrome at Conakry ...' De Gaulle agreed. 'I wish to insist to you personally and formally that the plan for the reconstitution of French Africa through Dakar should be upheld and carried out,' he told Churchill.[42]

Cunningham arrived at Freetown on 17 September and the meeting between the Admiral, Irwin, de Gaulle and Spears on the *Westernland* was tense. De Gaulle was determined to go ahead with the operation and Spears showed Cunningham his own signal to Churchill. Spears's diary describes de Gaulle going 'right into his shell'.[43] There was further disturbing news that the French cargo ship *Poitiers* had set herself on fire rather than surrender to the British cruiser *Cumberland*.

De Gaulle said that he had not suggested Operation Menace. 'It was decided by the Chiefs-of-Staff and by the British government. He then accepted it. Since then the only new fact that had arisen is the reinforcement of Dakar by three ships.' If the expedition was called off he would take a strong line. 'There is therefore only one thing for him to do and that is to take his force and ships to French territory and try as best he can to carry on alone without anticipating any further help from the British government.' Cunningham said sharply that the withdrawal of General de Gaulle to Duala 'was in fact one of that government's suggestions'.[44]

Eventually Cunningham and Irwin supported the pleas of Spears and de Gaulle. On 18 September they all had dinner together on the *Devonshire*, the evening spoilt by a row about the omission of de Gaulle's name from the orders, which mentioned only that Irwin and Cunningham were in command. Spears backed de Gaulle; at one stage the obstinate Cunningham said that 'the expedition might sail for Dakar without French contingent' and Spears suggested the discussion should be adjourned until the next day. 'So we left,' Spears noted, 'de G naturally deeply resentful – and this is fate of liaison officer always – not too keen on me though I had fought his case harder than he had.' The next day Cunningham climbed down gracefully and left out the offending paragraph, coming across to the *Westernland* to tell them. De Gaulle, armed with optimistic reports from his emissaries, was convinced that the people and soldiers of Dakar, but not the sailors, would rally to him.[45]

On the 18th a signal had come from the Admiralty giving the commanders on the spot the choice of going on with the operation or not. Later Churchill, to Spears's delight, wrote: 'it was very rare at this stage of the war for commanders on the spot to press for audacious courses. Usually the pressure to run risks came from home.'[46]

The attempt to take Dakar began on 23 September in thick fog. On the *Westernland* Spears and de Gaulle tried to interpret the signs of battle. Two Free French aeroplanes sent to seize the airfield were captured with their crews, and d'Argenlieu's mission to ask for the surrender of the town failed, the ex-monk barely escaping with his life. British naval aircraft were fired upon, some falling into the sea. De Gaulle broadcast at intervals to the city and John Stokes thought that his message, in which the bribe of more food was combined with the threat of bombardment by fifteen-inch guns, must have been deeply insulting to the defenders, who could not see the powerful force through the fog. Suddenly the shore batteries opened fire, to be answered by the overwhelming noise of the guns of the British fleet.

Spears felt powerless, claustrophobic in the confined space of the bridge of the *Westernland*. He had wanted to take part in the shore landing at Rufisque; then gunfire from the west showed that this was being opposed, not, apparently, with great force, but de Gaulle's untrained Fusiliers Marins were driven back by a small contingent of defenders and the commanders cancelled the main landing. The fog-shrouded *Westernland* was dangerously close to the shore, only some two miles from Rufisque, and Major Watson, Spears's personal assistant, ran on to the bridge to report that two fast Vichy cruisers had broken out of Dakar and might threaten them and the troops packed on the ship. In a rare occurrence, de Gaulle consulted Spears, who said they should turn away from the shore as soon as possible. That evening de Gaulle said that he intended to assume responsibility for having broken off the action. Spears said he would share it of course, and wrote later that the Frenchman's 'attitude in adversity compelled admiration while rejecting sympathy'.[47]

The only course left now was the bombardment of the defences of Dakar by the British fleet. Just after 11.00 p.m. the commanders told de Gaulle that they would begin this attack when an ultimatum expired at 6.00 a.m. on 24 September. Their signal mentioned a message from Churchill which was not transmitted clearly. In fact it had ordered them to go on to the end and 'stop at nothing'. De Gaulle asked Cunningham to make it plain to the Dakar authorities that the Free French were not involved in the bombardment. The next morning, 24 September, Spears heard the crash of the firing, which lasted until about 10.00 a.m., to be resumed for a short time in the early afternoon; later it became known that the guns of the coastal batteries had been taken over by the sailors of the cruisers recently arrived at Dakar, who were particularly hostile to Britain because of the attack on the French fleet at Mers-el-Kebir. At about 3.00 p.m. the fog lifted enough for Spears and de Gaulle to see the fleet: a sight that was 'extraordinarily dramatic', the great ships of war seeming to be 'the very embodiment of what Britain stands for'. But there was a presage of disaster when a small aircraft from the battleship *Barham* crashed into the sea.[48]

A whaler was lowered from a nearby destroyer to fetch Spears and de Gaulle and bring them to the *Barham*, where Admiral Cunningham had his command post. They boarded the battleship in a heaving sea, to find an unshaven and obviously exhausted crew; on the bridge, the conference resembled 'an old Irish wake at which the participants tried to pretend the corpse is not dead'.[49] But there were no recriminations and de Gaulle repeated his wish to share the responsibility for having pulled back from Rufisque. Both the Admiral and General Irwin felt 'the greatest admiration for a man with such quiet courage and with so cool and clear a brain' who listened calmly as Cunningham explained what had happened.[50] The Vichy guns had opened fire first, the *Cumberland* had been hit on 23 September and had had to retire, and two other destroyers had been slightly damaged. On the 24th the *Barham* and the *Resolution* had engaged the *Richelieu* and possibly hit her; this proved not to be true. During the afternoon, the *Barham* had been hit four times but without serious damage. The commanders seemed to wish to break off the action. De Gaulle thought the bombardment would have antagonised the inhabitants of Dakar and agreed it was too hazardous to attempt to land troops again. He reacted with dismay to the news that the battle cruiser *Strasbourg* had reportedly just sailed from Toulon and that Gibraltar had been bombed by Vichy aeroplanes. In a sign of tension, the Frenchman smoked heavily, scattering cigarette ends and matches over the bridge.

The conference broke up at 6.00 p.m., de Gaulle having been told that he could land his troops at Bathurst in Gambia. Back on the *Westernland* he told his staff that Dakar was over, and he did not permit any questions; later he unburdened himself to Spears about the failure of his West African dream, the 'morose roughness' of the sea depressing them both. Small operations were useless now, the General felt, and Vichy was entrenched in Senegal. He must save himself from the accusation that he was fighting Frenchmen and would take his men to Egypt, to fight the Italians. Spears disagreed, doubting he could get recruits in Egypt, except from Syria. At least in West Africa he could undermine Vichy; 'here he has an embryo empire'.[51]

On 25 September came another surprise. Perhaps mindful of Churchill's wish to stop at nothing, the commanders sent a signal to the *Westernland* to say that they would not break off operations. Air reports suggested that damage to Vichy ships and land defences had been more than they had thought and now the weather was perfect. Excited again, de Gaulle and Spears sent a cable to say that the Dakar operation 'in some form' should not be abandoned.[52] But the battleship *Resolution* had been hit during the morning's action by a torpedo from a Vichy submarine and at 1.00 p.m. Churchill signalled that the engagement should be broken off unless the commanders had an overwhelming reason to go on. The defences of Dakar were still effective and Vichy air patrols appeared increasingly self-confident.

British naval forces indicated that they could no longer cover de Gaulle's troops in Bathurst, so the entire force made for Freetown. The General seemed shaken. 'He keeps harking back to taking his troops to Egypt,' Spears wrote, 'and is so hypnotised by the fear of being

Lucy Hack, née Aylmer: Spears's beloved grandmother and a stable influence during his difficult childhood. He took great pride in her link with the Anglo-Irish 'Ascendancy' family of Aylmer.

His father: Charlie Spiers, the 'commission agent' and raffish resident of Paris.

The infant Spears on his mother's knee. Capricious and unstable, she soon turned against him.

His early patron, Francis Bennett-Goldney: Mayor of Canterbury and later Member of Parliament for that city. Generous but dishonest, Goldney both helped and swindled Spears. The girl is Jessie Gordon, Spears's jealous first love.

(opposite page) Voutenay, the château in Burgundy where the young Spears stayed often with his Rafinesque cousins. Memories of the idyllic life there contributed to his romantic love of France.

Field Marshal Sir Henry Wilson. Spears owed his early position in Anglo-French liaison to Wilson but came to hate him.

Field Marshal Sir John French, later the 1st Earl of Ypres: an admirer of Spears's work and courage during the great retreat of 1914.

Spears as a cavalry subaltern with his bulldog, Mrs Gamp.

With Winston Churchill and a group of French officers in France in December 1915. Spears is third from the left; Churchill is in the centre, wearing a French helmet.

'Poilus' on the western front. Spears greatly admired French soldiers' bravery and powers of endurance during the First World War.

At Calais in June 1917 with Paul Painlevé, the French Minister of War. Painlevé is in civilian clothes, looking at the camera; Spears is third from the left.

(opposite page) Spears in the garden of the rue Monsieur, Mary Borden's house in Paris, at the time of their marriage in early 1918.

Mary, or May, Borden, in her nursing uniform in 1915.

May greeting distinguished visitors to her Field Hospital on the Western Front.

Spears, the young politician, and May, the successful novelist,
with Michael, their son, and her three daughters by her first marriage.
The house is the haunted Bisham Abbey which they took in 1926.

The rivals: Nancy
Maurice, on the left,
and May, on the right,
in the early 1920s.

The Francophile Spears leading a group of British
members of parliament past the tomb of the unknown
soldier at the Arc de Triomphe in Paris during the 1930s.

May outside St Michael's Grange, the house near Bracknell
in Berkshire that they bought in 1933. Spears changed the
name from the more prosaic The Old Gables.

Yvonne de Lestrange. A great heiress, scientist at the Pasteur Institute, friend of André Gide and cousin of Antoine de Saint-Exupéry, she championed Spears and his books in France.

Spears visiting May and her unit and the local commander General Réquin at St Jean-Le-Bassel in 1940, before the fall of France. He is on the right, next to Réquin; May is fourth from the right.

Having lunch with General de Gaulle in London
1940, soon after the flight from Bordeaux.

De Gaulle and Spears on board the *Westernland*
during the disastrous attempt to take Dakar in
September 1940.

Handshake of humiliation. Pétain with Hitler at Montoire in October 1940.

May with Rosie Forbes in the desert in front of the tents of the mobile ambulance unit.

Churchill, Spears's
protector, talking to
Air Chief Marshal
Sir Sholto Douglas
at Cairo in 1943.
Spears is behind
and in the centre.

May beside one of the
jeeps of her mobile unit.

Madame Catroux's photograph, gracefully
inscribed for May. In fact they loathed each other.

Spears with General Catroux, his
French adversary in the Levant.
A characteristic pose.

In Beirut: a scene of unusual calm and apparent unanimity.
From left to right: Gilbert Mackereth, Spears, Tony Lambert,
Nancy Maurice, John Stokes.

At ease with Lebanese politicians.

The usual royal progress at the Ashanti mine. Spears is seated on the train on the right with May behind him.

Tiny Rowland, Ashanti's predator.

Nancy about to become
the second Lady Spears.

Spears: a late photograph.

accused of attacking Frenchmen that it is entirely vitiating his judgement. I told him he knew the risk before he started and must not give London the impression of vacillation. He answers that he never envisaged a pitched battle which is true, but that is only half the truth. He is brave, but is more of a gambler than a resolute man it turns out. For the moment he cannot see his way.' Then Spears thought of himself. 'I am sad to think of this flat failure and that I pressed for the expedition. I imagine what will be said concerning my telegram from Freetown urging action.'[53]

They arrived in Freetown on the 27th. Two days later the *Barham* came in towing the holed *Resolution*, and the great, damaged ship struck through to Spears's heart, 'for this helpless giant was one of England's hopes, and its plight was more shattering than any human loss could have been'.[54]

The men crowded into the bars and dance halls of the city built on the edge of malarial swamps, which would give the disease to so many of them. On the French sloops the anti-aircraft guns fired at Vichy aeroplanes in a way that was almost sporting, but the British colonial authorities showed an altogether less effective attitude, finding it convenient to appease Pétain's officials from the adjoining French possessions with whom they had worked contentedly before the war.

Spears looked back at the failure, overcome by melancholy. He wondered if any Frenchman was worth anything, then remembered the bravery of certain individuals. Perhaps some accommodation with Vichy had to come, if only to protect the British route to the Cape. Certainly the position of a France that collaborated with the Germans was terrible and shaming: the worst ever perhaps of any great power. His hope that some of his belief in her could be resurrected had been shattered by the refusal of Dakar to rally to the Free French; now his own reputation must suffer, for the British would probably abandon de Gaulle.[55]

'The days that followed were cruel for me,' the General wrote, recalling the 'long face' of Spears as they spoke of reported defections in London, then the efforts of the Englishman, 'his serenity somewhat restored', to encourage him by quoting Victor Hugo: 'le lendemain, Aymeri prit la ville.'[56] Spears knew that his future was irrevocably bound up with this awkward man, for whom he had fought the political and military establishments. But Dakar seemed to have changed de Gaulle, taking him beyond anyone's reach. Spears later denied that the General had contemplated suicide but observed how at Freetown, and later at Duala and Victoria, he became remote and cold: more like a potentate. De Gaulle seemed to be slipping from his grasp. The next

two months in West Africa, when he tried to help the General's efforts
to rally the French empire, were to be a time of difficulty and frustration,
exacerbated by the unhealthy, debilitating climate.

Others had no doubt where the blame for Dakar lay. In November
Anthony Eden spoke about Operation Menace to Miles Lampson, the
British High Commissioner in Cairo. Afterwards Lampson wrote in his
diary: 'as I suspected, Dakar was entirely Winston's doing just as in
the past the Dardanelles was.'[57]

14

Towards the Levant

In London, May endured the bombing. 'I don't think I am frightened,' she wrote on 17 September. 'The fatalistic idea seems to work well.' Biddy Carlisle abandoned her house in Chelsea. 'The tendency of the well-to-do is to scatter for safety,' May noted. 'But the poor huddle together.' 'Matelot' Fletcher repeated Lloyd George's view that Winston Churchill was not a lucky man.[1]

She had an astonishing visit from a Mademoiselle Nicolle, over from Paris, apparently with the consent of Vichy and with a permit from the Foreign Office to try to persuade Churchill to allow food ships from the United States into France. Mademoiselle Nicolle declared that she wanted to organise a section of French girls to work for de Gaulle and would see these on monthly trips from Paris, even though Vichy had condemned the Free French leader to death. The French disarray and frivolity infuriated May: 'Gen: de Gaulle's show is a game worth playing but his men are worth nothing.'[2]

After the failure of Dakar, she went to the headquarters of the Spears Mission, where Nancy Maurice and Somerville Smith, a member of the staff, said that they were not allowed to answer Spears's request for Whitehall's reaction. 'I saw suddenly that B might be sticking to de Gaulle,' May thought, 'urging him on, launching himself on a further hopeless quest without knowing how de Gaulle is already discredited.' They drafted a telegram, she tolerating the inclusion of Nancy's name alongside Michael's and her own to show the seriousness of the message: 'Nancy, Peti and I well but don't like reaction to Dakar and feel strongly that you personally should come back and get the facts.'[3] The Intelligence Committee forbade its despatch; May suspected that some people at the mission did not want Spears back, for old enemies were stirring. Lord Bessborough, who as Lord Duncannon had been Henry Wilson's devoted staff officer in the First War before serving as governor-general of Canada in the 1930s, had involved himself in French affairs and detested Spears.

On 5 October May heard that a redrafted version of the telegram would in fact be sent and should reach Spears three days later in Duala. At St Michael's Grange she studied a map of Africa, and Michael, home for the weekend, said: 'the socialists will have to win the war. They must defeat the German people. We can't hope to defeat the German army without America.'[4] His unexpected vehemence startled her. She then found that Nancy Maurice had not passed on a message from Spears, which was hurtful. 'NM is sensible and very loyal to him. But she is there between us – physically so placed that she gives me news of him and sends him news of me.' An American arrived from Paris with four cakes of soap. 'They think in France that we are starving and dirty.'[5]

On 9 October she heard from Spears that all was well and that he would return at the end of the month 'earliest'. Then came news that he was to stay out there; 'now I have such a sense of helplessness – as I have never had.' She blamed herself. 'Believing in my star I have had bad luck and carried bad luck. B and I have quarrelled – made each other wretched. Now he is gone.'[6]

Strathearn Place was hit by a bomb and there was glass everywhere and dust and scattered possessions. 'London begins to remind me of Ypres.'[7] Rain came in, soaking the stairs and the passages. She thought of the lighted candles in the dining room on the evening of Munich and Spears's eyes filled with tears for the Czechs. General Maurice told her that nothing could be made of French troops because their officers were so bad. There was however an optimistic statement by de Gaulle from the Belgian Congo: 'I wonder if B had a hand in it.'[8]

The effect of Dakar on public opinion was disastrous, particularly in France and her colonies. The press went into battle, the *Daily Mirror* declaring, 'Dakar has claims to rank with the lowest depths of imbecility to which we have yet sunk';[9] inside Germany, Ulrich von Hassell, a member of the beleaguered opposition to Hitler, despaired of British amateurism.[10] Roosevelt may have originally encouraged the plan but its failure diminished even further his opinion of de Gaulle, whom he thought had fascist tendencies. In Whitehall, some people said that Spears should be shot, Brigadier Beaumont-Nesbitt, Director of Military Intelligence, believing that he was the 'chief instigator' of an expedition 'which, at the moment, appears to have been as great a mistake as the attempt upon Norway'.[11] Lady Warwick, who worked at de Gaulle's London headquarters, described Spears as 'a born intriguer' who had been wrong to promote de Gaulle, 'too small and unknown a man to head the Free French forces'.[12] 'This may be the end of de Gaulle,' wrote John Colville, the Prime Minister's Private Secretary, and Lord

Bessborough declared that Spears's influence was 'pernicious': 'Winston has always had bad judgement.' Colville agreed: 'certainly it is true that Spears's emphatic telegrams persuaded the Cabinet to revert to the Dakar scheme after it had, on the advice of the Chiefs-of-Staff, been abandoned.'[13] On 28 September and 8 October Churchill defended Spears and de Gaulle to the House of Commons.

On 24 October Professor Louis Rougier, an envoy of Pétain, met Churchill at Downing Street, but the difficulties of dealing with Vichy were shown when the Marshal saw Hitler at Montoire on the same day. There were still hopes, discounted by de Gaulle, that Weygand might yet raise the standard in North Africa. To Spears these flirtations with a duplicitous and ugly regime were a mistake and he spoke out vigorously against them.

General de Larminat, who had helped to rally parts of West Africa for de Gaulle, tried tactfully to say how disastrous it would be for the Free French cause if the movement were seen to be too much under British control. Could Spears keep his mission as small as possible? Larminat believed part of the reason that the inhabitants of Dakar did not declare for de Gaulle was the obvious presence of the detested British fleet. There were messages from London about 'lack of organisation' and quarrelling among the Free French, and Desmond Morton's committee asked de Gaulle to return forthwith 'to put his house in order'.[14] Angry and frustrated, Spears worked his staff so hard that John Stokes came near to breaking point. 'Spears is utterly ruthless – great personal charm, but now I know him a most unattractive character,' Stokes told his wife. 'He is loathed by everyone ... he is completely vain, selfish and full of a politician's trickery.'[15]

While Spears remained mostly in Duala, de Gaulle flew to Fort Lamy in Chad, then to Brazzaville and Leopoldville. By 30 October Spears was dismayed by his behaviour and three days later sent a telegram to Ismay: 'I am horrified at de Gaulle's speeches and actions.'[16] At Brazzaville on 27 October de Gaulle, without telling the British, had issued a manifesto setting up a French Empire Defence Council and planned to send French troops overland to Cairo to fight against the enemy which, to Spears, would have 'ruined their material, wasted their time and risked the health of the men'. A small success came with the fall of Libreville and on 15 November de Gaulle visited the captured city though 'there was no enthusiasm for the Free French forces.'[17] The next day the Vichy Governor Masson committed suicide.

Churchill wondered if Spears and de Gaulle were on good enough terms to come back together, but on the 17th the two men left Africa for London. On the 24th Lord Lloyd, the Colonial Secretary, spoke to

Colville about the humiliation of Dakar: 'he expressed great hopes that the PM would be careful in his dealing with de Gaulle and Spears, who returned from Africa this weekend, and would at all costs not re-employ Spears.'[18]

In London Spears saw Winston Churchill in the cabinet war rooms underneath Whitehall. At first the Prime Minister was polite but distant, saying he had received the impression from de Gaulle that Spears and the Frenchman had quarrelled; Churchill seemed also to blame him for Dakar. Defending himself, Spears gave an account of the landing at Rufisque and Churchill, always the fighter, said that this should have been pressed home. 'I wish I had done what I originally intended and sent Roger Keyes in command,' the Prime Minister declared. 'He would have taken the place.' Spears admitted he had lost control of de Gaulle in West Africa by staying on at Duala to ensure the success of the attacks on Libreville and Port Gentil. 'There you were quite right,' said Churchill, more affectionate at last.[19]

One subject brought Spears and de Gaulle together: that of the futility of approaches to Vichy. In a series of coruscating memoranda, Spears attacked the idea of compromise with the Pétain regime and complained of Vichy elements operating behind the cover of the French consulate-general in London and of consulates throughout the British empire. Such people should be locked up, because 'if they are allowed loose must represent channels through which Germany can work in this country and in our colonies. To say the least they cannot be other than defeatist elements.'[20]

De Gaulle began to criticise Spears openly, telling Churchill at Chequers on 13 December that he was 'intelligent but egotistic and hampering because of his unpopularity at the War Office etc.', not adding that this unpopularity had come about partly because of Spears's efforts on his behalf. The Prime Minister declared on the same day that Dakar had been the worst of all the fiascos for which he had responsibility.[21]

Then came one of those glimpses of a more human de Gaulle. The Free French leader attended Midnight Mass on Christmas Eve at a French camp near Warfield and, as it was too late to go to Madame de Gaulle and the house they had in Shropshire, Spears asked him back to St Michael's Grange. De Gaulle looked enormous in the low-ceilinged rooms and the atmosphere was melancholy at the end of a year of defeat, but after lunch the General talked for an hour to Michael, their beloved 'Peti', and his face softened as they discussed Oxford and how Michael's friends felt about the war. When the Frenchman had left for London, the undemonstrative Michael came to

May and said: 'I would like to serve under General de Gaulle.'[22]

Such occasions were rare and Spears, weak with the fever and dysentery he had picked up in West Africa, felt sick at heart. Many of the French were now the enemy rather than representatives of a country that he loved and it seemed as if his hopes of creating an alternative to defeat had foundered on de Gaulle's obstinacy and failure to attract support. His anger rose. 'The refusal of the French to go on with the struggle in Africa was absolutely disgraceful,' he wrote, 'and the fact that none of those in power were ashamed to break their undertaking to us to carry on the war to the end together was unpardonable. The fact is they all expected us to follow them in the collapse. That we have carried on must be one of the bitterest crosses, or will be, to those responsible for the armistice.' He felt betrayed. 'The ease with which a greater part of the nation turned to detesting us can never be forgotten or forgiven. The feeling is made up of jealousy and atavistic delight.'[23]

Nineteen forty-one began badly. Documents showing that Vice-Admiral Muselier was a traitor were said to have been found, one proving a betrayal to Vichy of the plans for Dakar, and Churchill ordered his arrest, Muselier being seized in the early hours of 2 January when, so Spears later alleged, he was in bed with someone else's wife. Three days later de Gaulle handed Spears a memorandum which showed the documents to be forgeries. On the 8th the British admitted that the arrest had been a mistake and the forgers had confessed. They were men who had been introduced on British recommendation into the Free French security services, which heightened the General's suspicions. Winston Churchill apologised to de Gaulle personally.

De Gaulle neither liked nor valued Muselier except as a symbol of naval support. But, believing that the Admiral's accusers had worked with the connivance of British intelligence (though in fact their grudge against Muselier was personal), he ordered the dismissal of every British subject working for him, including the cleaners. Spears exerted all his persuasive powers and this decree was dropped.

He found himself divided between his public support for de Gaulle, hatred of Vichy and a growing mutual suspicion. Major-General John Kennedy attended one of the Ritz dinners on 21 January. 'De Gaulle and Spears never saw eye to eye,' Kennedy remembered, only slightly inaccurately. 'De Gaulle thought him too domineering to be a good liaison officer; he remarked to someone about this time, that he sometimes did not quite know who was running the Free French movement, himself or Spears.' Kennedy had to leave early and Spears walked with him to the lift. 'He remarked that de Gaulle was a very suspicious fellow, suspicious like a French peasant; that he did not know how to deal with affairs in London and needed careful handling.' To Kennedy this seemed odd; 'of the two men we had always regarded Spears as being much the more difficult.' Yet he admired his host: 'he was shrewd and intelligent, his French was perfect, and, as I wrote in my diary at the time, it was a good thing for the Foreign Office to have a few people like him who could speak to them bluntly.'[24]

De Gaulle was getting restive. Operation Marie, his plan for the Free French to capture Djibouti from Vichy, had had to be postponed and he suspected that the British wanted to build up the more emollient General Catroux in the Middle East at his expense. Now he wished to go to Africa to impose his authority on the Free French movement there, and Spears supported this. 'One of General de Gaulle's chief objects in going to Africa is to smooth things out between himself and General Catroux,' he wrote to Dill, the CIGS, 'and it is certainly in everybody's interests that this should be done.'[25]

First Spears saw Winston Churchill at Chequers. On 8 March he was among the guests there at a dinner that included de Gaulle, Menzies, the Prime Minister of Australia, and Duncan Sandys, then married to one of Churchill's daughters. They spoke of Germany and the Germans, de Gaulle saying that the French in occupied France should remain aloof: 'the Germans knew they were inferior beings and were susceptible on the point.' To Sandys's suggestion that Germany must be totally destroyed, even down to her books and libraries, to produce an illiterate generation, Spears said this would make the Germans more hardy and their conquerors effete on the fruits of victory. For Spears, Richelieu had shown the clearest understanding of the Germans by dividing them at the Diet of Ratisbon. Churchill also disagreed with Sandys; one could not have pariah nations now and Germany should be accepted into the family of Europe. As for Britain, the Prime Minister echoed the words of Spears's old schoolteacher: she was like Carthage, and the Carthaginians were vanquished because they had lost command of the sea.[26]

Churchill was warm. 'I felt close to him again, as I was 20 years ago,' Spears wrote, and 'I told him how good it was to serve and to serve someone one loved. He said how he deplored my role having been so restricted.' If France had not collapsed it would have been 'v great'. The Prime Minister said he had impressed upon de Gaulle his confidence in Spears.[27]

He left England still a sick man, having caught a chill which, exacerbated by exhaustion and the aftermath of fever, turned to pleurisy and bronchitis. There was a last, painful talk with May about Nancy Maurice and the importance to him of her loyalty and the way she could help him in London as his listening post; surely May must see this: 'it was torture' to sense 'unkindness to NM.'[28] On 14 March the flight was delayed by the weather, but eventually they reached Lagos after an 'agonising journey'.[29] It was on the 19th that May wrote to him before she left for the Middle East with her ambulance unit. He would not receive her letter until 30 December; it was, in a sense, an attempt to show what she too was doing for him.

> You cannot receive this for two months yet I can't go without writing ... I think you and I are both real fatalists about the war – I suppose because we have been through it before. But I am less completely so – for I am not about you – or the pud [one of their nicknames for Michael] and I have had a continual heartache when I carried through all these last arrangements, remembering your tired face. Dear little B, you are a great man, doing a great job. I can't bear to see you wearing yourself out – but to give every drop of your energy to this struggle – give your life – all of it every day – as you do – commands my deep admiration.

She meant to do the same with her unit: 'but think of me doing this job mostly in order to help you. I love you B – and shall be loving you day by day, at dawn and at night ...'[30] In her diary she noted: 'he was and is far from well.'[31]

From Lagos they flew to Fort Lamy and de Gaulle, apparently more amenable, talked again of the collapse of France and the British role. Sir Ronald Campbell, then the Ambassador, he thought 'v charming' but 'not up to the job and did not put his foot down enough'. Spears noted: 'he is right.'[32] At Khartoum Spears felt very ill: 'hospital was recommended but there was no time for that.'[33] De Gaulle wanted to see the Free French forces who were fighting in Eritrea and thought the British were trying to stop him; 'he is insufferable in that way,' thought Spears, whose relations with the Frenchman had briefly recovered, 'such a pity for he is such a nice man.'[34] They went to Keren, which had been recently captured from the Italians, and met the Foreign Legion Commander, Colonel Magrin-Verneret (alias Monclar), Spears recalling how the Colonel had answered a British complaint at Aldershot about unruly legionnaires by saying: 'excellent, the Legion has, I observe, been getting somewhat restive of late. I shall have two men shot tomorrow morning; an example is needed.'[35]

On 1 April they arrived in Cairo, the centre of British command for North Africa and the Middle East, to be met by General Wavell, the Commander-in-Chief; Air Marshal Longmore, the air force Commander;

members of the Free French Committee; and General Catroux, the former Governor-General of Indo-China and the most senior adherent to de Gaulle's cause. Six days earlier Catroux had asked Sir Miles Lampson, the British High Commissioner in Egypt, about Spears. 'I thought one might sum him up as being an arriviste filled with ambition,' Lampson wrote in his diary. 'At the same time I had no vestige of doubt he was out to do the best thing he could for his own country and for Free France.'[36]

The dapper and urbane Catroux, from a North African background of rich colonial planters, was very different from the puritanical de Gaulle. He collected furniture and antiques and his masterful wife had told Lampson that her proconsular existence in Indo-China had made it hard for her to live in anything less than a palace. Spears saw in Catroux a polished courtier who would have been at home in the complications of renaissance intrigue; more a diplomat than a soldier, he was content to allow de Gaulle to practise the arts of overt aggression. Madame Catroux lacked such subtlety and loudly criticised de Gaulle, saying that at least her husband had no French blood on his hands. It was not surprising that Catroux had a reputation for discreet affairs with other women. Spears would not always get his way with this feline individual.

De Gaulle, backed by Spears, wished to employ a combination of economic blockade and force against the French colony of Djibouti, where the Italians had the use of the harbour, but Wavell was reluctant to add war with Vichy to his other problems. April 1941 was a bad month for the British, with Rommel's successes in North Africa, the German invasion of Yugoslavia and Greece and the overthrow of the pro-British government of Iraq by the rebel Rashid Ali. Slowly the character of the region unfolded and on 7 April Spears was with de Gaulle in Jerusalem. 'Saw Mount Carmel and thought of La Fille de Jepthe. One is bowled over by industry of Jews, who, it seems, never smile.' At Nazareth he felt overwhelmed: 'same unchanged hills Christ had so often seen and grown up amongst and if had done what felt like doing would have knelt by side of road.'[37] They met the Governor of Palestine, Sir Harold MacMichael, and through him, Wavell and Lampson Spears heard of British attitudes towards the two largest French colonies in the Middle East: the Levant States of Syria and Lebanon.

Since the collapse of France, these had been a potential threat to British security in the region. Placed under a French mandate after the First War and the break-up of the Ottoman empire, they contained strong Arab nationalist elements, with Lebanon, and its divided population of Moslems and Maronite Christians, the more quiescent of the two. The French government had felt it should go at least some way to meeting demands for self-government and in 1936 had proposed terms that the Chamber in Paris refused to ratify. The Levant had a particular place in de Gaulle's heart for he had been posted there as a young officer between the wars and knew of the regional French colonial rivalry with Britain, which controlled Palestine and Trans-Jordan. Remembering Fashoda, the General believed that the imperial ambitions of the British were still strong and often perfidiously expressed.

Mers-el-Kebir and Wavell's caution prevented a declaration of the Levant States for de Gaulle and in its place came a curiously cosy relationship between the British and Vichy. The Foreign Office opposed any idea of stirring up the Syrian independence movement, believing that obvious connivance at the destruction of the French empire would arouse an even greater hatred for Britain in France.

In August 1940 this changed with the arrival of an Italian-controlled commission in Beirut and the decision, exemplified by Dakar, to take a more aggressive attitude to Vichy. But in September an abortive Gaullist coup in the Levant failed and the news of the disaster of Dakar dampened enthusiasm for more action. The British imposed an economic blockade but ships went between France and the Levant, London having the word of the French High Commissioner that they were merely repatriating troops. In fact these often carried not only goods for trade and supply but captured supporters of the Free French being sent back to prison. In December 1940 General Dentz arrived in Beirut to take the post of military commander and high commissioner in the Levant. Utterly loyal to Pétain, he detested de Gaulle and the Free French.

Both de Gaulle and Spears had fought for a stronger policy, objecting to the lax attitude to shipping, Spears calling in January 1941, against the advice of the Foreign Office, for action against the SS *Providence*, which was later found to be carrying not only Free French supporters in chains but aircraft parts as well. The German threat loomed with the visit of the diplomat Otto von Hentig to the region in January 1941; among the people he spoke to were representatives of the Jewish Stern gang who wanted to enlist his support in getting the British out of Palestine. But by March the British had decided to renegotiate the blockade because it was said to be causing too much pain in Syria and Lebanon.

In Egypt, at Alexandria, Spears himself saw the lax way in which the captured Vichy Admiral Godfroy and his sailors were treated while his ship was held in the port. 'As far as I was concerned the French sailors were just enemies since they behaved as such, printing and surreptitiously circulating pamphlets attacking de Gaulle and ourselves and creating a dangerous element of dissatisfaction among the mixed, uncertain population of the great port.'[38]

De Gaulle believed that his own movement would be strengthened by Syria and Lebanon, and Spears saw the Vichy threat to the British forces. The Levant had been 'England's Achilles heel for centuries',[39] Napoleon saying that the failure of the French to take Acre on the Syrian coast had wrecked his ambitions because the Middle East bisected the world. Now there were the additional prizes of the Suez Canal and oil from Persia and Iraq through the pipeline to Haifa. If the Germans controlled the Levant States, Egypt and Cyprus would come within easy range of air attack. Links with India and the Far East would be threatened.

On 15 April, the day before Spears and de Gaulle left again for West Africa, there was a conference on Syria at the embassy in Cairo. Catroux opened badly by saying, in response to Lampson's request for a French plan, that two British divisions, one of them mechanised, and the small Free French contingent should mass in Palestine on the Syrian border and then march into the Vichy-controlled territory.

Obviously this demand was impossible. The British could not spare two divisions, and an unprovoked attack with British troops would allow Dentz to rally the territory against foreign invasion. De Gaulle showed anger and Spears called for a tightening of the blockade and threats of intervention if Dentz took steps hostile to the allies. Air Marshal Longmore pointed out the danger of German planes landing at airfields in Syria on their way to supply Rashid Ali in Iraq with equipment or troops. De Gaulle thought it would be a sign of weakness at that moment for the Free French to support a declaration in favour of the independence of Lebanon and Syria in an attempt to win over the Arabs. He wanted to concentrate Free French troops in Northern Palestine.

Wavell was reluctant. 'If de Gaulle's people do anything, it must be a success,' he said to Spears afterwards, showing that he had little faith in the Free French.[40] De Gaulle, annoyed by Catroux's foolish suggestion, thought of sending him to the United States with a promise that he would be appointed high commissioner in the Levant if Syria and Lebanon rallied to the Free French.

Spears hated Cairo. He developed dysentery again and at Shepheards Hotel, where he stayed, the noise was terrible: trams, a shrieking cinema near by, bands playing till all hours. He worked to establish a branch of his mission but found the administration chaotic and was relieved to leave for West Africa with de Gaulle. Catroux came with them as far as Khartoum, hoping perhaps to atone for his mistakes. In West Africa Spears admired the well-planned French towns: 'the exact opposite of the sordid agglomerations the British allowed to grow up in their colonies'.[41] But the venality of some of the settlers shocked him; they did not seem to mind what government France had as long as they made money.

There were several revealing incidents. At Stanleyville airport in the Belgian Congo a shabby line of soldiers presented arms to the car in which de Gaulle and Spears were sitting and Courcel, the ADC, leant forward to point out the mark of respect, at which his master snapped: 'I forbid you to make a remark of that kind to me again. If I did not return the salute of those men, it is that I do not wish to do so. As an old soldier I see everything.' To Spears it was typical. 'This was part of his method – to freeze even his most devoted followers to a distance from which no sign could be made, no advice given, no suggestion offered.'[42] At Fort Lamy the General flared up at British attempts to dominate him. He would, he told Spears, close the airport, an essential air-link on the route from Nigeria to the Sudan and Egypt, to British planes, thus forcing them to take the detour around the Cape. Spears threatened to fly in troops and de Gaulle backed down.

On 3 May Spears was back in Cairo without de Gaulle but with the General's plan for a Syrian campaign which relied on huge British support, though leaving all the fighting to the small Free French forces. Spears wanted French participation, knowing also that the British would have to intervene in Syria: 'the sooner the better'.[43]

Cairo was better this time. He stayed at the embassy and lost no time in trying to impress Lampson. 'He told us all the latest gup from home,' the Ambassador wrote in his diary, 'a lot about Winston who was one of his great friends and to whom he has direct access.'[44]

British morale was low and the Prime Minister's son Randolph let off a broadside against the army at an embassy dinner on 6 May, saying it was not fighting as well as the air force, the navy or the Germans. 'He contends officers should be told exactly the point at which surrender is permissible,' Spears wrote in his diary. 'There may be something to it. We rely too much on people knowing by instinct. This may have been true in the past. With a wider basis to army more definite rules probably required. He said the first to surrender of the desert brigade was the brigadier. Hope not true. Says people not prepared to get killed.'[45]

Then at 10.30 May walked in, 'looking v well' but astonished to see her husband.

Her journey had begun on 21 March in the Clyde on the SS *Otranto*, with her British girls and the French commander Durbach. They sailed south to the Azores, down the west coast of Africa to Freetown, where she heard of German advances in Libya, Greece and Yugoslavia, 'the legend of German invincibility'; then the fall of Salonika: 'faced possibility last night of never getting home or seeing B again. And I started all this because I was convinced he didn't want me at home and would be glad to have me out of the way.' She felt guilty about leaving Michael, recalling also that Spears had not wanted her to go: 'it is wrong to have left them. A bad thing – done because of misunderstanding.'[46]

They went round the Cape and reached Durban, where the Coldstream and Scots Guards ('such nice boys. Charming to me') did an unimpressive march-past: 'I feel the Germans would have done it better.' There were 3,000 troops on board; 'what a stunted, flabby, ill-formed lot they are. Very disquieting to think this 3,000 is an average group of Britishers. As for the officers.' Then there were the French. 'What worried me most is the feebleness of Durbach and the FFF in general.' They landed at Suez on 2 May and she went to Cairo for two days to join Spears; 'B so very sweet. Wonderful to be looked after by a maid. It was all like a dream.' Then she called on Madame Catroux, whom she found 'even worse and more dangerous than I had expected'.[47]

Now there were terrible ructions. Wavell was reluctant to take action, even in Iraq against Rashid Ali, but Spears urged a show of force and the Chiefs of Staff agreed with him. On 2 May the RAF bombed the rebels and a British force assembled in Palestine to attack overland; on the 11th Spears had one of the most unpleasant interviews of his life, with Major-General Arthur Smith, Wavell's chief of staff, about his messages to Churchill criticising Wavell.

A furious Smith accused Spears of disloyalty, to which Spears answered that he was not responsible to Wavell and 'the only judge of my actions was the PM.' But Smith 'would he said tell me quite frankly I am viewed with extreme distrust, it was so wherever I went. All were unanimous: when will that fellow Spears go. As all thought alike I must be to blame'; to which Spears answered that he knew everyone at Middle East headquarters disagreed with him. 'I felt hit below the belt but happily kept confidence in myself.' He defended his record. 'When for instance I had kept the PM's friendship and confidence for over twenty five years it was just silly talk. My record of public service was second to none.' What Wavell and the other commanders detested, of course, was his direct access to Winston Churchill and the way the Prime Minister seemed almost always to heed what Spears said. Here, in their midst, was an outsider, probably a spy.

Then Wavell walked in and the atmosphere improved. 'He certainly exudes friendliness and frankness and there is little wonder that he is so much liked. When he is grumpy it is quite another matter.' Spears remembered what a member of his mission had told him: 'they are all terrified when they see me turn up as I represent something different.' The row had been painful: 'a severe moral strain but stood it without being downed'.[48]

On 13 May came the news that German planes were landing at Syrian airfields as part of an operation to support Rashid Ali. Vichy told Dentz to allow this and to attack any British incursions. Soon afterwards the British bombed the airfields and on the 21st the British war cabinet decided to invade Syria against Wavell's advice.

On the 15th Spears had visited May at a British field hospital in Palestine, where she was in bed with a bad boil on her shoulder. 'Felt dreadfully sorry,' he wrote. 'It was her birthday.'[49] Then he went to Jerusalem to see Catroux and the British General 'Jumbo' Wilson. An embittered French doctor had turned on May and said 'they had no need of my hospital.'[50] She told Spears, who spoke to Catroux and the matter was resolved. Madame Catroux was not so easy. 'I find it intolerable', she said, 'that English nurses should be allowed to nurse our dear wounded.'[51]

Spears suggested to London that to get local support for an advance into Syria the Free French and the British should give a solemn guarantee of absolute independence for the Levant States. On 20 May the Germans attacked Crete and five days later de Gaulle returned to Cairo from West Africa.

At first Spears liked 'Jumbo' Wilson, a large, jovial man with bright, small eyes who would command the expedition into Syria: 'big, frank, easy, understanding' – the opposite of Wavell, whom he had found 'full of inhibitions, wound tight like a ball of string'. After seeing May again he was worried, finding her 'v nervy and overwrought'. She must show a calm façade: 'she should not give the unit the impression of being forever worried to death and should talk to them'.[52] She still loved him. 'I don't belong here – am not interested,' she wrote. 'B interests me – I follow him in my mind through the sky – the immense and dangerous sky.'[53]

De Gaulle erupted again, demanding that Frenchmen who joined the RAF should be treated as deserters and shot if they landed in territories controlled by him. Spears felt exasperation: 'I get v tired of his eternal suspicions and of his attitude that we are always driving some deep scheme. Then again he is a bit silly, his attitude that FR is a great nation fighting G. He must keep up his own illusion I suppose.'[54] At the end of the month Rashid Ali's revolt collapsed.

Now Churchill hurt him. A message came that Spears's telegrams to London should go henceforth not direct to the Prime Minister but through the War Office. So Wavell had won his point. 'Want to throw in sponge. I see things more clearly here than anyone what is going on and all I can do is to influence this person or that generating hatred as I do. If I can't get the direct responsibility that suits me in this job or that wd be better off in parlt and looking after business.'[55] But he stayed.

The invasion force was ready. De Gaulle agreed to Churchill's request not to call Catroux high commissioner for Syria, a title given to the French representative under the mandate, and chose the names delegate-general and plenipotentiary instead. On 8 June at 2.00 a.m., British, Australian and Free French forces crossed into Syria and Lebanon. The same day Catroux issued his declaration of Syrian and Lebanese independence with a separate British endorsement and denial of any territorial ambitions in the area. It was this that foreshadowed the end of French rule in the Levant.

The invasion force consisted of 30,000 men: a mixture of Indian Army, British, Australian and Free French units and the Trans-Jordanian Frontier Force. It faced a Vichy army of 35,000–40,000 regular and native troops. The British naval blockade would stop any reinforcements or supplies, and Spears and de Gaulle hoped for only a token resistance from Dentz.

But Operation Exporter was a nasty campaign. The Free French Forces under General Legentilhomme met strong opposition and detachments of the Foreign Legion fought viciously against each other. Dentz called for German help, but even Vichy baulked at this, although the Luftwaffe attacked British warships off the Lebanese coast and the harbour at Haifa in Northern Palestine. The Germans, however, were preoccupied with their invasion of the Soviet Union, which began on 22 June.

The Vichy authorities were surprised at how hard their men fought, and Spears detested this new aspect of the France he had loved: 'that strange class of Frenchman who had developed a vigour in defeat which had not been apparent when they were defending their country'.

The defenders' tanks outnumbered Wilson's force and the Vichy officers shouted: 'the Germans will be along soon.'[56]

May moved up to the front line with her unit: an odd mixture of British nurses and drivers, Quaker assistants and French doctors and surgeons. She took in Vichy and Free French wounded, had difficulty in stopping them from murdering each other, and Spears again had to sort out a row with her French doctors; 'it is frightful to think of these FR, who would not be here but for her, behaving thus. They all hate us.' The ugly, badly planned campaign depressed him, reviving feelings of resentment; 'I want to have the opportunity of telling Winston I am fed up, working v hard and no thank you.'[57]

De Gaulle too was shocked by Wilson's ineptitude and told Spears he would never again place his troops under British command. 'As he says,' Spears wrote, 'one has impression there is no real command here,' with Wilson looking to Wavell and Wavell saying 'Jumbo is in charge.'[58] At least Spears felt near to the real war when he drove through beautiful stark country up to Damascus with the French General Legentilhomme, sensing a 'wild' longing for battle; 'it is after all what I have liked best in life and wd have done best.'[59] Now he was reinvigorated by this 'tiny spice of danger'.[60]

On 18 June Dentz asked for terms at last. A compromise, opposed by Spears, was worked out between de Gaulle and the commanders in Cairo, allowing the Vichy command to repatriate their personnel, as long as the Free French had a full part in the peace talks and could attempt to recruit among the Vichy troops. Lampson noted: 'I take my hat off to Louis Spears to whom I am sure we owe it that de Gaulle was so amenable in regard to our first draft.'[61]

Then there was another explosion. London sent a draft of the armistice proposals to Dentz, playing down the Free French right to take part in the talks or recruit and de Gaulle was furious. 'I don't think I will ever get on with Les Anglais,' he said. 'You are all the same, exclusively centred upon your own interests and businesses, quite insensitive to the requirements of others. Do you think I am interested in England's winning the war, I am not – I am interested only in France's victory.' Spears, who felt de Gaulle had a right to be angry, said they were the same. 'Not at all,' replied de Gaulle. This horrified the Englishman; 'even I, who know his mind and am not taken in by his occasional niceness about us, was taken aback.'[62]

On 1 July he heard that Oliver Lyttelton had been appointed Minister of State in Cairo and, as a member of the cabinet, would preside over meetings of the service chiefs and the Ambassador to give the direction Spears had felt to be lacking. An overpowering, ebullient man with a very good First War record, Lyttelton had gone into business and made money before Churchill took him into his government. An intelligent buccaneer, a gambler and a brilliant raconteur, he and Spears took to each other as fellow conspirators against the drab, the prim and the commonplace. It was Lyttelton who authorised Spears to visit Syria on 2 July.

From Jerusalem, where he heard that de Gaulle had discourteously taken off for Brazzaville without telling him, he went to Aleppo and Damascus, thrilled by the wild country. Syrian political leaders said they would have preferred a British occupation but would accept the Free French because of the British endorsement of the guarantee of independence. 'There was some affection left for France,' he noted, although their colonial officials had often been corrupt.[63] Both British and French prestige had suffered from the ineptitude of Operation Exporter, one ex-Prime Minister of Syria saying that Hitler would be in Moscow before the British were in Beirut. There were many stories of the hatred of the two French sides for each other. In the big French military hospital in Damascus, the doctors and nurses who had worked for Vichy refused to look after the Free French wounded, even when the town had been captured by the allies.

Spears joined May in Damascus, where her unit was in the old Italian hospital. Catroux asked them to the French residence, then they went to a party to celebrate the remarriage of a Druze prince and a Syrian Minister for War, the Emir Suleiman Attrache, to his Emira, a singer and beauty, once a British agent. In Jerusalem, on the way back, he heard that de Gaulle had put a French officer under house arrest for going to see Wavell off.

Cairo seemed better. Lyttelton he liked and now there was a new commander-in-chief, Auchinleck (Wavell having been moved to India), who said to Spears: 'You know as much about soldiering as anyone.' 'Feel atmosphere completely different,' he wrote in his diary, 'now Wavell gone.' Lyttelton said he wanted 'a big man' to be the British representative in the Levant States. Would Spears go? 'Said could not do that': he had too much work with de Gaulle and the Free French.[64]

On 14 July they heard of the armistice terms agreed by 'Jumbo' Wilson at Acre. To Spears these were 'quite preposterous';[65] to de Gaulle they were 'a pure and simple transference of Syria and the Lebanon to the British'.[66] The Free French were virtually ignored, although Catroux was there; all Vichy troops and equipment were handed over to the British, and Wilson and Dentz signed a secret protocol to allow the repatriation of Vichy troops to France without any contact with Gaullist recruiters. Anxious to settle matters quickly,

Wilson had gone out of his way to smooth Vichy sensibilities, and Churchill had sent Lyttelton a telegram on 12 July, favouring a rapid settlement no matter what the Free French might want. Spears told Lyttleton he thought the armistice 'so wet that cress could be grown on the paper on which it was written'. The Minister agreed and said that Spears should fly to Levant to try to modify 'these appalling documents'.[67]

In Damascus Wilson defended his work, whereas Catroux, frightened of de Gaulle, tried to deny it. Spears believed that his talks with them had changed the spirit of the secret protocol. Then on 20 July de Gaulle returned to Cairo from Brazzaville. To Spears, whom he saw that afternoon for two and a half hours, he was courteous but obviously very angry, saying he would withdraw his troops from British command in Syria. Spears felt sympathy and let him talk. 'I rather flattered myself that I had taken the edge off his spite.'[68]

This was wrong. The next day de Gaulle, with General de Larminat, called on Oliver Lyttelton, and Spears was the only other person present. What followed is justly famous. Lyttelton thought there was a touch of theatre about it, that de Gaulle was attempting to exploit the English dislike of scenes, but Spears's memory was of a man tormented by fury and injured pride: 'he looked frightful as if he had not slept for a week, he was completely intransigent and often extremely rude.'[69] He handed Lyttelton a document which declared that at 12.00 noon on 24 July the Free French troops in Syria would no longer be under British command. Lyttelton tore it up, de Gaulle let off another tirade and the meeting was adjourned until 6.00 p.m.

Spears and Lyttelton consulted Lampson, who thought Spears 'even more violently disposed against de Gaulle than the others. He even suggested deposing de Gaulle in favour of Catroux, if necessary locking him up.'[70] But at 6.00 p.m. de Gaulle was more amenable, and the outcome was the Lyttelton–de Gaulle accords, drawn up on the 25th. These owed much to Spears and allowed the Free French to take over part of the Vichy equipment and the right to rally as many Vichy forces as they could to their cause. Operational command went to the British and local territorial command to the Free French. De Gaulle set off on a tour of the Levant, both he and Lyttelton claiming victory. But for Spears disenchantment, previously near, had set in. Frankenstein was appalled by his monster.

By 25 July Spears was back in Palestine, heading for Beirut with an ADC, Lord Oxford, Henry Hopkinson of the Foreign Office and several others. At a café just inside Lebanon a party of drunken

Australian troops broke some glasses and tried to leave without paying the bill, whereupon Spears confronted them with his revolver. 'Get back and pay up,' he ordered, and the NCO in charge sheepishly obeyed.[71] Later Catroux would complain of Australian brutality; apparently a soldier had been found with two pairs of Vichy ears in his knapsack.

Spears had now agreed to be temporary head of the British mission to the newly liberated Levant States, and in Beirut he found the Free French, Vichy and the British at loggerheads. The armistice commission was headed by the British Major-General Chrystall, who appeared to have been seduced by representatives of the Vichy General de Verdilhac, cavalry officers of the old French army whom the British liked. In the countryside the Free French felt threatened by the British, particularly by the intelligence officers, whom they saw as innumerable potential 'petits Lawrences'.[72] There were particular difficulties in the Jezirah, a rich country bordering on the Euphrates, where British political officers established themselves in the aftermath of the invasion and were welcomed by the inhabitants, the Druze, who reminded Catroux how they had destroyed a French column of 3,000 troops in 1925 and wished now to join Trans-Jordan. In Soueida, the Djebel Druze capital, the British had hoisted the Union Jack and the French commander demanded, and got, its replacement by the tricolour. In the Jezirah, French-controlled police packed eighty men into a hall so small that several were suffocated. Wilson, exasperated by these quarrels, threatened to impose martial law.

Vichy's people, although supposed to have withdrawn to Tripoli, were in evidence throughout Syria and Lebanon: in the French officers' club in Damascus, in the Hôtel Normandie in Beirut and particularly in the bazaars, where they bought as much food, ornamental goods, clothes and silks as possible to take back to France as part of their very generous baggage allowance. Vichy troops still lived comfortably in barracks, while the Free French, British and Indians camped out in mosquito-infested groves. At Baalbek, the Vichy officers lounged in the Hôtel Palmyra while the Black Watch fought insects in the open country.

The chances of Spears taking a calm view of all this were lessened by his health. A Beirut doctor told him that one lung had been badly affected by pleurisy and that he had an enlarged liver with some malarial infection. The dysentery still troubled him: 'feel extremely unwell'.[73] But now, determined to impose order on the chaos, he wanted to be made the permanent head of the Levant branch of the Spears Mission. The irony was that de Gaulle had supported him for the post, perhaps because Wilson, for whom the General had no respect, seemed to dominate the scene.

De Gaulle felt that his bullying tactics were working; these had been 'very successful', he told Spears in early August, who thought Lyttelton was too accommodating to the General when the Minister came to Beirut on the 17th.[74] Then there was the ridiculous way in which the defeated forces were treated. It was soon clear that most longed to return to France, 'to their families, their houses, their pensions', while de Gaulle could offer only exile. On General de Verdilhac's departure from Beirut, two companies of Australian infantry stood to attention, a band played the Marseillaise, and the General bade an ostentatious and graceful farewell to various women whose favours he had enjoyed. Chrystall found himself moved to tears, but Catroux and the Free French were furious.

De Gaulle tried to persuade Spears to come to London with him in an attempt to get his new adversary out of the Levant, but he would not leave. The General's reaction was to order Catroux not to have any direct dealings with Wilson, to whom Spears reported; de Gaulle himself would deal with Levantine affairs in London. At Brazzaville he gave an interview to an American newspaper in which he was very critical of British planning and aims in Syria and Lebanon. Churchill, furious, considered replacing him as leader of the Free French but, after an initial explosion, they repaired their rift.

On 9 September the Prime Minister spoke to the House of Commons of British intentions:

> we have no ambitions in Syria. We do not seek to replace or supplant France or substitute British for French interests in any part of Syria ... However I must make it quite clear that our policy, to which our Free French allies have subscribed, is that Syria shall be handed back to the Syrians, who will assume at the earliest possible moment their independent sovereign rights ... There is no question of France maintaining the same position which she exercised in Syria before the war ... There must be no question, even in war-time, of a mere substitution of Free French interests for Vichy French interest.

There was, however, a sop to the French. 'I conceive that France will have special arrangements with Syria.' But 'the independence of Syria is a prime feature in our policy.'[75]

De Gaulle tried to persuade the British government to make Spears ambassador to Syria and Lebanon rather than chief of the British mission to the Free French there, hoping to entangle him in the thicket of diplomatic restrictions. Meanwhile Catroux, desperate to maintain

French influence in the administration, took on former Vichy officials without extracting an oath of loyalty to Free France. The statistics tell the story: 48 per cent of Vichy officials in the Levant chose to stay at their posts without rallying to de Gaulle; 30 per cent pledged allegiance to him, and 22 per cent returned to France.[76] Spears seized on this, proposing that Britain should take over direct control of the two countries. The British, he believed, were being fought 'at every stage with greater venom, one cannot help feeling, that either Vichy or the Germans would arouse'.[77] Churchill was disturbed and but for Lyttelton, who was in London at this time, might have taken Spears's advice.

Catroux moved slowly to give meaning to the promise of independence. He appointed Sheikh Taj al-Din, a wily reputedly pro-French politician, to be president of Syria and on 27 September issued a unilateral declaration of Syrian independence, de Gaulle informing the British that this could be only provisional for France was not yet governed by the Free French. In November 1941 he made Alfred Naccache, Dentz's choice as head of government, president of the Lebanese Republic.

In Lebanon the population was divided between Maronite Christians, who saw the French as their protectors, and Moslems; the British disliked French attempts to promote the minority Christians at the expense of the Moslem majority. In the countryside Spears's political officers soon found themselves in conflict with their French equivalents on a series of matters like tribal revolts against taxes and French suspicion of British imperial ambition. 'The truth of the matter', wrote Charles Mott-Radclyffe, Wilson's intelligence officer, 'was the traditional French jealousy of Britain, injected in large doses into the veins of all Frenchmen in the Levant ever since 1918, constituted a far stronger factor in their psychology than any loyalty to their own service or to any anti-Nazi feeling.'[78] Spears saw the country handed over more and more to the new French rule, which he feared would not resist the Germans. But the Foreign Office thought him far too alarmist; the diplomats agreed to the issuing of the proclamation of Lebanese independence on 29 November without most of the changes that the British had pressed for and they hoped other differences of opinion could be sorted out on Spears's forthcoming visit to London.

May would never forget her first journey from Damascus to Beirut, soon after the Vichy surrender. She had heard that Spears was there and on an impulse, driven by Rosie Forbes, took the road through the long sweep of the Bekaa Valley, then towards the white, distant shape of Mount Hermon, imagining how alongside the Bedouin encampments lay the grave of the prophet Elijah and the valley where Adonis was said to have died in the arms of Venus. The Levant fascinated her: 'the nights are made for love. Yet there is no time for love in this war world.'[79] Someone told her about an emira who had left her husband for a local sheikh, then poisoned him and been condemned to death by stoning. At Baalbek she found the Hôtel Palmyra reserved for Vichy officers and thought of the pride of the Romans or the Crusader castles: 'we have not such faith in ourselves or the future.'[80]

In Beirut, they settled into the old Japanese consulate, a large house reminiscent of a Venetian palazzo, with the Spears Mission's offices in the former headquarters of the colonial French commander and the Hadfield–Spears Hospital next door in what had been the General Hospital. After 'old, proud, moody and violent' Damascus with colours 'like running flames', she found Beirut 'soft, luscious as ripe fruit'. Pale Jesuit fathers or dusky Maronite bishops were not as romantic as Arab chiefs.[81]

General Catroux, high commissioner in all but name, occupied the Grand Serail, and Madame Catroux aspired to be the First Lady of Beirut and Damascus, where their residence had Louis XV furniture, cool gardens with soothing fountains and an air of French civilisation and power. Catroux seemed mournful but kind and his wife suddenly friendly, almost coquettish, when she confided that she and 'Georges' had first met in Syria. For the summer they offered Spears the house at Aley, above Beirut, which General Dentz had used as his hot-weather residence; later May found out that Madame Catroux had given this up for a larger mansion. Madame Catroux put her arm around May's shoulder. 'Georges likes your General so much,' she murmured. 'Her manner was effusive,' May recalled, 'but there was a dangerous gleam in her eye.'[82]

Catroux had the title Commandant en Chef des Armées du Levant but commanded only the Free French forces and the local 'Troupes Speciales', who had French officers. The British Ninth Army, under the overall command of 'Jumbo' Wilson, was the chief occupying force.

Madame Catroux tried to get May's unit under her control, failed and set up a rival one. The two mobile hospitals chased each other across North Africa, Italy and France in a not always friendly rivalry. 'If she outran me in the rapidity with which she moved across continents,' May remembered, 'we far outdistanced her in the number of men we looked after.'[83]

Usually at Aley they ate out on the terrace, with the mountains at sunset changing from pale pink to crimson. From here May saw the Vichy forces leaving for France: more than 35,000 officers and men went, with only 3,000 rallying to de Gaulle, mostly because they had business interests in the Levant. The rich and exotic Beirut society proved heady for some of the British, and at Madame Catroux's reception in August for the visiting de Gaulle May noticed the beautiful Druze Emira Attrache sitting with the British General Evetts 'like sweethearts'. The aristocratic Madame Sursock entertained in her garden: 'sumptuous, luscious, very well done with candles lighted in lovely Louis-Philippe abat-jours and the half moon above the trees'.

The Emira spoke freely to May. Evetts was not the only British officer to be infatuated with her; an Air Commodore Buss talked of 'their' rooms, 'their' luggage, and May thought she had made a complete fool of him. Then the Emira took off for Turkey, and Spears had her stopped at the frontier. 'Her story is pathetic,' May thought, 'in the shilling shocker style.' It seemed extraordinary that the British had paid her £300 a month as an agent and then cut this off suddenly because her job appeared to be over. A French officer joked of visiting the Emira's apartment and seeing Buss under the bed, Evetts in it and Spears suspended from the chandelier.[84]

May was glad to be with him. 'Actually it is the first time in many years and almost the first since Peti was born that I have been mistress in his house. The relief is enormous. And I think he realises that I am after all quite a useful pleasant person.' She cherished their ties: 'memory, purpose, love'.[85] But his health worried her as she played bridge in grand houses and ate the rich food, for there were no shortages among the gilded Lebanese; never happy for long to lead a sybaritic life, even as a break from work with her unit, she helped to organise clinics in the villages, petitioning 'Jumbo' Wilson for help.

On 13 December Spears set off for London. May knew that when he returned she would be with her unit in the Western Desert, for she felt this was now her duty. Nancy Maurice would come back with him. 'The gossips will say I have left him – and he too may well imagine a grievance – whereas the truth is that he neither needs me nor wants me when she is at hand. Well, we had seven months together. Such a happy time – with Miss M removed to the other side of the world. Now she comes back – presumably. That at any rate is what she and he are determined will be – and I go. So once again I have made a beautiful house for her to enjoy with him. The queerest part of it all is that he is fond of me.'[86] But there could be no denying Nancy's role or usefulness to him in this strange division of power.

In Cairo Lampson and Lyttelton wondered if Spears was the right man to be minister plenipotentiary in the Levant, for this was the post that

London had decided to create. Both felt he could not be cast aside: 'Louis has done very good work.' But he was unpopular with British military authorities, his own staff and Catroux; and Lampson had no doubt there would be 'perpetual friction'. Lyttelton said he would send Spears, who was 'a very sick man', on a full two months' leave. There was always the possibility that he would refuse the appointment; 'that, if it happened, might simplify matters a great deal.'[87]

On the way to London, he worried that the job might be a way of kicking him upstairs, for Nancy Maurice had warned that both de Gaulle and Morton wanted him out of the way; 'on the other hand someone must be accredited to the Levant States and there is no room for a Minister and the mission.' He did not like the idea of having to resign his directorships. Also 'worried about Nancy whom I need badly here and who would help and relieve me greatly – but who is the only person I can rely upon in England to inform and guide me and look after my interests'.[88]

He stopped in Lisbon and at the embassy, where Sir Ronald Campbell was now ambassador, recalled May's scathing tongue when Lady Campbell turned on her husband: 'made some v cutting remarks about the poor little man's cough'. The next day he saw another quarrelling couple. 'Marriage is really dreadful in most cases and women are worse. They score and hit because they feel safe and yet their only protection is a man's chivalry.'[89]

15

'That Charlatan Spears'

In December 1941 the war was still going badly for the British. In the desert, Auchinleck attacked in November but did not succeed in breaking Rommel's forces. In the Mediterranean the Royal Navy had suffered losses, including an aircraft carrier and a battleship. In the Far East, the Japanese threatened Malaya and Singapore and on 10 December their bombers sank two warships, the *Prince of Wales* and the *Repulse*. There were, however, two good omens: in Russia the German offensive halted near Moscow and on 7 December the Japanese attack at Pearl Harbor brought the United States into the war. But it was France that preoccupied Spears. On 27 December, he wrote of 'heartbreaking' times in Syria; 'I would not have thought it possible to see 32,000 Frenchmen electing to sail back to France rather than to fight their country's enemy.'[1]

He came to London bearing gifts of silk for Mrs Churchill and a bag for her daughter Mary. The Prime Minister once again proved to be a loyal patron. The London-based Spears Mission was replaced by a Foreign Office liaison section, but Churchill allowed Spears to stay in charge of liaison with the Free French throughout the Middle East as well as becoming the minister, with ambassadorial status, to Syria and Lebanon. Spears also kept his directorships, in a break with diplomatic practice, and effectively wrote his own instructions, which were 'to foster the independence of the republics while maintaining the Free French shop front'.[2] As chief of the mission to the Free French he would report to the Minister of State, at that time the sympathetic Oliver Lyttelton, but as minister to the Levant he reported to the Foreign Office, an arrangement that would lead to rows of titanic proportions.

Spears was open now in his dislike of de Gaulle, 'that warrior monk', and told Hugh Dalton he felt unhappy at the Foreign Office taking over his liaison work in London: 'the diplomats always stick together and find each other jobs.' Desmond Morton he condemned as 'the fifth wheel on any coach'. Michael, who had left Oxford in the hope of doing war work, was declared unfit for the army and became a temporary member of the Foreign Office staff. He came with his father to see Dalton, who thought him 'very Jewish looking'.[3]

With Spears's new position came a knighthood, a KBE, and de Gaulle sent him a congratulatory telegram. He heard that President Roosevelt, influenced by Sumner Wells and the State Department, now wanted to make up to Vichy instead of de Gaulle: potentially, as a member of Spears's London Mission observed, 'a mortal blow for the Free French movement'.[4] Spears knew how much de Gaulle's position depended upon the goodwill of Winston Churchill and therefore valued greatly the fact that he could communicate directly with the Prime Minister.

On 10 March 1942, eight days before his return to the Middle East, he wrote a letter to Churchill, to be delivered in the event of his death. It shows the emotion with which he viewed their friendship and the sense of insecurity, of unreturned affection, that often clouded his life.

What worried him was May's position if he was killed, for he had no army pension. 'When I resigned I did so in the belief that I had completed 15 years service, which would have entitled me to a pension. I discovered afterwards that having been on half pay for some time owing to a bad polo accident this disqualified me and I only received a gratuity. In the case of my death my wife and my son Michael, who is your godson, would be very badly off.' His business income, averaging £15,000 a year, would vanish and they had saved almost nothing. 'It would certainly not be possible to keep Michael at the Foreign Office where he is now unless a reasonable pension is allowed to my wife.' He looked to his old friend for help with May if the worst happened. To have been made answerable to the Foreign Office seemed a betrayal. 'It was with deep regret that I found myself working no longer directly under you. I always felt a much deeper affection for you than you perhaps realised.'[5]

His old friend Brendan Bracken, now Minister of Information, sensed his anxiety. 'I am sure Winston knows that if anything goes wrong in Syria it will be no fault of yours,' Bracken wrote on 6 March. 'No-one is better qualified than yourself to solve the thorny problem of the Levant States.'[6] On the 18th Spears left London with his new ADC, Francis Stonor, and Nancy Maurice. The aeroplane was packed with VIPs, among them the King of Greece and Stafford Cripps on his way to India. The new Envoy Extraordinary and Minister Plenipotentiary was still suffering from dysentery and often in pain.

Spears returned to a position not far short of that of a viceroy. To the

Lebanese and Syrian politicians who wished to be rid of the French, he, as representative of the British empire and personal friend of Winston Churchill, was potentially a very powerful ally; he might succeed, they said flatteringly, where T. E. Lawrence had failed and lead the rebirth of a free Arab world. The French were wary of him but he represented their paymaster: the British government.

His mission to the Levant States had grown. The different sections included military, press, propaganda, censorship, naval, economic and financial with legations in Beirut and Damascus; there were some 100 political officers in the field, almost as many as the Free French, with duties ostensibly of liaison with French and local authorities but also of intelligence gathering. It all cost approximately £300,000 a year. The Free French, faced with this evidence of British imperial weight, felt that their position as the colonial power was under threat and Spears himself deprecated the role of mere liaison. 'The word liaison should be avoided or qualified,' he told Lyttelton. 'It has only a precise sense when applied to illicit relations between the sexes. If liaison means Cupid in the sentimental world, it only denotes some sort of postman in the military one.'[7]

How did his staff look upon this new proconsul? Reactions varied, from the fury of a secretary who felt his hand up her skirt when the lights went out to an intelligence officer's respect for a man of 'utmost consideration, frankness and kindness'. What alarmed those who did not know him was his reputation. The secretary, Belinda Ruck-Keene, was told of 'quite a tiger' and the intelligence officer, Charles Mott-Radclyffe, heard about 'a tortuous intriguer and a most difficult character to deal with'. To his Arabist adviser John Hamilton, however, he was 'a brilliant man'.[8] Spears certainly had an eye for quality. An early ADC was Lord Oxford, who had taken a double first at Oxford, and the young Quintin Hogg, later Lord Hailsham, did intelligence work for him. The Foreign Office provided Dan Lascelles, a brilliant draftsman, whose speciality was politician diplomats; earlier he had gone with Stafford Cripps to the Soviet Union. Spears worked them hard, not least because of the flood of telegrams he despatched, almost always with a copy to the Prime Minister.

By March 1942 he had decided to attack the French. It was as if personal feelings of betrayal and exclusion had come together in an obsessive fury, abetted by a warrior instinct all the stronger for his subconscious sense that it had been denied by his work out of the front line in both wars. The intense disappointments of the defeat of June 1940, the failure of Dakar and the ingratitude and rudeness of de Gaulle combined to sharpen his determination not to allow the French to thwart the fulfilment of his mission to bring independence to the Levant States; in this role lay his chance of lasting achievement, even greatness.

Patrick Coghill, the new head of the British Security Mission in Beirut, was shocked by an 'evident determination to thwart, bully and browbeat' an ostensible ally 'on every possible occasion'. He found Spears both baffling and exotic. He saw a thick-set man, quite tall, with thinning hair touched with grey, a strong nose and a frightening mouth: 'a rat-trap gash'. He could not place his new master. 'Quite unaccountably my reaction was that he was a Jew – and I am not Jew conscious – it was only later that I heard the speculative gossip that his original name was Speier and that he was a Jew from Alsatia.' Coghill was awed by 'his tireless energy and drive' and his 'quite ruthless and equally unscrupulous' methods.[9]

These methods worked well in his control of the Wheat Office, or Office des Céréales Panifiables, which supervised the distribution of wheat and barley throughout Syria. Because the British Treasury paid for this, and the Syrian government of Taj al-Din baulked at French control, Spears could defeat attempts by Catroux to interfere with his decisions, which in any case were made with the backing of the British army. Hoarding was overcome, landowners released their stocks and by the end of the war Syria became not only self-supporting but an exporter of wheat and barley, with immense savings in the costs of shipping and imported foods. In addition for three years running Spears bought the entire wool clip of the area for battledress and revived the Lebanese silk industry to make parachutes.

All this made Spears seem, to Coghill, a remarkable man: 'of great gifts and power and some charm when he chose – but I never felt I could trust him'. At Aley the dinner parties of fourteen to eighteen people were beautifully done with good, simple food and the host talking easily in French or English: 'a first rate raconteur', yet often able to eat only dry toast because of his dysentery. Coghill remained perplexed: 'really a very odd man'.[10]

The two countries to which Spears was accredited were very different, not least in the sizes of their populations, Lebanon having 1,626,000 people and Syria 5,500,000. Syria was the more nationalistic and the Lebanese more attached to the French, who had, since the nineteenth century, been the traditional protectors of the Maronite Christians. In February and March of 1942 the Syrian nationalists, encouraged partly by the nationalist Wafd party's success in Egypt, held demonstrations and strikes, the position being exacerbated by food shortages. Spears, against the advice of the cautious diplomats on his staff, took up their cause and demanded a date from the French for early elections. The nationalists saw how they might exploit the rift between the British and Catroux.

The Foreign Office, conscious of the German threat in the Western Desert, did not want turmoil in the Levant as well and discouraged Spears's push for elections. But he put pressure on the two presidents, Taj al-Din in Damascus and Naccache in Beirut, whom he thought were too subservient to the French. In Cairo, the Middle East War Council supported him, as did the new Minister of State, the Australian Richard Casey, who had replaced Lyttelton.

Catroux knew that the Foreign Office was worried by Spears's undiplomatic methods, which had led to complaints from de Gaulle. But on 11 and 13 May in Cairo Spears and Casey bullied Catroux into saying that he would announce elections within six weeks. The French feared that a victory for the nationalists would make their position very difficult; both Catroux and de Gaulle believed that the British wanted this so that they could supplant France as the dominant western power in the Levant.

Catroux was saved by Rommel's startling offensive of June and July. To risk elections and unrest in the Levant at this time was obviously unwise, as even Spears admitted. In the middle of June de Gaulle spoke in London, reaffirming the French mandate. In the same month Spears and Casey came to London, where Spears told Churchill and all who would listen about 'the incredible attitude' of de Gaulle.[11]

In Beirut he and his staff drafted a note for the Foreign Minister Franjieh to send to President Naccache demanding a repudiation of de Gaulle's statement; Naccache rejected the note and the Foreign Office called it 'senseless agitation'.[12] In July Spears demanded a say in the formation of a new Lebanese cabinet to be formed after more bread riots, wanting particularly to block a notorious smuggler Ahmed al-Assad, whom Catroux looked upon with favour, and, if possible, to bring about the departure of Naccache. Catroux refused to reconsider the appointments, having broken off communications with Spears, who treated the Frenchman's two aides, Boegner and Baelen, with open contempt, pointing out that both had worked for Vichy.

The Foreign Office protested. The British envoy had apparently fallen out with both Catroux and President Naccache. Such a bellicose approach was idiotic: 'a complete negation of a diplomatic representative. It is also dangerous.'[13] Churchill defended his protégé yet sanctioned a formal rebuke. But Spears got his way and Ahmed al-Assad was kept out of the government. At the end of August Casey managed to get Spears and Catroux speaking again. The Foreign Office tried to curb the power of the mission, but Churchill's loyalty stood in the way. Spears, his former admirer the diplomat Oliver Harvey noted, 'is a hopeless misfit but he is a protégé of the PM. Any professional diplomat would have been sacked, and rightly, for a third of what he has done.'[14]

In August de Gaulle returned to the Middle East. Rommel's offensive lost its edge and the Free French fought well in the desert, particularly under Koenig at Bir-Hakim. Casey was turning against Spears's methods and there were plans to have him recalled. But then de Gaulle's hectoring manner, shown during a tour of Syria and Lebanon, made the dismissal of Spears impossible. He accused Spears and the British of plotting to gain control of the two countries and demanded their almost complete exclusion from the administration. Even Catroux was shocked, telling Lampson that de Gaulle was 'a very difficult man'.[15]

In late August Churchill came to Cairo and Spears was summoned to see him. 'Louis Spears has a great many enemies,' the Prime Minister declared at lunch, 'but he has one friend' and hit his own chest.[16] He told Spears not to report so much or send so many telegrams as these gave the Foreign Office opportunities to get at him. Spears spoke of the 63,000 tons of wheat accumulated under the wheat scheme and Churchill was obviously pleased; 'he looked as if he were the proud mother of a small daughter who has recited her piece of verse nicely.'[17] But the Prime Minister raised a report sent by the acting American Consul in Beirut, who blamed Spears for the tension with Catroux.

In fact de Gaulle's behaviour had saved him. 'If only de Gaulle had controlled himself,' Harvey noted, 'we could have got Spears out by now thanks to the complaints we have received from all sides.'[18] But some of the criticism stuck. Wendell Willkie, the American presidential candidate who was touring the Middle East, heard that Spears was 'a British imperialist of the most rigid type' who was 'trying to promote British interests in Syria to the exclusion of all else'.[19]

British diplomats wanted de Gaulle to leave the Levant. He refused to come to London at first, then capitulated when told that the plans to attack Madagascar would go forward without him. Spears was disappointed. He had hoped that de Gaulle might stay and behave so badly that Churchill would replace him with Catroux. In London on 30 September Churchill and de Gaulle had an explosive meeting. Harvey said, 'it couldn't have gone worse', the Frenchman imputing to the British the worst motives in the Levant. 'Behind all this stands

the evil influence of that charlatan Spears who has said he is out to
smash de Gaulle.'[20]

Spears saw matters differently and told Ismay of his sense of getting
no support at home: 'the peoples of the Levant and the immense
Arab populations behind only have me to express their fears and
apprehensions.' He deprecated de Gaulle.

> I think all this talk about de Gaulle's influence in France is just my eye,
> but he is such a very clever blackmailer. Such reports as I have, and on
> the French side we are not ill-informed here, is that opinion in unoccupied
> France is turning steadily against us. Our sacrifices to keep de Gaulle in
> a good temper do not seem to have paid in that area. In the occupied
> zone the only thing the people care about is getting rid of the Germans,
> and food. They do not care two hoots about Syria. It is really rather
> ridiculous to find de Gaulle making speeches about the sensitive ear
> France turns to events in the Levant when she did not react to our
> attacking the country a year ago, or to our attack on Madagascar. France
> dislikes us thoroughly I am sorry to say, but detests the Germans more.[21]

The diplomats tried to salvage a settlement and the result was a
botched compromise in which the Free French recognised Britain's
rights to be involved in political and military decisions in the Levant
and the British granted the French a formal say in the administration
of British areas of control in the Middle East. Casey objected to the
latter, as did Spears, and Catroux and de Gaulle felt the former went
too far.

In November the allies landed in North Africa, the Germans occupied
Vichy France and the Levant left the limelight. On 10 December, in a
secret session in the House of Commons, Churchill expressed his
impatience with de Gaulle. The General, he declared, was 'one of those
good Frenchmen who have a traditional antagonism engrained in
French hearts by centuries of war against the English'. The 'trail of
anglophobia' left on his Syrian visit of 1941 had been repeated in
August 1942; 'his whole object seemed to be to foment ill-will.'[22] The
Prime Minister told Spears that in hindsight, the most dangerous
moment in the war was in June 1940 when France might have
accepted his own offer of union with Britain, thus creating an inevitable
morass of mutual suspicion and dislike.

May had left Beirut in a convoy on New Year's Day 1942 and in
Cairo, on her way to the desert, Michael Knox, representative of the
Spears Mission there, said that her husband had 'more enemies than

he thinks'. She knew how he felt about the Free French: 'B is more completely disillusioned than anyone knows.'[23]

On 25 January the unit set out for Tobruk, to find the British in retreat. An angry Larminat was against the withdrawal and there were rumours that General Ritchie had been about to abandon the whole of Cyrenaica when Auchinleck stopped him.

They stayed until the middle of May in a British military hospital just outside Tobruk. May deduced from the wounded that 'the men had lost confidence in their chief';[24] a visit by the dour Auchinleck did little to raise spirits. One officer told her what was wrong with the army; 'they want to go home,' he said, 'they don't think of the Empire.'[25] Rommel was a hero, even to the British. The news of the fall of Singapore depressed her even more.

Nick Alderson, one of the Quaker conscientious objectors in the unit, was killed while sheltering from bombs in a slit trench and was buried there; his head was never found. She had thought him 'so gentle, so muddle-headed, so charming': someone 'really pursuing the good life, a life of sacrifice'. The officers seemed too callow. 'Nice young men in the mess, but I can't see them fighting the Germans and I don't think they did.'[26] Bir-Hakim, held by the French, was a terrible place for sandstorms, but the girls drove bravely between there and Tobruk. The soldiers were astounded to see such glamour near the front line. 'Am I dreaming or do I hear the voice of angels speaking?' one asked.[27]

May left for Beirut to see Spears present his credentials as minister and did not return to the desert until June, when General Koenig came into her hospital with his wounded from Bir-Hakim. None of the French criticised the British tactics to May or her nurses, whom they called 'Les Spirettes', but Koenig's stand was one of the few reasons for pride in the rout of the allies which included the fall of Tobruk, its garrison of 30,000 men (including the Guards Brigade) and a mass of stores and equipment. In Cairo, GHQ began to burn its files, expecting Rommel's victory.

The unit reached Mena camp in July on the outskirts of the city and Rommel's advance stopped at El Alamein. In Cairo May found a friend: Mae Casey, an Australian who liked painting and was married to the new Minister of State in the Middle East. They would cling together during the next year. Then she went back to Beirut, where she liked the legation's staff: John Hamilton, who complained of the depravity of the French; Robin Hutchins, head of the Military Section ('such good legs'); Hamish Mackenzie; the fastidious exacting Lascelles; 'our beautiful, languid' Tony Lambert.[28] They were loyal to Spears. She worked again to organise clinics in the countryside with Bayard and Mary Dodge of the American University and tried not to cross the formidable Madame Catroux.

When de Gaulle came on a royal progress, they were granted a chilling audience one evening at the French residence, having been excluded from the party on the same night. At a lunch May told the General about Koenig and his wounded in her hospital after Bir-Hakim and he thanked her for the information but not for what her nurses had done for the Free French. 'Neither then, nor at any time during the war,' she wrote, 'did he say anything that could be construed as a tribute to the work we had done.'[29]

May returned to her unit, where the nurses said the troops seemed quite different from last summer: much more confident under the Eighth Army's new commander, General Montgomery. A part of the unit had gone to a forward position under Vernier, its senior French medical officer. On 23 October the battle of El Alamein began and the onrush of wounded: then a victory at last. News came through of the allied landings in North Africa and the capitulation of the Vichy forces in Algiers after three days' fighting. May was in the Levant for Christmas at her husband's side.

Beirut was the easier of the two cities, for in Damascus they had no official residence at first and, for a year, had to stay in a hotel on their visits. Lebanon had a rich cosmopolitan set, many of whom were Christians, used to yearly visits to Paris, fluent in French and bored by being imprisoned by the war in their own country. Some were bankers or landowners; others made money from growing hashish and May, perhaps wrongly, included Emile Eddé, the French candidate for the Presidency, among them. Horse racing and cards, or imitating French culture and civilisation, were what they liked and May saw how easily they could be snubbed by Madame Catroux or Madame de Larminat. There were bridge parties and Arab horse races on Sundays on a track in the midst of umbrella pines with snow-covered peaks in the distance. It was an elegant, idle and self-indulgent society, content to watch while the nationalists tried to play the British off against the French. Madame Catroux urged May to be friends with her but she noticed that young French officers who became too close to the British were removed from Beirut.

She painted in the city gardens, then escaped to the mountains or the Barada river or the Arab palace of Bet el Dene, where Lamartine had once lived, or the sea, where Spears shared a boat with Robin Hutchins. Dan Lascelles came with her, slowly beginning to relax, and she found 'pure happiness' in the soft full light.[30] Not until early

February 1943 did she rejoin the unit, which by then was back at Tobruk.

Throughout the early part of 1943 the Free French were preoccupied with the rivalry between de Gaulle and General Giraud, whom the British and Americans had put in charge of French colonial North Africa. Catroux spent more time in Algiers and an acting delegate-general was appointed to look after French interests in the Levant: Jean Helleu, Vichy's former Ambassador to Turkey. Helleu, with his previous subservience to Pétain, exemplified the unfortunate history of many of the French officials in the region. He continued to rely on the advice of two other former Vichyites: Baelen and Boegner.

Spears despised Helleu, who was an alcoholic. 'He made me think', he wrote later, 'of an ant-eater because of his long nose, which, unlike that of the animal, was red at the tip, but seemed to be forever sniffing for something. His voice was plaintive and he wore a continuous simper.' Crises did not suit Helleu; 'he would disappear to a shed at the bottom of his garden armed with a large bottle of whisky.'[31] To May he seemed 'small and feeble'; his wife was correct and statuesque, obviously once good-looking but now very unhappy. 'It wasn't long', May noted, 'before Boegner held everything French, including his miserable chief, in his scrawny, prehensile, fanatically anti-British hands.'[32]

Helleu's weakness suited Spears. He told Churchill that Boegner had been found by British intelligence to be corresponding with a Vichy agent in Ankara and backed the request by Lépissier, the pro-British Secretary-General of the French Delegation, that Helleu should permanently replace Catroux, whom Lépissier thought represented the authoritarian, even potentially fascist, side of the Gaullist movement. The Levant in early 1943 was a hive of imperial and personal rivalries and intrigue. 'I am not surprised they collapsed,' Coghill wrote despairingly of the French. 'I am only surprised they ever ranked as a great power. They are selfish, short-sighted, narrow-minded, ungenerous, grasping, dishonest, provincial and quite incapable of unity except possibly against England (which they cannot forgive for not cracking) and the USA.'[33]

In February Catroux returned to the Levant to prepare for elections in Syria and Lebanon. This time Spears approved of his choice of politicians. In Beirut he replaced Naccache as president with Dr Ayub Tabet, a protestant Christian, and in Syria approached the ex-President Hashem al-Atasi, essentially a front-man for the nationalist Shukri al-Quwatli. Having received al-Atasi's promise of a return to relations with the French after the elections on the basis of the 1936 treaty, Catroux appointed a politically neutral interim government in Syria under Ata al-Ayubi. In return he had said the French would not interfere with the nationalists' election campaign. 'He has in fact been extremely responsive to my suggestions,' Spears wrote smugly to London. 'The result justifies the very hard and prolonged struggle I have had in the past.'[34]

The old tensions soon surfaced again. In Lebanon the Free French were said to be trying to block pro-British or strongly nationalist candidates and in Tripoli their preferred man was Rashid Mukaddam, whom the British arrested after he had been found smuggling drugs with the help of some bribed British officers. French complicity in the drug trade was notorious but the French were angry that the arrests left the way open for a nationalist candidate reputedly in the pay of the British. Helleu and Spears began to fall out. In June Catroux moved to Algiers to be a member of the new French Committee of National Liberation and Helleu was appointed delegate-general of Lebanon and Syria, with the elections planned for early July.

There were two sets of British views on the future of the Levant. One was held by the imperialist administrators of the area, of whom Glubb Pasha, the Commander of Trans-Jordan's Arab legion, and Harold MacMichael, the High Commissioner in Palestine, were typical. They wanted an Arab federation under British tutelage encompassing Palestine, Trans-Jordan and Syria and Lebanon. The French stood in the way of this, but their departure from the region might make it possible after the war. Casey, the British Minister in Cairo, liked the idea, as did the Middle East War Council, and of course, Spears.

Such sentiments horrified the Foreign Office, which thought in European terms of the restoration of post-war France to democracy and stability. De Gaulle had been promised predominance in the Levant. Any scheme of Arab federation merely increased French suspicions of British imperialist plots. The diplomats thought also that a precipitate French departure would create instability in the region and rob Britain of an ally against anti-colonialist pressure from the United States.

The diplomats saw Spears as a particularly disruptive influence: ruthless, sly and close to Churchill. They believed that he dominated Casey and that no agreement with France would be possible until he went. At about this time there was an extraordinary scene in Cairo at a dinner party where Spears and May were guests of honour when a drunken Randolph Churchill, the Prime Minister's son, attacked his policy in the Levant, echoing Whitehall's criticism in a display that showed his furious jealousy of his father's friend. Another guest pitched into Churchill afterwards for his rudeness to distinguished British public servants; Randolph's response was to burst into tears.[35]

At the end of June Casey and Spears came to London for talks. Spears sent off a long memorandum at the start of July, putting forward the theory that a de Gaulle–Giraud right-wing imperialist regime would be much more likely to frustrate British interests in the Middle East than a left-wing government of the Léon Blum variety, which would co-operate with the British in giving early independence to Syria and Lebanon. If the French refused full partnership in the Levant, Britain should unilaterally take over the economic and financial affairs of the two states. Winston Churchill approved. 'This is a very powerful and able paper,' he told Eden. 'I had no idea the French were behaving so tyrannically.'[36] The diplomats were furious, Oliver Harvey noting: 'Spears is here on leave, intriguing and spreading poison.'[37] Spears was equally scathing about them; after seeing Maurice Peterson, Head of the Foreign Office's Eastern Department (whom Lampson had also called 'a proven dud'), and his assistant Baxter, he wrote: 'Peterson is not at all what I had expected, big, flabby, with sunken eyes, cloaked with a hostility that will I feel never disappear. Baxter is the wettest thing I have ever come across.'[38]

Helleu's highhandedness helped Spears. At a ridiculous trial, the French acquitted the drug smuggler Mukaddam, who had been handed over to them by the British, and protected him from General Holmes, the British military commander, when Holmes demanded that he be arrested again or expelled from the area. Helleu refused to have elections in Lebanon before September and said Mukaddam should be allowed to stand. Holmes backed down. 'We are being knocked about unduly and unfairly by the French,' Churchill complained.[39] 'There is no doubt that the army commander gave in because he was doubtful of support from home.'[40] In fact Helleu had antagonised even France's closest friends in London and made the removal of Spears impossible. On his return, Spears had his way; Mukaddam withdrew as a candidate and was deported by the British to Cyprus.

Spears had been apprehensive about the London trip and found his son 'not looking too well. He has some bother with his leg. He is very untidy in his appearance.' There was bad news about SOAG, a company of which he was a director, where German refugee staff might have passed information to the enemy. On 26 June he went to Chequers, where the Prime Minister's welcome seemed cool at first but became 'much more friendly'. Churchill asked him about the Levant and they touched on Zionism, about which they did not quarrel although Spears, now a romantic arabophile, disagreed with the Prime

Minister's sympathy for this cause. The next day he went to St Michael's Grange, where Biddy Carlisle came to dinner and said that Michael was mixing with 'undesirable' people at Oxford: a bad omen.[41]

On 7 July he met Churchill and Casey in London. The Australian praised Spears's work and the Prime Minister was 'in the friendliest mood'. Then they saw Massigli, the new Free French Committee's Foreign Affairs representative, and Churchill told him the British had no designs on the Levant. Spears seemed to be in the ascendant. The Foreign Office could find no job in London that might tempt him to come home and he scorned the instructions issued to him on his departure. 'Casey and I both came to the conclusion independently that the new set of instructions were an attempt to handcuff me,' he wrote in his diary. 'They are full of loopholes anyhow.'[42]

Events in the Levant helped him. At the end of July, the nationalists had an overwhelming victory in Syria and, on his return from London, Spears brought the local Moslem and Christian leaders in Beirut together in a deal that had eluded Helleu. In the Lebanese elections, Helleu backed Eddé, a man of European culture and inclinations, against Bishara al-Khoury, who had much closer ties to the Moslem community. To the horror of the Foreign Office, these elections turned into a Franco-British contest, with Helleu doing all he could to help Eddé and Spears supporting al-Khoury. Both sides spent money freely, the French harassed al-Khoury supporters and stuffed ballot boxes and the British sent military police to stop interference at polling stations by French troops.

The results were predictably a defeat for Eddé, the only consolation for Helleu being that it was not overwhelming. Al-Khoury became president, with the nationalist Riad al-Solh prime minister, and the way seemed clear to Lebanese independence, especially as the election victors felt sure of the support of Spears and the British. Helleu had abandoned the subtleties of Catroux, and Spears gleefully followed him.

On 12 August, sickened by the recriminations and point-scoring, Coghill wrote: 'I long to be out of this atmosphere.' By October it was worse. 'Spears quite impossible,' he declared. 'I fear in his desire to thwart the French and to increase his own personal position he will encourage the native governments to ask for the earth and the moon.'[43]

It was the height of his imperial power. John Stokes, who had been at Dakar and came to be Spears's ADC in Beirut in September, observed this: the colossal Buick car with two Union Jacks, the hut at the French Bain Militaire by the Mediterranean where lunch was served by a waiter in a jacket emblazoned with the royal coat of arms; His Majesty's

Minister's exotic clothes of a white suit, dark blue shirt, yellow tie and co-respondent shoes; his habit of carrying a fly whisk. Then in the summer the tension relaxed over dinner on the terrace at Aley over-looking a precipice, with the hills outlined in the moonlight and the distant gleam of Beirut, where few Lebanese observed the blackout. At the other residences in Damascus and Beirut Spears insisted on pomp, which he thought impressed the Arabs.

He rose late, was at his desk soon after 10.30, having inspected a guard of honour, and worked until 2.00 p.m.; then, if he was in Beirut, he went to lunch and bathed at the Bain Militaire, returning to the office at 4.30 p.m. and not leaving until 8.00 p.m. or later. There followed the extensive ritual of dinner, talk afterwards and late to bed. Several people had advised John Stokes not to take the job, although others thought it would be fascinating; but the young Captain's previous dislike of his master turned to admiration, even if the General could be terrifying when presented with shoddy work.

May had come back from the desert and her appearance shocked Stokes, who compared her to one of the witches from Macbeth: dyed black hair, long and parted in the middle, large eyes shaded in brown, thick lips bright with lipstick, decaying teeth. The French joked about her being one of the famous ruins of the Lebanon; to Stokes she seemed 'a completely sexless creature'.[44] But she and Spears were affectionate to each other as they talked of writers, French poetry or their memories of the First War. She could be domineering, but the ADCs pitied her, particularly when Nancy Maurice was around. Nancy's looks had also gone; she was 'wizened' according to Stokes, although her devotion remained, and the shadow of a past romance. 'I think there must have been something once,' Stokes thought.[45] May complained to him about Nancy, of her 'hard, masterful character', the way she answered for the General and tried to keep Spears to herself. 'They hate each other,' Stokes told his wife.[46] Spears he found an absorbing mixture: the driving ruthlessness, then an immense charm away from work. This complex, vain man who quoted Musset and Flaubert was, he decided, 'by no means a typical General'.[47]

16

'The Odious Intrigues of England'

The Lebanese elections lit a fuse. On 7 October Riad al-Sohl, the new Prime Minister, addressed the Chamber of Deputies, calling for national sovereignty free of the mandate and an end to French as the official language. Crowds gathered outside the parliament building and Spears was delighted when Helleu's protests were ignored by the new government. The Foreign Office, dreading chaos in the region, thought the Lebanese were being too provocative and muttered denials of Spears to the French.

But the French were divided. Helleu, urged on by Baelen and Boegner, wished to use force to maintain French power whereas Catroux and Massigli, in Algiers, favoured a more circumspect policy. De Gaulle saw British conspiracies everywhere. Meanwhile the humiliations continued. On 8 November a French-inspired boycott of the Beirut Chamber of Deputies was supported only by Emile Eddé and one other.

On the 9th Spears was told that the French were loading bombs on to a Blenheim bomber lent to them by the British. That same day Helleu returned to Beirut from Algiers, where he had seen de Gaulle. Apparently inspired to action, he cancelled the Lebanese cabinet's invitations to the forthcoming Armistice Day parade on the 11th, whereupon President al-Khoury announced that he would boycott the ceremony, as did the diplomatic corps at the instigation of Spears.

On the 10th Spears was with Helleu at the airport in the welcoming party for the young King of Yugoslavia, and found the French Delegate 'his usual, amiable, tiddly self, without apparently a care in the world'.[1] That night King Peter, who was staying at the French residence, came to dinner with the British Minister, accompanied by Monsieur and Madame Helleu.

During the evening May looked at the agonised Madame Helleu and the glassy-eyed, bibulous Delegate. 'General de Gaulle had chosen strange people to represent him in the Levant,' she thought.[2] She remembered the joy and simplicity of Voutenay with the eccentric

Rafinesques and the sophistication of the rue Monsieur in post-war Paris; only Catroux, she decided, came near to representing this other France. It was the laughter that she missed. French colonials did not laugh; they sniggered or winked like Helleu.

The French had feelings of equal hostility. Both Catroux and Helleu believed Spears had told the Lebanese nationalists that they could rely on British support. Some of his staff shared this view. Patrick Coghill knew that the Foreign Office had told Spears to dissuade the Lebanese government from provoking the French. 'He had at least two days,' Coghill thought, 'and boasts that Riad al-Solh the Prime Minister did nothing without his advice. So I firmly believe he could have stopped them. But no. He merely quoted French history and the famous meeting of the States General in the tennis court.'[3]

After dinner Spears took Helleu into his study, confident that he would dominate the apparently insignificant diplomat. Would Helleu give him his word that there would be no precipitate French intervention? The Delegate quickly assented. 'Je vous donne ma parole d'honneur.'[4] Afterwards May saw her husband's obvious relief.

It did not last long. In the early hours of the morning of 11 November, Spears awoke to find the eldest son of President al-Khoury in his bedroom. His face covered in blood, the boy said that soldiers had entered his parents' room where his mother was ill in bed and dragged his father off, also beating the boy with the butts of their rifles, shouting, 'son of a dog, son of an Englishman.' The President had called out to him as he was carried off: 'Go to General Spears and tell him.'[5]

Spears, hearing shooting outside and the sound of aeroplanes overhead, telephoned Casey in Cairo to tell him what had happened. Then Helleu came on the radio to say that he had suspended the constitution, dissolved the Chamber of Deputies and appointed Emile Eddé to be the head of a new government.

The French had staged a coup, arresting the President, the Prime Minister and most of the cabinet. The troops, many of whom were black Senegalese, had burst into the bedrooms, roughly separating the men from their wives. But the affair had been bungled, for two ministers had fled to the mountains near Beirut and were still free.

By seven o'clock, the house was, in May's words, 'like a railway station'.[6] Deputations poured in, among them the Maronite Archbishop of Beirut, the Moslem Grand Mufti and Madame Chamoun, 'fair as a ripe wheat field in sunshine, her immense blue eyes ablaze', whose husband, the pro-British Camille Chamoun, had also been seized.[7] Senegalese soldiers and their French officers cruised the streets in lorries, firing apparently indiscriminately. Later in the day May went to call on the President's wife to show support and found that troops had killed people outside the al-Khourys' house; Madame al-Khoury, clearly terrified, moved for a night to the British residence with her children. The Lebanese looked to Spears to restore their freedom.

In Algiers, Catroux and Massigli were horrified. Helleu had revealed France to the world as brutal and, even worse, inept. The anglophobic de Gaulle was much more sympathetic and may even, during the Delegate-General's recent visit to Algiers, have encouraged Helleu to act. But it was Spears's hour.

In Beirut there was a general strike. The French tried to impose a news blackout and put up posters of de Gaulle and Stalin to assert that they had the Soviet leader's support. Spears and the American Consul George Wadsworth said they would have nothing to do with Edde; the British Minister had a group of journalists flown up from Cairo to counteract Helleu's censorship. Soon stories of French brutality featured in the world's press, but Helleu stood firm. Answering Spears's official letter of protest, he wrote of its 'discourteous' terms and how he needed no lessons in honourable behaviour.[8]

Spears asked Cairo to allow him to declare martial law and let the British take over the running of the country. Casey refused this and the Foreign Office, Peterson especially, was horrified at his request to fly the two fugitive ministers to Cairo for safety. But even the diplomats knew that the French had to be forced to back down, if only because the Helleu coup had hit at British prestige in the Middle East. Harold Macmillan, the British Minister resident in Algiers, was told to get the Lebanese politicians released and Helleu removed from Beirut.

On 12 November there was a huge demonstration in Beirut culminating in the delivery to the British residence by Madame Chamoun and Klodagh Tabet of a message for Winston Churchill asking for British help. At the American legation the women were dispersed by Senegalese troops, a curfew was set for 6.30 and tanks faced angry crowds; machine-gun fire echoed in the streets. British troops were confined to barracks. 'I shall never feel the same about the French again,' John Stokes wrote to his wife. 'They've behaved simply outrageously.' Spears he found 'magnificent'; 'the ladies this evening went wild when he addressed them.'[9] When May called on Madame Riad al-Solh, the Prime Minister's wife, French troops in lorries fired at the crowds outside and people climbed on to her car, seeking British protection. She discovered that a French officer had offered children money to throw stones at her.

On 13 November Spears heard how the French had used Bren-gun carriers to break up a demonstration in Tripoli, killing at least eleven people, seven of whom were children under eight, their bodies mutilated and unidentifiable. In Sidon too they had fired on an unarmed crowd and in Beirut ten students were wounded by French marines. On the 15th, as he was being driven back to his house at 9.15 in the evening, Spears was held up by French troops, one brandishing a revolver. Dan Lascelles and Nancy Maurice were with him and he recalled that Nancy herself had deflected the weapon. 'The Gen behaved like a roaring lion,' wrote Stokes, who was in the car behind, 'took part himself in the fight and smashed his walking stick.'[10] The next day a French officer called to apologise. Spears asked the press not to publicise the incident, for the French were emerging badly enough to the world even if, to Spears's fury, the BBC continued to carry their communiqués. General Holmes ordered an armoured brigade to Beirut from the Suez Canal and sent soldiers to protect the residence.

To an objective observer Helleu seemed little more than a pawn. Characterising him as 'more yielding, more anglophile but more lax' than Catroux, Delcoigne, a Belgian diplomat in Beirut, thought the Delegate-General was influenced by anglophobes like Boegner 'who commit error after error'. Delcoigne had no doubt that Britain sought to replace France in the Levant. 'Lawrence must be smiling in his tomb.' France he thought was her own worst enemy: 'isolated, unpopular and practising the politics of arrogance'. But there was one hope. A Free French source told Delcoigne that Stalin would intervene in the Levant within two or three months because he wished to sustain France as a great power.[11] First, however, the Soviet leader had to deal with the more pressing matter of trying to evict the Germans from his own country.

Catroux went to Beirut, stopping in Cairo on the way to threaten Casey. If the French were humiliated in the Lebanon, they would get out, leaving Britain alone as the colonial power to cope with the chaos. Spears wanted precisely this to happen, for it would leave him as the virtual Viceroy of the Levant, but the British knew they must not show signs of imperial greed, especially to Roosevelt; also they lacked the resources to hold the two countries.

The personalities worried Harold Macmillan, the British Minister in Algiers, who held cabinet rank and was senior to Spears in the Mediterranean hierarchy. 'I feel that Spears is out for trouble and personal glory,' he wrote in his diary, 'and Casey is so weak as to be completely in his pocket.' Macmillan felt that at a sign of British aggression the French would rally to de Gaulle's hard line. When he saw Winston Churchill in North Africa he tried to persuade the Prime

Minister to remove Spears; 'PM did not much like this.' Macmillan believed he could get the French to reverse Helleu's idiotic coup without humiliating them. 'Spears wants a Fashoda; I do not.'[12]

On 17 November Catroux called on Spears in Beirut. The Frenchman was courteous but refused to let him see the imprisoned ministers or commit himself to their release; 'I knew he detested me,' Spears wrote.[13] At the mission, the atmosphere was tense: 'Lascelles and Miss Mo [Maurice] overworked and distraught,' John Stokes told his wife, 'and Lady S a mass of nerves, so that when I light her cigarette her hand trembles.' The visiting Frenchman, however, put up a calm front. 'Catroux is a gentleman and has immense charm,' Stokes thought.[14]

Casey arrived on the 19th. He told Catroux that the British demanded the release of the ministers and recall of Helleu by the 22nd, otherwise there would be a military takeover. Catroux said: 'This is Fashoda.'[15] What Spears did not know was that in the event of martial law being imposed General Holmes would have been put in charge, with himself pushed to one side as a mere ambassador. Massigli thought that the inspiration for Spears's behaviour came from Churchill himself, and de Gaulle insisted that any recall of Helleu should be ostensibly for consultation, because a disavowal of the Delegate-General had been made impossible by the 'odious intrigues of England'.[16]

As a concession to the French, the deadline for the reinstatement of the ministers was extended on 24 November. In Beirut the strikes continued, bombs were thrown at French installations, posters of de Gaulle were slashed and a French air force patrol fired on a car, killing a British major. French casualties were low: four in hospital and one fatality, the dead man a soldier shot by an officer for refusing to fire on an unarmed crowd, or so Spears claimed.

At last on the 22nd the French released the ministers. A huge crowd celebrated outside the British legation and when Spears went to call on the liberated President he was carried shoulder high by ecstatic Lebanese and embraced by al-Khoury, who said that May had been like a sister to his wife and a mother to his children. The rejoicing reminded a delighted Spears of Paris on the armistice day of 11 November 1918; others thought of the Fall of the Bastille. 'Everyone is hysterically happy,' Stokes wrote, 'because for the first time in history the whole Lebanon is united – Christian, Moslem and Druze and it has taken the French to do it.' Spears, 'the absolute hero of the whole country', was compared to Byron in Greece, an inspiration in the struggle for freedom.[17]

Catroux accepted the humiliation with dignity; he had had the ministers released without the approval of de Gaulle, the General detesting the idea of a retreat forced by the British. Reinstated in their former positions, the ministers refused to make any concessions and some of the local French were so furious that Catroux warned Spears of the possibility of them both being assassinated. Boegner and Baelen left for Algiers, and Helleu was replaced temporarily by his former deputy Chataigneau. The Syrians began moves to change their constitution and break away from the French mandate.

It was the apotheosis of Spears. 'At the moment there is absolute pandemonium in the French ranks,' he told Beaverbrook.[18] He had a tremendous reception at Sidon on a visit to a local politician and feudal lord when he was escorted by over a hundred mounted Arabs, firing rifles and waving scimitars. Flowers and scent were thrown at the British cavalcade and choirs of schoolchildren sang as he passed; so great was the crush that it took his car an hour and a quarter to reach his host's house. Over a thousand people came to the banquet that followed, a huge feast with roasted sheep and long speeches in Arabic, to which Spears replied in French. The guests included George Wadsworth, the American Consul, and the Ministers of Belgium, Egypt and Iraq, but there was no doubt about who took the place of honour. 'Our popularity here is so great that it is almost alarming,' Stokes wrote.[19]

The French dropped those who had failed. 'It seems to me very desirable that Helleu leaves Beirut', Massigli wrote to Catroux, 'as quickly as possible and Baelen and Boegner also.'[20] Eden and Macmillan sought to lower the expectations of the Lebanese and the Syrians, the Foreign Office wanting to leave negotiations entirely to the French and the locals. Spears, of course, was not prepared to bow out, arguing that French outrages had made such contacts impossible. 'I cannot help thinking that being a popular hero in the Levant has rather gone to his head,' Harold Macmillan wrote. 'I cannot believe he was ever so cheered and applauded in Carlisle.'[21]

In Algiers, Massigli realised how low the reputation of France had fallen in the Levant, partly because of her defeat in 1940 but also through the 'selfishness, lack of education and mediocrity of the local French'.[22] Count Stanislas Ostrorog, a French diplomat, reported from Beirut that Spears exercised 'a veritable fascination' over the locals, although 'this will not last.'[23] Catroux took the long view, feeling that traditional divisions and rivalries in the region would return after the war, allowing France to regain her influence.

At a conference in Cairo at the start of December Eden and Macmillan put their case. The aim should be to bring about treaties between Free France and the Levant States of a similar type to those negotiated earlier between Britain and Iraq. Spears disagreed: 'It would be folly, it would be suicidal, to attempt to put back the Levant States into French strait jackets.'[24] On 22 December, in Damascus, Catroux signed an agreement with Syrian and Lebanese representatives that pointed to the French handover of power and the end of the mandate. But May sensed, for all Spears's apparent triumph, a dismal echo in one corner of his heart, because he knew that the French were out for his blood. 'Does it matter? Does he mind? No, not really. But he did love France, and when France went back on us, there was de Gaulle and the Free French, but now de Gaulle has done this and there is no-one.'[25]

'Life here is very dull and the weather extremely bad,' John Stokes wrote to his wife from Damascus on 21 January 1944. 'The Lady S– Miss M friction has reached unpleasant heights and I have to listen to Lady S pouring out her woes to me by the half hour.' The strain showed on Spears. 'His bad points are glaring,' Stokes thought. 'Colossal selfishness, childish vanity.' Yet there was another side. 'He's kind,' Stokes wrote, 'extremely easy to talk to and he does treat one as an equal. In spite of being a bad man, he has a heart.'[26]

In Beirut they did not go to French houses but were entertained by the rich Lebanese: the Tabets, Sursocks and Chamouns. When Spears flirted with others in this cosmopolitan society May showed jealousy, but Nancy blamed May for taking him out too much in the evenings. 'She is a dull, extremely unsympathetic type of woman,' Stokes wrote of the adoring Miss Maurice. 'Her only conversation is of S and her work.' When May asked him once why Spears had invited Nancy to a dance in Beirut he answered: 'Oh I think he is sorry for her'; to which she said: 'I wish he were sorry for me sometimes.' She told the ADC that she might leave Spears for the whole summer and stay with her unit. 'Miss M is becoming quite intolerable and possessive in a demoniac sort of way,' Stokes noted on 11 May. But by June they were close again and he might have been writing about a different person: 'Lady S is in simply marvellous form these days, looking really lovely when she makes up well at night (and that is so extraordinary because she normally looks appalling but sometimes at night she looks radiant) and talking with a brilliance that I've never heard anywhere else before.'[27]

She spoke of her days as a suffragette, of Korda's offer of £4,000 to film *The King of the Jews*, of how she did not blame unfaithful wives of absent soldiers. Spears and May dazzled their young ADC. 'They certainly have character and really are most remarkable people, great faults and yet very loveable, terrible errors of judgement in simple things and yet such brilliance. Tremendous vitality ... infinite charm, wonderful talkers – they've lived immensely full lives.' Then he came back to earth. 'And yet, they've no friends, are at bottom insincere and selfish, while he of course (like Disraeli) is decidedly un-English in some things. But oh how interesting.'[28]

In January 1944 Duff Cooper arrived in Algiers as British ambassador to the Committee of French National Liberation. Although they had both opposed the Munich agreement, the new Ambassador did not like his old parliamentary colleague; and Spears would later recall Cooper's ugly outbursts of temper and how his biography of Talleyrand was based on a French author's research for a similar study not published in English. Duff Cooper was an ardent, sentimental francophile who looked forward to being the British Ambassador to a liberated France. He agreed with Harold Macmillan, Anthony Eden and the Foreign Office that no settlement was possible in the Levant until Spears left.

The two sides were still far apart. So shocked had May been by French behaviour that she had considered not returning to the Hadfield–Spears unit, still attached to the Free French forces; only Spears's encouragement had made her join them for several weeks near the Bay of Tunis in response to messages from the unit's Commander, Colonel Vernier. In January Spears saw Chataigneau, acting Delegate-General since the departure of Helleu, and flourished a congratulatory telegram from Churchill to show his friendship with the British Prime Minister.[29]

Locally, the atmosphere was one of intense suspicion. The energy and resourcefulness of Spears induced feelings of fascination and horror in the French. The arrival of the new Delegate-General, General Beynet, in February led to another row when the Levant governments demanded that he should be reduced to the status of an ambassador. Eventually it was agreed that he could be delegate-general but with an ostensible reduction in the military power of the position. The Syrians were asking for control of the 20,000 Troupes Speciales, which they looked upon as their army, and the French refused to concede this, hoping also to push Eddé forward again and revive the ancient Lebanese Christian–Moslem antagonism. On 31 March, with the encouragement of Spears, a motion was passed overwhelmingly in the Beirut Chamber to expel Eddé for his activities during the Helleu coup. Beynet's protests were in vain.

Spears seemed uncontrollable. Duff Cooper had written to Churchill from Algiers on 21 February, after a visit from May:

conversation with her has left me in no doubt that she and her husband believe that the main object of their mission is to maintain the rights of the native populations of the Levant against the dominant power, and even to encourage the natives to assert these rights. That is not my view, nor I believe, the view of His Majesty's Government. We have surely enough native problems of our own to face without stirring up native problems for others. I think we should try to help the French rebuild both their country and their Empire and by our encouragement win their friendship. Spears, owing to what I think is a mistaken view of his local objective, seems to have altered the whole of his European policy and to have become definitely, if not violently, francophobe. He is certainly considered so by all the many branches of French opinion.

The letter ended with a reference to current criticism of members of parliament whose outside work prevented them from attending to their parliamentary duties. 'Perhaps consideration could be given to the three years' disenfranchisement that has befallen the burghers of Carlisle.' Churchill's answering telegram disappointed Cooper: 'nothing doing about burghers of Carlisle.'[30]

On 7 March Spears, aware of this hostility, asked Brendan Bracken if he should come home. Could he be suggested for a peerage, which would take care of any criticisms of his parliamentary absence for then he could give up his seat? Before Bracken could answer, Churchill wrote on the 10th, reminding Spears that it was not government policy to destroy French influence in Syria and Lebanon: 'You are however going further than I wish and anyone can see you have become bitterly anti-French.' He sweetened the admonishment with praise: 'Admire efficiency and vigilance in your work but "surtout pas trop de zèle".'[31] Bracken's answer was discouraging. The government would not risk a by-election in Carlisle until the end of the war, when Spears might have a choice between the Lords and the Commons. Perhaps in the meantime he should take some leave to catch up on what was happening. 'I think we in London may not appreciate the difficulties with which you are confronted in your vast parish.'[32]

The French were encouraged in April by the victory of Joseph Karan, a Christian Maronite supporter of Eddé, in the Tripoli by-election. His triumphant entry into the Chamber in Beirut was planned for 27 April and Spears discussed ways of thwarting this with the Lebanese cabinet. The police stopped Karan's supporters, a riot took place outside the parliament building, a Lebanese-born French non-commissioned officer was shot dead while trying to hoist the tricolour and the al-Solh government arrested ninety suspected supporters of the French. Unlike

Helleu, Beynet showed restraint and most of the prisoners were soon released.

It was about this time that a despatch from Spears to Duff Cooper was delivered by mistake to Massigli in Algiers. An extraordinary tirade, it recounted rumours that Catroux's staff had been penetrated by Vichy agents; that Madame Catroux's banker brother, to whom she wrote frequently, handled the transactions of the German armies in France; that Count Ostrorog, apparently an opium addict, also had Vichy sympathies; that Boegner had been trained secretly as a right-wing terrorist and Baelen, less dangerously, was 'a feeble pseudo-aesthete'. Massigli told London how shocked he was by such francophobic paranoia and Churchill defended Spears but agreed he should not have sent the letter by ordinary post.[33]

May passed through Algiers often on her way to and from the Levant and saw Catroux, now the Governor-General. 'Tell me, May,' Margot Catroux said, 'all about that wretched Helleu.' French policy seemed to be to put all the blame for the November débâcle on this inadequate little man, and Madame Catroux said that May would like the Beynets. 'Algiers was ashamed,' May wrote, 'of the poor show their people had made in the Levant.'[34]

In May, the Foreign Office moved against Spears. Dan Lascelles, who had supported his hard line against the French, was replaced by Gilbert Mackereth, once Consul in Damascus and a reputed francophile. On the 25th the new couple came to dinner, the other guests being what Stokes called 'the family': those members of the staff particularly sympathetic to May and Spears. Mackereth was 'short, bald and very unimpressive in looks' and his wife 'the school marm type'. There seemed to be nothing to fear but tedium.[35]

In June Spears announced his intention of giving the Syrian-controlled gendarmerie rifles and other equipment, to the fury of the French, who had only 3,000 mostly Senegalese troops in the region. Massigli thought this a deliberate disruption of Anglo-French relations in the run-up to D-Day, Duff Cooper having suggested that Lebanon and Syria should be abandoned to the French in return for their promise to work with Britain in a liberated Europe.

On 15 July in Algiers, Madame Catroux telephoned Cooper to say she had heard on Vichy radio that Spears had been assassinated. He did not believe it, but realised how much it would have eased his task, although 'it would be a misfortune if it were done by a fanatical Frenchman.'[36] Spears organised a diplomatic boycott of the French military review that was to take place in Beirut on Bastille Day, 14 July, and encouraged the Lebanese and Syrian governments to forbid their officials to attend any of the French ceremonies. Eventually Churchill submitted to Eden's pressure and called him back to London to report. The Foreign Office hinted to Massigli and others that Spears would not last much longer, and that Britain would work for a satisfactory treaty between France and the Levant States.

The French reported with glee that Spears had had the right to two places on the aeroplane to London and had taken Nancy Maurice with him instead of his wife; also that General 'Jumbo' Wilson had said that Winston Churchill had two weaknesses: his son Randolph and Louis Spears. They hoped, 'by the grace of God', that their tormentor might not return to the Levant and noted how worried the Lebanese and Syrian governments were by this possibility.[37]

In London it was Brendan Bracken who alerted Spears to a new danger, this time from within; 'we are getting some very queer telegrams from that fellow who is acting for you in Beirut,' he said.[38] At the behest of the Foreign Office, Gilbert Mackereth, in Spears's absence, reported very critically on his master's ideas and actions. Eden told Spears to help with any negotiations between the French and the Levant governments, in spite of his furious riposte that the French could not be trusted. Spears might have only two more months in his present post, the Foreign Secretary suggested. Spears of course asked Churchill to ensure 'that I am not asked to leave my post until the end of the war with Germany, and that I be allowed to ask to be relieved when the time comes'. Dreading public humiliation, he begged that his old patron should 'prevent action being taken which would be interpreted by the outside world as a sign that you considered I had failed'.[39]

This time the response was reproachful. 'I had great difficulty in securing your return to your post,' Churchill answered. 'You did not take my advice to try to keep your Francophobia within reasonable bounds and there is no doubt that great irritation is felt by the French.' Two or three months more would be granted, that was all. 'I will however arrange that, when the time comes, you will be given the opportunity of asking to be relieved instead of being abruptly super-seded. That is the best I can do.'[40]

In Beirut, May represented Spears at the pathetic celebrations arranged by the French to mark the liberation of Paris which had taken place on 25 August. Beynet, she claimed, had to hire a crowd to shout 'De Gaulle! De Gaulle!' and it turned nasty, invading his house at Aley to steal the spoons and electric lights set up for the party. Radio Levant, under French control, dressed the news up as a great French victory, but Beirut divided into two camps: one saying, 'one cannot blame them. It means so much to them,' while the other asked, 'were there no British troops in Normandy? No Americans to march on Paris?' She felt an extra fury for she knew of the danger to her unit as it advanced from the south of France up towards Lyon.[41]

Spears returned to Beirut on 6 September. To his fury Mackereth was not at the airport to meet him, another insult to add to the attempts at sabotage. 'There will be a colossal row,' John Stokes told his wife: 'nothing of course S loves better!' Some of his staff had made their peace with the new man after rumours that Spears would not come back from London: 'quite disgusting', thought Stokes.[42] Now Spears dismissed Mackereth, who refused to go; eventually Eden saw that the diplomat could not be in such blatant discord with the head of the mission and recalled him in October, giving Spears what seemed like a victory. But the Foreign Office stood by its instructions that Spears should promote a treaty between France and the Levant States.

Events seemed to reinforce the prejudices of both sides. The Syrian government threatened a public row if the Troupes Speciales were not under Syrian control when the parliament met in Damascus on 5 October; the Foreign Office though that Spears was at the back of this, whereas he claimed to be restraining the Syrians. Eden called again for Spears to be dismissed and Churchill answered that the promised two or three months had not yet passed. The French heard of an interview Spears had given to a journalist in which he spoke of chasing 'a decadent' France from the Levant and seemed to see himself as the new Cecil Rhodes.[43]

He knew, however, that he had little time left. To a French observer he seemed like a bear pacing up and down its cage, and John Stokes heard rumours: 'things have boiled up so much of late that I shouldn't be surprised if S didn't resign at any moment.' The atmosphere affected May, who oscillated between irritation and viceregal graciousness and fought with Spears, especially about Nancy Maurice: 'my goodness how she goes for him,' Stokes declared. As for Nancy, she became a caricature of herself: 'she blows smoke in one's face, wears the oldest shabbiest clothes and is so hard and coarse in conversation.'[44]

Both General Paget, the British Commander in the Middle East, and Lord Moyne, the Minister in Cairo, felt that the French might launch another coup. Eden thought the French had every right to occupy the Levant States and compared their claims to those of the British in Egypt. When Moyne said how hated the French were in these countries, the Foreign Secretary argued that there was the same dislike for Britain in Egypt, 'where however we had every intention of remaining.'[45] The

Foreign Office was determined not to spoil the forthcoming meeting in Paris between Churchill and de Gaulle.

In November Lord Moyne was murdered in Cairo by Jewish terrorists. Moyne had warned Spears that his removal had been confirmed when Eden and Churchill had stopped in Egypt in October on their journeys to and from Moscow. As a known friend of the Arabs, Spears had his guard strengthened. 'S is so popular in this country', John Stokes thought, 'that any attackers would have a thin time from the crowd.'[46]

Churchill received a tumultuous welcome in Paris. His talks with de Gaulle seemed to go well and a cloudy compromise emerged on the questions of the gendarmerie in the Levant and the transfer of the Troupes Speciales, which would involve more discussion. On Spears, there was no definite decision. He tried to make it hard for Churchill. 'I do not believe you wish me to be a burnt offering to de Gaulle,' he wrote and mentioned again the potential humiliation. 'All I am asking for is to be given time to prevent the work I have done being destroyed, and that when I go the world will have no reason to say that I have failed, or that the French have obtained my recall.'[47] Then on 23 November Spears received the telegram from Churchill. He could, the Prime Minister said, resign for political reasons citing his wish to resume his parliamentary duties; in any event the resignation should take effect from 15 December. This at least gave him the dignity of an ostensibly voluntary departure. De Gaulle had obtained his scalp at last.

'You can imagine the wild whoop of joy that will go up from the French,' John Stokes told his wife.[48] To his staff, Spears seemed not broken but deeply unhappy and they noticed that May became more loving to him, showing the loyalty that always emerged in moments of crisis. At Beirut dinner parties, women wept openly and Spears himself broke the news to the Lebanese President, who burst into tears. John Stokes's cynicism reasserted itself. 'The Ss are worshipped,' he thought, 'and how they enjoy it!'[49]

With the end came a sense of liberation. 'From that time on,' Spears recalled, 'I considered myself a free man and began to make very open speeches.'[50] He assured Syrian and Lebanese leaders that he would support them against the pro-French leanings of the Foreign Office by speaking in parliament and writing in the newspapers. In his last report home, he wrote of the collapse of French prestige in the Levant, where British influence could be sustained only by helping Syria and Lebanon find their freedom. This was what he had worked for: 'a solid position for ourselves which would buttress the whole structure of our influence in the Middle East'.[51]

The farewells were tremendous: a huge reception in Damascus; a dinner to which the Syrian President came, in a gesture previously shown only to King Faisal and Allenby; the gift of the Syrian Order of Ommayed with Stars, hitherto given only to heads of state: then in Beirut a further presidential dinner; the Highest Order of the Cedar of Lebanon; speeches in parliament and elsewhere; popular acclaim in the streets. 'Never has any Ambassador or Minister had a send-off like this,' wrote John Stokes.[52]

Spears's speeches showed his romantic view of the Levant. 'Damascus has always been the ultimate destination of the desert,' he said in the Syrian capital. 'The caravans dreamed of the coolness of her oasis, the merchants of her bazaars, the conquerors of her riches, and the poets of her gardens ... Henceforth there will be another man to dream of Damascus and of the day of his return. In my place in Parliament, enveloped in the mists of London, I shall only have to close my eyes to conjure up your sunlight, your blue sky and your teeming streets.' In Beirut he spoke of freedom: 'I am certain of little Lebanon's welcome among the noble company of those who have dared all for freedom and who, refusing to accept defeat, are witnessing at last the dawn of the day of triumph, of victory won at the cost of such blood, many tears and great sacrifice.'[53]

He had lunch with General Beynet, who was cordial, although the Frenchman had not come to any of the farewell functions. Then on 15 December May and he left Beirut, after inspecting a British guard of honour, and drove through Palestine, heavily guarded against the Stern gang, killers of Lord Moyne, to Jerusalem. Spears flew back to Europe, passing over a cloud-covered France to arrive at Poole at 5.15 p.m. on 21 December. There followed an exhausting slow journey in a train that reached London at two o'clock in the morning. He caught 'flu and went to bed at the Ritz, where he spent Christmas, upset also that the Foreign Office seemed to have no further use for Michael, who had been working in the embassy in Greece. There was contact with another world when Fagalde wrote from a prison camp in Germany to say he had heard of his assassination.

How should he approach Churchill? First he drafted a letter of complaint, 'a very frank grouse', which he toned down in response to Beaverbrook's advice.[54] Camille Chamoun, now the Lebanese representative in London, and his wife were in a house in Little College Street to remind him of his former battles, and Desmond Morton gave a picture of a chaotic France where de Gaulle might be ousted. Spears thought of founding an Arab Club to use oil as a lever against the Foreign Office and had lunch with the board of Shell to discuss this.

He was determined to keep up the façade of a voluntary resignation and forced *The Times* and the *Sunday Dispatch* to publish corrections to stories about his dismissal by threatening legal action.

In the Levant, the new Minister, the diplomat Terence Shone, lacked Spears's personality and ambitions. Even Patrick Coghill, never an admirer, felt that a gigantic figure had gone: 'with his departure, the States will realise that we are relatively broken reeds and our stock will go down.'[55] For May, there were the memories of their last day in Beirut: an angry but clear sea; the winter sun; palms lashed by the wind; the mountains of Lebanon covered with snow.

17

Defeat

Christmas 1944, the first after Spears's recall from the Levant, was bleak, although the Prime Minister's answer to his letter seemed friendly if a little distant. 'I am greatly pressed with all kinds of disagreeable affairs at the present time,' Churchill wrote on 7 January 1945, 'but I hope we may meet one day in the House of Commons so that I may congratulate you on your return home after so much hard and difficult work.'[1]

In Carlisle, at least, Spears felt encouraged. 'I found the position even better than I had dared to hope,' he told Casey on 16 January after a trip to his constituency, 'and I think that as far as anything can be foreseen in a seat where Labour is so strong, I am safer than I have ever been.'[2] Westminster seemed a haven after Beirut. 'I find it much more fun being a Member of Parliament than a diplomat,' he wrote to Henry Hopkinson.[3]

In January he gave a lecture on the Levant to the Royal Empire Society and Harold Nicolson, asked to open the discussion, was irritated by an interpretation slanted 'as if Syria and the Lebanon were British colonies which had been granted their independence, amid rapturous demonstrations of the populace, by Louis Spears'.[4] Nicolson, to applause, declared his sympathy for France's position, comparing Spears's policy to the hypothetical case of an American minister supporting Rashid Ali's rebellion against British involvement in Iraq. Spears was furious, particularly as Camille Chamoun and his wife were in the audience, but his criticism of the Foreign Office had reached Churchill's ears. 'I am told that you are still in receipt of pay for deferred leave from the Government,' the Prime Minister wrote on 28 January, 'and I confess it seems to me that while this continues it is not correct that you should pursue a course of action hostile to the Government by whom you are still in effect employed...'[5]

Early in the New Year they glared at each other in the lobby of the House of Commons and then had two conversations in the smoking room. At the first Churchill emphasised the extent of French anger;

the second was more cordial, the Prime Minister promising that one day he would fire a broadside at de Gaulle to remind the French leader that Spears had brought him out of France. But he was cautious about the Levant. 'He said', Spears noted, 'the French could obviously not keep their position or indeed remain in the Middle East but we ought not to be the people to push them out.'

Spears set out his complaints. 'I told him I thought I had been treated shamefully and that it was particularly objectionable that he should thus have dealt with me because I was so fond of him and was such an old friend.' Churchill either misunderstood this or affected not to hear. 'I ask for no special favours,' he repeated. 'You can shoot at me as much as you like'; and he reminded Spears of what he had said in Cairo: that Louis Spears had many enemies but could always be sure of his friendship. Then the Prime Minister recalled former days. 'Nothing will alter the fact that you were a very brave officer in the last war and you did much useful work in this.' Eden too tried to be conciliatory, asking what Spears thought of the official statements about the Levant. He answered that they might have been worse.[6]

In January, May returned to France, reaching Paris in a snowstorm, awestruck to think that Spears's great adversary, General de Gaulle, was in the same city as head of the provisional government. At a hotel to meet her was Rosie Forbes, perhaps the member of the unit to whom she felt closest; the next morning they set out for Hohwald in Alsace to find the hospital.

Colonel Vernier, the unit's chief medical officer, had written to May in Beirut to say that he had resisted General de Lattre de Tassigny, the Commander of the French division to which Hadfield–Spears was attached, who had ordered a change of name, probably as an excuse to drop the detested word Spears. Were the French turning against her too? Nurses on leave had spoken of a marked anglophobia.

In the pretty, snow-covered village of Hohwald she lodged at Madame Eboué's pension and inspected the unit. Vernier was clearly uneasy and the personnel had changed, having been greatly added to by new French recruits whose roles during the German occupation were still mysterious. Many of the older staff, the British nurses and the Quakers, were shocked that people were often hostile or affected to have no interest in the war. Hohwald, someone told May, had been openly pro-German.

Vernier felt ashamed to have to bring up the proposed change of name. May went directly to General Garbet, the divisional Commander, who said, 'The hospital is known and loved as "Spears" throughout the Division,' but he passed the responsibility on to General Guerriac, the Medical Inspector, at Belfort.[7] She set off for Belfort on an excruciating drive in the snow, to be told by Guerriac that he did not know of any attempt to change the unit's name. Back at Hohwald, Vernier showed her the order from Guerriac to say that de Lattre de Tassigny and the French Minister of War, Diethelm, wished the name to be changed. Both Vernier and she decided to ignore this.

In a show of support, officers of the French Foreign Legion and the Chasseurs Alpines asked May and the British nurses to their mess near by, providing a huge cake with 'Spears' spelt out in icing sugar on its top. They told her how depressed they were by what they found in France, particularly at the occasional comment on how good the German occupation had been for business. The adulteration of the country dreaded by de Gaulle revealed itself in odd details. The fields around Madame Eboué's pension were strewn with unexploded German and American mines and higher up, with views towards Strasbourg, stood the former German concentration camp of Struthof, where 20,000 people had been killed. Madame Eboué's niece pointed to the gas chamber, saying she had found the screams frightening at first but became used to them. May noticed white particles scattered over the soil of the vegetable garden made for the Commandant; the niece said calmly that these were human bones from the camp incinerator, useful as fertiliser.

She compared the reality of Hohwald to the hopes of British soldiers and diplomats in Paris who declared that France had been sick and needed only to be nursed back to health. In the capital she detected a note of petulance, the not always unspoken sentiment that at least under the occupation the city had worked. De Gaulle, she felt, was not loved for his attempts to kill the past.

At the end of March the unit was ordered south, to join the Army of the Alps near the Mediterranean. On the way she passed through Voutenay, to find that the empty house had been pillaged by the Germans because of the family's English connections, or so Marcel Rafinesque told her perhaps a little reproachfully. The hospital was installed at Beaulieu, in the Hôtel Bristol, and the wounded soon began to arrive.

In the south the atmosphere was even stranger. The locals compared the invading armies of the last four years, the Free French being the least popular because of their poverty. The hairdressers worked hard, with no shortage of nail varnish or scent. In one rich house, over tea served by an English butler, an old woman told May how her daughter had been tortured by the Germans and then shot. She herself had been locked up in the same prison for ten days, hearing the girl's screams while they flogged her, burnt her arms, throat and breasts with red-hot irons, her face with lighted cigarettes. 'All the more bloody of the populace on this coast to live as they are living,' May thought. The British Consul hated his job. 'France is as corrupt as ever,' she wrote, 'and so beautiful. The peach and plum all in bloom. The people are rotten.'[8] On VE-Day she and Rosie Forbes listened to the wireless in a hotel, depressed because the populace on the riviera seemed to have no interest either in the war or in the victory.

Vernier suggested that the unit should join in the campaign against the Japanese, but May said she must return to Spears and the forthcoming British election. An order came to go to the Paris area to take part in the victory parade on 18 June. To please Vernier, she wrote to de Gaulle, offering to take the unit to the Far East, but received only an acknowledgement from his aide Gaston Palewski. Then from her new base at Trilport on the Marne she went into the capital and called at the British embassy to see the Ambassador Duff Cooper, who told her about the extraordinary events in Syria.

Terence Shone felt overshadowed by his predecessor. 'His remarkable personality,' Shone wrote of Spears, 'his great talents – not least his aptitude for public speaking in French as well as in English – his tireless energy, his gift of personal appeal to people in these countries in all walks of life and, above all, his championship of the cause which is closest to their hearts – their independence – had won him a position here which was altogether exceptional for a foreigner.' May too, he said, had gained 'the esteem and affection of the States to a remarkable degree'. It was hard for the career diplomat. 'His place here was not easy to take.'[9]

The French had felt encouraged by Spears's departure. Against British protests, they sent troops to the Levant, for de Gaulle wished to show French power to France and the world. But the spirit of the states could not be curbed and Syria now took the lead, while Lebanon reverted to comparative calm. Full-scale fighting broke out and General Oliva-Roget ordered the bombardment of Damascus on 29 and 30 May, causing hundreds of civilian casualties including one member of the Spears Mission. Senegalese soldiers seized the parliament building, killing twenty-three Syrian gendarmes apparently after the Syrians had surrendered. Shone reported a reign of terror. It was a direct challenge. On the 31st General Paget assumed territorial command and British soldiers took control of the city, French troops being confined to barracks. Washington cabled support for the British action. Even de

Gaulle realised that it would be folly for France and Britain to fight each other in the streets of Damascus. French power in the Levant was at an end.

De Gaulle summoned Duff Cooper to the Elysée and spoke with cold fury. 'We are not, I admit, in a position to open hostilities against you at the present time,' he said. 'But you have insulted France and betrayed the West. This cannot be forgotten.'[10] On 2 June de Gaulle gave a press conference at which he castigated Spears, blaming him and his policies for the bloody finale, saying also that he had asked Churchill for his recall. Even as anglophile and dispassionate observer as the diplomat Hervé Alphand believed the débâcle to have been brought about by one man: 'a time bomb, set up three years ago by Spears and his accomplices'.[11]

Churchill defended his old friend in the House of Commons. The reason Spears had left the Levant was because he wished to resume his parliamentary duties; 'the suggestion that he was recalled to please General de Gaulle is entirely unfounded.' Then came a personal reference in which he added another wound to the four Spears had actually received in the First World War. 'I may say that my honourable and gallant friend was selected by me for this appointment in the Lebanon because, among other qualifications, he wears five wound stripes gained in his work as liaison officer between the French and British armies in the last war. He is the last person on whom General de Gaulle should cast reflections, because he personally secured General de Gaulle's escape to England from Bordeaux in his motor-car and airplane on 18th June 1940': a point which the Gaullists would later dispute.[12]

Britain's popularity sank in France. At a gala at the Paris Opéra Duff and Diana Cooper were booed and the French cancelled a football match arranged between the RAF and the French air force. The euphoric welcome given to Winston Churchill in Paris in November 1944 died away. An opinion poll taken in June 1945 showed that 65 per cent of those asked put the blame on Britain for what had happened in Syria, with the figure rising to 74 per cent in the Paris region, where Pétain's popularity had been shown as recently as April 1944 when crowds had greeted him with wild hysteria.[13]

In Paris, Duff Cooper gave May the reports to read. De Gaulle's belittling of the British at the press conference seemed grotesque; 'when the French went into Syria they had taken British troops with them,' she thought. Cooper said: 'He's in a bloody temper these days. I usually give back as good as I get when he turns rough but it didn't achieve anything in my last interview.'[14] No wonder her offer to go to the Far East had received only a perfunctory acknowledgement.

Cooper gave May a letter from Spears that urged her to take part in the parade of 18 June. The Ambassador added his encouragement, saying that her unit must fly the British flag. She wondered if de Gaulle was deliberately setting out to quarrel with Britain partly to please Vichy supporters. In the unit, Vernier stuck to his belief that Spears loved France and expressed shock at the insulting way the French command treated May. To Marcel Rafinesque and his wife Susie she explained the British position and Marcel said: 'one must admit that England is right.'[15] Another French friend was less receptive. 'Tell me,' she asked May, 'what has B done to us in Syria?'[16] A French nurse from the hospital told her that half Paris was against England, half against de Gaulle, and the first half said it was all the fault of General Spears.[17]

Twelve vehicles from the unit took part in the parade on the 18th and were sent explicit orders by the French organisers about how they should line up. The two staff cars carried two small pennants each, one British and one French.

At noon they set out from the avenue de la Grande Armée, divided behind the Arc de Triomphe and came together again to sweep down the Champs Elysées. On her right May saw Rosie Forbes, 'a delicately moulded Amazon', some officers in a jeep beyond and Vernier ahead. As they entered the place de la Concorde, there was Koenig, now Governor of Paris, 'standing like a very ancient warrior', on the pavement in front of the grandstand where de Gaulle stood with the white-robed Sultan of Morocco and other guests. Duff Cooper was the only British representative, another snub having been administered when de Gaulle forbade the participation of British troops. May thought again of earlier days. 'It is queer that B should not have been there. He was literally responsible, next to de Gaulle, no not next, even before de Gaulle, for today. It was his idea not de Gaulle's.' She recalled what Spears had said to her the night she had reached London on 1 July 1940. 'I saw that the French nation subject to continuous German propaganda would take up arms against us – unless we had a French force fighting with us.'[18]

As de Gaulle saw the Union Jacks fluttering alongside the tricolours and summoned Koenig to the stand, a group of old patients of the unit, waiting at the end of the Champs Elysées, many in bandages, on crutches or still in plaster, let out a tremendous cheer: 'Voilà Spears! Vive Spears!' By this time de Gaulle had heard of the identity of the unit and the reason for the British flags. He turned to the Minister of

War and ordered that the Hadfield–Spears ambulance should be closed down immediately and its British members repatriated as soon as possible.

The unit had served France since the beginning of the fighting and had treated over 20,000 patients. Its existence had been made possible by money raised through May's efforts and the reputation of her work during the First War. Vernier, who received the order, felt ashamed and attempted expiation by calling the whole unit together to relay de Gaulle's personal anger at seeing the flags. The French doctors and surgeons reacted by saying that if they had known this would happen they would have flown even more Union Jacks.

The division gave the unit a farewell party at the French Officers' Club and three Fusiliers Marins protested personally to de Gaulle's private office. Packing up took several days and it was not until 23 June that they left Trilport with a Foreign Legion band adding poignancy to the early-morning farewells. May flew to Carlisle to take part in her husband's election campaign, while the rest of the British drove to Dieppe for the cross-Channel journey.

May felt great emotion when she thought of the people who had worked with her, and a certain humility. What had she given? 'I suppose I had something, some quality, perhaps it was good judgement. But I suppose I gave martial inspiration. But the fine record of the unit is in no sense due to me. And I will never stop wondering at how little I have done with it, with such good results.'[19]

She wrote to de Gaulle, accusing him of discourtesy not only to the British members of the unit but to its French officers and staff, and received a lofty denial. To this, on 5 July, she replied, from the Crown and Mitre Hotel in Carlisle, Spears's constituency. Her hurt at the 'brutality' of his order is a sad epitaph for her work for the French. 'From you I have had no recognition since February 1941, when you inspected the unit on its departure for the Middle East, until today, but I know I am speaking for my entire British staff when I say that our four years with the 1st Free French Division have bound us to the officers and men of that Division with bonds that can never be broken.'[20]

In his election campaign, Spears spoke of his role in winning freedom for the Levant States, hardly a popular cause in Carlisle. 'I can assert with complete truth', he declared, 'that the numerous Arab nations, so important to us as customers and as friendly custodians of our vital Imperial highways, have become our friends largely owing to my efforts. Thirty million Arabs will be watching with keen interest – even anxiety – the result of the electoral contest in the City of Carlisle.'[21]

Sensing at last the unpopularity of the Conservatives in the industrial constituency, he called himself the 'National Candidate' to show his links with Churchill and the now disbanded national government. Probably nothing could have brought him victory and the result was a Labour majority of over 5,000. At the count Spears showed his disappointment in a way which led to accusations that he was a bad loser. The Liberal candidate had split the vote, he declared, a strange charge when Liberal support stood at only 4,845, with Labour on 18,505 and Spears with 13,356. He called the Labour victory 'a national disaster';[22] others disagreed, Duff Cooper expressing himself to be 'delighted' at Spears's defeat.[23]

Spears tried to console Winston Churchill after his government's humiliation: 'your fame will be unaffected by the odium that is bound to come to any government holding office at this period. It is absolutely certain that your greatness and legend will grow by leaps and bounds.'[24] His own plans had been shattered. He had seen himself as a supporter of the Arab cause in parliament and a businessman who would use his connections and reputation in the Middle East. The seat at Westminster was vital to this, an outward sign of influence and distinction. He asked Winston Churchill to recommend him for a peerage in his resignation list, but Churchill declined to do this because of the limited number of recommendations available to him; he may also have been conscious of the controversial reputation of his old protégé. Perhaps he might buy an interest in a newspaper that could promote the Arab cause; certainly he would resume his business interests, added to now by the chairmanship of Ashanti Goldfields.

There was another worry: that of his son. Having failed to establish himself at the Foreign Office, Michael seemed to be sinking into a condition of inertia. This was partly physical, an echo of his former illness, but it was also psychological. Sometimes his father's barely concealed disappointment and impatience erupted, to be smothered quickly, for Spears tried to be sympathetic. With May it was different, for she fussed over Michael, nagged and praised in a way that grated; she felt guilt because of her long absences during his childhood and adolescence. Michael's condition and his parents' reaction to this fed upon one another to create a deepening unhappiness. His reaction was silence; May's to fuss, to nag, and Spears's to adopt an external resignation that concealed disappointment and regret. Michael seemed almost to taunt his parents with a mixture of weariness and contempt, in spite of being reliant on their financial support. He had seen the domestic quarrels, knew of the strange triangle formed with Nancy; whether he felt irritation or misery about this is impossible to say.

What perhaps also hurt him was the early memory of adoring expectation, which still flickered in May and Spears, and the impossibility of his living up to this. His one passion was chess and his decision to try fruit farming in Kent lacked enthusiasm or hope. He would haunt the rest of his parents' lives.

Now the obvious purpose of the war years had ended. 'May is very unsettled and does not know what she will do,' Spears told Richard Casey, his old colleague in the Middle East.[25] He fought on, getting damages and costs from the *Sunday Dispatch* because the newspaper had said Winston Churchill had recalled him from the Levant at the behest of General de Gaulle. He tried to further his business career by asking his doctor to write to a fellow patient who was a director of several companies to suggest to this man that he should resign from their boards for health reasons; the man had promised some time ago to nominate Spears as his successor. 'I think it would be a tactical error,' the doctor answered. 'It might raise the idea that my letter was inspired.'[26]

In October he went to Brussels, in his capacity as chairman of SOAG Machine Tools, travelling by ferry with a chauffeur-driven car. There he carried out what he saw as a rescue mission, for his niece Béatrix, the daughter of his sister Kathleen and the poet Christian Beck, had made her way to Belgium from France with her infant daughter. Spears heard the story of her war years, of her work in French factories, and of how her Polish husband Naum Szapiro had been killed. She and her daughter must accompany him back to England, he said. She could help in the house at St Michael's Grange; that would be a fair return for the security he could offer. A fascinated Béatrix observed the characters of her new existence: Spears, May and Michael. The results, delayed for some twenty years, would be devastating.

18

'Life Here Is Really Very Unpleasant'

In the autumn of 1946 May published *Journey Down a Blind Alley*, her only volume of autobiography. It tells of the Hadfield–Spears unit's long journey from the first winter of the war, through the flight to Bordeaux and Arcachon and the return to battle in the desert; then, as a sub-plot, May's own experiences in the turbulence of the Levant and Spears's relationship with de Gaulle.

The book is less constricted than her novels, perhaps because the real-life drama was more powerful in itself than anything within the range of her imagination. She shows passion and anger, and some of the vignettes are unforgettable, such as that of de Gaulle in 1940 or the stillness at the convent of St Jean-Le-Bassel before it was hit by war. Spears is never far away, a domineering force, and the book questions neither his brilliance nor his tactics. Publicly May and he face the world together, as they had done since their meeting near the front line of the Somme.

Spears felt the lack of a parliamentary seat and the platform this had given him. He was turned down by several constituencies, where his approach could be tactless. 'As you and I are of almost exactly the same age,' he told the Chairman of the Wokingham Conservative Association, 'I do not think you yourself can contend that my age should deter the Association from forming its own views on my suitability as a candidate.'[1] The newspapers at least gave him an outlet, the *Daily Telegraph* in particular providing a forum for his views on the Middle East. In October and November of 1946 he went on a trip that included Cairo, Damascus, Beirut, Baghdad, Amman and Jedda. In Beirut he was received with affection by the President, but the Syrians were less effusive; it was known that his days of power were over and grand official welcomes in Baghdad and Amman could not hide the fact that the Arabs thought of Spears as a man of the past. There were even newspaper reports that he was no help to the Arab cause because he was of Jewish origin and married to a Jewess. Inevitably he found himself afflicted by melancholy. 'Am doing too much,' he wrote to

Nancy Maurice from Beirut, 'and rather tired but this place is even more lovely than we remembered it.'[2]

The violent side of the end of empire hit Spears in June 1947 when he was sent a letter bomb by Zionist extremists angry at his opposition to a Jewish state in Palestine. His habit of passing interesting stamps on to his Rafinesque cousins, who collected them, saved him because a close look at the parcel revealed the ominous wires. Inevitably the past seemed increasingly glorious; in 1946 he had celebrated his sixtieth birthday. 'I often think of all our affairs together,' Churchill told him on 8 October 1946, 'especially the walk round Vimy Ridge and your spirited encounter with Pétain on our visit to Paris. Life slips away, but one fights with what strength remains for the things one cares about. I expect that is your position too.'[3]

In France Spears was perhaps the most detested foreigner of the time. Marshal Juin had apparently said that if Sir Edward Spears set foot in his country he would have him assassinated; characteristically in the summer of 1946 Spears borrowed a Cadillac and chauffeur, insured his life and set out for Burgundy and Poitou, accompanied for part of the journey by Yvonne de Lestrange. 'You have never known occupation, this leper,' she told him. 'When I think of my country I have tears in my eyes, my poor country that you loved also.'[4]

Chitré had been taken over by the Germans, who had accidentally set fire to part of it, and Yvonne herself had spent most of the war in Paris, working at the Pasteur Institute, which she claimed had been committed to resistance. She had heard of Spears's activities in the Levant and, before his journey there in 1946, wrote: 'explain why it is absolutely necessary that you go to the Levant if everyone wants to kill you there? And why do you occupy yourself with what we do there? I am sad that you see yourself against our poor country.' She urged him to write another book, to settle down. 'In this country opinion about you has been made by the German newspapers,' Yvonne thought. 'People have kept something of it and forgotten where they read it. Naturally everyone holds that you are Jewish; my protestations count for nothing.' But she wanted to see him: 'It would not matter if this did not make your coming to France difficult.'[5]

At least she had survived. Helbronner, Spears's Jewish friend from the First War, had been murdered by the Nazis, and Yvonne's beloved cousin Antoine de Saint-Exupéry had disappeared while on a flight over southern France in 1944. On one of his post-war visits to her, Spears and she talked of 'Tonio'. Had he, she asked, ever read *The Little Prince*, Saint-Exupéry's last masterpiece? They bought a copy in a bookshop in a small town in Périgord and Spears, reading it that night, was transfixed by the mystical tale of thwarted innocence. Henceforth the book would be always at his bedside, perhaps partly because it evoked the tender feelings he had had for the young Michael.

When the story emerged of the way Marshal Pétain had been treated in France where only a year before he had been received in Paris with hysterical enthusiasm, even Spears, who detested Vichy, was shocked. Recalling Verdun and the mutinies of 1917, he felt disgust at the inability of de Gaulle to see that there were two Pétains: the hero of the First War and the head of the abysmal regime that had negotiated with Hitler in 1940: or, in human terms, the kindly, gifted soldier and the deluded, vain old man.

Pétain's trial in 1945, at the age of eighty-nine; the way he and his wife were treated as common criminals; the insulting manner of the prosecuting counsel; the obviously political nature of the court; the refusal to allow Madame Pétain to share a cell with her infirm husband when even the Nazis had allowed Léon Blum to live with his wife in separate quarters in the middle of an extermination camp: all these seemed to Spears to show de Gaulle at his most vindictive and inhumane. The death sentence was not carried out; an opinion poll taken in France soon after the fall of Vichy showed that 58 per cent of those questioned thought that no punishment should be inflicted on Pétain, thus showing the outcry that would have followed an execution.

Spears looked favourably upon the later attempts of the Marshal's junior defence counsel Jacques Isorni to rehabilitate Pétain's reputation. Isorni came to see him in London and told of the petty punishments inflicted upon the old man: how, when the Marshal was imprisoned in a fortress in the Pyrenees, Madame Pétain was allowed to stay in a hotel in a nearby village for only fifteen days at a time and had to walk the three miles to and from her husband's gaol to visit him. On the Ile d'Yeu, his last prison, the room in the hotel was so cold that she slept in her clothes.

A myth grew around Pétain: that of sacrifice, of the martyrdom of a pathetic old man whose motives had been those of patriotism and self-denial. Spears found himself perhaps unwittingly supporting this in a way that was paradoxical because most of the surviving Pétainists of the French right abominated him for his Jewish blood, putative theft of a part of France's empire and early championing of de Gaulle. It would be revealed also that, in recollection, the Marshal had had a cold and suspicious view of this clever young Englishman.

His reputation held among some. In February 1947, when Spears landed at Duala on the way to Ghana and the Ashanti mine, he found a French guard of honour drawn up on the tarmac. 'It must be for you,' a passenger said, to which he answered that if it was it could only be a firing squad. In fact a French general was expected, but the officer in command said: 'If I had known General Spears was on board I would have presented arms. Here we know what France owes him.'[6] General Gérard wrote in 1949, encouraging Spears and May to visit France: 'you have many friends there ... and no one has forgotten the great devotion of Lady Spears to our wounded.'[7]

Then there came a sad plea. In March 1948 his old colleague Fagalde wrote that he had been ruined. Was there any chance of a British pension in recognition of his First War service in the War Office in London? Alas, it was not so simple. Fagalde, captured in 1940, stood accused of having offered to fight in the SS in order to obtain his freedom. Although he held the CB, the CMG and the MC, the Frenchman could expect nothing more from Britain, Ismay told Spears.

The vituperation continued to echo across the Channel. The diaries of Cambon, French Ambassador in London during the First War, were published and included a passage in which the diplomat warned Paris of this shrewd Jewish spy Spiers whom the British had cunningly infiltrated into the French War Office. Prince Poniatowski, another old colleague from the First War, said in his autobiography *D'un siècle a l'autre* that Spears, encouraged by his British masters, had read secret papers in Clemenceau's room. When Spears protested, the Prince answered that he had raised the episode for one reason: 'the nature of your activities in French politics during the subsequent years called for my absolute disapproval.'[8] It was the initial support for de Gaulle which the Prince detested, thus showing that Spears was disliked for different reasons by Gaullists and anti-Gaullists. Then the spirit of Vichy lingered also, as in Jacques Mordal's 1956 work *La Bataille de Dakar*, which described him as 'an evil genius' whose memoirs were 'the most astonishing collection of tittle-tattle ever to have emerged from the pen of an allied general'.[9]

In such an atmosphere, the battle of the memoirs was bound to be vicious. Winston Churchill asked him to wait for a few years before he gave his view of 1940, but Churchill himself was quick into the field. In the six volumes of the former Prime Minister's history of the war that appeared between 1948 and 1954, Spears found himself praised for his role in June 1940. Two sentences gave him particular pleasure. 'When Frenchmen and Englishmen are in trouble together,' Churchill wrote, 'and arguments break out, the Frenchman is often voluble and vehement, and the Englishman unresponsive or even rude. But Spears could say things to the high French personnel with an ease and force which I have never seen equalled.'[10] Churchill describes the events in the Levant and shows exasperation with French conduct and policy there. On Spears's own activities, however, he passes no judgement.

General Catroux's *Dans la bataille de Méditerranée*, published in 1949, showed no such reticence and devoted a whole chapter to Spears. The picture is that of a man of frustrated ambition: someone who boasted of his knowledge of France when he had only a superficial understanding of her history and her remarkable powers of recovery; a vain intriguer who could not forgive de Gaulle's refusal to let him dominate the Free French movement.

The shafts are only slightly blunted by gratitude for his part in persuading Wavell to allow the invasion of Syria in 1941 and to include Free French troops in the campaign: 'I have nothing but praise for Spears for that.' Catroux emphasises the distrust felt for this outsider. 'Soldiers in general showed no great liking for a politician who had become a Brigadier-General at the age of 30 in World War I: a man better equipped with contacts than with knowledge of soldiering.' He also mentions the personal antipathy. 'The main thing was we didn't trust him and as the animal in La Fontaine we didn't like him being near us. We feared the effects of his vindictive and combative temperament, his quick temper, his suspicious authoritarianism and his snap judgements, all of them more dangerous because he had Churchill's ear.'

Spears's francophilism, Catroux claimed, had been a mere feeling for Parisian society, friendships with statesmen and pride in his ability to declaim French poetry; the reality was a typical Anglo-Saxon enemy of France, interested in her only when she was powerful: 'narrow mindedly British if not by birth and upbringing at least by his idiosyncratic view of politics'; an adherent also of the ancient British aim of evicting France from the Levant: 'the master plan'. For Spears, morality had no place in politics; he was completely ruthless. To Catroux, his every move had been governed by his personal animosity towards de Gaulle and the Free French. 'The wounds inflicted on vanity are the worst. Spears was inordinately vain.'[11]

The memoirs received immense publicity in France and were serialised in *Le Figaro*, one extract appearing under the headline: 'General Spears, a man of inordinate ambition'.[12] Spears sent a detailed refutation, to be told by Pierre Brisson, *Le Figaro*'s Director-General, that his letter would not be published: 'the insolence that you show in it to our country is only equalled by the cynicism of your treachery.'[13] In the event the paper printed letters from Oliver Lyttelton, 'Jumbo' Wilson, Casey and General de Larminat challenging various aspects of the book; Spears had to content himself with giving a press conference in London to put his point of view. *Le Monde*'s reaction was also hostile, especially towards Spears's call for elections in the Levant. 'We should like to know in what country, apart from the United States, "Free Elections" could be held in wartime. Unless we are mistaken Great Britain herself postponed hers until the end of the war.'[14] Yvonne de Lestrange advised detachment. 'The memoirs were boring enough,' she wrote to Spears about *Dans la bataille de Méditerranée*, 'and one has certainly forgotten them. Would not the best thing be silence?'[15]

The attacks did not always come from France. In 1953 Duff Cooper, now Viscount Norwich, completed his own memoirs, called *Old Men Forget* and published by Rupert Hart-Davis's own firm, into which Spears had put money. Knowing his litigious nature, the author and publisher sent him the passages dealing with the Levant. Spears's reaction seemed to be to accept a difference of opinion. 'I expect you realise', he wrote to Duff Cooper, 'that I felt you were making things as difficult for me as you consider I made them for you.' But he laughed at the prospect of conflict. 'Monsieur le Vicomte, tirez le premier.'[16]

The final copy, however, infuriated him, particularly a passage which claimed that Spears had acted against the wishes of the British government. A clash of lawyers followed; neither Duff Cooper nor Rupert Hart-Davis would back down and publication went ahead. Then on 1 January 1954 Cooper died suddenly, and Spears turned on Rupert Hart-Davis as the surviving offender. Their relationship deteriorated into mutual hostility, from which it would never recover.

Spears disliked the new socialist Britain. 'Life here is really very unpleasant,' he told General Irwin, his old Dakar colleague, now stationed in West Africa. 'One feels frustrated at every turn. The streets are full of young men in khaki, their caps on the back of their heads, their hair falling over their eyes, and their hands in their pockets, which has driven me to the conclusion that the Army Council has handed over to the British Council.'[17] Shortages he particularly loathed. 'What are you to do in a country where literally the only topic of conversation is food in any milieu anywhere?' he wrote to General Sir Bernard Freyberg, who was the Governor-General of New Zealand.[18] The Freybergs obliged with food parcels, and Spears did what many people do when faced with changes they find incomprehensible or unsympathetic: he created a controllable world of his own.

His redoubt was Ashanti Goldfields, the company of which he had become chairman in July 1945. Situated at Obuasi in what was then called the Gold Coast, now Ghana, near the town of Kumasi in the

Ashanti region, the mine held gold of a higher quality even than that of the Reef mines of South Africa. The concession had been granted to the company at the end of the nineteenth century; Ashanti Goldfields Ltd was quoted on the London Stock Exchange and had its head office in the city. Associated with Ashanti, and run from the same head office, was the poorer mine of Bibiani, about fifty or sixty miles away. A separate company, Bibiani also had Sir Edward Spears as its chairman. He would increase his involvement by becoming managing director of the two companies in February 1950.

Spears's work for Ashanti led to a further increase in the power of Nancy Maurice. Utterly loyal and fanatically possessive, she had, unlike May, a good head for the intricacies of commerce and it was to Nancy, whom he involved in every facet of his post-war business life, that he wrote to describe his first visit to Ashanti in November 1945. The mine was in a landscape of green hills and forest, reached after a long railway journey from Accra: 'the country beautiful, wonderful trees of all kinds, v hilly. At all stations v colourful natives, exquisite taste in exotic clothes.' Ashanti employed over 4,000 people, with between 100 and 150 British and South African expatriates in managerial positions. He was met by the heads of the various mine departments and a large, intimidating crowd. 'Dear Nancy, I wish you were here. It wd all be so much easier.'[19]

His health was still bad and he felt tired, suffering from arthritis and lung trouble; inevitably age weakened him in his sixtieth year. Almost as soon as he arrived, a general strike began, for no apparent reason. 'This folly of trying to start unions is at the bottom of all the trouble,' he told Nancy on 24 November. 'The Natives don't begin to understand what it is all about.' He went down the mine, to the deepest part: 'rather proud because Mine Captain says that when he comes back from leave he can't do what I did today – but it can't be good for me. My heart hurts and pumps, but this is evidently only temporary. The heat was intolerable. The air in parts is very poor. It is essential to improve conditions. Men can't work down there.'[20]

He found the area oddly magical: 'yesterday in the forest. Beautiful and strange.' Bibiani appealed to him as well: 'a dream'. Nancy was told of the reaction: 'the acting manager Russell (he was once a Scotch working miner – I like him) says my visit is the greatest experience he has ever had and he wd not have believed it possible anyone cd get down to it so quick.' He had to restrain his instinct to dominate. 'I am exercising great control in not taking over show.'[21]

At the Bibiani mine he spoke to the workers. 'There are certainly some agitators amongst them,' he told Nancy. 'Most of them were all right but at one time I told them off good and proper.'[22] He was assiduous in his attentions to the local Chief, bringing gifts of whisky and watches. But the Chief interrupted Spears, who lost his temper; this 'worked like magic' and the African asked for forgiveness. 'The best way to treat these people is as if they are children,' he told the other directors, 'but reasonable children to whom one endeavours to explain things.'[23]

The African visit became an annual event, lasting usually for about six weeks in January and February. Writing to Nancy from the Gold Coast in February 1947, Spears contrasted proudly the restrictions in post-war Britain with Ashanti's efforts on behalf of its employees. 'It is curious to think that in spite of all difficulties, having to import everything, we are building the most charming European homes by the score at £1,200 and are planning a whole town just because it is private enterprise. And it is Africans who are benefiting.'[24] Nor did he neglect the entertainment of the workers, asking Yvonne de Lestrange for illustrated records of Provençal festivals 'as I am introducing a carnival for the Blacks on the Gold coast'.[25]

A new existence came out of his involvement with Ashanti: that of the pasha. For six weeks of the year, accompanied by May and sometimes by Nancy, he escaped the gloomy winters of post-war Britain, where Huguet's prophecies of decline seemed to be coming true. A ritual evolved: the first-class flight on BOAC; no trouble at Accra with customs or passport control, simply a quick way out with a mountain of luggage to the waiting Armstrong Siddeley limousine, which took him to the house of Ashanti's representative in the capital, a comfortable establishment with at least fourteen servants. Good cooks were scarce in West Africa, so the company sent large Fortnum and Mason hampers on ahead with cases of wine.

The representative in Accra would rather dread these visits. Spears could be charming but was an exacting guest and liked an audience to stay up late to listen to his anecdotes. He demanded also a precise account of the local political scene. The morning after his arrival, the Armstrong Siddeley would take him up to the mine, a four-hour journey of about 150 miles on atrocious roads, the food having been sent on in advance. At Obuasi, he built a large bungalow, supposedly for guests of the company, although he called it 'my house' and forbade anyone to stay there without his permission. Its style was Islamic, with arches and courtyards, a reminder of his days of power in the Levant.

The management of Ashanti fell into two parts: the running of the mine, about which Spears knew little, and the attempt to calm the turbulence that accompanied a new African nationalism, where he felt his political and diplomatic experience could help. His weekly meetings with the heads of departments were unproductive, occasionally a farce, as he had absolutely no technical knowledge and was cautious to the point of being unhelpful on the complex matter of Africanisation of the senior staff. There would be an element of the royal visit in his inspection of new buildings or machinery or an excursion to the less profitable Bibiani mine, where another 2,000 miners and 60 expatriate staff worked.

The Gold Coast, in common with the rest of colonial Africa, was changing with the rise of nationalism. At first Spears complained about this, and the high taxation on profits which he blamed on an appeasing colonial government. The strikes he thought had their origin through the policy of instilling trades unionism into the African miners through government labour officers: 'the equivalent of giving a loaded revolver to a child of five'.[26] In 1951 he was scornful of the Gold Coast elections: 'the people themselves had not the faintest idea what was going on, and could not have cared less.' The appointment of black ministers did not please him, for he saw a serious lack of qualified Africans to fill humbler administrative posts. At least the new ministers had been given princely salaries. 'There is just a possibility that to keep the boodle they may do what they are told,' he told Freyberg, 'that is follow all the suggestions that are made to them by English officials.'[27] The nationalist leader, Kwame Nkrumah, he believed to be 'entirely subversive'.[28]

Nkrumah had been a student in Britain and the United States before returning to the Gold Coast in 1947. Imprisoned for agitation in 1950, he was elected to the Gold Coast parliament while still in gaol and became prime minister and in 1960 president of the newly independent Ghana. Known as the 'Ghandi of Africa', Nkrumah spoke out against white domination, while Spears associated nationalism with communism and potential chaos. 'It is a rather ridiculous Punch and Judy show,' he told General Irwin in 1953, 'with African ministers strutting about with Europeans pulling the strings while the marionettes boo them to the immense satisfaction of the population.'[29] But in the same year he found Nkrumah 'highly intelligent and much more moderate as a result of his experience of government',[30] and he told the annual general meeting of Ashanti Goldfields: 'It is always a pleasure to meet this very intelligent, pleasant man who exercises such a sway over his followers.'[31] An extraordinary relationship had begun.

Spears exemplified a type strongly represented in boardrooms during the first two decades after 1945: the retired senior officer or politician used to receiving a deference granted by rank. Mostly ignorant of the technical aspects of their companies, or of the complexity of modern financial management, such people were very different from the technocrats and engineers then making their way to the top of German or French industry.

In 1947 he became involved with the Institute of Directors, believing that, at a time of excessive government regulation, this organisation could be a voice of propaganda for free enterprise. Although it had been granted a royal charter in 1906, the Institute was moribund, with the share of a one-room office in a gaunt Victoria Street block and only 400 members. In 1948, Spears became chairman and enlisted Oliver Lyttelton, who had worked in industry before entering politics, to help him; by 1951 there was a membership of over 4,000. Spears hoped the public could be taught how damaging socialism was. 'To do this,' he told General Freyberg, 'we are going to adopt novel means of advertising in the socialist papers and the sort of papers the nincompoops who have the votes today actually read, or rather they don't read much. We shall have to go in for strip cartoons.'[32]

The post-war world brought a sense of dislocation. Now his wish to belong to an easily identifiable part of British life would never be fulfilled. His military career had been too involved with politics and diplomacy for him to be thought of as a soldier; in any case he had not commanded men in the field. He came too late to the career of a full-time businessman and was seen by his associates there more as a general, politician and diplomat who had turned in retirement to commerce: someone with powers of broad leadership and useful contacts but without detailed knowledge or technical skill.

A peerage would at least have given him a platform in the House of Lords. In 1952 he felt hopeful as Oliver Lyttelton, Duncan Sandys, Ismay and Brendan Bracken approached Winston Churchill on his behalf. But the old enemies surfaced again and Jock Colville noted consternation at Churchill's wish to honour 'Bomber' Harris and Spears. In 1953, the year of the coronation, he was made a baronet: a small consolation. Casey wrote: 'The opposition at the Foreign Office is, I expect, a formidable hurdle.'[33]

There was still his writing, one achievement that had won him almost unanimous praise. By 1951 he had a draft ready of a book about the fall of France in 1940 which Sir Ronald Campbell, the former British Ambassador in Paris, pronounced to be accurate. To Rupert Hart-Davis the book seemed 'first rate' but needed drastic pruning. Angry, Spears took the book away from him and showed it to Collins and Jonathan Cape, where it was turned down on account of its length; then in

September 1952 Heinemann agreed to publish the entire work in two volumes.[34] Winston Churchill refused to write a foreword, having become Prime Minister again in 1952. 'I fear that in my present position', he told Spears, 'it would not be suitable for me to write a preface to your new book, as it raises so many points of controversy with the French. Also I think it is too flattering for me. I must admit, however, that I could not put down the proofs you sent me.'[35] Spears secured an advance of £250 on each volume and suggested the title *Katabasis*, the Greek word for a descent or military retreat, but Heinemann thought this too obscure, opting for his other idea: *Assignment to Catastrophe*.

A few last changes were made. Spears cut a favourable reference to Duff Cooper because of his anger at *Old Men Forget* and the libel lawyers advised him to remove the name of the Baroness von Thyssen, the German woman who it had been suggested was planted on the Belgian King Leopold by the Nazis; also he should not say that the Marquise de Crussol had been Daladier's mistress. On 8, 9 and 10 June 1954 extracts from the first volume were published in the *Daily Telegraph*, increasing the sense of excitement at the prospect of this account by a brilliant observer of an intensely dramatic moment in modern European history.

Assignment to Catastrophe, the title given overall to the two volumes, *Prelude to Dunkirk* and *The Fall of France*, is different from Spears's two earlier books, *Liaison 1914* and *Prelude to Victory*. Written with the author as the central figure, it is about personal disillusion as well as national tragedy and has no more telling passage than the description of his feelings as he drives through Touraine after the French defeat. 'During this horrible, depressing journey I endured the kind of sorrow that withers faith. All that I had believed in, worked and hoped for during so many years, could not now be recalled without pain. The finger of memory touching the past hurt as if probing a wound.'[36] *Assignment* is the story of a love affair ending in pitiful disappointment, with only the last flight from Bordeaux in the company of de Gaulle as a sign of hope. The book is permeated also with the unspoken bitterness of what happened later in the Levant.

Yvonne de Lestrange found it too partial. 'Have you noticed that the English of which you speak are all remarkable, efficient and heroes naturally, as for the French ... The only one who wins your favour is your chauffeur.'[37] In Britain, however, the critics were enthusiastic. Harold Nicolson, R. C. K. Ensor, Lord Hailsham and Michael Howard all praised the first volume, Howard noting only that Spears clearly was not a man to be modest about his own talents and achievements.

Obviously *Assignment* is deficient as a work of impartial history. Spears accepted the hysterical rumours of German fifth-column activity and the justice of Reynaud's unfair condemnation of the wretched King of the Belgians. He also played down the incontrovertible fact that Britain had been able to give little help in the French moment of desperation. But A. J. P. Taylor offered an accolade that delighted the author: 'Sir Winston Churchill and Sir Edward Spears are the only men who have written books of superlative excellence about both wars.'[38]

Spears has his villains: Weygand, Baudouin, Madame de Portes, others who worked later with Vichy. On Pétain he is not so hard; the impression is of a man moving with pathetic vanity in and out of the fog of senility. The heroes are fewer: Mandel, repellent but brave; Reynaud, raised beyond the capacities of his character; de Gaulle, a figure still in the shadows but with a sense of inevitable growth. Some of the portraits are memorably sharp, like that of the 'slight oiliness' of Gaston Palewski, aide to Reynaud and de Gaulle and later the lover of Nancy Mitford, whose hands clasped each other 'in unexplained and inexplicable self-congratulation'. The francophile Nancy hated *Assignment*, perhaps because of this tilt at Gaston: 'funnily enough he fancied himself as a ladies' man.'[39]

Assignment to Catastrophe poses a still unanswered question. The rot at the top Spears could comprehend, although its extent had come as a surprise to him; far more shocking was the way this had extended downwards apparently to the level of a whole people. For him, the tension was one between memory and reality, between emotion and fact: a gap shown in the contrast between Pétain as the saviour of France in 1917 and the disgraced leader of Vichy. To the essentially rootless Spears, France had given an identity and an ideal which had vanished in 1940. Now, after what had happened in the Levant, memories of her were besmirched by disappointment, even hatred.

He stipulated that the book should not yet be translated into French, believing it to be too soon for his account to be given a fair reception in France. But, inevitably, there was comment on the English edition from across the Channel. In *Le Monde*, Henri Pierre praised the work a little grudgingly and one commentator let loose an anti-semitic jibe about Spiers and Dreyfus, two Jews who were enemies of France.[40] The journal *Combat* suggested that Spears had known only the French *gens du monde*, the country's landscape and its restaurants. *Assignment*, it said, appealed to the British fascination with 1940 without attaching any blame to the British government; and its author in his relationship with France resembled the two-headed Janus: first faithful friend, then implacable foe. Counterblasts of greater force came from Randolph

Churchill in *Truth* and *Le Figaro* where he accused Spears of conceit, of spitting in the face of a country he had once loved, of not realising that the defeat had its origins in the failure of Britain and the United States to guarantee French security after the First World War.[41]

The correspondence that followed the publication of *Assignment* allowed Spears to enlarge upon the faults of those whom he disliked. He told Field-Marshal Montgomery that Marshal Juin had declared at Pétain's table in 1941 how happy he would be to fight under Rommel against the British in North Africa. Weygand, he said, was probably not the illegitimate child of the Empress of Mexico, as some rumours suggested, but the son of a Belgian gardener.[42]

19

Fighting Back

In 1950 Michael married a divorcee called Margery Eynon and went to live with her on a fruit farm in Kent. Spears had come to rely more and more on the boy's old nanny to act as a bridge to his son and was pleased when she approved of the match; Margery, she said, understood the boy's quietness. In fact the marriage lasted barely two years, although they were not divorced until 1956. Michael seemed to have little wish to see anyone except to play chess; then a manservant moved in to look after him and there were hints of homosexuality to complete the shattering of his parents' conventional wishes.

May began to visit the United States again, where her nephew Adlai Stevenson became governor of Illinois and, in 1952, the Democratic presidential candidate. She adored Stevenson, and the memory of Joyce's suicide, the reality of an unresponsive Michael and an increasingly neglectful Spears seemed momentarily far away. 'She says America is far more exhilarating and pleasanter to live in than England,' Spears wrote in October 1954, 'which I can well believe; but I am so busy myself that it does not very much matter where I am.'[1]

In 1950 May published her first post-war novel, called *For the Record* in Britain and *Catspaw* in the United States. Its background is the communist takeover of a central European state, obviously based on Czechoslovakia and the tragedy of Jan Masaryk, an old friend of Spears, who died in mysterious circumstances after falling from a window in Prague in 1948. The hero is Prince Louis, famous for his part in the anti-Nazi resistance, who returns to his country with Isabel, his beautiful American wife, to join the first post-war government. Suspense comes from the knowledge that Alex, the Prince's secretary and a psychological cripple, is a communist working secretly to bring about a revolution.

The tone is that of a political operetta hardening only occasionally into its author's idea of realism: a fairyland of princes, princesses, gothic castles, hobgoblins and foul fiends. The sexual link between Louis and Isabel fascinates the impotent Alex; 'the effort not to think of them together in the intimacy of their bedroom was unspeakably exhausting'. Louis, though, is not faithful: 'how could a man who enjoyed lolling on the big breasts of a street-woman go from her to his wife's bed?' One observation came straight from the author's heart: the way 'married lovers quarrel and then make it up without settling anything'. If *For the Record* now seems a rather simplistic vision of fanaticism facing naivety, it is a brave attempt to show the link between personal trauma and political extremism.[2]

May's fascination with idealism showed also in her other notable post-war novel *Martin Merriedew*, published in 1952: an account of how a Christ-like figure might be treated in the modern world. The book begins in an English village where Lady Barbara Patche, the squire's daughter, observes the life of Martin Merriedew, the son of the local doctor. Martin becomes a doctor himself, then disappears to the east before returning to Britain to reveal also as a charismatic religious leader. In the war he joins the Red Cross, helps German prisoners to escape and tries to persuade British soldiers to lay down their arms. For this he is tried for treason, the judge being the man who has married Barbara, and during the trial, as Martin's story unfolds, she feels ashamed of the compromises of her own unsatisfying life.

Martin Merriedew has the usual autobiographical aspects. Barbara Patche's brother, the weakling Francis whose mother has wished him 'to rule the British race', has echoes of the author's son Michael. Why do children 'always detest their parents'? May asks. By this time Michael had descended into truculent silence. But it was belief that intrigued May; and in the courtroom Barbara wants to believe in Merriedew. 'If one could be certain about God, Charles, we would be safe,' she tells her dull husband. At the end she settles for the prospect of a safe, if bleak, old age: 'I have Charles. I stick to Charles.'[3]

Now May and Spears were together more than during the war and the strains showed. Her appearance could be disconcerting; she had lost weight again and become alarmingly thin with hair dyed either dark or pale brown and with brightly painted nails. She smoked ceaselessly and her hands shook but her clothes could be exquisite and the eyes were still huge, of extraordinary depth and colour, fixing people with a gaze of stern fascination. Cyril Connolly compared her to an exotic bird. The voice had softened, deepened by incessant smoking, and had lost its child-like insistence. As she seemed to shrink with age, so Spears appeared to become larger, not only tall but now broad, his presence even more insistent.

May's two anxieties were her son Michael and Nancy Maurice. She felt agonised when Spears's irritation and disappointment with the boy sometimes, if rarely, erupted; 'whatever you may feel about him even if you hate him,' May wrote despairingly once, 'he is your son.'[4]

She usually accompanied Spears for at least a part of his annual six-week visit to the Gold Coast and the Ashanti mine, but knew that he took short holidays with Nancy, often as extensions of business trips. In August 1955 May became upset about one of these, partly because it coincided with an especially bad period with Michael. 'Have you forgotten the morning when he came upstairs to your bedroom door and you only consented to let him come in when I begged you to – and then turned on me in fury and said: "I will not have Peti foisted on me,"' May wrote. 'Miss Maurice turned up a few moments later and I left.' She heard Nancy telling one of the directors at Bata Shoes that she was going to the Adriatic: 'how far you travelled together is of no consequence. It is enough to know that when my deepest feelings run counter to her wishes and convenience, I am not worth considering.'[5]

May seems always to have been faithful to Spears; even the affair with Claude Rome between the wars was almost certainly only a romantic friendship. Gossips, especially French gossips, imputed a lesbian side to Madame la Générale in her feelings for some of the members of her unit but here again the intensity was emotional, with no evidence of physical relationships. Since 1916 she had loved her husband in all his complex moods and ambitions, and stayed loyal to him. She loathed her rival. 'She used some of her coarse expressions the other day at the cottage about someone else,' May told Spears. '"O, yes," she said, "he will eat any amount of dirt." She has quite possibly said the same of me. She has certainly thought it each time you have proved to her that she has the right to despise me.' She feared for Michael in the event of a separation or divorce. 'Where and how am I to live without damage to you and him? Am I to go on eating dirt to feed N.M.'s appetite? I remember her saying "Nothing amuses me so much as doing somebody down."' May had seen Nancy's gradual invasion of their life. 'She has got everything she wanted except your name. I am a cypher.' She tolerated Nancy because of her importance to Spears. 'She collaborates with you and there is no more to be said.' To upset Michael might be fatal; 'I do not exaggerate.' The personal dilemma overwhelmed her. 'I must find a way. I await your suggestions and I dread your return.'[6]

Michael's attempt at running the fruit farm went badly. Then in August 1956 he had a brain haemorrhage and was unconscious for a month, forcing May to return from the United States, where she had been helping Adlai Stevenson's presidential campaign. At the end of the year Michael, while recovering, went down with pneumonia and May nursed him day and night at the house at Warfield. She knew her son would want to move into a flat of his own when he recovered and her feelings were divided between the hope that he would get better and a dread of losing him. 'She told me last night that her heart was broken,' Spears wrote to her sister Joyce, 'and I think this is really true.'[7] The anxiety made her lose even more weight. In August 1962 Michael was back in hospital with high blood pressure, raising her fears once more.

None of this stopped May from playing a large part in the structure of Spears's post-war domestic life. 12 Strathearn Place, a big house in Paddington, was where they entertained: large, rather formal black-tie dinners with food cooked by the French chef from the Institute of Directors. The guests were usually politicians, diplomats, journalists and businessmen: Lords Boothby and Chandos (as Oliver Lyttelton had become) and Colin Coote from the old guard; Duncan Sandys, Julian Amery and Peregrine Worsthorne from a younger group with the new generation represented by Edward du Cann, Robert Carr, the Liberal Jeremy Thorpe or the trades unionist Vic Feather. There might be Americans like Adlai Stevenson, perhaps some grand Lebanese, but seldom any French. Spears would sit at the head of the table, drinking in even the most outrageous flattery as if it were vintage champagne.

At St Michael's Grange, the house at Warfield, it was quieter. Here, from 1957, Spears and May were looked after by Mrs Reichart, a German refugee who became devoted to them both. She noticed Spears's affection for his dogs, a poodle and an Alsatian, and his fury when this was not returned. Once, in the garden, the poodle would not leave Mrs Reichart to come to him and he ordered her to fetch a whip so that he could punish the disobedient creature. She refused and a furious row started, ending only when May shouted: 'Stop it, both of you!'

Spears could never conceal the domineering side of his character. He directed work in the garden and controlled the household arrangements. Most mornings in the country he wrote in his ground-floor study, finding it increasingly hard because an old head wound from the First War had flared up again to interfere with his concentration. Mrs Reichart thought him a kind man, but quick tempered and strong in his dislikes; he spoke courteously to her sometimes in German. Often she would hear him reciting poetry and he enjoyed children, especially May's grandchildren and great-grandchildren. He seemed fatalistic about Michael's illness; May was much more obviously distraught. Mrs

Reichart watched them both grow old: May, frail and thin, the General solid and rather deaf but still sharp and with dyed black hair.

Sometimes Nancy would come to St Michael's Grange at the week-end when May was there; Mrs Reichart disliked her and adored May. There was a further addition to the household when Kwesi Manu, a Ghanaian who had worked at the Ashanti residence, came to England to be the General's valet in 1971. Apparently Spears made it clear that Kwesi and his wife Stella should not have children for this would lead to noise and discord. Mrs Reichart and Kwesi loathed each other. He thought she was a witch and she dreaded being alone with the Ghanaian, especially after she had once seen him glance significantly at a bread knife.[8]

Mrs Reichart thought that May and Spears remained close, in spite of their quarrels. On his eightieth birthday, in August 1966, he was on holiday alone in Corfu; May had stayed behind because Michael was ill again. She sent him a telegram of congratulation and love and wrote on 7 August: 'I have thought of you a great deal today.' But there was no message from him and she put the worst interpretation on the silence, dreading that he 'wanted to be rid' of her 'for good and all'. Michael sank further; 'you will never know how cruel this 3 weeks experience has been'. Then at last Spears's letter arrived, having been delayed in the post. 'The unnecessary suffering is over,' May told him, 'and I breathe again, awaiting your return with unfailing love.'[9] On his side, too, there was still real feeling. 'I really hated leaving you my little May & I think & worry about you all the time', Spears wrote in 1964, 'my very dear love' for 'my little circle is very much centred on you.'[10]

But his post-war letters show how important Nancy had become to him. She had the studio in Battersea, 'the stud', where they would play records of his favourite French songs. Away from this, Spears charged her with neglect. Signs were terribly important. 'You might have done something about my birthday,' he wrote in 1946 from Chitré. 'It is the first time you have not. Dear Nancy, you are my very dear Nancy.' In 1957 he wrote from Haroué, the Prince de Beauvau-Craon's huge château in eastern France: 'the spring of my wrist watch has broken. I wonder if it is an omen on my birthday?' Nancy had gone to Majorca to rest an injured leg. 'I think of you constantly,' he told her, 'so much so that you might be here, so much so that my mind does not miss you tho' my heart does. I have not faced up to your being a long way away. You will come quickly if I send for you, won't you?'

At Haroué he could not sleep. 'I feel quite stunned and something torn out of me. You can't think how lonely I am.' Some Pétainists came to lunch and it was intimated that he might be an embarrassment, so he went out for the day. Nancy's telegram from Majorca to say that she had arrived safely relieved him: 'I am sick with fear when you are in the air.' Then he felt guilty at not having brought her on the trip to France. 'I suddenly saw myself as having driven you off, away from me, into a kind of exile and the macabre of it got me by the throat. That I should drive my love away seemed to exceed the worst jokes Hell ever devised.'

She wrote to say that her leg did not seem to be getting better. Her plaintive tone annoyed him and he pushed May forward as an example of one who did not complain in spite of the trouble with Michael. 'In contrast to you May is as good as gold and making a real effort not to worry me.' He felt a dread that he had failed with her. 'If I were eliminated as I no doubt will be soon, wd you be happier? At least you would not worry.' He went on to Chitré, where Yvonne seemed preoccupied. 'Y says she has "a grande indifference" for everything – and it is true'; in 1953, her only son had died of leukaemia. Spears needed constant outward signs from Nancy. 'Your letters are wonderfully descriptive but – I may be wrong, I searched them but did not find that brimful love which made me so happy in your first ones.'

The French trip ended with what would be almost his last visit to Voutenay, because the Rafinesques sold it in 1958. Here, one hot afternoon when the family was away, he lay down by the river and slept, then walked in a wood across the valley from the church where he had a good view of his grandmother's grave. Here at last he felt peace.[11]

From France, however, came an unexpected public note of family discord. Béatrix Beck, the daughter of his tragic sister Kathleen, had been unhappy in England, where Spears had taken her after the war. She had worked as a housekeeper at St Michael's Grange and for Michael on his farm in Kent but found the language difficult. Her own daughter Bernadette detested the convent in Folkestone where Spears paid for her education.

Béatrix began to write and in 1946 won the Belgian Prix de Brabant for some short stories. On leaving England, she and Bernadette went to Paris, where André Gide took an interest in her because of his early friendship with her father Christian Beck and an admiration for her work. She became his last secretary, then in 1952 won the Prix Goncourt with *Léon Morin, prêtre*.

Béatrix Beck's novels are precise studies of character and atmosphere, often based on her own experiences. *Des accommodements avec le ciel*, published in 1954, is about Barny, a young girl who has moved at the end of the war from France to Belgium with her infant daughter, as Béatrix Beck had done. Here she is rescued by her uncle, the English General Sir Edgar Deirdree, sometimes called Lord Deirdree: a preposterous figure dressed in tweeds and speaking a particularly pompous type of French. As soon as he is driven off the ferry by his chauffeur Sir Edgar starts to give orders. She must change her name, he says, from that of her dead husband who had been a Jew. If she comes to England to cook for his son Warren, as he wishes her to do, this will be essential for it would be a catastrophe for him and Warren to have a niece with a Jewish name.

'Why are you anti-semitic?' Barny asks. 'Because I am not Jewish,' he answers, in a way that seems to her to be a demonstration of English pragmatism. His blue eyes are pitiless and sparkle with amusement. Victorious as usual, he persuades her to come back with him and at the end of the book Barny's child observes how sad it is to go to the country of the people who killed Joan of Arc.[12]

In France, where *Des accommodements avec le ciel* received respectful reviews, no connection seems to have been made between Spears and the grim Sir Edgar. But with *Le Muet*, the book's sequel, published in 1963, there was public recognition of the origins of the fictional English General. For *Le Muet* is a detailed account of life in the household of Sir Edgar, his American wife Maude and Michael, the mute of the title.

In the novel the character Barny is again in a position once experienced by Béatrix: this time as housekeeper to Warren, the invalid son of Sir Edgar and Maude. She does not understand the language or the culture of this strange land. Maude, or May, might tell her that she likes England because it is simultaneously practical and poetic, but to Barny it seems silent and brutal.

For her, the brutality lies in the silence. Warren has never heard the truth about his sister's suicide. He will not read Maude's novels because he dreads having to tell her if he does not like them; of Sir Edgar's latest book, *The Secret Battles*, he says only that it is rather clichéd. He plays chess brilliantly and is clever but speaks hardly at all, not even to his mistress Belinda. Maude chain-smokes, has wounded eyes and a detached adoration for her son, again unexpressed. Sir Edgar Deirdree, who has changed his name from the less impressive Deirdry, surrounds himself with photographs of the royal family and cuts short all conversation about his political views, which are expressed mostly in the form of anti-semitic jibes. Silence permeates *Le Muet* in much the same way as it does *Three Pilgrims and a Tinker*, May's novel about

English life. But in *Le Muet* the silence is that of anger and disappointment; for Warren it takes the form of an almost religious
renunciation of the world.

Barny returns to France, taking her daughter with her. Sir Edgar
has been kind to the little girl, in the same way that Spears was often
good to children. In Paris she sees the Countess Hermine de Drolla,
modelled on Yvonne de Lestrange, who tells her that Warren has
married and divorced, and that she finds Sir Edgar bigoted and lacking
in culture; once he scolded her for going to the theatre with an Indo-
Chinese friend. If ever he comes to France, the Countess says, one
would scratch his eyes out after what he has written about the French.
The novel ends with the news that Warren has suffered a cerebral
haemorrhage and become one of the living dead. Sir Edgar and Maude
are apparently seeing no one.[13]

In France, the newspapers picked up the autobiographical aspect, *Le
Monde* putting at the top of its review: 'Another portrait of England
featuring General Spears'. The critic, Jacqueline Piatier, praised the
painterly approach of the author: 'she does not write novels, she
composes pictures.' It was the picture of England that intrigued the
French: a country of reserve, puritanism, hidden tension, crudity, silent
vanity and eccentricity, of human alienation and despair. Why has
Warren, or Michael, settled for the life of a mute? Does the reason lie
in the brutality of a boarding-school education, the suicide of his sister
or the long illness of his youth? *Le Monde* felt that Béatrix Beck had
avenged the damage done to France by Spears's description of the bad
days of 1940.[14] *Le Nouveau Candide* went even further; if all English
families are like the one portrayed in *Le Muet*, its correspondent wrote,
General de Gaulle was right not to allow Britain into the Common
Market.[15]

Spears read *Le Muet* and was horrified. He cut off all contact
with Béatrix but still cherished his memories of her infant daughter
Bernadette. His efforts to entertain the girl had not always been
appropriate, he recognised, as when he had taken her to *Waiting for
Godot*, but she had aroused that sympathy he had always had for
children. There was an epilogue in 1981 when Bernadette Szapiro
published a novel of her own about her childhood, *La Première Ligne*.
The loneliness of her time in the Folkestone convent is one of its
themes; and her relief at her eventual return to France with her mother
to escape the silence.[16]

In post-war Britain Spears swung to the right. Among his dislikes were
a possible Channel Tunnel, membership of the Common Market, the

Greek-Cypriot nationalist leader Archbishop Makarios, the trades unions and immigration. In 1958 he shocked the editor of the *Daily Telegraph* by proposing that the part of Cyprus thought to harbour terrorists should be evacuated and the whole area soused with poisonous gas: 'a difficult technical problem but not an impossible one'. Donald McLachlan, the acting Managing Editor, wrote back: 'the suggestion you make in your second paragraph is so reminiscent of methods used by the Germans in Europe and by the Russians that I cannot believe that you would wish to advocate it in public without further consideration.'[17]

In 1958 de Gaulle returned to power in France and Spears sent him a telegram: 'in souvenir of June 17 I send you my good wishes for the accomplishment of your heavy task. I believe you will succeed.' The General answered on a card, in his own handwriting: 'Merci, mon cher Général. On fera ce qu'on pourra. Avec témoins souvenirs.' When de Gaulle came on his state visit to Britain in 1960 he wrote beforehand to Spears to say how memories of 1940 would be in his thoughts. As for Spears and May, he said, he had written in his memoirs what he thought suitable and fair, although Spears had challenged de Gaulle's version of what had happened in the Levant. But the past could sometimes rear up in a more personal way.[18] In 1960 Spears battled through lawyers with Randolph Churchill over a biography of Lord Derby in which Churchill had included slighting remarks Derby had made about Spears and raised the matter of his putative Alsatian origins, always a touchy point; the text was changed to give a more anodyne view and the reference to Spears's foreign blood left out.

At the Institute of Directors, he fought with the present, launching a pamphlet in 1959 which claimed that the socialists planned to nationalise over 500 major industrial companies. Harold Wilson is said to have believed that it lost Labour the election and the party devoted an entire political broadcast to its refutation.

The basis of the Institute was Spears's wish to have an organisation that could speak up for free enterprise. In 1950 the headquarters moved to 51 Palace Street, Westminster and then to Chips Channon's old house in Belgrave Square, with a grand dining room and a French chef. A magazine, the *Director*, added weight to the propaganda battle. Encouraged by Lord Chandos, Spears imposed a military style of management on the Institute. Sir Richard Powell, a baronet and wartime Welsh Guards officer who had escaped from a German prison camp and worked with the French resistance, became its first director-general in 1954. Membership then stood at just under 20,000; Powell devoted his energy and piratical style to increasing this and the standing of the Institute. His toughness appealed to Spears. 'I trust everyone until they do me a dirty trick,' he said once. 'And if that happens then I kick them in the teeth.'[19]

Spears was an active chairman from 1948 until 1966, the year of his eightieth birthday. In 1955 the Institute's Annual Convention moved to the Royal Festival Hall and was attended by 2,500 people, who were addressed by Sir Walter Monckton, the Minister of Labour, and Vic Feather, the Assistant General Secretary of the TUC. Motions were passed calling for reductions in taxation, the restoration of incentives and a reversal of the drift to collectivism and the destruction of individual wealth and property. In 1957 Harold Macmillan, the Prime Minister, was one of the speakers.

By 1961 membership had reached 38,000 and the Annual Convention moved to the Albert Hall. These gatherings received much press attention, not least because of the lavish lunch boxes given to each person who came. In 1962 3,000 members had to be turned away because of lack of space: the speakers were the Duke of Edinburgh on his Award Scheme; Dr Beeching on the future of the railways; the Archbishop of York on ethics in trade and industry; Professor Goodhart on Anglo-American relations; Lord Home, the Foreign Secretary, on the communist threat to international peace; Lord Chandos on the Common Market and unofficial strikes; and Spears himself on the Commonwealth. In 1965, Spears's last year as chairman, James Callaghan, then Chancellor of the Exchequer, and Edward Heath, the Leader of the Opposition, spoke. In 1966, after Spears had made it plain that he felt he had been forced out, the post of chancellor of the Institute of Directors was created for him and he held this until his death in 1974.[20]

Inevitably there were criticisms. The huge commissionaire outside the Belgrave Square offices, Sergeant-Major Vonk, seemed to reflect the slightly intimidating atmosphere inside of social exclusivity and distance from the shop floor. Of the governing council few had come up through the ranks of industry and there was a slight sense of an old boys' network. But the effort could not be faulted; the flood of pamphlets extolling free enterprise and low taxation attested to this.

Golden Evening

Spears watched de Gaulle's daring foreign policy with fascination, certain that the French President had malevolent intentions towards Britain. 'I look upon it as our only chance that when he dies there will be nobody to take his place,' he wrote in February 1964. 'He has shaken himself free of America. All he has to do now is to trample over our remains.'[1] In June he felt the presidential power when a long interview he gave to French television about the departure from Bordeaux on 17 June 1940 was not shown because it might have contradicted the elevated image that the General wished to convey at election time.

In France, however, he had a new ally. The French rights to *Assignment to Catastrophe* had been bought by Les Presses de la Cité and, to his delight, Spears found himself dealing with Thérèse de Saint Phalle, a young editor there who wrote novels and could cope with even the most awkward of his demands. Translated as *Témoignage sur une catastrophe*, *Assignment* was serialised in five extracts in *Le Nouveau Candide* from 24 August until 2 October 1946, ten years after its appearance in Britain.

Sam White, the *Evening Standard*'s correspondent in Paris, thought the national resurgence under de Gaulle made the shameful revelations of *Assignment* bearable to the French: 'it could not conceivably have been published here much earlier because it would have been rather like pouring vinegar into still open wounds'.[2] The French response was not too hostile, *Le Monde* carrying only a fairly anodyne piece. In *Nouvelles Littéraires* Pierre Desvernois described the book, which he said might offend some French, as a captivating portrait of the psychology of Britain and how the country awoke to the dangers of Hitler; *L'Humanité* accused Spears of having no idea of the practical politics of the Communist party.[3] In *Figaro Littéraire* François Mauriac commented on Spears's opposition to a Channel Tunnel by echoing Huguet's earlier thoughts in *Great Britain and the War*. To Mauriac, it was absurd to think of isolation, a Victorian concept, in the age of the aeroplane and the atomic bomb.[4] Sales were slightly disappointing: 5,000 copies of each volume by November 1965 against original British sales of 13,000 for *Prelude to Dunkirk* and 12,000 for *The Fall of France*. But he began to get hints from across the Channel of the renaissance of his reputation.

A television appearance, timed to coincide with the publication, was a triumph. The first point put to Spears was that the British army had let down the French at Dunkirk, to which he answered that as British troops were under French command at the time any complaints should be addressed to that quarter. Speaking perfect French, he fielded several questions of this kind, to be clapped loudly at the end by the studio technicians and the interviewer.

'How I wish I could have been present at your television interview,' Lord Ismay wrote. 'Winston always said you could be rougher with the French and get away with it than anyone else.'[5] It was, of course, to Churchill that Spears owed his chance of observing the events of 1940: to Churchill also his decision to enter politics after the First War and protection until 1944 for his contentious activities in the Levant.

After 1945, and Spears's public criticism of government policy, the relationship changed. Churchill made no serious move to help Spears get back into the House of Commons, and when the Conservatives returned to power in 1951 no official position was offered to him. His baronetcy in 1953 seemed a poor substitute for the longed-for peerage. But Spears still cherished glimpses of his hero: at the Other Club or in stories relayed by the great man's staff or family or those who had heard Churchill talk fondly about his friend Louis. Then an increasing decrepitude showed that the end was near; and on 24 January 1965 Winston Churchill died.

Spears could not come to the great state funeral in St Paul's Cathedral because he was on his annual visit to Ghana. 'Even here the impact of Winston's funeral has been tremendous,' he told Churchill's last secretary, Anthony Montague Browne. 'It is quite clear that he served England magnificently in death as in life.' He had heard that Churchill had asked in his will for a small token to be given to those of his friends who desired it. 'I should very much like to be considered one of these.' He looked back to the early days. 'I think the thing I am proudest of in my life is that Winston asked me to be his second in command when he commanded the Royal Scots Fusiliers in 1915.'

Lady Churchill sent him a silver box and an appreciative note. But he felt he should thank Montague Browne for this, and 'for the way you have always acted as my interpreter to the Churchill family': a further sign of the decline in intimacy since the war.[6]

Spears dreaded retirement, partly for financial reasons, because he still had the cost of Michael's medical treatment; also he liked a life of comfort, even luxury. Fortunately his astonishing energy survived the ailments of old age. In 1956 he was seventy and the next decade brought prostate trouble, thrombosis of the leg and congestion of the lungs; even if these entailed short spells in hospital he managed to throw them off. The House of Lords, of course, would have been perfect as a place to advance his views and another source of income. His stream of letters to the newspapers on subjects that included the Common Market, the Rhodesian Unilateral Declaration of Independence, de Gaulle and the leftward-leaning BBC could not have the same resonance. 'A letter from Spears? Not a bit surprised,' says a character in Nancy Mitford's *Don't Tell Alfred* on hearing of the contents of an edition of *The Times*.[7] His friends felt for him. 'I was always sad', Ismay wrote, 'that Winston didn't offer you a peerage.'[8]

There was still his writing. In September 1965 he received an advance of £500 for a book on Pétain and de Gaulle that would include the Marshal's own account of the French mutinies of 1917 which he had written in 1926 and given to Spears. He had already done most of the work for this when he read an unpleasant reference to him in a book about Pétain, resurrecting the charge that he had been a British spy. 'He was all the time on my back keeping me under surveillance,' the Marshal had apparently said, referring particularly to a summer between the wars when Spears and May had rented a house near Pétain's property in the south of France.[9]

This did not apparently affect the mostly laudatory account in his new book, *Two Men Who Saved France*. In *Two Men* Spears does not mention the metaphysical bond between de Gaulle and Pétain detected by some. He denies also that de Gaulle had any concept of himself as a rebel in 1940, asserting the General always believed in the absolute legitimacy of what he was doing. Sympathetic, even affectionate, towards both men and written with Spears's usual *élan*, the book has some obvious dislikes: the pusillanimity of Whitehall, French trades union agitators, the nauseating ethos of Vichy. Although more sketchy than his previous works, *Two Men* has thrilling evocations of the palpable tension of Paris in June 1917 or the meetings by moonlight at sea on the way to Dakar: also those telling details at which its author excelled like the glimpse of a French naval signalman on the bridge of the *Westernland* awakening the ghosts of the Breton fishermen of his childhood.

For Spears, the two men's essential greatness was displayed best by Pétain in his treatment of the mutinies and by de Gaulle after his country's humiliation in 1940. There is no comparison of their achievements or characters; and, with de Gaulle, only a hint of the later quarrel: 'de Gaulle and I finally parted company over his attitude towards the Levant States, whose independence we had guaranteed. But that is another story.'[10] Two photographs were included, both inscribed, Pétain's declaring: 'Au Général Spears avec mes sentiments affectueux'; de Gaulle's, signed in August 1940: 'Au Général Spears, témoin, allié, ami.'

The book had a good reception when it came out in October 1966, with a note of indulgence towards an old man. 'As with all Spears, one longs for more,' Alistair Horne wrote in the *Sunday Telegraph*. In the *Observer* Malcolm Muggeridge detected that the author had a greater sympathy for Pétain, perhaps because of de Gaulle's unforgiving nature, and Frank Giles in the *Sunday Times* found the book 'penetrating and very funny'. But D. C. Watt in the *Spectator* called *Two Men* 'a much slighter volume' than Spears's earlier works, with the author's 'particular brand of High Toryism' too much in evidence, precluding any sympathy for the mutineers. 'I wish he could be persuaded to write of his experiences in Syria in the Second World War,' Watt wrote. 'It would be a major service both to literature and to history.'[11]

Thérèse de Saint Phalle had bought *Two Men Who Saved France* for Les Presses de la Cité, and on 30 November and 1 December *Le Figaro* carried two extracts. In December Spears was in Paris to promote the book. *L'Aurore* wondered if de Gaulle would invite him to the Elysée and a journalist wrote in *Noir et Blanc* that he thought Spears one of the most intelligent and brilliant people he had met, a man who spoke their language better than most French. A review in the left-wing *Nouvel Observateur* by Daniel Mayer was more grudging. Mayer felt the comparison between de Gaulle and Pétain had been done for commercial reasons and expressed his belief that the Gaullist regime resembled Vichy in its growing authoritarianism.[12]

By 9 January 1967 the English edition of *Two Men Who Saved France* had sold 2,097 copies and plans were finalised with his new publisher, Maurice Temple-Smith of Secker and Warburg, for a book of autobiographical essays called *The Picnic Basket*. It starts with his childhood in France and ends with a fanciful description of the battle of Poitiers which Spears claimed had unfolded in his mind's eye during a visit to the battlefield with Yvonne de Lestrange, called Simone in the narrative. Of his grandmother and Voutenay he writes with unashamed feeling, resurrecting also the Celtic tales of his Breton nursemaid Gaidic; then comes a roseate view of the life of a cavalry subaltern before 1914. The First World War features through the experience of a Belgian woman caught up in the German advance and also in his reconstruction of a cavalry engagement at Néry in September 1914 which he claimed destroyed the enemy's scouting power and allowed a trap set by Joffre to become the victory of the Marne.

The book's tone is discursive, resembling a series of anecdotes told as much for the pleasure of the writer as for that of his audience. The Poitiers essay is taken mostly from Froissart, with Spears also drawing on his knowledge of the weapons of the Hundred Years War. Again the critics were indulgent, the *Times Literary Supplement* alone complaining of the book's blandness, its occasionally absurd metaphors, and the fustian language of the account of Poitiers. 'Few pre-Mons cavalry officers have the gift of grooming their readers as skilfully as their chargers,' Cyril Connolly wrote in the *Sunday Times*. 'General Spears blends good judgement with unusual observation.'[13] In July John Terraine, the distinguished historian, did a programme on BBC radio about Spears's books, a celebration of 'one of the most admirable, elegant and lucid writers on military matters in the language'.[14]

In April 1968, Eyre and Spottiswoode brought out a new edition of *Liaison 1914* with some additions by Spears reiterating his claim that Joffre rather than Gallieni had brought about the victory of the Marne. A new generation of military historians praised the book, led by John Terraine, Correlli Barnett and John Keegan; to the latter *Liaison* was 'one of the golden windfalls of history' in which the author shows 'a mastery of the English language and of the narrative form'.[15] Only Liddell Hart, old champion of Gallieni, dissented, saying that the additional material had not changed his mind. A. J. P. Taylor remained fervently admiring: 'it is a marvellous book which seems to get better with the passage of time.'[16] Arthur Bryant wrote a eulogistic piece in the *Illustrated London News* about *The Picnic Basket* and *Liaison 1914* under the headline 'A Twentieth Century Froissart'. Spears sent copies of Bryant's article to more than ninety of his friends and associates.[17]

In August 1968 he broadcast about the flight from Bordeaux on 17 June 1940 with de Gaulle. Afterwards came a new excitement, the chance to kill the French claim that the aeroplane had not been at his command, when he received a letter from a Wing-Commander E. B. Fielden who was living in a caravan in South Devon. Fielden believed he might have been the pilot, but his story differed slightly from previous versions. He said he had landed at Bordeaux in his Flamingo on 16 June not with de Gaulle but carrying a king's messenger from Algiers; then he thought it possible that he had taken Spears and de Gaulle on to London on 17 June. This is doubtful, for Fielden's diary shows that his flight to London took place on 16 June, a day earlier, and observers at Jersey remember de Gaulle landing in a De Havilland, not a Flamingo. Unfortunately Fielden's logbook had been lost. Spears did not know that these facts, discovered later, contradicted Fielden's genuine belief that he had carried Spears and de Gaulle. Sensing triumph, he gave Fielden lunch at the Institute of Directors in March 1969 and, at Spears's behest, an account of the meeting appeared, with a photograph, in the *Daily Telegraph*. The identities of Fielden's passengers from Bordeaux remain a mystery.[18]

On her annual trips to the United States May would go to Princeton to see Bayard Dodge, who had been President of the American University in Beirut, and his wife Mary. Here she sought out Albert Einstein to ask if he believed in God. Einstein waited only a moment before answering. 'Yes,' he said, 'but God is a concept that I cannot explain and I have no proof. You understand, there is no proof. You can never be sure. You can only say that you are not sure.' May asked how this affected him: 'if you are not sure of anything, if you are only floating in a dream, how can you be so serene?' Einstein laughed: 'floating in a dream is too floating a statement.'[19]

Adlai Stevenson provided more certainty, even if it was only about the present. He confided in May, knowing that she understood his problems with his wife, and her relation, Ellen, who suffered from paranoia and drank. An anglophile, Stevenson was consoling in 1956 about the deterioration of the Anglo-American alliance as a result of Suez and assured May in 1960 that John Kennedy would make a better president than Richard Nixon: 'one of the few people in my life I really deeply dislike and distrust'.[20]

In 1965 Adlai Stevenson dropped down dead in a London street. To May it was a terrible shock at a time of unhappiness and exhaustion with Michael. She began to feel a sense of displacement, of doubt about how much she had ever understood her adopted country. In October 1966, when she was eighty, she was asked to be an honorary fellow of the new Mugar Memorial Library at Boston University, to which she had given her manuscripts and papers. She did not feel strong enough to cross the Atlantic for the celebratory dinner and gave her thanks by telephone from a prepared text. 'I love England,' she said, 'and believe in the British people, stalwart, unbeatable when roused, but after trying to understand them for forty years, they remain baffling. My home is on your side – and I need to come home again.'[21]

May never visited the United States again. Increasingly frailty kept her from travelling, but in January 1968 Spears took her with him on his annual trip to Ghana where she fell at Obuasi and broke a hip.

Flown by helicopter to Accra, she was put on an aeroplane to London, accompanied by Spears and Nancy Maurice.

Two trained nurses moved into Strathearn Place. Word reached Freya Stark, an old admirer of them both from the Levant days, that May had died. 'She was a very dear, brave and sincere person,' she wrote, 'and you must feel very lonely.' Spears told her that she had been misinformed and that May had had an operation in London for an artificial hip and was learning to walk again: 'her courage has been tremendous.'[22] But by the summer of 1968 May could walk only with two sticks. Michael lived mostly in his own flat in London, cared for by a manservant: 'I am afraid', Spears said, 'he is sinking more and more into a completely physical life.'[23] May, always outspoken, quarrelled with one of her nurses; then, with the coming of winter, went into decline. On 2 December she died with her hand in Spears's. 'She had not found a solution to the question that she had hoped Dr Einstein would help her to resolve,' Spears wrote later, but she seemed serene. He remembered, above all, her courage, which he thought resembled the spirit and toughness of the early settlers in America.[24]

The Times obituary compared her novels to those of Edith Wharton: 'both were American born, both identified themselves with Europe while retaining something of distinctly American temper, and both seemed to take novel-writing in their stride while leading lives of conspicuous and purposeful social distinction.' It noted that her fiction had been confined to the circumstances of the very rich and remarked upon 'a certain conventionality of outlook'. On 5 December Rupert Hart-Davis wrote to *The Times* to remind its readers 'in fairness to her grandchildren and great grandchildren' that she had been married first to Colonel George Douglas Borden-Turner. He praised the way she had faced disaster after the Wall Street crash: 'she was entirely without self-pity and never referred to her losses.'[25]

Spears was furious. Hart-Davis and he had already quarrelled over Duff Cooper's memoirs and Rupert had later left Comfort, who had forsworn sexual relations after the birth of their third child, for his third wife Ruth. Spears despatched a stinging letter. 'I am deeply shocked that in your notice in *The Times* concerning "Miss Mary Borden", you, who after over 30 years of marriage deserted one of her daughters, should have given yourself the right to invoke "justice" for her grandchildren and great grandchildren.'[26] This exacerbated Hart-Davis's loathing of Spears and of Nancy Maurice, whom he saw as the encourager of such vindictiveness: 'the only really evil person I ever knew'.[27]

At this moment of loss, General de Gaulle wrote to his old ally. He and his wife, de Gaulle said, offered their sincere condolences. He had not forgotten the welcome given to him by Lady Spears at the beginning of the heroic times or what she and her unit had done for the Free French Forces. Spears asked Courcel, now French Ambassador in London, if he might make the letter public but was told this would not be appropriate.

A memorial service was held at St Paul's Church, Knightsbridge, on 7 January 1969. The French Minister of Defence, Pierre Messmer, sent over a group of twenty-five soldiers from the division to which May's ambulance unit had been attached; their standards gave a military air to the occasion. Madame de Larminat, widow of the General, came, as did the British Field-Marshals Alexander and Templer. Madame la Générale seemed to be in the ascendant over Mary Borden, popular novelist. The ambassadors of the United States, France, Switzerland, Turkey, Kuwait, Lebanon and Saudi Arabia reflected other aspects of her past and the years of entertaining at Strathearn Place. Almost all the living 'Spirettes' were there and that ghost at May's window, Nancy Maurice.

Lord Boothby gave the address, and Cyril Connolly offered ideas about what he might say. Boothby spoke of May's flair for people; of how she sifted genius from talent; of her deep, extraordinary eyes; of the childlike, drawling, irresistible voice. She had been a woman of elegance: chic, simple, cordial, ironic and brave. He mentioned the links with de Gaulle and Spears's own gifts: 'she married a man who, in my judgement, is one of the great living masters of English prose and, through him, was connected with another man who is, perhaps, the greatest living master of French prose. I will not mention his name, but he is very eminent and he is a great master of the art of language – the French language, just as Louis Spears is a great master of the art of English language. They must all have given much to each other.'[28]

May was remembered also in the *Revue de la France Libre*, where Médecin Général J. F. Vernier, once the medical chief of the Hadfield–Spears ambulance unit, wrote an eloquent obituary. The Quakers and conscientious objectors in the unit, Vernier recalled, had been devoted to her, so much so that when the peace came one of them had uttered the *cri de coeur*: 'Merde! The war has ended.'[29]

Michael's death came on 12 January 1969, five days after May's memorial service. 'I am only thankful that he died after and not before May,' Spears wrote to a friend, 'as she would have died heartbroken instead of happily and peacefully.'[30] On 3 May her ashes and those of Michael were buried in the cemetery of Warfield Parish Church. A rumour went out that May had left a great fortune to Spears and he worried that her children might think he had cheated them. In fact the sum came to £27,000, earned mostly from her writing.

After May's death Nancy Maurice expected to marry the man to whom she had been devoted for almost fifty years. But her manner had become insufferably domineering and he seemed reluctant to lose his new independence. His fending off of her took an often unsubtle form; certainly his asking John Tusa of Bata Shoes in front of Nancy whether Tusa advised him to marry her or not was neither tactful nor kind. One can, however, imagine the irritation she induced in a tired old man.

By October 1969 Nancy had had enough of his procrastination and bad temper. 'Your treatment of me during the last four weeks has been such that I shall have a breakdown if I do not get away,' she wrote. She complained of scenes, of threats to dismiss her and constant nagging about her very heavy smoking. In fact she knew that her control of much of his life, from his tax return to every aspect of his business interests, made her irreplaceable. 'I am prepared to come back as an experiment to see whether we can live together without destroying each other,' she told him, 'but I should have to have an assurance from you that there will be no threats, no scenes and that you will accept that if I give you my word I shall keep it.' They were married on 4 December 1969 at St Paul's Knightsbridge, one year and two days after May's death, with Sir Richard Powell, the Director-General of the Institute of Directors, as best man. Nancy moved into Strathearn Place and St Michael's Grange to take up her position as the second Lady Spears.[31]

There were other, more placid friendships to illumine old age. In 1955 he had received a letter from Dame Mary Moriarty, the Mother Superior at Stanbrook Abbey near Worcester, explaining that she was a relation of his through her paternal grandmother who had been a sister of his grandfather, Edward Louis Hack.

Spears and May came to Stanbrook to see Dame Mary, who admired his writing. Siegfried Sassoon visited the abbey too and Dame Mary thought Spears and Sassoon were masters at conveying sympathy through their writing. 'Are you aware of all the affection you have inspired in those who knew you or read your books?' she asked him in 1969. 'You have had plenty of glory too but affection is worth more than glory.' She saw, however, another side to him. 'I would like to talk to you about that tiger we all have inside us but tamed and chained up by religion and civilisation.'[32]

Visits to Yvonne de Lestrange became more difficult when Marc Allegret, the film director and former companion of André Gide, moved into Chitré. Spears and Allegret did not like each other and the link to Yvonne began to loosen, although on his side the devotion remained; 'the next world without Yvonne has got little attraction for me,' he told her.[33]

Then came a new admirer, from the beautiful renaissance château of Touffou, near Chitré, that had been immaculately restored by the brilliantly successful advertising man David Ogilvy. Having read *The Picnic Basket*, Ogilvy wrote in delight to the author and in 1969 Spears stayed at Touffou for the first time. Enchanted with his room in a high tower, he was at his best, fascinating Ogilvy and others with a series of anecdotes about his long, extraordinary life.

He was working on an account of his wartime experiences in the Middle East. 'I am very rude to everybody in this book,' he wrote to Thérèse de Saint Phalle, 'English and French alike.'[34] Much of modern Britain set him in a rage: the strikes, the attempts to propitiate de Gaulle in order to get into the Common Market, the changes in what he had previously looked upon as immutable institutions and states of mind. At the Carlton Club he was shouted down when he criticised its management; never, he said, had he known an exhibition of worse manners, not even in the roughest districts of his Carlisle constituency.

In August 1969, Spears would be eighty-three. Inevitably his past kept being resurrected, through newspaper articles, books, interviews on the radio and television appearances in programmes like *The Great War* or *Le Chagrin et la pitié*, the French documentary about the defeat and occupation. Then a challenge came to his one remaining position of real power: that of chairman of Ashanti Goldfields.

The story of Spears's activities in Ghana shows his extraordinary force of character and determination to mould change to his own wishes. At first it seemed as if he might succeed, if only by cautious shrewdness. He thought Kwame Nkrumah, the African nationalist leader of Ghana, unreliable but knew he had to get on with him. He tried, however, through the influence of Ashanti, an increasingly important part of the Ghanaian economy, to build up Dr Kofi Busia, a gentle academic unsuited to the rough world of Ghanaian politics, who despised Nkrumah as 'an adventurer ready to hop from adventure to adventure, relying on good luck and manoeuvring skill, plus his power over a section of the masses'.[35] Busia came from the Ashanti region; Spears hoped to keep him incorruptible, refusing all his requests for loans or financial assistance.

Although it was a public company, Ashanti seemed at times to be Spears's personal fief: a tribute again to his domineering personality.

He assembled a board of directors more noted for their past or other distinctions than for knowledge of mining: Sir David Waley, previously a civil servant at the Treasury; Lord Ismay, Churchill's former chief of staff; the Earl of Ranfurly, once Governor of the Bahamas; the politician Duncan Sandys; the retired colonial administrator Sir Miles Clifford; the financier Harley Drayton. To Spears 'the technicians' or engineers had no place on the board; 'technical knowledge and the power to direct are two entirely different matters.'[36] His old friend Lord Winster (as 'Matelot' Fletcher had become) was engaged to write a column in the *Ashanti Times*, a newspaper owned by the company. May enlisted Adlai Stevenson's help over American support for the huge Volta river project and dam.

With this personal style came personal responsibility. There were frequent crises with the African labour and trades unions that often boiled over during his yearly visit. At the end of 1955 a fourteen-week strike took place at the two mines. When it ended in February 1956 Spears gave a party to celebrate, but a number of workers stayed away because they had been told by the witch doctors that a spell in the White Man's cakes would prevent them from ever striking again. That year he collapsed from heat stroke while inspecting the depths of the mine, a not surprising fate for a man of seventy.

He claimed that Ashanti was the Commonwealth's richest gold mine, and in January 1959 the company declared a rise in net profit to £795,755. He was proud of having been made a chief of the Ashanti tribe and portraits of Africans adorned his office in Old Jewry. Of Nkrumah and his ministers he said: 'they are my personal friends.'[37]

Spears needed his powers of diplomacy, particularly after 1957 when, under Nkrumah's leadership, Ghana became independent. In March 1961 Spears told the annual general meeting of Bibiani, 'a dying mine', that the company had been sold to the Ghana government. He personally received £7,500 in compensation, but the next year came the shock of Nkrumah's dismissal of his British chief of the army, General Henry Alexander, who had boasted that he had Nkrumah in his pocket. 'He has been going from extreme to extreme,' Spears wrote to Ismay of the Ghanaian leader. 'I have been very worried about the effect on the Ashanti mine.'[38]

Spears feared that the Ghanaian government would either take over the mine or extract crippling amounts in tax. There were also increasing difficulties in getting money out of Ghana to pay the dividends in London and obtaining import licences for mining equipment. It was an achievement to get an audience with Nkrumah and this he could almost always do. With the Ghanaian leader he deployed charm and flattery, arriving with gifts from London: glass, expensive china, silver gilt and toys for the Nkrumah children. Once an aide entered to find Spears and the President on their knees trying out one of the more elaborate model trains; another time, perhaps in an intimation of the coming of a military regime, the Chairman brought a group of toy soldiers that, at the press of a switch, presented arms and marched in strict formation, to the sound of a drum. In 1962, after one of these meetings, Spears wrote of a 'really quite affectionate' Nkrumah who had declared that 'he looked upon me as a real friend' and spoke of the interests of Ashanti and Ghana as being 'identical'. The Chairman had brought the usual presents, 'but I firmly refused to let him see them until I had gone through the business part of the talk.'[39]

He thought constantly of his small kingdom. Having admired the scenery of a production at the Covent Garden opera house, he wrote to ask the Chairman if he might send a draughtsman round to look at it; 'I would like to do something of the same kind for the Ashanti Goldfields Corporation gardens in Ghana.'[40] His approach to the employees at Obuasi was paternalistic and he, May and Nancy moved among the people showing not only graciousness but concern. 'At every turn of every road – or conversation – you crop up spontaneously and fervently,' Lady Ranfurly told him after her first visit to the mine in 1964. 'You have built up something here which is far more than Gold could ever be.'[41] Spears spoke proudly of the company's record of building houses, clinics and schools, but critics claimed later that more could have been done, particularly with the profits that the Ghanaian government would not allow Ashanti to take out of the country.

By 1964 his main complaint was that the government took 77.3 per cent of Ashanti profits and expatriate workers would not stay at the mine because of the high taxation. But Nkrumah, who had embarked on a seven-year development plan, was not sympathetic, particularly as in the previous year the company made a record profit before tax of two million pounds and still had few senior African staff. The Ghanaian leader, wooed by the Soviet Union and the Chinese and 'quite insatiable of flattery', moved steadily to the left.[42] Then on 24 February 1966 he was toppled in a coup while on a visit to China, to be succeeded by General Ankrah, a former sergeant in the West African Frontier Force.

Soon afterwards Spears saw Ankrah, who promised to release money said to be owed to Ashanti Goldfields by the Bank of Ghana and allowed some disputed import licences to be granted as well. When the General said he would review the tax position, Spears was overjoyed and declared: 'well, he's a soldier, you see.'[43] The new regime seemed 'pro-west, pro-capital, pro-private enterprise' and without the old 'half baked Socialism'. Spears boasted of his past diplomacy, claiming that 'under the Nkrumah regime we did better as regards getting the dividends out, getting import licences etc: than any other company.'[44] But he quickly distanced himself from Nkrumah and sued the author of a book on Ghana who claimed he had been an intimate adviser of the former President. Ashanti's Accra representative, however, warned him of the poor perception of the company locally as being 'reactionary', 'overborne with expatriates' and 'not keeping pace with modern Ghana'.[45]

In 1965 the company moved to new offices in the City, at Moor House in London Wall, where Spears installed a diorama view of the mine in the boardroom, together with a balcony decorated with African plants. He held his press conference before the annual general meeting in this exotic setting. An extensive buffet would be laid on, with free-flowing drink, and the occasion was described as 'an annual event which London's financial journalists try hard not to miss'. In 1967 one commentator thought that Spears, then aged eighty-one, looked twenty years younger. Nancy in a leopardskin coat and hat, was there to help, interrupting sometimes to put him right; 'it was 75 per cent when you paid the final oil tax but it's only 73 per cent now.' The Chairman turned to his guests. 'You see, gentlemen, I've got a secretary who knows too damn much. Perhaps we had better have two press conferences next year.' He did not say that earlier in the year he had presented the two senior members of the new military regime with the same marching toy soldiers he had given Nkrumah the year before.[46]

Spears's almost viceregal position at Obuasi seemed indestructible. One year he had his Rolls-Royce flown out from London so that he could be driven around in even greater style. A new primary school was named after him in 1965, and May opened the Lady Spears Day Nursery. Each year there was a presentation by the Chairman of long-service medals and watches to employees of the mine. It was this that he enjoyed: the reassuring mixture of deference, comfort and power. The financial rewards were never huge; his director's fees and salary of approximately £6,000 a year scarcely changed between 1946 and 1967 and his share options brought only a small annual addition to this.

But a predator was eyeing Ashanti. In 1968 'Tiny' Rowland, the able and daring Managing Director of the trading company Lonrho, persuaded the Ghanaian Minister of Mines, Silvan Amagashi, that the Europeans had too much control at Ashanti. He suggested that the government should end Ashanti's ninety-year lease, granted in colonial times, and give Lonrho a new fifty-year lease in return for 20 per cent of the new company being ceded to the government of Ghana, with an option to buy a further 20 per cent for which, if it was exercised, Lonrho would receive £1 a share. Lonrho would be paid an annual management fee in Ghanaian currency.

In London, the movement towards takeover began in October 1968. Lonrho offered £15 million, but the key to the success of the bid was a statement by Amagashi that an independent Ashanti lease would not be renewed. Spears and his board seemed to have no choice. Rowland flew the four African directors of Ashanti to London and put them up at the Dorchester.[47]

Lonrho had wooed the Ghanaians assiduously, particularly Amagashi, with whom Spears had not always concealed his temper. One explosion in December 1968 led to a threat by the Mines Minister to ban Spears and Nancy from Ghana; Amagashi contrasted his belligerence with the 'very sympathetic' Lonrho board who in 1969 made the Ghanaian a consultant. Naturally the Lonrho bid succeeded. The *Financial Times* thought Ashanti 'could hardly do better than agree to Mr Rowland taking over the reins'; the newspaper also said of the company that 'its continued success in Ghana during recent years has owed a great deal to the Chairman, Sir Edward Spears, whose diplomacy has resulted in shareholders being given a reasonably fair deal even during the difficult days of the Nkrumah regime.' In the last year Ashanti had made pre-tax profits of £3.03 million, but 75 per cent of these had been paid in tax to the government of Ghana.[48]

At first Spears felt drawn to his new associate, saying, 'I liked Rowland very much and am impressed with his ability.'[49] He knew of Rowland's German origins and his internment on the Isle of Man during the war. It was to his credit, Spears thought, that he had worked as a railway porter and valet at the Connaught Hotel. His previous successes in Africa were undeniable. Rowland treated Spears generously. He made him a director of Lonrho and encouraged the annual visit to Ghana and the use of the residence at Obuasi, apparently perpetuating his extraordinary position with the company.

Then industrial troubles blew up into riots that threatened Lonrho's new business. Soon after May's memorial service and the death of Michael, Spears flew out to Ghana with Nancy to face the crisis. In the course of the demonstrations five men were shot by police. Lonrho paid three months' backpay to the workers to end the strikes, and Spears returned exhausted, believing that he still had the dominant role at the mine. But he could not come to terms with the new African directors, who, he complained, tried to 'meddle in the running of the mine' or with his loss of supremacy. In May 1969 Rowland wrote of his anxiety 'about the present relationship between the staffs of our two companies and indeed between yourself and myself'. In Ghana, where their visits coincided briefly in the same year, Rowland showed his lack of deference; an observer wrote: 'I had never before heard anyone speak so directly to the General.'[50]

The visit revealed a change in atmosphere. Spears thought his position had been strengthened when his old protégé Kofi Busia became Prime Minister of Ghana in 1969. But the new management looked askance at a chairman who was well into his eighties. In Ghana, in 1971, he found himself no longer the undisputed magnifico but watched over by two Lonrho men, Alan Ball, a director of the London board, and Major-General 'Jock' Anderson, once Commander of the Rhodesian army.

The Prime Minister greeted him with warmth. 'Are you not the man who believed in me when no one else did?' Busia said. 'Did you not say that I should be one day where I am now, in this chair?' When Spears complained that the Mines Minister had been rude to him, Busia said: 'This is the sort of thing I am up against. I will deal with it at once.' General Anderson's reaction was rather different. To Spears's tale of ministerial bad manners, he said merely: 'I am sorry. We will need him.' Spears then spoke in the style that had characterised his reign at Ashanti. 'Those who deal with us must learn to do so politely.'

Alan Ball told him that the Ghanaian members of the Ashanti board would agree to any proposal that Lonrho made and Spears wondered if this had been the intention when they were appointed; 'was it not rather that they should watch over Ghanaian interests?' Then, in the presence of Duncan Sandys, Ball declared, near to tears, how painful it was for him to have to say that, as a result of a cabinet decision, the Ghanaians would vote against Spears's re-election to the board. The most dignified course would be for him to resign from the chairmanship of Ashanti Goldfields after his eighty-fifth birthday and be made non-executive president for life.

Spears knew that he could not refuse. He told Alan Ball that he wished to continue his annual visits to the mine. Ball agreed to this but said that, after his resignation, he would be looked upon as a guest of the company. Some days later Spears saw Busia, who said the matter had never been discussed with him, nor had it come before the cabinet. Busia declared Ball's claim to be 'a lie, an absolute lie'.[51]

The last battle came two years later. In December 1972 the Ghanaian government had assumed control of the mine, with a minority share-holding and the management remaining in the hands of Lonrho. Spears approached Duncan Sandys, now Chairman of Lonrho, to ask when he might go in the new year to 'my' house at Obuasi. Sandys passed on the question to Derek Power, the company's chief consulting engineer.

Power's reply was not encouraging. Apparently the residence was now used often by Government officials and the new Ghanaian Chairman and directors. A Ghanaian army officer lived permanently at the mine and reported daily to the Commissioner for Lands and Mineral Resources. There had been much recent criticism, perhaps 'unfortunate and unfair', in the Ghanaian press of the past management of Ashanti Goldfields. Power felt Spears would find the present conditions unpleasant: 'for these reasons I must reluctantly recommend that the visit be postponed for the time being.' Upset, Spears did not go to Ghana.[52]

It was perhaps not surprising that he joined a group of Lonrho directors who that year rebelled against what they saw as the dictatorial behaviour of Tiny Rowland. With Spears, they planned a boardroom coup to force Rowland's resignation. 'The straight eight', as they were called, had a majority on the board but Rowland secured an injunction to prevent his dismissal. The struggle attracted public attention partly because another director, and former ally of Rowland, was Angus Ogilvy, married to Princess Alexandra, who resigned, fearful of the publicity of the impending court action.

Some reports spoke of an outsider's battle against the establishment; others cast doubt on Rowland's business methods. On 8 May 1973 the trial began. Rowland claimed that only the shareholders could dismiss him: not the board of directors. There was a flurry of affidavits from supporters and opponents of Rowland; among these was one from Major-General Sir Edward Spears.

With the diminution of his power at Ashanti, Spears's affection for Rowland had turned to dislike and disdain. At Ashanti, he claimed, Rowland had shown himself to be vindictive and wrong. 'Care was taken to eliminate me. I was too popular and knew too much and many schools are named after me.' Spears asserted that the Ghanaian government had been virtually given the mine, with Lonrho left only as a minority shareholder. 'If Mr Rowland's methods prevail there will soon be no European investment in Africa.'

Spears spoke of his own thirty-nine years of experience in business; 'I have never in the whole of that time experienced the kind of dictatorial behaviour which Mr Rowland seems to regard as normal in his relations not only with his subordinates but with his co-directors.' He cast doubt on Rowland's sanity. 'His conduct has in recent months been so uncontrolled, his language so immoderate, and his displays of excitement when contradicted so hysterical that I have been seriously led to wonder whether he is entirely responsible for his actions.'

Rowland countered by arguing that Spears's knowledge of Africa was out of date; 'he is now over 85 years of age.' Major-General Anderson was harsher, particularly about the proconsular tours. 'I was left in no doubt that these visits upset the staff of the mine and the then Ghanaian directors of Ashanti Goldfields had often made mention of the "off-hand" way in which Major-General Spears treated them.' Anderson said he had told Rowland of this, saying also that the Ghanaians had asked that Spears should not make such visits: 'Mr Rowland, however, always insisted that he could not bring himself to be unkind to so elderly a man.' To Anderson, this kindness was 'typical' of Rowland and should be contrasted with Spears's own vindictive resentment. 'Major-General Spears told me personally that he resented the fact that Mr Rowland had negotiated the "take over" of Ashanti Goldfields.'[53]

On 14 May Rowland lost his bid in the High Court to prevent his dismissal. He decided to appeal over the heads of the board to the shareholders and a meeting was set for the 31st. A propaganda war began in which Rowland told a journalist that he had nothing against Spears, who had never forgiven him for taking over Ashanti: 'we still provide him with a Rolls, a chauffeur and £10,000 to £12,000 a year.' Nancy said this sum was made up of his Ashanti pension of £4,000, £6,000 salary as President of Ashanti and £800 basic annual fee as a Lonrho non-executive director. The Rolls was ancient: 'rather like a hearse.'[54]

On 28 May the Managing Director of Ashanti in Ghana reported that the Ghanaian Commission of Lands and Mineral Resources had ordered the removal of the name of Spears from all public places in Obuasi; these included the Spears shaft, the Spears school, the Lady Spears Memorial Clinic, Spears Road, the Lady Spears Estate, the General Spears Primary School, the Lady Spears Day Nursery School and the Spears House at Obuasi Technical School. Spears believed that he knew who had inspired this. 'I hope you will suggest to Rowland that he should erect a statue to himself at Obuasi,' he wrote to Alan Ball, an ally of Rowland. He hoped that the memorial to May would remain in the cemetery; 'I shall ask friends on the mine to see that it is tended.'[55] An anonymous correspondent sent him a Ghanaian newspaper report of a statement by the mining trades union that 'the Spears era was one of misery and suppressed anger which cannot be allowed to return'.[56]

The mine was producing more gold and making higher profits than ever before. Spears claimed this had its origin in the programme of investment started by him; he believed also that the British shareholders could get little benefit from the success because the Ghana government had taken a majority stake in the company. His arguments, however, were of little use. The votes of the shareholders had been counted before the meeting on 31 May. Twenty-eight million voted for the dismissal of the eight, eight million for their retention. Rowland himself cast over thirteen million votes; the rest came from an extraordinarily loyal collection of shareholders, often individuals, for whom he had made money over the years.

The meeting, in a packed Central Hall, Westminster, turned into a triumph for Rowland. Duncan Sandys, the Chairman, moved the dismissal of Spears with that of the other seven directors. 'I put this resolution with great personal pain, because he has been a very old friend of mine for very many years,' Sandys declared. The proxy votes were overwhelmingly against Spears and a shareholder asked from the floor why Sir Edward would not resign. Eventually a show of hands took place, with an uncertain result, but because of the size of the proxy vote Spears volunteered to go, to the applause of the audience. Later he asked a question about Ashanti's present production and how much Lonrho received for this: 'Ashanti Goldfields produces between £750,000 and £500,000 a week and not one of you have received a penny of that.' Fred Butcher, the Finance Director, gave some figures and said: 'I am surprised that he does not know. After all he was a director until a few months ago.'

Sandys thanked the defeated directors: 'in particular I would like to mention my old friend General Sir Edward Spears who built up the Ashanti Goldfields.' Spears returned the compliment later in the meeting when Sandys's £130,000 consultancy fee was discussed. 'We all consider ourselves very fortunate in having him as our chairman,' he declared.[57]

Immediately after his victory, Rowland announced that he held no grudges against the eight who had sought his dismissal and shook hands publicly with their leader, Sir Basil Smallpeice. The next day, however, he spoke of paying them 'not one penny'. Spears claimed not to be surprised: 'the man is a cad.'[58] In the event he continued to receive £4,000 pension and £6,000 a year for life as non-executive president of Ashanti Goldfields, although it was decreed that his Rolls-Royce and chauffeur were to be taken away.

The car became a matter of bitter contention. The chauffeur left, but Spears locked the Rolls-Royce up in a garage near Marble Arch.

Rowland thereupon cut off the annual payments of £10,000 and Spears issued a writ against him. He died while the writ was being prepared and Nancy heard that the remaining instalments of the pension would be paid. The fate of the car is unknown.

His friends offered sympathy. 'At least one can be proud that half the board put principle before profit,' Jock Colville wrote.[59] The year ended with a coalminers' strike, the imposition of a three-day week by the embattled Heath government and prophecies of economic and industrial disaster, even of revolution and a military coup. In December Spears and Nancy put an announcement in the Court Circular of *The Times*: 'Sir Edward and Lady Spears send affectionate greetings to their friends and hope that one day we shall all emerge from the surrounding gloom.'[60]

In January, Spears had a severe haemorrhage in his colon. Rushed to hospital at Ascot, he endured a two-and-a-half-hour operation which seemed to have been successful. The doctors and surgeon were astonished at his vitality; soon he was sitting up in a chair and taking soup. Then he had a coronary, recovered briefly but sank again, to die at nine o'clock in the morning of 27 January 1974, aged eighty-seven.

Nancy was devastated. 'I am completely shattered,' she told Antonin de Mun. 'I know I am lucky to have had his society for fifty four years but the blank is enormous and now I have nothing to look forward to but death.'[61]

On 7 March there was a memorial service at St Margaret's Westminster. Jeremy Thorpe gave the address. He emphasised Spears's great gifts: as a writer, diplomat, businessman, politician. He brought up the case of Thomas Parker as an example of his humanity and spoke also of Nancy's devotion. It would have been wrong to have avoided the difficult side, that determination to follow campaigns and quarrels to the very end: the vindictiveness born out of the belief that he was alone and had always to fight for himself. 'Louis was a controversial figure,' Thorpe said. 'He has his opponents and critics'; he then claimed that these enemies had been 'the right ones'. The trumpeters of the 11th Hussars sounded a fanfare and the French and Lebanese ambassadors were there. Afterwards Nancy kissed Thorpe in a way that some found embarrassing. It was impossible not to realise the immensity of her loss.[62]

His death led to sonorous public obituaries and private mutterings about his complicated character. To the charge of anti-semitism, Claud Calmon, himself Jewish, wrote a denial in the *Director*, the magazine of the Institute of Directors. 'Nothing could be further from the truth,' he declared. 'Little is known of his generous help given to many Jewish and political European refugees though obviously General Spears was too modest to talk about it.' Calmon had had an office next to that of Spears and had observed this: 'in fact I believe I was of some help on one particular occasion.'[63]

Spears's grave is at Warfield, alongside those of May and Michael. In his will he left £41,228, showing that, in spite of his long involvement in business and the City, he had never made a fortune. Nancy gave up Strathearn Place, sold its contents and moved to St Michael's Grange, which had been left to her for her lifetime. When there, she tried to visit the grave of her loved Beaucaire every day. She went on a last tour of France in the summer of 1974, to Spears's old haunts of Chitré, Touffou and Haroué, where she was received with sympathy and forbearance rather than enthusiasm. She began to smoke again and to drink heavily to dull the pain.

'Things are in a bad way with me,' she told Yvonne de Lestrange in January 1975. 'I cannot live without Beaucaire and have not yet succeeded in escaping to death.'[64] That year she died and at St Michael's Grange, Mrs Reichart heard a long, high wail come from where Kwesi, the African valet, lived with his wife. It was the cry of Ashanti mourning, and she found its unyielding sound haunting and strange.

His battles continued even after death. To the French of the wartime generation, Spears remained a conspiratorial, treacherous figure: someone whose knowledge and love of France made his apparent determination to destroy French interests doubly inexcusable. The controversy revived when his account of his time in the Middle East, *Fulfilment of a Mission*, was published posthumously in 1977. Less objective even than *Assignment to Catastrophe*, it depicts its author as carrying out almost in the spirit of a simple soldier the task entrusted to him by Winston Churchill to free Syria and Lebanon from French colonial rule in accordance with the promises of the allies. De Gaulle and the former supporters of Vichy who stayed on to represent France in the two countries appear as the main obstacles to this, together with the pusillanimous, timid, absurdly francophile British Foreign Office. There is only a faint echo in the book of his own hopes of creating a British sphere of influence in the region that after the war would look to London for guidance and venerate Spears himself for having realised the dreams of T. E. Lawrence.

The Levant was one of the times that Spears felt himself to be exercising a power worthy not only of his great ambitions but in furtherance of a profoundly justifiable cause: others included his work on behalf of de Gaulle and the Free French movement and his pre-war advocacy of resistance to Nazi Germany. In Syria and Lebanon his disappointment with a defeated and shameful France and anger towards an obstinate, ungrateful de Gaulle led him to discard diplomacy and work to get the French out of their former colonies. De Gaulle had a similarly wounded pride, determination and singlemindedness, a similar strength of will, also the outsider's sense that he could ultimately depend only on himself; and a clash became inevitable. Confrontation of some kind would have happened no matter who had been the British representative with the Free French and in the Levant. But the complicated emotions Spears brought to the task meant that the position became exacerbated by the personal animosity, vanity and obsessiveness of two exceptionally strong personalities. As the diplomats had feared, it poisoned Anglo-French relations in the immediate after-math of the war and left a lingering bitterness, particularly in France.

To reason with him was hopeless; once set on a course, Spears would not respond to pressure or influence. Isolated since his early days as an Englishman in France and a Frenchman in England, he liked to work alone, away from orders or clearly defined limits. This is shown in his career as an often elusive liaison officer during the First World War, as an independent member of parliament, as the representative answerable only to Churchill in France in 1940, as the dominant head of Ashanti Goldfields and the Institute of Directors, as the writer of brilliant and idiosyncratic autobiography and history. His marriage to an equally strong character went sour when May's love for him made her critical as well as loyal. Their life together suffered from his need for the absolute unquestioning devotion that he received from Nancy Maurice; and the illness of his son, the adored Michael, added tragedy to the existing tensions.

Spears began life with two countries: France and Great Britain. Like Peter Ibbetson, the hero of one of his favourite books, he found himself cast out of the France of his youth with only the memory of his former trust and admiration. His story shows disillusion: it also reflects the turbulent relations and misunderstandings between those two countries during his own lifetime. But the boy from outside the hard circle of the late-Victorian governing class, who joined an obscure Anglo-Irish militia regiment at the age of sixteen, went on to become an intimate of the great: an often controversial but always courageous soldier, diplomat and politician; an extraordinary survivor in business and the dying world of British imperial influence; and a matchless chronicler of his times. This was the achievement of Major-General Sir Edward Spears.

NOTES

1
A Divided Boyhood

1. Spears Churchill College acc 545 box 35.
2. Spears Churchill College 1/75.
3. Spears Churchill College acc 545 box 35. Notes by Spears on his early life.
4. Ibid.
5. See *Dictionary of National Biography* entry for Alexander Spiers. For the unsuccessful legal action, see *The Times* of 26 February 1858.
6. PRO HO1/4. 25 June 1803.
7. Ibid. 1 and 10 August 1803.
8. Spears Churchill College acc 643 box 5.
9. E. L. Spears, *The Picnic Basket*, p. 15.
10. Spears Churchill College acc 545 box 35. Notes.
11. Ibid.
12. Ibid.
13. Spears Churchill College 2/27. February 18 1889.
14. Spears Churchill College acc 545 box 35. Notes.
15. Spears Churchill College 1/45. No date. Lecture by Spears on 'The French and British Character'.
16. E. L. Spears, *The Picnic Basket*, p. 23.
17. Ibid., pp. 105–6.
18. Spears Churchill College acc 545 box 35. Notes.
19. E. L. Spears, *The Picnic Basket*, p. 108. For the dog incident, see ibid., p. 45. See also Spears Churchill College acc 545 box 35. Notes.
20. Spears Churchill College acc 545 box 35. Notes. Also for the information on Goldney. I am grateful to Ann M. Oakley for further details of Goldney's life, character and career.
21. Spears Churchill College 1/257. 14 January 1952.
22. For Horsley, see P. Upton, *Man of Barts*, p. 15. Also *Dictionary of National Biography*.
23. Spears Churchill College acc 545 box 35. Notes.
24. Spears Churchill College 2/29. 23 May 1913.
25. C. Andrew, *Secret Service*, p. 127.
26. W. Churchill, *The World Crisis*, vol. 5: *The Aftermath*, p. 55.

27. See *The Times* obituary of Macdonogh of 16 July 1942. For more on Macdonogh, see Kirke papers, VII 382–92.
28. Spears Churchill College 1/20. 2 July 1968.
29. James Edmonds papers, 111/5/11–27.
30. Ibid.
31. E. L. Spears, *The Picnic Basket*, p. 159.
32. O. Sitwell, *Great Morning*, p. 131.
33. Spears Churchill College 1/311. 7 May 1948.
34. E. L. Spears, *The Picnic Basket*, p. 147.
35. L. R. Lumley, *History of the Eleventh Hussars*, p. 11.
36. E. L. Spears, *The Picnic Basket*, p. 78.
37. Spears Churchill College acc 545 box 35. Notes.
38. Ibid.
39. Ibid.
40. E. L. Spears, *The Picnic Basket*, p. 155. Also E. L. Spears, *Liaison 1914*, p. 394.
41. Spears King's 2/3/21. Letter of 16 May 1919.
42. Spears Churchill College acc 545 box 35. Notes.
43. E. L. Spears, *Liaison 1914*, p. 13.
44. Spears King's 2/3/21. Letter of 16 May 1919.
45. W. Lewis, *Blasting and Bombardiering*, p. 56.
46. Ibid., p. 58.
47. J. Meyers, *The Enemy*, p. 72.
48. 'Bridget Maclagan', *The Mistress of Kingdoms*.
49. 'Bridget Maclagan', *Collision*.
50. Aylmer Collection. Fragment of a draft memoir. N.D.
51. Mary Borden. Mugar box 25.
52. Aylmer Collection. Court depositions in connection with the custody case of 1921.
53. J. Meyers, *The Enemy*, p. 72.
54. Lewis collection, Cornell. N.D.
55. Ibid. N.D.

2
Liaison 1914

1. Spears Kings 2/3/21. Letter of 16 May 1919.
2. E. L. Spears, *Liaison 1914*, p. 37.
3. Ibid.
4. Edmonds papers. 111/5/11–27.
5. E. L. Spears, *Liaison 1914*, p. 74.

6. Ibid.
7. French papers. PP/MCR/C32.
8. E. L. Spears, *Liaison 1914*, p. 84.
9. Ibid., p. 88.
10. Ibid., p. 138.
11. Ibid., p. 149.
12. Ibid., p. 154. See also Spears King's 2/3/21.
13. Ibid., p. 171.
14. Ibid., p. 188.
15. Ibid., p. 201.
16. Ibid., p. 211.
17. Ibid., p. 227.
18. Ibid., p. 240.
19. Ibid., pp. 266–7.
20. Wilson diary. DS/Misc/80. 28 August 1914.
21. Spears Churchill College 2/2.
22. E. L. Spears, *Liaison 1914*, p. 300.
23. Ibid., p. 325.
24. Ibid., p. 351.
25. Ibid., p. 397.
26. Ibid., p. 415.
27. Ibid., pp. 416–17.
28. Ibid., p. 419.
29. Ibid., p. 432.
30. Ibid., pp. 464–5.
31. Ibid., p. 473.

3
'Think I Will Shoot Myself'

1. E. L. Spears, *Liaison 1914*, p. 68.
2. Ibid., p. 220.
3. Spears King's. Album. 21 October 1914.
4. Spears Churchill College acc 545 box 59. Journal 27 October 1914.
5. E. L. Spears, *Liaison 1914*, pp. 455–62.
6. Spears Churchill College acc 545 box 59. Journal 31 October 1914.
7. Ibid., 16 November 1914.
8. Ibid., 26 November 1914.
9. Ibid., 27 November 1914.
10. Ibid.
11. Ibid., 6 December 1914.

12. Ibid., 20 December 1914.
13. Ibid., 21 December 1914.
14. Ibid., 22 December 1914.
15. Ibid., 25 December 1914.
16. Ibid., 26 December 1914.
17. Ibid., 5 January 1915.
18. Ibid.
19. Ibid., 18 March 1915.
20. Ibid., 17 March 1915.
21. Ibid., 5 April 1915.
22. Ibid., 21 April 1915.
23. *Sunday Telegraph*, 24 October 1971. Review by Spears of Martin Gilbert's *Winston S. Churchill*, vol. 3.
24. Spears Churchill College acc 545 box 59. Journal 5 May 1915.
25. Ibid., 9 May 1915.
26. Spears King's 1/2. Journal 28 May 1915.
27. Ibid.
28. Spears Churchill College acc 545 box 59. Journal 13 June 1915.
29. Ibid., 8 June 1915.
30. Ibid., 21 June 1915.
31. Ibid., 23 June 1915.
32. Ibid.
33. Ibid., 22 June 1915.
34. Ibid., 25 June 1915.
35. Spears King's 1/3/4. 23 July 1915.
36. Spears Churchill College acc 545 box 59. Journal 9 July 1915.
37. Ibid., 25 August 1915.
38. Ibid., 21 August 1915.
39. Ibid., 31 August 1915.
40. Ibid., 29 September 1915.
41. Ibid., 9 October 1915.
42. Ibid., 17 October 1915.
43. Ibid., 5 December 1915.
44. Ibid., 6 December 1915.
45. Ibid., 7 December 1915.
46. M. Gilbert, *Winston S. Churchill*, vol. 3, p. 600.
47. Spears Churchill College acc 545 box 59. Journal. 14 December 1915.
48. Ibid., 16 December 1915.
49. Ibid., 20 December 1915.
50. Ibid., 29 December 1915.
51. M. Gilbert, *Winston S. Churchill*, vol. 3, p. 625.
52. Spears Churchill College acc 545 box 59. Journal 13 January 1916.

53. Ibid., 22 February 1915.
54. Ibid., 5 March 1916.
55. Ibid., 9 March 1916.
56. Ibid., 10 March 1916.
57. Ibid., 14 March 1916.
58. Ibid.
59. E. L. Spears, *Prelude to Victory*, pp. 126–7.
60. Dillon diary. 16 May 1916.
61. Ibid., 10 July 1916.
62. Ibid., 18 June 1916.
63. Ibid., 26 May 1916.
64. Spears Churchill College 1/19. 25 May 1916.
65. Spears Churchill College acc 545 box 59. Journal 17 June 1916.
66. Dillon diary. 19 June 1916.
67. Spears Churchill College acc 545 box 59. Journal 24 June 1916.
68. Ibid., 1 July 1916.
69. E. L. Spears, *Liaison 1914*, p. 107.
70. Ibid.
71. Spears Churchill College acc 545 box 59. Journal 7 July 1916.
72. Ibid., 9 July 1916.
73. Ibid., 10 August 1916.
74. Spears Churchill College 1/7. 26 August 1916.
75. Spears Churchill College acc 545 box 59. Journal 9 August 1916.
76. Spears King's 1/7. 11 August 1916.
77. Ibid.
78. Spears King's 1/7. 24 August 1916.
79. Spears Churchill College acc 545 box 59. Journal 18 September 1916.
80. Spears King's Album 24/5. 14 November 1916.
81. Spears Churchill College acc 545 box 59. Journal 15 September 1916.
82. M. Gilbert, *Winston S. Churchill*, vol. 3, Companion Documents part 2, p. 1578. 27 October 1916.
83. Spears Churchill College acc 545 box 59. Journal 20 October 1916.
84. Ibid., 2 December 1916.
85. Ibid., 18 December 1916.
86. Ibid., 25 October 1916.
87. Ibid., 17 January 1917.
88. Ibid., 18 January 1917.
89. E. L. Spears, *Prelude to Victory*, p. 100.
90. Spears Churchill College acc 545 box 59. Journal 19 January 1917.
91. Ibid., 23 January 1917.
92. Ibid., 25 January 1917.
93. Ibid., 18 February 1917.

94. Spears King's 1/8. 13 March 1917.
95. Spears Churchill College acc 545 box 49. Journal 28 March 1917.
96. Ibid., 6 April 1917.
97. Ibid., 21 April 1917.
98. Ibid., 27 April 1917.
99. PRO FO 371/2937. 2 May 1917.
100. Spears Churchill College acc 545 box 59. Journal 14 April 1917.

4
'The Most Dangerous Job in Europe'

1. See correspondence in PRO FO 800/191.
2. Spears Churchill College acc 545 box 59. Journal 4 May 1917.
3. Ibid., 5 May 1917.
4. Ibid.
5. PRO FO 800/191. 22 May 1917.
6. Spears Churchill College 2/2/6. N.D., p. 2.
7. Ibid.
8. Ibid., p. 4.
9. Ibid., p. 5.
10. E. L. Spears. *Two Men*, p. 37.
11. Spears Churchill College 2/2/6. N.D., p. 8.
12. Ibid., p. 9.
13. Ibid.
14. PRO CAB 27/6. June 11 1917. See also Spears King's 1/13/1. 14 June 1917.
15. Spears Churchill College 2/2/6. N.D., p. 10.
16. Ibid.
17. Spears King's 1/13/1. 29 June 1917.
18. Ibid., 1/13/1. 7 July 1917.
19. PRO FO 800/191. 29 June 1917.
20. Mary Borden, *Journey*, p. 10.
21. G. Stein, *The Autobiography of Alice B. Toklas*, p. 185.
22. Mary Borden, *The Romantic Woman*.
23. Spears Churchill College 2/29. N.D.
24. V. Brittain. *The Testament of Youth*, p. 292.
25. Spears Churchill College 2/29. 26 May 1917.
26. Ibid., 26 May 1917.
27. Ibid., 8 July 1917.
28. Ibid., 11 August 1917.
29. Ibid., 7 August 1917.

30. Ibid., 9 August 1917.
31. Ibid., 11 August 1917.
32. Ibid., N.D.
33. Ibid., 8 September 1917.
34. Ibid., 9 September 1917.
35. Ibid., 11 September 1917.
36. Ibid., 12 September 1917.
37. Ibid.
38. Ibid., 18 and 20 September 1917.
39. Ibid., 21 September 1917.
40. Ibid., 6 October 1917.
41. Ibid., 8 October 1917.
42. Ibid.
43. Spears King's 1/13/1. 18 August 1917.
44. Ibid., 14 September 1917.
45. Spears Churchill College acc 545 box 33. 'Poincaré', p. 3. N.D.
46. Spears King's 1/17. 23 November 1917.
47. E. L. Spears, *Assignment*, vol. 1, p. 57.
48. R. Watt, *Dare Call It Treason*, p. 239.
49. E. L. Spears, *Assignment*, vol. 1, pp. 57–8.
50. Hankey diary. 27 November 1917. Quoted in S. Roskill, *Hankey: Man of Secrets* vol. 1, pp. 464–5.
51. Spears King's 1/13/1. Letters of 2, 12 and 18 December 1917.
52. Wilson diary. DS/Misc/80. 23 December 1917.
53. Aylmer Collection. Diary. 25 December 1917.
54. Ibid., 30 November 1917.
55. Ibid., 1 December 1917.
56. Ibid., 15 December 1917.
57. Ibid., 2 January 1918.
58. Spears Churchill College 2/29. 14 January 1918.
59. Ibid., N.D.
60. Ibid., 2 February 1918.
61. Ibid., 10 February 1918.
62. Ibid., 11 February 1918.
63. Aylmer Collection. Diary. 25 January and 1 February 1918.
64. Ibid., 3 February 1918.
65. Ibid., 4 February 1918.
66. Ibid., 5 February 1918.
67. Ibid., 7 February 1918.
68. PRO FO 372/1125. 12 February 1918.
69. Spears Churchill College 2/29. 15 February 1918.
70. Aylmer Collection. Diary. 16 February 1918.

71. Spears Churchill College acc 545 box 33. 'Lord Bertie', p. 3.
72. Spears Churchill College 2/29. 17 February 1918.
73. Ibid., 17 February 1918.
74. Aylmer Collection. Diary. 18 February 1918.

5

'The Honour of One's Country Is a Costly Thing'

1. Aylmer Collection. Diary. 21 February 1918.
2. Ibid., 24 February 1918.
3. Ibid., 26 February 1918.
4. Ibid.
5. Wilson diary. DS/Misc/80. 27 February 1918.
6. Aylmer Collection. Diary. 27 February 1918.
7. Wilson diary. DS/Misc/80. 27 February 1918.
8. Aylmer Collection. Diary. 27 February 1918.
9. Spears Churchill College 2/29. 28 February 1918.
10. Aylmer Collection. Diary. 6 March 1918.
11. Ibid., 2 March 1918.
12. Ibid., 16 February 1918.
13. Spears Churchill College 2/29. N.D.
14. Aylmer Collection. Diary. 4 March 1918.
15. Ibid., 24 March 1918.
16. Ibid.
17. Ibid., 23 March 1918.
18. N. Maurice, *The Maurice Case*, Introduction by Spears, p. 12.
19. Spears Churchill College acc 643 box 4. 30 March 1918.
20. Spears King's 1/18. 31 March 1918.
21. Aylmer Collection. Diary. 4–7 April 1918.
22. Spears King's 1/13/2. 17 April 1918.
23. Aylmer Collection. Diary. 14 April 1918.
24. R. Churchill, *Lord Derby*, pp. 360–1.
25. Ibid., p. 363.
26. Spears Churchill College 1/19. 24 April 1918.
27. P. Cambon, *Correspondence 1870–1924*, vol. 3, p. 254.
28. S. Roskill, *Hankey: Man of Secrets*, vol. 1, p. 535.
29. Aylmer Collection. Maurice letter to Spears of 3 June 1918.
30. Ibid. Diary. 30 May–1 June 1918.
31. Spears King's Album. 18 May 1918.
32. Spears Churchill College acc 643 box 4. 6 June 1918.
33. Derby diary. 28/1/1. 29 June 1918.

34. Wilson diary. DS/Misc/80. 28 June 1918.
35. Aylmer Collection. Diary. 17 July 1918.
36. Ibid., 15 August 1918.
37. Spears Churchill College acc 643 box 2. 3 August 1918.
38. Derby diary. 28/1/1. 27 July 1918.
39. Aylmer Collection. Diary. 19 August 1918.
40. Ibid., 30 August 1918.
41. Derby diary. 28/1/1. 13 September 1918.
42. Ibid., 14 September 1918.
43. R. Churchill, *Lord Derby*, pp. 365–6.
44. Aylmer Collection. Diary. 8 October 1918.
45. Ibid., 7 November 1918.
46. Ibid., 12 November 1918.
47. Ibid.
48. Spears Churchill College 2/29. 29 October 1918.
49. Ibid., N.D.

6
'Winston's Spy'

1. Spears King's 1/14. 29 November 1918.
2. Aylmer Collection. Diary. 29 November 1918.
3. Spears King's 1/14. 3 December 1918.
4. Wilson papers. 2/14k/33. 8 December 1918.
5. Mary Borden, *Journey*, p. 11.
6. Derby diary. 28/1/4. 2 December 1918.
7. Spears Churchill College 1/54. 18 November 1918.
8. Spears Churchill College 1/75. 19 April 1960.
9. Spears King's 1/21/1. 6 March 1919.
10. Spears King's 1/12. 16 March 1919.
11. Spears King's 1/21/1. 18 April 1919.
12. Aylmer Collection. Diary. 11 April 1919.
13. Ibid.
14. Ibid.
15. Spears King's 1/14. 26 April 1919.
16. Spears King's 1/21/2. 2 May 1919.
17. Ibid., 8 May 1919.
18. Spears Churchill College 2/25. 'Savinkov'. N.D., p. 1.
19. Wilson papers. 2/14M/39. 11 May 1919.
20. Spears Churchill College 1/76. 12 May 1919.
21. Ibid., 15 May 1919.

22. R. Churchill, *Lord Derby*, pp. 367–8.
23. Spears Churchill College 1/342. N.D.
24. Wilson diary. DS/Misc/80. 29 May 1919.
25. Ibid., 14 June 1919.
26. Ibid., 17 June 1919.
27. Ibid.
28. Spears Churchill College 1/342. 22 and 23 June 1919.
29. Spears Churchill College 1/310. 29 June 1919.
30. Spears Churchill College 1/76. 22 July 1919.
31. Wilson diary. DS/Misc/80. 6 August 1919.
32. Spears Churchill College 1/218. 15 August 1919.
33. Wilson papers. 2/14N/2. 3 October 1919.
34. Wilson diary. DS/Misc/80. 16 October 1919.
35. Ibid., 17 October 1919.
36. Ibid., 20 October 1919.
37. Spears Churchill College 1/76. 1 November 1919.
38. Spears Churchill College 1/107. 11 November 1919.
39. Spears Churchill College 1/76. 18 November 1919.
40. Wilson diary. DS/Misc/80. 5 December 1919.
41. Ibid., 13 February 1919.
42. Spears Churchill College 2/29. 4 March 1920.
43. PRO FO 371/3770. 10 June 1919.
44. Spears Churchill College 2/29. 6 and 20 August 1920.
45. Ibid., 14 October 1920.
46. Ibid., 20 October 1920.
47. Ibid.
48. Spears Churchill College 1/218. 21 December 1920.

7
Post-War and Parliament

1. Spears Kings Album.
2. Aylmer Collection. Papers and depositions of the 1921 custody case.
3. Ibid. See also D. Stuart, *Dear Duchess*.
4. Spears Churchill College 2/4. Diary. 18–22 April 1921.
5. Ibid., 2 and 13 May 1921.
6. Ibid., 5 July 1921.
7. Ibid., 24 May 1921.
8. Ibid., 13 June 1921.
9. Ibid., 6 July 1921.
10. Ibid., 5 July 1921.

11. Ibid., 18 and 19 June 1921.
12. Ibid., 2 July 1921.
13. Spears Churchill College 1/301. 2 January 1967.
14. Spears Churchill College 2/4. Diary. 9 July 1921.
15. Ibid., 13–17 July 1921.
16. Ibid., 23 July 1921.
17. Ibid., 2 August 1921.
18. Ibid., 16 September 1921.
19. Ibid., 2 October 1921.
20. Ibid., 18 October 1921.
21. Ibid., 21 October 1921.
22. Ibid., 19 October 1921.
23. Ibid., 5 November 1921.
24. Ibid., 23 November 1921.
25. Ibid., 10 November 1921.
26. Ibid., 22 November 1921.
27. Ibid., 15 November 1921.
28. Ibid., 29 November 1921.
29. Ibid., 1 December 1921.
30. Ibid., 19 December 1921.
31. Ibid., 31 December 1921.
32. Spears Churchill College 1/76. 3 January 1922.
33. Spears Churchill College 2/5. 11 January 1922.
34. Ibid., 12 January 1922.
35. Ibid., 20 January 1922.
36. Ibid., 30 and 31 January 1922.
37. Ibid.
38. Ibid., 31 January 1922.
39. Ibid., 5 February 1922.
40. Ibid., 25 February 1922.
41. Spears Churchill College 1/143. 4 April 1922.
42. Mary Borden papers. Mugar box 22. 10 February 1922.
43. Spears Churchill College 2/5. Diary. 12 June 1922.
44. Ibid., 13 July 1922.
45. Ibid., 8 September 1922.
46. Ibid., 2 August 1922.
47. Ibid.
48. Spears King's 2/3/40. 10 September 1922. See also Spears Churchill
    College 1/124. 11 September 1922.
49. Spears King's 2/3/46. 15 November 1922.
50. Spears Churchill College 1/76. 21 May 1973.
51. Ibid.

52. Ibid.

53. Spears Churchill College 1/76. 18 November 1922.

54. E. L. Spears, *Liaison 1914*, pp. 521–7.

55. Spears Churchill College 1/230. 2 March 1923.

56. Spears Churchill College 1/206. 21 August 1923.

57. Quoted in J. H. Marshall-Cornwall, *Geographic Disarmament*, pp. 149–54.

58. Spears Churchill College 1/144. 6 December 1923.

8

A Loss of Faith

1. Mary Borden, *Jane Our Stranger*.

2. Spears Churchill College acc 545 box 33. 'The Marquis de Castellane,' p. 1.

3. *Punch*, December 1923; *Manchester Guardian*, 14 December 1923; *Guardian* review, 21 December 1923 (M. Borden album, Aylmer Collection).

4. *Daily Telegraph*, 1 April 1924.

5. *Queen*, 5 March 1924.

6. Aylmer Collection. August 1924.

7. Ibid.

8. Ibid.

9. Ibid.

10. Ibid.

11. Hansard, vol. 160, cols 735–41. 19 February 1923.

12. Hansard, vol. 162, cols 614–21. 28 March 1923.

13. Hansard, vol. 171, cols 2057–62. 1 April 1924.

14. Hansard, vol. 170, cols 2688–95. 13 March 1924.

15. Hansard, vol. 176, cols 86–93. 14 July 1924.

16. Hansard, vol. 165, col. 2290. 27 June 1924.

17. Hansard, vol. 176, col. 2068. 20 July 1924.

18. Aylmer Collection. 14 October 1924.

19. Spears Churchill College 1/257. 22 November 1924.

20. Spears Churchill College 1/166, 2 December 1924; 1/261, 4 and 18 December 1924.

21. Aylmer Collection. December 1924.

22. Spears Churchill College 1/76. 25 May 1925.

23. Ibid., 2 July 1925.

24. Spears Churchill College 1/331. 9 November 1925.

25. S. Leslie, *The Jerome Connexion*, p. 98.

26. Spears Churchill College 1/87. 2 May 1927.

27. C. Headlam, *Parliament and Politics in the Age of Baldwin*, 30 May 1927, p. 122.
28. Spears Churchill College 1/87. 2 June 1927.
29. Spears Churchill College 1/76. 16 June 1929.
30. Spears Churchill College 1/168. 8 June 1926.
31. Spears Churchill College 1/218. 11 February 1928.
32. Spears Churchill College acc 545 box 33 and 34. N.D.
33. D. Pryce-Jones, *Cyril Connolly*, pp. 171–2.
34. Mary Borden papers. Mugar box 23. July 1929.
35. Mary Borden, *Four O'Clock*.
36. Mary Borden papers. Mugar box 9.
37. Mary Borden, *A Woman with White Eyes* and *Sarah Gay*.
38. Mary Borden, *The Forbidden Zone*.
39. Mary Borden papers. Mugar box 23. 1930.
40. E. L. Spears, *Liaison 1914*, p. ix.
41. Ibid., p. 33.
42. *Morning Post*, 22 September 1930; *News Chronicle*, 22 September 1930; *Daily Express*, 3 October 1930; *Sunday Referee*, 5 October 1930; Spears King's 6/1/4, 22 September 1930.
43. *Times Literary Supplement*, 2 October 1930.
44. Spears Churchill College 2/2. 4 November 1930.

9
The Greatest Possible Anxiety

1. Spears King's 6/1/4. 5 February and 3 March 1931.
2. Spears Churchill College 1/56. 23 March 1931.
3. D. Pryce-Jones, *Cyril Connolly*, pp. 264–5.
4. Mary Borden papers. Mugar box 23. May and July 1931.
5. Spears Churchill College 1/230. 5 November 1931.
6. Spears Churchill College 1/309. 15 December 1931.
7. Spears Churchill College 1/348. 7 January 1932.
8. Reviews in *Le Figaro*, 25 January 1933; *L'Action*, 9 April 1933; *Mercure*, 15 August 1933; *La Liberté*, 19 April 1934. Gillot letter, Spears King's 6/1/4. 29 January 1933.
9. Spears Churchill College. 19 March 1969.
10. Mary Borden papers. Mugar. 'Michael' album.
11. Hansard, vol. 279, cols 1836–53. 30 June 1933.
12. *Cumberland News*, 5 August 1933.
13. Spears Churchill College 1/154. 27 April 1933.
14. Spears Churchill College 1/331. 19 November 1933.

15. Spears Churchill College 1/146. 2 and 4 December 1933.
16. *Sunday Express*, 17 and 24 December 1933.
17. Mary Borden papers. Mugar. 'Michael' album.
18. D. Pryce-Jones, *Cyril Connolly*, p. 265.
19. Mary Borden, *Mary of Nazareth* and *The King of the Jews*.
20. Mary Borden papers. Mugar box 6.
21. Mary Borden, *Action for Slander*. See also Mary Borden papers, Mugar box 9. For earnings, see Spears Churchill College 2/30.
22. Mary Borden, *The Black Virgin* and *Passport for a Girl*.
23. Mary Borden, *The Technique of Marriage*.
24. Mary Borden, 'Personal Experience and the Art of Fiction', in *Essays by Divers Hands* (Royal Society of Literature), vol. 29, pp. 87–96.
25. J. Colville, *The Churchillians*, pp. 203–4.
26. Spears Churchill College 1/31. 10 February 1934.
27. Spears Churchill College acc 545 box 46. Local press clippings of the campaign.
28. Spears Churchill College 1/21. 26 May 1935.
29. Spears Churchill College 1/103. 11 February 1936.
30. H. Macmillan, *Winds of Change*, p. 466.
31. Mary Borden, *Journey*, p. 12.
32. Spears Churchill College 1/137. 'Aide-Mémoire on Pierre-Etienne Flandin'. N.D., p. 2.
33. Spears Churchill College 2/1. 'Abdication Crisis'. 1936.
34. Spears Churchill College 1/96. Also *Sunday Referee*, November 1938.
35. A. Roberts, *Eminent Churchillians*, p. 163.
36. R. Hart-Davis, *The Power of Chance*, pp. 67–8.
37. Hansard, vol. 281, cols 655–9. 13 November 1933.
38. Hansard, vol. 270, cols 618–23. 10 November 1932.
39. Hansard, vol. 284, cols 1516–19. 21 December 1933.
40. Hansard, vol. 276, cols 555–7. 23 March 1933.
41. Spears Churchill College 1/76. N.D.
42. Spears Churchill College 1/41. 14 March 1938.
43. E. L. Spears, *Assignment*, vol. 1, p. 105.
44. Mary Borden papers. Mugar box 20. 'Diary during the Crisis'.
45. Ibid.
46. Ibid.
47. Ibid.
48. Ibid.
49. M. Gilbert, *Winston S. Churchill*, vol. 5, p. 997.
50. Spears Churchill College 1/245. 2 November 1938.
51. Spears Churchill College 1/2. November 1938.
52. Spears Churchill College 1/46 and acc 545 box 41, November 1938.

53. Spears Churchill College 1/76. July 20 1939.
54. E. L. Spears, *Assignment*, vol. 1, p. 4.
55. Ibid., p. 12.
56. Ibid., p. 17.
57. Ibid., p. 22.
58. Ibid., p. 24.
59. Ibid., p. 26.

10
'If the Real Thing Begins'

1. Aylmer Collection. Diary. 6 September 1939.
2. Ibid., 17 September 1939.
3. Ibid., 27 September 1939.
4. Ibid., 30 September 1939.
5. Ibid., 8 October 1939.
6. Spears Churchill College 1/76. 26 September 1939.
7. Spears Churchill College 1/159. 29 September 1939.
8. E. L. Spears, *Assignment*, vol. 1, p. 42.
9. Dalton diary. 5 September 1938.
10. *Spectator*, 10 November 1939.
11. Spears Churchill College 2/18/1. Diary 31 October–6 November 1939.
12. Reviews: *Daily Telegraph*, 3 November 1938; *New Statesman*, 18 November 1938; *Daily Sketch*, 4 December 1939; Buchan, Spears Churchill College 21/17, 9 January 1940.
13. Spears Churchill College 2/17. 1 February 1940; *Horizon*, February 1940; *Observer*, 5 November 1939.
14. Spears King's 6/2/3. 28 October 1939.
15. Ibid., 27 October 1939.
16. Ibid., 28 December 1939.
17. Spears Churchill College 1/323. 7 January 1940.
18. E. L. Spears, *Assignment*, vol. 1, p. 69.
19. Spears Churchill College 1/31. 2 February 1940.
20. Spears Churchill College 1/140. 23 May 1940.
21. E. L. Spears, *Assignment*, vol. 1, p. 75.
22. Spears Churchill College 2/18/1. Diary. February 1940.
23. Mary Borden, *Journey*, p. 25.
24. Spears Churchill College 1/61. 13 March 1940.
25. Spears Churchill College 2/18/1. Diary. 5 April 1940. See also E. L. Spears, *Assignment*, vol. 1, p. 99.
26. E. L. Spears, *Assignment*, vol. 1, pp. 99–101.

27. Spears Churchill College 1/183. 7 May 1940.
28. E. L. Spears, *Assignment*, vol. 1, p. 121.
29. Ibid., pp. 129–34.
30. Aylmer Collection. Diary. 29 April 1940.
31. Mary Borden, *Journey*, p. 32.
32. Aylmer Collection. Diary. 29 April 1940.
33. Mary Borden, *Journey*, p. 36.
34. Ibid., p. 39. See also Aylmer Collection. Diary. 17 May 1940.
35. Spears Churchill College 2/29. 18 May 1940.
36. Aylmer Collection. Diary. 28 May 1940.
37. Ibid., 26 May 1940.
38. Spears Churchill 2/29. 27 May 1940.
39. Aylmer Collection. Diary. 28 May 1940.
40. Spears Churchill College 2/29. 30 May 1940.
41. Aylmer Collection. Diary. 10 June 1940.
42. Mary Borden, *Journey*, p. 72.
43. Ibid., p. 96.
44. Ibid., p. 102.
45. Ibid., p. 107.
46. E. L. Spears, *Assignment*, vol. 1, p. 144.
47. Ibid., p. 153.
48. Ibid., p. 154.
49. Ibid., pp. 161–2.
50. Ibid., p. 165.
51. Ibid., p. 170.
52. Ibid., p. 173.
53. Ibid., p. 174.

11
'A Crack in the Crystal Cup'

1. Spears Churchill College 2/18/1. Diary. 25 May 1940.
2. E. L. Spears, *Assignment*, vol. 1, p. 179.
3. Ibid., p. 189.
4. Spears Churchill College 2/18/2. 25 May 1940. Also see diary of that date.
5. E. L. Spears, *Assignment*, vol. 1, p. 216.
6. Ibid., p. 222.
7. Ibid., p. 223.
8. Ibid., p. 229.
9. Spears Churchill College 2/18/2. 27 May 1940.

10. Ibid.
11. Ibid.
12. E. L. Spears, *Assignment*, vol. 1, p. 248. Also Spears Churchill College 2/18/1. Diary. 28 May 1940.
13. E. L. Spears, *Assignment*, vol. 1, p. 253.
14. Ibid., p. 261.
15. Ibid., p. 271.
16. O. Harvey, *War Diaries*, p. 372.
17. Spears Churchill College 2/18. 29 May 1940.
18. E. L. Spears, *Assignment*, vol. 1, p. 274.
19. Ibid., p. 291.
20. Ibid., p. 316.
21. Ibid., p. 318. Also O. Harvey, *War Diaries*, p. 374.
22. E. L. Spears, *Assignment*, vol. 2, p. 5.
23. Ibid., p. 19.
24. Spears Churchill College 2/18/1. Diary. 3 June 1940.
25. E. L. Spears, *Assignment*, vol. 2, p. 27.
26. Ibid., p. 48.
27. Ibid., p. 53.
28. Ibid., p. 79.
29. Ibid., p. 75.
30. Ibid., pp. 83–91.

12
Flight

1. E. L. Spears, *Assignment*, vol. 2, pp. 95–6.
2. Ibid., p. 99.
3. Ibid., p. 112.
4. Ibid., p. 113.
5. Ibid., p. 126.
6. Spears Churchill College 2/18/1. Diary. 11 June 1940.
7. Ibid.
8. E. L. Spears, *Assignment*, vol. 2, p. 131.
9. Spears Churchill College 2/18/1. Diary. 11 June 1940.
10. E. L. Spears, *Assignment*, vol. 2, p. 138.
11. Ibid., p. 139.
12. Spears Churchill College 2/18/1. Diary. 11 June 1940.
13. Ibid. Also E. L. Spears, *Assignment*, vol. 2, p. 151.

14. Spears Churchill College 2/18/1. Diary. 11 June 1940.

15. E. L. Spears, *Assignment*, vol. 2, p. 157.

16. Spears Churchill College acc 545 box 34, Waddington letter of 1955. See also E. L. Spears, *Two Men*, p. 143.

17. E. L. Spears, *Assignment*, vol. 2, p. 161.

18. Ibid., p. 164. See also Spears Churchill College 2/18/1. Diary. 12 June 1940.

19. E. L. Spears, *Assignment*, vol. 2, p. 164.

20. Spears Churchill College 2/18/1. Diary. 12 June 1940.

21. Ibid. See also E. L. Spears, *Assignment*, vol. 2, p. 170.

22. Spears Churchill College 2/18/1. Diary. 12 June 1940.

23. E. L. Spears, *Assignment*, vol. 2, pp. 175–7.

24. Ibid., p. 182.

25. O. Harvey, *War Diaries*, p. 387.

26. E. L. Spears, *Assignment*, vol. 2, p. 204.

27. Ibid., pp. 214–15.

28. Ibid., p. 218.

29. Ibid., pp. 219–20.

30. Ibid., pp. 228–9.

31. Ibid., p. 237.

32. Spears Churchill College 2/18/1. Diary. 14 June 1940.

33. E. L. Spears, *Assignment*, vol. 2, p. 241.

34. Spears Churchill College 2/18/1. Diary. 14 June 1940.

35. E. L. Spears, *Assignment*, vol. 2, p. 243.

36. Ibid., p. 258. See also Spears Churchill College 2/18/1. Diary. 15 June 1940.

37. E. L. Spears, *Assignment*, vol. 2, p. 265.

38. Ibid., p. 269.

39. Ibid., p. 280.

40. Ibid., p. 291.

41. Spears Churchill College 2/18/1. Diary. 16 June 1940.

42. E. L. Spears, *Assignment*, vol. 2, p. 294.

43. Ibid., p. 303.

44. Ibid., p. 305.

45. Lady Gladwyn. Diaries. p. 361.

46. Spears Churchill College 2/18/1. Diary. 16 June 1940.

47. Ibid.

48. Ibid.

49. Ibid.

50. Ibid.

51. Ibid., 17 June 1940.

52. Ibid.

53. E. L. Spears, *Assignment*, vol. 2, p. 323. For the flight, see E. Petit, 'Le
    Pilote du Général', *Icare*, issue 141, pp. 40–9.
54. C. de Gaulle, *The Call to Honour*, p. 86.

13
The Warrior Monk

 1. J. Lacouture, *De Gaulle*, vol. 2, p. 156.
 2. Ibid., vol. 1, p. 258.
 3. Spears Churchill College 1/134/2. N.D.
 4. Ibid., 1 July 1940.
 5. Dalton diary. 28 June 1940.
 6. E. L. Spears, *Two Men*, p. 162.
 7. Ibid., p. 165.
 8. Spears Churchill College 1/136. 4 July 1940.
 9. E. L. Spears, *Two Men*, p. 165.
10. Spears Churchill College 1/137/2. 11 July 1940.
11. Spears Churchill College 1/135. 10 July 1940.
12. Spears Churchill College 1/134/2. 11 July 1940.
13. Ibid., 22 July 1940.
14. H. Colyton, *Occasion*, pp. 162–3.
15. E. L. Spears, *Two Men*, p. 148.
16. Spears Churchill College 1/134. See also E. L. Spears, *Two Men*, p. 170.
17. Aylmer Collection. Diary. 17 August 1940.
18. Spears Churchill College 1/350. 22 February 1952.
19. PRO PREM 3/276. 5 July 1940. See also Spears Churchill College 1/376.
20. Spears Churchill College 1/136/5. 26 August 1940.
21. Spears Churchill College 1/134/3. 26 August 1940.
22. Spears Churchill College 1/137/2. 28 August 1940.
23. Spears Churchill College 1/136. 5 July 1940.
24. Spears Churchill College 1/136/5. 25 August 1940.
25. E. L. Spears, *Two Men*, p. 183.
26. Mary Borden, *Journey*, pp. 113–14.
27. Aylmer Collection. Diary. 17 August 1940.
28. A. Marder, *Operation Menace*, p. 37.
29. Spears Churchill College 2/21. 7 November 1973.
30. PRO CAB 84/19. 19 September 1940.
31. Aylmer Collection. Diary. 30 August 1940.
32. J. A. Watson, *Echec à Dakar*, p. 51.
33. Spears Churchill College 2/6. Dakar diary.
34. Stokes papers. 6 September 1940.

35. E. L. Spears, *Two Men*, p. 186.
36. Spears Churchill College 2/6. Dakar diary.
37. Ibid.
38. Ibid.
39. PRO WO 178/10. 14 September 1940.
40. Ibid., 15 September 1940.
41. W. S. Churchill, *The Second World War*, vol. 2, p. 427.
42. PRO WO 178/10. 17 September 1940.
43. Spears Churchill College 2/6. Dakar diary.
44. PRO WO 178/10. 17 September 1940.
45. Ibid., 18 September 1940. See also Spears Churchill College 2/6. Dakar diary.
46. W. S. Churchill, *The Second World War*, vol. 2, p. 428.
47. E. L. Spears, *Two Men*, p. 202.
48. Ibid., pp. 202–3.
49. Ibid., p. 205.
50. A. Marder, *Operation Menace*, p. 137.
51. E. L. Spears, *Two Men*, p. 208. See also Spears Churchill College 2/6. Dakar diary.
52. E. L. Spears, *Two Men*, p. 209.
53. Spears Churchill College 2/6. Dakar diary.
54. E. L. Spears, *Two Men*, p. 209.
55. Spears Churchill College 2/6. Dakar diary.
56. C. de Gaulle, *The Call to Honour*, pp. 133–4.
57. Killearn diary. 4 November 1940.

14
Towards the Levant

1. Aylmer Collection. Diary. 17 September 1940.
2. Ibid., 24 September 1940.
3. Ibid., 2 October 1940.
4. Ibid., 5 October 1940.
5. Ibid., 8 October 1940.
6. Ibid., 10 October 1940.
7. Ibid., 15 October 1940.
8. Ibid., 27 October 1940.
9. Quoted in F. Kersaudy, *Churchill and de Gaulle*, p. 102.
10. U. von Hassell, *Diaries*, p. 141.
11. Dalton diary. 29 September 1940. See also R. E. Lee, *London Observer*, p. 76.

12. R. E. Lee, *London Observer*, p. 87.
13. J. Colville, *The Fringes of Power*, pp. 295 and 326.
14. PRO WO 178/10. 13 October 1940.
15. Stokes papers. 16 October 1940.
16. PRO WO 178/10. 30 October 1940. See also Spears Churchill College 1/136/7. 2 November 1940.
17. PRO WO 178/10. 4 and 21 November 1940.
18. J. Colville, *The Fringes of Power*, p. 354.
19. Spears Churchill College 2/7. Diary.
20. Spears Churchill College 1/136/8. 3 December 1940.
21. J. Colville, *The Fringes of Power*, pp. 370–1.
22. Mary Borden, *Journey*, p. 115.
23. Spears Churchill College 1/143/1. 28 December 1940.
24. J. Kennedy, *The Business of War*, p. 64.
25. Spears Churchill College 1/136/9. 5 February 1941.
26. J. Colville, *The Fringes of Power*, pp. 432–3.
27. Spears St Antony's 1. Diary. 13 March 1941.
28. Ibid.
29. E. L. Spears, *Fulfilment*, p. 3.
30. Spears Churchill College acc 545 box 60. 19 March 1941.
31. Aylmer Collection. Diary. 15 March 1941.
32. Spears St Antony's 1. Diary. 23 March 1940.
33. E. L. Spears, *Fulfilment*, p. 4.
34. Spears St Antony's 1. Diary. 29 March 1941.
35. E. L. Spears, *Fulfilment*, p. 6.
36. Killearn diary. 26 March 1941.
37. Spears St Antony's 1. Diary. 7 April 1941.
38. E. L. Spears, *Fulfilment*, p. 24.
39. Ibid., p. 30.
40. Ibid., p. 37.
41. Ibid., p. 43.
42. Ibid., p. 42.
43. Ibid., p. 55.
44. Killearn diary. 3 May 1941.
45. Spears St Antony's 1. Diary. 6 May 1941.
46. Aylmer Collection. Diary. 10 April 1941.
47. Ibid. 24, 27 and 28 April and 11 May 1941.
48. Spears St Antony's 1. Diary. 11 May 1941.
49. Ibid. 15 May 1941.
50. Aylmer Collection. Diary. 20 May 1941.
51. Mary Borden, *Journey*, p. 133.
52. Spears St Antony's 1. Diary. 29 May 1941.

53. Aylmer Collection. Diary. 29 May 1941.
54. Spears St Antony's 1. Diary. 1 June 1941.
55. Ibid., 7 June 1941.
56. E. L. Spears, *Fulfilment*, pp. 11 and 102.
57. Spears St Antony's 1. Diary. 14 and 15 June 1941.
58. Ibid., 18 June 1941.
59. Ibid., 6 July 1941.
60. E. L. Spears, *Fulfilment*, p. 110.
61. Killearn diary. 19 June 1941.
62. Spears St Antony's 1. Diary. 20 June 1941.
63. E. L. Spears, *Fulfilment*, p. 115.
64. Spears St Antony's 1. Diary. 10 and 11 July 1941.
65. E. L. Spears, *Fulfilment*, p. 123.
66. C. de Gaulle, *The Call to Honour*, p. 194.
67. E. L. Spears, *Fulfilment*, pp. 127–8.
68. Ibid., p. 133.
69. Spears St Antony's 1. Diary. 21 July 1941.
70. Killearn diary. 21 July 1941.
71. H. Colyton, *Occasion*, p. 194.
72. See A. Roshwald, *Estranged Bedfellows*, p. 89.
73. Spears St Antony's 1. Diary. 29 July 1941.
74. Spears St Antony's Ic/2. 16 August 1941.
75. Hansard, vol. 374, col. 76. 9 September 1941.
76. PRO FO 371/27318/E7988. 1 December 1941. See also A. Roshwald, *Estranged Bedfellows*, p. 91.
77. PRO FO 371/27318/E7988. 23 September 1941.
78. C. Mott-Radclyffe, *Foreign Body*, p. 108.
79. Aylmer Collection. Diary. 18 July 1941.
80. Ibid., 22 July 1941.
81. Mary Borden, *Journey*, p. 149.
82. Ibid., p. 150.
83. Ibid., p. 153.
84. Aylmer Collection. Diary. 4 and 5 August, 11 September 1941. See also H. Colyton, *Occasion*, p. 196.
85. Aylmer Collection. Diary. 11 September 1941.
86. Ibid., 23 December 1941.
87. Killearn diary. 13 October 1941.
88. Spears St Antony's I. Diary. 11 December 1941.
89. Ibid., 15 and 16 December 1941.

15
'That Charlatan Spears'

1. Spears Churchill College 1/15. 27 December 1941.
2. Spears St Antony's II/6. 29 January 1942.
3. Dalton diary. 8 January 1942.
4. Spears Churchill College 1/137/2. 6 February 1942.
5. Spears Churchill College 1/76. 10 March 1942.
6. Spears Churchill College 1/50. 16 March 1942.
7. PRO FO 371/2713/E6479. 9 October 1941.
8. Belinda Ruck-Keene manuscript. See also C. Mott-Radclyffe, *Foreign Body*, p. 110.
9. Coghill papers, pp. 15–16.
10. Ibid., pp. 17–18.
11. E. L. Spears, *Fulfilment*, p. 212.
12. PRO FO371/31473/E3654. 19 June 1942.
13. PRO FO 371/31473/E4441. 25 July 1942.
14. O. Harvey, *War Diaries*, 26 July 1942, p. 144.
15. Killearn diary. 12 September 1942.
16. E. L. Spears, *Fulfilment*, p. 216.
17. Ibid., p. 217.
18. O. Harvey, *War Diaries*, 14 September 1942, p. 156.
19. Spears Churchill College 1/1437/2. 11 September 1942.
20. O. Harvey, *War Diaries*, 1 October 1942, p. 164.
21. Spears Churchill College 1/180. 4 October 1942.
22. M. Gilbert, *Winston S. Churchill*, vol. 7, pp. 277–8.
23. Aylmer Collection. Diary. 4 January 1942.
24. Mary Borden, *Journey*, p. 167.
25. Aylmer Collection. Diary. 8 February 1942.
26. Ibid., 7 March 1942.
27. Mary Borden, *Journey*, p. 172.
28. Ibid., pp. 183–4.
29. Ibid., p. 188.
30. Ibid., p. 204.
31. E. L. Spears, *Fulfilment*, p. 208.
32. Mary Borden, *Journey*, p. 213.
33. Coghill papers, pp. 26–7.
34. PRO FO 371/35176/E1602. 19 March 1943.
35. H. Colyton, *Occasion*, p. 206.
36. PRO FO 371/35178/E3893. 12 July 1943.
37. O. Harvey, *War Diaries*, 6 July 1943, p. 271.
38. Spears St Antony's I. Diary. 25 June 1943.

39. PRO FO 371/35178/E3893. 12 July 1943.
40. PRO PREM 3/422/12. 28 June 1943.
41. Spears St Antony's I. Diary. 24, 26 and 27 June 1943.
42. Ibid., 15 July 1943.
43. Coghill papers, pp. 31 and 33.
44. Stokes papers, 9 October 1943.
45. Ibid., 25 October 1943.
46. Ibid., 23 November 1943.
47. Ibid., 22 October 1943.

16
'The Odious Intrigues of England'

1. E. L. Spears, *Fulfilment*, p. 226.
2. Mary Borden, *Journey*, p. 128.
3. Coghill papers, pp. 34–5. 28 November 1943.
4. E. L. Spears, *Fulfilment*, p. 225.
5. Ibid., pp. 226–7.
6. Mary Borden, *Journey*, p. 222.
7. E. L. Spears, *Fulfilment*, p. 230.
8. French Foreign Ministry, Londres–Alger CFLN–GPRF 1468. 16 November 1943.
9. Stokes papers. 12 November 1943.
10. Ibid., 15 November 1943.
11. French Foreign Ministry, Londres–Alger CFLN–GPRF 1468. 16 November 1943.
12. H. Macmillan, *War Diaries*. 16, 17 and 19 November 1943, pp. 294–6.
13. E. L. Spears, *Fulfilment*, p. 261.
14. Stokes papers. 19 and 20 November 1943.
15. E. L. Spears, *Fulfilment*, p. 263.
16. French Foreign Ministry, Londres–Alger CFLN–GPRF 1468. 21 November 1943.
17. Stokes papers. 23 November 1943.
18. Beaverbrook papers, C301. 25 November 1943.
19. Stokes papers. 29 November 1943.
20. French Foreign Ministry, Londres–Alger CFLN–GPRF 1468. 25 November 1943.
21. H. Macmillan, *War Diaries*. 26 November 1943, p. 306.
22. French Foreign Ministry, Londres–Alger CFLN–GPRF 1468. 8 December 1943.
23. Ibid., 14 December 1943.

24. E. L. Spears, *Fulfilment*, p. 281.

25. Mary Borden, *Journey*, p. 235.

26. Stokes papers. 21 January, 7 and 18 February 1944.

27. Ibid., 9 February, 4 March, 11 May and 5 June 1944.

28. Ibid., 5 June 1944.

29. French Foreign Ministry, Londres–Alger CFLN–GPRF 1001. January 1944.

30. E. L. Spears, *Fulfilment*, p. 292.

31. Spears St Antony's II/7. 10 March 1944.

32. Spears Churchill College 1/137/2. 11 March 1944.

33. PRO PREM 3–423/15. 22 May and 11 June 1944.

34. Mary Borden, *Journey*, p. 244.

35. Stokes papers. 25 May 1944.

36. Duff Cooper diary. 15 July 1944.

37. French Foreign Ministry, Londres–Alger CFLN–GPRF 1003. 1, 2, 3 and 8 August 1944.

38. E. L. Spears, *Fulfilment*, p. 296.

39. Spears St Antony's II/7. 2 September 1944.

40. Ibid., 3 September 1944.

41. Mary Borden, *Journey*, pp. 250–1.

42. Stokes papers. 6 September 1944.

43. French Foreign Ministry, Londres–Alger CFLN–GPRF 1003. 3 August 1944.

44. Stokes papers. 4, 9 and 20 October 1944.

45. Spears St Antony's II/6. 11 October 1944.

46. Stokes papers. 8 November 1944.

47. Spears St Antony's II/7. 24 October 1944.

48. Stokes papers. 26 November 1944.

49. Ibid., 30 November 1944.

50. Spears St Antony's I. Diary. January 1945.

51. PRO FO 371/4037/E7799. 8 December 1944.

52. Stokes papers. 12 December 1944.

53. Mary Borden, *Journey*, p. 261.

54. Spears St Antony's I. Diary. December 1944.

55. Coghill papers. Diary January 1945, pp. 38–9.

17

Defeat

1. Spears Churchill College 1/76. 7 January 1945.

2. Spears Churchill College 1/65. 16 January 1945.

3. Spears Churchill College 1/167. 23 February 1945.
4. Spears Churchill College 1/254. Quotes Nicolson letter of 17 January 1945.
5. Spears Churchill College 1/76. 28 January 1945.
6. Spears St Antony's I. Diary. 2–10 January 1945.
7. Mary Borden, *Journey*, p. 273.
8. Aylmer Collection. Diary. 6 April 1945.
9. PRO FO 371/45564/E3122. 30 April 1945.
10. C. de Gaulle, *Salvation*, p. 192.
11. H. Alphand, *L'Etonnement de l'Etre*, p. 185.
12. Hansard, vol. 411, col. 694. 5 June 1945.
13. *Institut Français d'Opinion Publique*. Bulletin no. 13. 16 July 1945.
14. Aylmer Collection. Diary. 12 June 1945.
15. Ibid.
16. Mary Borden, *Journey*, p. 292.
17. Aylmer Collection. Diary. 14 June 1945.
18. Ibid., 18 June 1945.
19. Ibid.
20. Mary Borden, *Journey*, p. 296.
21. Spears Churchill College acc 545 box 1.
22. Spears Churchill College 1/76. 26 July 1945.
23. Duff Cooper diary. 26 July 1945.
24. Spears Churchill College 1/76. 27 July 1945.
25. Spears Churchill College 1/65. 4 August 1945.
26. Spears Churchill College 1/304. 22 September 1945.

18
'Life Here Is Really Very Unpleasant'

1. Spears Churchill College 1/87. 16 November 1948.
2. Spears Churchill College acc 545 box 28. 24 October and 14 November 1946.
3. Spears Churchill College acc 545 box 13. 8 October 1946.
4. Spears Churchill College 1/202. N.D.
5. Ibid., August 1946.
6. Spears Churchill College acc 545 box 38. February 1947.
7. Spears Churchill College 1/144. 6 June 1949.
8. Spears Churchill College 1/143/1. 26 April 1949.
9. J. Mordal, *La Bataille de Dakar*, p. 103.
10. W. S. Churchill, *The Second World War*, vol. 2, p. 97.

11. G. Catroux, *Dans la bataille de Méditerranée*, Chapter 23, 'Sur le Général Sir Edward Spears', pp. 191–8.
12. *Le Figaro*, 9 September 1949.
13. Spears Churchill College 1/255. 11 October 1949.
14. *Le Monde*, 19 October 1949.
15. Spears Churchill College 1/202. December 1949.
16. Spears Churchill College 1/255. 29 April 1953.
17. Spears Churchill College 1/180. 1 April 1947.
18. Spears Churchill College 1/139. 26 November 1947.
19. Spears Churchill College acc 545 box 38. 20 November 1945.
20. Ibid., 24 and 29 November 1945.
21. Ibid., 29 November, 1 and 6 December 1945.
22. Ibid., 13 December 1945.
23. Spears Churchill College 3/2. November–December 1945.
24. Spears Churchill College acc 545 box 38. February 1947.
25. Spears Churchill College 1/202. 3 January 1946.
26. Spears Churchill College 1/139. 26 November 1947.
27. Ibid., 10 April 1951.
28. Spears Churchill College 3/8. 1 July 1949.
29. Spears Churchill College 1/180. 22 April 1953.
30. Spears Churchill College 3/14. 8 January 1953.
31. Spears Churchill College 3/17. April 1955.
32. Spears Churchill College 1/139. 10 April 1951.
33. Spears Churchill College 1/65. 24 June 1952.
34. Spears Churchill College 2/17. N.D.
35. Ibid., 1 November 1952.
36. E. L. Spears, *Assignment*, vol 2, p. 237.
37. Spears Churchill College 1/202. N.D.
38. *Observer*, 12 December 1953.
39. E. L. Spears, *Assignment*, vol. 1, pp. 92–3.
40. Jewish jibe in *Aspects de la France, La Vie Politique*, 18 June 1954.
41. *Le Figaro*, 30 November 1954; *Truth*, 3 December 1954.
42. Spears Churchill College 1/239. 10 and 28 December 1954.

19
Fighting Back

1. Spears Churchill College 1/143/1. 25 October 1954.
2. Mary Borden, *For the Record*.
3. Mary Borden, *Martin Merriedew*.
4. Spears Churchill College 2/29. 12 August 1955.

5. Ibid., 18 August 1955.

6. Ibid.

7. Spears Churchill College 1/25. 30 September 1957.

8. Richard Usborne, notes of 1984 interview with Mrs Reichart.

9. Spears Churchill College acc 643 box 1. Letters of August 1966.

10. Aylmer Collection. N.D. 1964. 26 October 1964.

11. Spears Churchill College acc 545 box 38. Letters of August 1946, 7, 10, 17 and 18 August 1957.

12. B. Beck, *Des accommodements avec le ciel.*

13. B. Beck, *Le Muet.*

14. *Le Monde*, 29 June 1963.

15. *Le Nouveau Candide*, 26 June 1963.

16. B. Szapiro, *La Première Ligne.*

17. Spears Churchill College 1/101. 5 and 7 August 1958.

18. Spears Churchill College acc 643 box 1. Card of 1958 and letter of 13 April 1960.

19. See *A Brief History of the Institute of Directors* in *Direct Line* (IOD 1983).

20. Ibid.

20
Golden Evening

1. Spears Churchill College 1/234. 24 February 1964.

2. *Evening Standard*, 27 November 1964.

3. *Nouvelles Littéraires*, 7 January 1956; *L'Humanité*, 25 May 1965.

4. *Figaro Littéraire*, 4 November 1964.

5. Spears Churchill College 1/180. 12 November 1964.

6. Spears Churchill College 1/176. 19 February and 30 June 1965.

7. Nancy Mitford, *Don't Tell Alfred.*

8. Spears Churchill College 1/180. 14 November 1965.

9. Spears Churchill College 1/279. 1 February 1965.

10. E. L. Spears, *Two Men*, p. 217.

11. *Sunday Telegraph*, 9 October 1966; *Observer*, 9 October 1966; *Sunday Times*, 9 October 1966; *Spectator*, 14, 21 and 28 October 1966.

12. *L'Aurore*, 2 December 1966; *Nouvelle Observateur*, 21 December 1966.

13. *Sunday Times*, 6 July 1967.

14. E. L. Spears, *Fulfilment*, Introduction, p. x.

15. *British Book News*, 21 May 1968.

16. Spears Churchill College 2/19. 29 April 1968.

17. *Illustrated London News*, 19 July 1968.

18. *Daily Telegraph*, 29 March 1968. Also E. Petit, 'Le Pilote du Général', *Icare*, issue 141, 1992.
19. Spears Churchill College 2/25. N.D. 'On a Paper by Mary Borden'.
20. Aylmer Collection. 28 July 1960.
21. Mary Borden. Mugar Collection.
22. Spears Churchill College 1/316. 13 and 22 March 1968.
23. Spears Churchill College 1/109. 12 July 1968.
24. Spears Churchill College 2/25. N.D.
25. *The Times*, 3 and 5 December 1968.
26. Aylmer Collection. 9 December 1968.
27. Richard Usborne interview with Hart-Davis. October 1985.
28. Spears Churchill College 2/31. Copy of the address. For correspondence about the service and de Gaulle's letter of 6 December 1968, see Spears Churchill College 2/30.
29. *Revue de la France Libre*, January 1969.
30. Spears Churchill College 2/31. 13 January 1969.
31. Spears Churchill College acc 545 box 38. 20 October 1969.
32. Spears Churchill College 1/240. 21 August 1969 and 20 July 1970.
33. Spears Churchill College 1/202. 10 February 1970.
34. Letter in the possession of T. de St Phalle. 27 February 1973.
35. Spears Churchill College 3/12. 16 December 1952.
36. Spears Churchill College 3/39. 25 November 1963.
37. *Time & Tide*, 31 January 1959.
38. Spears Churchill College 1/180. 6 April 1962.
39. Spears Churchill College 3/36. 10 February 1962.
40. Spears Churchill College 1/111. 30 May 1963.
41. Spears Churchill College 3/45. February 1964.
42. Spears Churchill College 3/34. 23 May 1961.
43. *Guardian*, 2 April 1966.
44. Spears Churchill College 3/48. 5 July 1966.
45. Ibid., 25 November 1966.
46. *West Africa*, 8 April 1967.
47. See T. Bower, *Tiny Rowland*, pp. 113–14.
48. *Financial Times*, 26 October 1968.
49. Spears Churchill College 3/55. October 1968.
50. Spears Churchill College 3/59, 26 June 1969; 3/60, 22 May 1969; 3/65, 23 March 1969.
51. Spears Churchill College 1/210. E.L.S. note of 1971 conversations.
52. Ibid., 9 March 1973.
53. For the affidavits, see Spears Churchill College 1/210.
54. *Western Mail*, 15 May 1973.
55. Spears Churchill College 1/210. 14 June 1973.

56. Spears Churchill College 3/63. 31 May 1973.
57. For the meeting, see *Financial Times* of 1 June 1973. Further information in Spears Churchill 1/209–10 and Spears Churchill acc 545 box 27.
58. *Daily Mail*, 2 June 1973.
59. Spears Churchill acc 545 box 36. 14 June 1973.
60. *The Times*, 19 December 1973.
61. Spears Churchill College 1/244. 28 January 1974.
62. Aylmer Collection. Typescript of Thorpe's address.
63. *The Director*, 9 March 1974.
64. Spears Churchill College acc 545 box 31. 14 January 1975.

BIBLIOGRAPHY

1. Manuscript sources

The main source for any biography of Spears is his own papers. These are to be found in three places: Churchill College, Cambridge has his personal, political, business and family papers; King's College, London has material to do with the First World War; and The Middle East Centre at St Antony's College, Oxford, has papers linked to his service in the Levant. The division is not exact; for example, there is First War material, notably the diaries that Spears kept from 1914 to 1917, and Middle Eastern papers at Churchill, which has by far the largest collection (337 boxes in all). King's has some Second War papers, although often there are copies of these at Churchill College, and also one book of the First War diaries.

The papers of Mary Borden (Lady Spears) in the Mugar Memorial Library at Boston University and those still in the care of Colonel Anthony Aylmer, Nunwell House, the Isle of Wight, have also proved to be an important source. I am grateful to the librarian of Cornell University, New York, for sending me copies of letters from Mary Borden in the Wyndham Lewis collection there.

I have also consulted British government documents in the Public Record Office and French government papers in the military archives at Vincennes and the diplomatic archives at the Quai d'Orsay.

In addition I have used the following collections of personal papers:

Lord Beaverbrook. The House of Lords Record Office
Lord Bertie of Thame. The British Library
Viscount Chandos (formerly Oliver Lyttelton). Churchill College, Cambridge
Major-General Sir Sidney Clive. King's College, London
Lieutenant-Colonel Patrick Coghill. The Middle East Centre at St Antony's
　　College, Oxford
Duff Cooper (later Viscount Norwich). The Viscount Norwich
Hugh Dalton. The London School of Economics
The Earl of Derby. The Liverpool Record Office
Viscount Dillon. The Imperial War Museum
Sir James Edmonds. King's College, London
Viscount Esher. Churchill College, Cambridge
Field-Marshal Sir John French (later the Earl of Ypres). The Imperial War
　　Museum

Lord Hankey. Churchill College, Cambridge
Sir Basil Liddell Hart. King's College, London
Lord Harvey of Tasburgh (formerly Oliver Harvey). The British Library
Lieutenant-General Noel Irwin. The Imperial War Museum
General Sir Walter Kirke. The Imperial War Museum
Sir Miles Lampson (later Lord Killearn). The Middle East Centre at St Antony's College, Oxford
Sir Robert Bruce Lockhart. The House of Lords Record Office
Walter Milner-Barry. The Imperial War Museum
Belinda Ruck-Keene. Extracts from an unpublished autobiography lent to me by Belinda Ruck-Keene
Sir John Stokes. Sir John Stokes
Field-Marshal Sir Henry Wilson. The Imperial War Museum

2. Books and articles

Alexander, Martin. *The Republic in Danger: General Maurice Gamelin and the Politics of French Defence 1933–1940* (Cambridge 1992)
Alphand, Hervé. *L'Etonnement d'être* (Paris 1977)
André Gide et Christian Beck, Correspondance, ed. Pierre Masson (Geneva 1994)
Andrew, Christopher. *Secret Service* (London 1985)
Anglesey, Marquess of. *A History of the British Cavalry 1816–1919*, volume 4: *1899–1913* (London 1986)
Barnett, Correlli. *The Swordbearers* (London 1963)
Baudouin, Paul. *Private Diaries: March 1940–January 1941* (London 1948)
Beck, Béatrix. *Des accommodements avec le ciel* (Paris 1954)
——. *Le Muet* (Paris 1963)
Bédarida, François. 'La Rupture Franco-Britannique de 1940', *Vingtième Siècle Revue d'Histoire*, no. 25, 1990
Beevor, Antony and Artemis Cooper. *Paris After the Liberation* (London 1994)
Bertie, Lord. *The Diary of Lord Bertie 1914–1918*, 2 volumes (London 1924)
Bidault, Georges. *D'une résistance à l'autre* (Paris 1965)
Bond, Brian. *France and Belgium 1939–1940* (London 1975)
Bonham-Carter, Victor. *Soldier True* (London 1963)
Borden, Mary (as Bridget Maclagan). *The Mistress of Kingdoms* (London 1912)
——. *Collision* (London 1913)
——. *The Romantic Woman* (London 1916, republished in 1924 under the name of Mary Borden)
—— (under her own name). *Jane Our Stranger* (London 1923)
——. *Three Pilgrims and a Tinker* (London 1924)
——. *Jericho Sands* (London 1925)

——. *Four O'Clock and Other Stories* (London 1926)
——. *Flamingo* (London 1927)
——. *Jehovah's Day* (London 1928)
——. *The Forbidden Zone* (London 1929)
——. *A Woman with White Eyes* (London 1930)
——. *Sarah Gay* (London 1931)
——. *The Technique of Marriage* (London 1932)
——. *Mary of Nazareth* (London 1933)
——. *The King of the Jews* (London 1935)
——. *Action for Slander* (London 1936)
——. *The Black Virgin* (London 1937)
——. *Passport for a Girl* (London 1939)
——. *Journey Down a Blind Alley* (London 1946)
——. *No. 2 Shovel Street* (London 1949)
——. *For the Record* (London 1950)
——. *Martin Merriedew* (London 1952)
——. *Margin of Error* (London 1954)
——. *The Hungry Leopard* (London 1956)
——. 'Personal Experience and the Art of Fiction', 1956 lecture in Royal
Society of Literature, *Essays by Divers Hands*, vol. 29 (1958)
Bower, Tom. *Tiny Rowland: Rebel Tycoon* (London 1993)
Brittain, Vera. *The Testament of Youth* (London 1979, paperback edition)
Bryant, Arthur. *The Turn of the Tide* (London 1957)
——. *Triumph in the West* (London 1959)
Cadogan, Alexander. *Diaries of Sir Alexander Cadogan 1938–1945*, ed. David
Dilks (London 1971)
Callwell, Sir Charles. *Field Marshal Sir Henry Wilson*, 2 volumes (London
1927)
Cambon, Paul. *Correspondance 1870–1924*, vol. 3: *1912–1924*, ed. Henri
Cambon (Paris 1946)
Castellane, the Marquis de. *Confessions* (London 1924)
Catroux, G. *Dans la bataille de Méditerranée* (Paris 1949)
Chandos, Viscount. *Memoirs* (London 1962)
Channon, Henry. *'Chips': The Diaries of Sir Henry Channon*, ed. Robert Rhodes
James (London 1967)
Charmley, John. *Duff Cooper* (London 1986)
Churchill, Randolph. *Lord Derby* (London 1959)
Churchill, Winston. *The World Crisis*, 5 volumes (London 1923–31)
——. *Great Contemporaries* (London 1937)
——. *The Second World War*, 6 volumes (London 1948–54)
Colville, John. *Footprints in Time* (London 1976)
——. *The Churchillians* (London 1981)

——. *The Fringes of Power*, 2-volume paperback edition (London 1986 and 1987)

Colyton, Henry. *Occasion, Chance and Change* (Norwich 1993)

Cooper, Artemis. *Cairo in the War* (London 1985)

Cooper, Duff. *Old Men Forget* (London 1953)

Coote, Colin. *Editorial* (London 1965)

Dalton, Hugh. *The Fateful Years* (London 1957)

——. *The Political Diary of Hugh Dalton 1918–40, 1945–60*, ed. Ben Pimlott (London 1986)

——. *The Second World War Diary of Hugh Dalton 1940–45*, ed. Ben Pimlott (London 1987)

D'Argenlieu, T. *Souvenirs de guerre* (Paris 1973)

Direct Line. October 1983 issues (London 1983)

The Director, journal of the Institute of Directors (London 1947–74)

Duprey, Jacques. *L'Ambulance Hadfield–Spears ou la drôle d'equipe* (Paris 1953)

Edmonds, Sir James. *History of the Great War Based on Official Documents, Military Operations, France and Belgium 1914, 1915*, 4 volumes (London 1922–8)

Farrar-Hockley, Anthony. *The Somme* (London 1964)

French, David. 'Who Knew What and When? The French Army Mutinies and the British Decision to Launch the Third Battle of Ypres', in Lawrence Freedman, Paul Hayes and Robert O'Neill (eds), *War, Strategy, and International Politics* (Oxford 1992)

Foch, Marshal. *The Memoirs of Marshal Foch* (London 1931)

Foot, M. R. D. *S.O.E. in France* (London 1966)

Fraser, Peter. *Lord Esher: A Political Biography* (London 1973)

French, Field-Marshal Viscount. *The Despatches of Lord French* (London 1917)

——. *1914* (London 1919)

Gaulle, Charles de. *War Memoirs*, vol. 1: *The Call to Honour 1940–1942* (London 1955); vol. 2: *Unity 1942–1944* (London 1959); vol. 3: *Salvation 1944–46* (London 1960)

——. *War Memoirs. Documents*, 3 volumes (London 1955–60)

——. *Lettres, notes et carnets*, 3 volumes (Paris 1981–3)

Gaunson, A. B. 'Churchill, de Gaulle, Spears and the Levant Affair, 1941', *Historical Journal*, no. 27, 1984

——. *The Anglo–French Clash in Lebanon and Syria, 1940–1945* (London 1987)

Gilbert, Martin. *Winston S. Churchill*, vols 3–6 (London 1971–1988)

Gillois, A. *Histoire secrète des Français à Londres* (Paris 1973)

Gladwyn, Cynthia. *The Paris Embassy* (London 1975)

——. *Diaries*, ed: Miles Jebb (London 1995)

Glubb, Sir John. *The Story of the Arab Legion* (London 1948)

——. *Britain and the Arabs 1908–1958* (London 1959)

Griffiths, Richard. *Marshal Pétain* (London 1994 edition)

Hailsham, Lord. *A Sparrow's Flight* (London 1990)

Harman, Nicholas. *Dunkirk: The Necessary Myth* (London 1980)

Hart-Davis, Rupert. *The Power of Chance* (London 1991)

Harvey, Oliver. *The Diplomatic Diaries of Oliver Harvey 1937–1940*, ed. John Harvey (London 1970)

———. *The War Diaries of Oliver Harvey 1941–1945*, ed. John Harvey (London 1978)

Hassell, Ulrich von. *The Von Hassell Diaries* (London 1948)

Headlam, Cuthbert. *Parliament and Politics in the Age of Baldwin and Macdonald: The Headlam Diaries*, ed. Stuart Bell (London 1992)

Holmes, Richard. *The Little Field Marshal* (London 1981)

Horne, Alistair. *To Lose a Battle* (London 1969)

———. *The French Army and Politics 1870–1970* (London 1984)

———. *Macmillan 1894–1956* (London 1988)

Huguet, V. *Great Britain and the War* (London 1928)

Ismay, Lord. *Memoirs* (London 1960)

Isorni, Jacques, with Jean Lemaire. *Requête en revision pour Philippe Pétain* (Paris 1950)

———. *Souffrance et mort du Maréchal* (Paris 1951)

———. *C'est un péché de la France* (Paris 1962)

———. *Pétain a sauvé la France* (Paris 1964)

———. *Correspondance de l'île d'Yeu* (Paris 1966)

James, Robert Rhodes. *Winston Churchill: A Study in Failure 1900–1939* (London 1970)

———. *Anthony Eden* (London 1986)

Juin, A. *Mémoires*, vol. 2 (Paris 1960)

Kedourie, Elie. *England and the Middle East* (London 1956)

Keegan, John, ed. *Churchill's Generals* (London 1991) (see the essay on Spears by G. D. Sheffield)

Kennedy, Major-General Sir John. *The Business of War* (London 1957)

Kérillis, Henri de. *De Gaulle Dictateur* (Montreal 1945)

Kersaudy, François. *Churchill and de Gaulle* (London 1981)

Khoury, Philip. *Syria and the French* (Princeton 1987)

Kirk, George. *The Middle East in the War* (London 1953)

Lacouture, Jean. *De Gaulle the Rebel: 1890–1944* (London 1990)

———. *De Gaulle the Ruler: 1945–1970* (London 1991)

Lamb, Richard. *Churchill as War Leader* (London 1991)

Lampson, Miles (Lord Killearn). *The Killearn Diaries*, ed. Trefor E. Evans (London 1972)

Lanrezac, General C. *Le plan de campagne français* (Paris 1920)

Larminat, Edgard de. *Chroniques irrévérencieuses* (Paris 1962)

Ledwidge, Bernard. *De Gaulle* (London 1982)

Lee, General Raymond E. *The London Observer: The Journal of General Raymond E. Lee, 1940–1941*, ed. James Leutze (London 1972)

Leslie, Seymour. *The Jerome Connexion* (London 1964)

Lewis, Percy Wyndham. *The Letters of Wyndham Lewis*, ed. W. K. Rose (London 1963)

——. *Blasting and Bombardiering* (London 1967 edition)

Lloyd George, David. *War Memoirs*, 2 volumes (London 1938)

Lockhart, R. H. Bruce. *Memoirs of a Secret Agent* (London 1932)

Lockhart, Robin Bruce. *Ace of Spies* (London 1967)

Longrigg, Stephen. *Syria and Lebanon under French Mandate* (Oxford 1958)

Lumley, L. R. *History of the Eleventh Hussars (Prince Albert's Own) 1908–1934* (London 1936)

Macmillan, Harold. *Winds of Change* (London 1966)

——. *The Blast of War* (London 1967)

——. *War Diaries* (London 1984)

Marder, Arthur. *Operation Menace* (Oxford 1976)

Marshall-Cornwall, Major-General J. H. *Geographic Disarmament* (London 1935)

Maurice, Nancy. *The Maurice Case*. With an introduction by Spears (London 1972)

Maurier, George du. *Peter Ibbetson* (London 1896)

Mengin, Robert. *No Laurels for de Gaulle* (London 1967)

Meyers, Jeffrey. *The Enemy: A biography of Wyndham Lewis* (London 1980)

Mitford, Nancy. *Don't Tell Alfred* (London 1960)

——. *The Letters of Nancy Mitford*, ed. Charlotte Mosley (London 1993)

Mockler, Anthony. *Our Enemies the French* (London 1976)

Monroe, Elizabeth. *Britain's Moment in the Middle East* (London 1981 edition)

Moran, Lord. *Winston Churchill: The Struggle for Survival* (London 1966)

Mordal, Jacques. *La Bataille de Dakar* (Paris 1956)

Mott-Radclyffe, Charles. *Foreign Body in the Eye* (London 1975)

Murphy, Robert. *Diplomat among the Warriors* (London 1964)

Nicolson, Harold. *Letters and Diaries*, ed. Nigel Nicolson, 3 volumes (London 1966–8)

Ogilvy, David. *Blood, Brains and Beer* (London 1978)

Painlevé, Paul. *Comment j'ai nommé Foche et Pétain* (Paris 1924)

Passy. *Souvenirs*, vols 1 and 2 (Monte Carlo 1947); vol. 3 (Paris 1951)

Pedroncini, Guy. *Les Mutineries de 1917* (Paris 1967)

——. *Pétain, Général en Chef 1917–1918* (Paris 1974)

Peterson, Maurice. *Both Sides of the Curtain* (London 1950)

Petit, Edmond. 'Le Pilote du Général', *Icare, Revue de l'Aviation Française*, issue 141, 1993

Philpott, William. 'Britain and France Go to War: Anglo–French Relations on the Western Front 1914–1919', *War in History*, vol. 2, no. 1, 1995

Playfair, I. S. O., C. J. C. Molory and Sir William Jackson. *The Mediterranean and the Middle East*, 6 volumes (London 1954–88)

Porch, Douglas. *The French Secret Services* (London 1996)

Pryce-Jones, David. *Cyril Connolly: Journal and Memoir* (London 1983)

Ranfurly, The Countess of. *To War with Whitaker* (London 1994)

Repington, Lt-Col. C. A. C. *The First World War* (London 1920)

Reynaud, Paul. *La France a sauvé Europe* (Paris 1947)

——. *In the Thick of the Fight* (London 1955)

——. *Mémoires: Venue de ma montagne* (Paris 1960)

Roberts, Andrew. *Eminent Churchillians* (London 1994)

Roberts, Brian. *Randolph: A Study of Churchill's Son* (London 1984)

Robertson, Field-Marshal Sir William. *From Private to Field Marshal* (London 1921)

——. *Soldiers and Statesmen*, 2 volumes (London 1926)

Rose, Norman. *Vansittart: Study of a Diplomat* (London 1978)

Roshwald, Aviel. 'The Spears Mission in the Levant: 1941–44', *Historical Journal*, no. 29, December 1986

——. *Estranged Bedfellows: Britain and France in the Middle East during the Second World War* (Oxford 1990)

Roskill, Stephen. *Hankey: Man of Secrets*, 3 volumes (London 1970, 1972, 1974)

——. *The War at Sea 1939–1945*, vol. 1, *The Defensive* (London 1954)

Sachar, Howard. *Europe Leaves the Middle East, 1936–1954* (London 1974)

Saint-Exupéry, Antoine de. *The Little Prince* (London 1995 edition)

Saint Phalle, Thérèse de. 'Le Petit Lion' in *Histoires Brèves 1* (Paris 1981)

Schiff, Stacy. *Saint-Exupéry* (London 1994)

Sitwell, Osbert. *Great Morning* (London 1948)

Spears, E. L. *Lessons of the Russo–Japanese War*. Translated, as E. L. Spiers, from the original French of General F. O. de Négrier (London 1906)

——. *Cavalry Tactical Schemes*. Translated, as E. L. Spiers, from the original French of Colonel Monsenergue (London 1914)

——. *Liaison 1914* (London 1930)

——. *Prelude to Victory* (London 1939)

——. *Assignment to Catastrophe*, vol. 1: *Prelude to Dunkirk*, vol. 2: *The Fall of France* (London 1954)

——. *Two Men Who Saved France* (London 1966)

——. *The Picnic Basket* (London 1967)

——. *Fulfilment of a Mission* (London 1977)

Stein, Gertrude. *The Autobiography of Alice B. Toklas* (London 1966 paperback edition)

Stirling, W. F. *Safety Last* (London 1953)

Stuart, Denis. *Dear Duchess* (London 1982)

Szapiro, Bernadette. *La Première Ligne* (Paris 1981)

Taylor, A. J. P. *English History 1914–1945* (Oxford 1965)

Terraine, John. *Mons: The Retreat into Victory* (London 1960)

——. *Douglas Haig: The Educated Soldier* (London 1963)

——. *The Western Front* (London 1964)

Thomas, R. T. *Britain and Vichy* (London 1979)

Thompson, R. W. *Churchill and Morton* (London 1976)

Tuchman, Barbara. *August 1914* (London 1962)

Ullmann, Richard. *Anglo–Soviet Relations*, 2 volumes (Princeton 1961–8)

Upton, Peter. *Man of Barts* (London 1989)

Waley, Daniel. *British Opinion and the Italian–Abyssinian War 1935–6* (London 1975)

Watson, D. R. *Georges Clemenceau* (London 1974)

Watson, John A. *Echec à Dakar* (Paris 1968)

Watt, Richard. *Dare Call It Treason* (London 1964)

Webster, Paul. *Antoine de Saint-Exupéry* (London 1993)

Werth, Alexander. *The Last Days of Paris* (London 1940)

Weygand, General M. *Recalled to Service* (London 1952)

Williams, John. *The Guns of Dakar* (London 1976)

Wilson, Field-Marshal Lord. *Eight Years Overseas* (London 1948)

Wingate, Ronald. *Not in the Limelight* (London 1959)

Woodward, E. L. *British Foreign Policy in the Second World War* (London 1970)

INDEX

Ranks and titles are generally the highest mentioned in the text